S0-BOH-337

RAILWAYS OF THE WORLD

FODOR'S MODERN GUIDES
Founded by Eugene Fodor

EDITORIAL STAFF

New York
ROBERT C. FISHER
editor

LESLIE BROWN
managing editor

DOROTHY FOSTER
research director

London
RICHARD MOORE
executive editor

EUROPEAN PRODUCTION STAFF

EILEEN ROLPH
managing director

ADVERTISING STAFF

New York
E. W. NEWSOM
director

RAILWAYS OF THE WORLD:

Editorial Contributors: HUGH BALLANTYNE, RON BUTLER, MURRAY
  HUGHES, K. WESTCOTT JONES, P. M. KALLA-BISHOP, LT. COL. A. A.
  MAINS, J. N. SLATER, DAVID D. TENNANT
Editorial Assistant: SUSAN D. POOLE
Drawings: JANUSZ HORODECKI
Map: DYNO LOWENSTEIN
Production: C. R. BLOODGOOD, DONALD W. STRAUSS

FODOR'S RAILWAYS OF THE WORLD

ROGERS E.M. WHITAKER
("FRIMBO")
consultant editor

ROBERT C. FISHER
editor

LESLIE BROWN
managing editor

Introduction by Paul Theroux

DAVID McKAY COMPANY INC.

NEW YORK

© 1977 FODOR'S MODERN GUIDES, INC.
ISBN 0-679-00186-7 (McKay, cloth edition)
ISBN 0-679-00187-5 (McKay, Traveltex edition)
ISBN 0-340-22404-5 (Hodder edition)
No part of this book may be reproduced in any form without permission in writing
from the publisher

The following Travel Books edited by Eugene Fodor are current in 1977:

AREA GUIDES:
EUROPE
CARIBBEAN, BAHAMAS
   AND BERMUDA
INDIA
SOVIET UNION

JAPAN AND KOREA
MEXICO
SCANDINAVIA
SOUTH AMERICA
SOUTH-EAST ASIA

FODOR'S U.S.A. (1 vol.)

COUNTRY GUIDES:
AUSTRIA
BELGIUM AND
   LUXEMBOURG
CZECHOSLOVAKIA
FRANCE
GERMANY
GREAT BRITAIN
GREECE
HOLLAND
HUNGARY*

IRELAND
ISRAEL
ITALY
MOROCCO
PORTUGAL
SPAIN
SWITZERLAND
TUNISIA*
TURKEY
YUGOSLAVIA

USA GUIDES:
NEW ENGLAND*
NEW YORK AND
   NEW JERSEY*
MID-ATLANTIC*
THE SOUTH*
INDIAN AMERICA

THE MID-WEST*
THE SOUTH-WEST*
ROCKIES AND PLAINS*
THE FAR WEST*
HAWAII
OLD WEST*

CITY GUIDES:
LONDON   PARIS   PEKING
VENICE*   VIENNA

LANGUAGE GUIDE:
EUROPE TALKING*

TRANSPORTATION GUIDES:
CRUISES EVERYWHERE*   RAILWAYS OF THE WORLD

LATEST ADDITIONS TO THE SERIES:
CANADA   EGYPT   IRAN

*Not available in Hodder and Stoughton editions
MANUFACTURED IN THE UNITED STATES OF AMERICA

CONTENTS

CONTENTS

CONTENTS

WORLD RAILWAYS

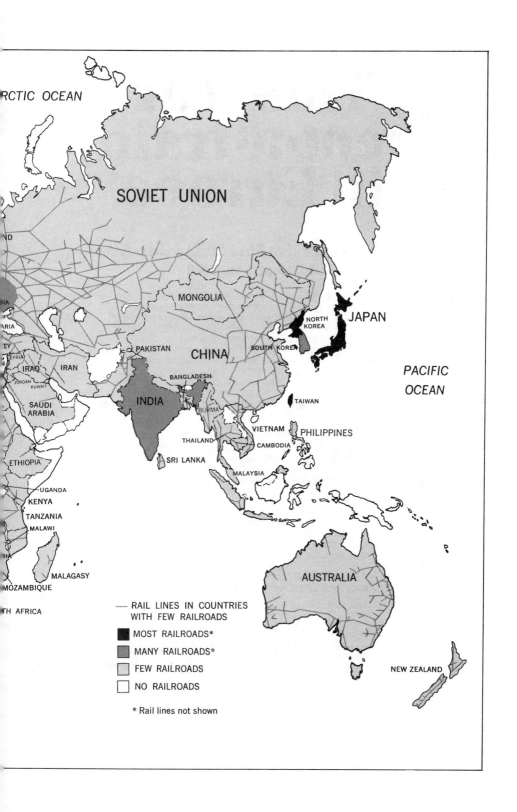

ARCTIC OCEAN

SOVIET UNION

MONGOLIA

NORTH KOREA

JAPAN

PAKISTAN

CHINA

SOUTH KOREA

BANGLADESH

INDIA

BURMA

TAIWAN

VIETNAM

PHILIPPINES

THAILAND

CAMBODIA

SRI LANKA

MALAYSIA

IRAQ

IRAN

JORDAN
KUWAIT

SAUDI
ARABIA

SYRIA

ETHIOPIA

UGANDA

KENYA

TANZANIA

MALAWI

MALAGASY

MOZAMBIQUE

TH AFRICA

PACIFIC
OCEAN

AUSTRALIA

NEW ZEALAND

— RAIL LINES IN COUNTRIES
WITH FEW RAILROADS

■ MOST RAILROADS*

■ MANY RAILROADS*

FEW RAILROADS

NO RAILROADS

* Rail lines not shown

This year rent·a·train in Europe.

2 weeks unlimited First Class train travel, 13 countries, $170

Renting a car in Europe can be pretty expensive, and driving on strange roads isn't everyone's idea of a carefree vacation. Compare that with Eurailpass "Rent-a-Train" (you're not really renting a train, of course, just getting a pass that lets you enjoy all the train travel you like).
You ride fast, clean, punctual trains that run often, and whisk you right to the heart of cities. While you sit back and relax, Europe unfolds from your window. You dine and sleep on board. You can ride Europe's deluxe trains without paying extra for them. You can take lots of ferry and steamer trips, even some motorcoach jaunts—your Pass covers them. You can get to know Europeans; they prefer going by rail, too.
Can your trip be as spontaneous as when you drive? Just about. With a Eurailpass you can improvise, take locals to out-of-the-way places, stop where you like, move on at whim. There's never any problem. You don't have to queue up for tickets. Just a flick of your Pass and you're on your way.
When you think how pleasureable train travel in Europe is, and how easy and economical with a Eurailpass, you can understand why more and more Americans are switching from rent-a-car to "Rent-a-Train."
Be sure to get your pass from your Travel Agent here, it's not for sale abroad. A three-week Pass costs $210. One-month, $260. Two-months, $350. Three-months, $420. Students under 26 get a Student-Railpass for two-months unlimited Second Class rail travel, $230.
See your Travel Agent or write for free brochures.
Eurailpass, Dept. 269-404, Box Q, Staten Island, New York 10305

Fares subject to change.

AUSTRIA
BELGIUM DENMARK
FRANCE
GERMANY HOLLAND
ITALY LUXEMBOURG
NORWAY PORTUGAL
SPAIN SWEDEN
SWITZERLAND

EURAILPASS

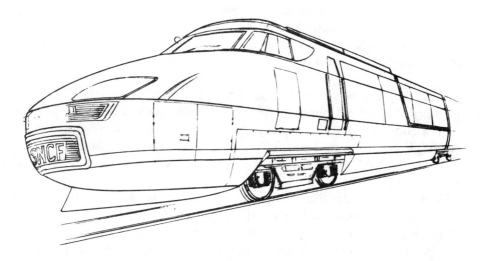

THE WORLD AT GROUND LEVEL

Beating Phineas Fogg by One Month

By Rogers E. M. Whitaker

The author, who writes frequently under the name of "Frimbo", is probably the best-known American railways critic, and certainly one of the most-travelled. Mr. Whitaker is also a contributing editor at the New Yorker.

TIME was running out, we kept telling George and Meredith Payne-Grayson, who, because they are English, are forever traveling the globe. They had circled it twice in cruise ships. Now, Kate and I hoped, they were ready for circling the globe our way—by land (a whole lot), by ship (upon occasion), and by plane (hardly at all). Time was running out because the railways of the United States (or so it seemed but a few years ago) would soon afford us no passenger trains at all, and the railways of certain other countries seemed moribund. Amtrak, in the United States, and a railway resurgence in other parts of the world have rather changed all that, but how could we know then? "Then" was at the end of a very long conference the four of us had been attending in San Francisco. We could, I had calculated, carry out our scheme in under fifty days (thirty days less than Jules Verne gave his Phineas Fogg to circumnavigate the globe in "Around the World in Eighty Days," and a great deal more comfortably). Find us a couple of cruise ships, I had said to the Payne-Graysons, and leave the rest to me.

We set off one morning from San Francisco on a train called the *Coast Daylight,* and through the windows of our parlor car we watched a day-long panorama of inland California and then coastal California as—high above the blue Pacific—we made our way to Los Angeles. Next, at seven one evening, we moved east in two double bedrooms on the *Super Chief,* whose glass-topped dome car kept us upstairs all day and deep into two moonlit nights before we turned in. The Payne-Graysons were really seeing the United States for the first time at close range, and how they enjoyed it!

A five-minute taxi ride through Chicago brought us to the *Twentieth Century Limited,* no longer in the best of health, but still willing to provide a glass-ended observation car and lobster souffle in the dining car for the overnight run to New York. There were strawberries for breakfast as we rolled south from Albany down the Hudson River, past scenery as fine as the eye could wish.

As a bonus, we duplicated the run to Albany a day later in a train called the *Laurentian,* once more in a parlor car, and added another bonus in the magnificent journey along the western shore of Lake George en route to Montreal, where we arrived in the early evening. On the following evening, aboard the *Ocean Limited,* we set forth on a run to Halifax, in Nova Scotia. The *Ocean Limited* travelled on the rails of the Canadian National, a line owned by the government, and the story always is that a government cannot operate anything well. But the *Ocean Limited* (scallops appeared on the luncheon menu next day, and a wide-windowed club-bar car offered an early-morning view of the St. Lawrence and an afternoon view of the Baie de Chaleurs) proved the fallacy of the story.

We were in Halifax in the evening, and after a night in the commodious station hotel, we backtracked a bit to the west next day and then moved north across the Cape Breton portion of the Maritime Provinces—a view wherever one looked—on our way to North Sydney, a not particularly eventful town, but the town from which we were to begin our island-hopping across the Atlantic. A government railway steamer, plain but serviceable, took us—under cover of night—across as turbulent a body of water as any of us had ever crossed; we quickly understood why there were two stout leather straps across each berth. This was the Cabot Strait, which isolates mainland Canada from Newfoundland. Arriving next morning at the tiny town of Port aux Basques, our eyes beheld the beginnings of one of the most astonishing toy railways in the world—the old Reid Newfoundland, by then under the benign administration of the Canadian National. A narrow-gauge train, but one accoutered with all the amenities—sleeping cars with toy drawing rooms for the Payne-Grayson/Whitaker entourage, a dining car, also toy, but serving human-sized meals, and at the rear end an open observation platform, also toy, from which to survey a countryside that often resembles the ends of the earth. At toy speeds (it took us nearly a day to manage the 547 miles to St. Johns) we studied the gnarled landscape at leisure, and slept well indeed after our night on the Cabot Strait.

Island-hopping

St. Johns is the easternmost point in the Western Hemisphere, and no railway will ever attempt the long leap across the Atlantic to Ireland—our next island. Very few ships do, either, but Meredith Payne-Grayson had found a freighter (hardly the cruise ship she had gaily promised) that had six two-berth cabins and was due away east in a couple of days. The towering headland on the north side of the tiny bay on which St. Johns lies made the Kilgarriff, the freighter that was to transport us to Cork, in southern Ireland, look even more minute than she really was. But, once aboard, we discovered that we would take meals with the ship's officers, and could visit the engineroom of this venerable coal-burner, visit the bridge and the captain's quarters. It was family-style all the way to Cork.

We had now used up—and used well—fourteen of our fifty days. So we pushed on, by day express train, to Dublin. The gentle, everlasting ruins of Ireland welcomed us, and the countryside was clean and fresh and green. Irish bacon, Irish eggs, Irish butter, and Guinness stout kept the interior man and woman properly nourished en route to Dublin and thence to Belfast. (A glance at any atlas will reveal the fact that we four were taking a rather long way around the world!) An early-morning run north to the beautiful harbor of Larne, only an hour away, and then by steamer to the next of our islands—Great Britain (more precisely, the part of that island that is occupied by Scotland). Two or three hours across the Irish Sea, and we were in the harbor of Stranraer, whence a train up the Scottish coast put us in Glasgow in the afternoon.

The overland journey from Scotland to London can be done almost *ad lib,* but we chose from Glasgow the morning train that rolls up hill and down dale through spectacular, sparsely populated countryside to Carlisle, on the border between England and Scotland, and then across even more starkly beautiful moors to the huge city of Leeds, then mile after mile of handsome Yorkshire countryscape en route to London.

We had finished, for the moment, with islands; our next objective was a continent—Europe, across the English Channel, but no problem for our railway group. From Victoria Station in London, there departs every evening a fleet of Wagons Lits sleeping cars, old and lumbering but comfortable, and with a restaurant car ready for any late diners, down to Dover. There the cars go aboard a ferryboat and at just about daybreak they come ashore on French soil, in the harbor of Dunkerque. Not long after, the cars (some for Brussels, some for Paris) are rolling south, and not long after that (if one wishes) the sleeping-car attendant appears with a Continental breakfast, to be consumed in one's bedroom. No "security measures" as at an airport, no customs inspection, no standing in line for anything at all.

From Paris, the classic route to the southeast is the railway along first the Seine and then the Rhone to the Mediterranean and then east along the Riviera, and the classic daytime train is *Le Mistral,* which is almost a small resort on wheels, with a menu and a wine cellar of resort caliber. It is evening for the journey along the Riviera to Nice, but the continuous band of lights along the towns, the hills, and the shore make the journey rather like a pageant. A day in Nice, and then dinner on a mid-evening train, the *Ligure,* into Italy (customs and immigration inspection, on board the train, are almost imperceptible—in sharp contrast to what one can undergo crossing an international boundary by automobile). The *Ligure's* staff is Italian, and so, generally, are the menu and the wines—absolutely no grounds for complaint. And the pageant of lights continues.

Overnight in Genoa, and then by a morning train down the Italian Riviera to Rome, and what a sight that coastal run is! The view inland offers a glimpse of the Leaning Tower of Pisa, by the way. There was, and still is, a restaurant car on that train, for which our thanks. Next day, an early-afternoon express with a deluxe restaurant car by way of Firenze and Bologna to Venice—itself an island, but so close to shore that our train took us right in. An early dinner next day, and then aboard our sleeping car to Trieste, almost on the border of Yugoslavia, and on across the border (the Yugoslavian frontier inspection is usually as polite as can be).

Eastern Europe

Soon after eight in the morning we were in Belgrade, the capital, and home of some of Eastern Europe's best chefs. Our hotel provided us after breakfast next day with a carry-on packet of food and drink to sustain us in our journey, in a carefully reserved set of first-class seats, on the *Marmara Express.* We rolled east shortly before ten o'clock on a nine-hour daytime journey to the Bulgarian border (here the customs and immigration operation was formal and long-drawn-out, but courteous) and the Bulgarian capital, Sofia, across a great variety of countryside and past examples of architecture that became increasingly Oriental. Sofia is Oriental, though Westernized enough for a trolley car to run right underneath an Oriental mosque in the center of the city.

Our next move, toward another international boundary, set us off, again armed with food and drink, at a little after eight in the morning, and again in carefully reserved seats, on the eleven-hour journey into Romania and its capital city, Bucharest. Here our school-days French, which had been at rest since we left Paris, was again called into play; French is the second language in the best hotels and the restaurants. The crossing of the border, at about four in the afternoon, was somewhat more cheerful than our crossing into Bulgaria, but almost as long. Bucarest was hot and dusty that summer, but our hotel was airy, and a vast orchestra made dinner music of nineteenth-century perfection. Romanian champagne, slightly too sweet but a great dust-quencher, took care of the evening.

We slept in for a day or so, preparing for a truly great leap—scientists would call it a quantum leap—the entry into Russia, whose border formalities can be exhaustive and exhausting. The *Danube Express* was to be our vehicle, out in the late evening from Bucharest, in a four-berth sleeping car—an arrangement, for two couples, far less formal than the civilities at the Russian border, which we reached next morning at what would have been breakfast time had there been a restaurant car. There wasn't, but passengers who turned out to be Russian school teachers who understood English heard us discussing our predicament and insisted on giving us black bread, cheese, cucumbers, and beer to keep us alive on the long run to Kiev, perhaps, at least in its more ancient parts, one of the most beautiful cities in the world. Kiev is Ukrainian, handsomely sited on a huge bluff above a river, and our two days there, and our first sampling of chicken a la Kiev, erased our memories of the border formalities and the dinerless run from the border. At the border it was, by the way, the first time we had undergone the eerie experience of sitting, locked in our sleeping car, as we slowly rose several feet in the air while the wheels on which we had come from Bucharest were removed and another set of wheels, set to the wider gauge of Russian railways, was rolled under us as replacements.

Two days in Kiev, mostly walking through the old town or along the river, and then by night to Moscow, in sleeping cars with two-berth compartments and of far less utilitarian surroundings than graced the car in which we had left Bucharest.

The Trans-Siberian

A day's rest and meditation, broken only by a night of opera at the Bolshoi Theater, and then aboard the *Russia,* the train that makes the longest journey on this globe—nearly 6,000 miles across Russia and Siberia to the Yellow Sea, where we were to resume our island-hopping. At that time, the *Russia* had not acquired the two-berth compartment cars now in service, so we were chock-a-block again in a four-berther, with our Intourist girl guide, a most useful and intelligent guardian, berthed elsewhere in the huge train. She it was who saw that we got breakfast, luncheon, and dinner precisely when we wanted it; she it was who translated the dining-car menus (unsalted Caspian caviar appeared three times on the *breakfast* menu during our seven-day journey as far as Khabarovsk). Between meals and afternoon tea in the dining car, which seemed never to close, we tried to converse—mostly in sign language—with the Japanese and Chinese and Mongols and Bulgarians and Poles we encountered, standing side by side with us as we gazed hour by hour at the steadily changing countryside and the strange villages and towns. No other overland journey can quite match this experience. In Khabarovsk, steaming in our first real bath in seven days, we talked only of our last day's trip, along the very edge of northern China, where, after dark, we could see the floodlights of a Chinese military air base. A welcome day of ease, and then a final night's journey in a more luxurious train to the seaport of Nakhodka, on the Yellow Sea—two-berth compartments, with a washroom and needle shower between each pair of compartments, two dining cars, and—of course—a champagne supper with our guide. In the morning, the coast—dark and brooding, a range of ominous mountains stretching far to the north.

A proper setting, those mountains, for our next spate of island-hopping, because the first night out on our neat, comfortable, and well-appointed

Russian passenger ship, the tail of a typhoon began rolling our vessel from side to side in a manner that made our voyage across the Cabot Strait a tame evening at sea. Typhoon weather pursued us through the second night, and then, as we approached the northern coast of Japan, we had a peaceful passage south to Yokohama. An elegant little bar helped us hardened travelers through the stormy weather, and there was a movie in which the *Russia,* the train in which we had crossed Siberia in summer, crossed Siberia in the middle of winter—more picturesque, and far more authentic, than the train journeys in the movie "Dr. Zhivago." We asked that it be shown again the second night out, and it was.

Across the Pacific

One last great obstacle, the Pacific Ocean, now interposed itself between us and home. Passenger ships across this broad expanse are rarely to be found at the time one wants them, but before we embarked upon our only flight on our round-the-world journey, we took an easy breather in Japan— not rushing south from Tokyo to Osaka on the celebrated Bullet trains, but going down the coast of the main island in a comfortable, leisurely series of trains whose restaurant cars, each run by a famous Japanese hotel that prided itself on its cuisine, presented us with true delicacies—baked eel, for example, so rich and delicious that we all ordered a second round. A day or so at the great Japanese hot-springs town of Beppu, and then by steam-ship and local trains up the magnificent Inland Sea on our way back to Tokyo and the flight to Seattle.

Then followed two nights aboard the *Empire Builder,* a train flush with good food and a glass-topped dome car from which we viewed some of the very best of the Wild West, and a daylight trip down the Mississippi River from Minneapolis and St. Paul en route to Chicago. What turned out to be our very last trip on the *Broadway Limited* was an all-Pullman occasion. It still had an observation car, and a so-called master room, or pair of master rooms, each with a shower—the perfect way of ending our circling-the-globe holiday.

The train across Newfoundland has gone to its reward, and so, I suspect, has the venerable steamer Kilgarriff, but the rest of our journey can still be made exactly as we made it, in part or in whole, and with some changes of name here and there. Be sure to try it before you dare say to anyone, "I have seen it all and done it all."

That is not all there is, of course, for the traveler who likes the notion of riding the rails in other countries. There are, for example, the daytime trains up the east and west coasts of England from London to Scotland; the nighttime *Blue Train* from Paris to the French Riviera; the great fleet of Trans-Europe Expresses across and up and down Western Europe, which—linked together—will carry you from Paris in the west into Belgium, Holland, Western Germany (as far as Munich), as well as into Switzerland, Italy, and as far south as Palermo, in Sicily. Not to mention the real race horses of Western Europe—such as *L'Etendard* (Paris-Bordeaux) and the twice-a-day *Le Capitole* (Paris-Toulouse) and the *Settebello* (Milan-Rome). All are but samples of the great galaxy of trains. And, if it is essential to pop from one major city to another overnight, there are expresses with sleeping cars, more and more of them air-conditioned, from nearly anywhere in this part of the world to anywhere else.

The Balkans, India, Asia—all these are for the railway adventurer, or for the cautious traveler who goes only where there are sleeping-car and daytime coach reservations to be had. The Balkan capitals may all be reached from the west by sleeping car; restaurant cars are more often absent than present. Adventure in India is at its best if you join a cruise ship that puts in, say, to Bombay and charters a train, sleeping cars, restaurant cars and all, for a land "cruise" of several days. There are a few sleeping cars from the west all the way to Athens, and two a week to Istanbul. In Asian Turkey, there are sleeping-car trains and a few day expresses that can properly feed you, serving the important cities.

Far-flung indeed is Australia, but its cross-the-continent *Indian Pacific* provides showers in every sleeping car, and the double bedrooms all have their own showers. The classic Australian train, however, is still the *Southern Aurora,* nightly between Sydney and Melbourne—for comfort, dining, wining, and just plain delight, it is one of the world's best. The North Island of New Zealand, a country in which every prospect, every landscape pleases, is an unlikely place in which you could expect to travel overnight between Auckland and Wellington, on a mountain-climbing railway of distinctly narrow gauge, in a train that gives you a full breakfast in bed (compliments of the management), provides you with showers, air-conditioning, and a staff whose sole aim is make the customer happy. One sleeping car, usually reserved for V.I.P.'s, offers a suite with a bedroom, living room, and real bathroom. Such elaborateness is the keynote of the *other* Blue Train, the one that runs once or twice a week (depending on the time of year) through South Africa, from Pretoria to Johannesburg and Cape Town. It is an overnight train, but so much of its run takes place during daytime, at both ends, that many miles of this stunningly beautiful country are visible in broad daylight. It is quite possible that, at the moment, this is the best-run, best-staffed, most comfortable train any of us are ever going to travel. Once you have made *this* journey, you can with truth tell your friends that "I have seen it all, done it all."

WHY RAILWAYS?

Travel, Not Just Transportation

By Paul Theroux

The author, an American resident of London, wrote his best-selling The Great Railway Bazaar *after an extended train trip from Waterloo Station to Tokyo and back. His latest book is* The Family Arsenal, *a novel.*

When travelers, old and young, get together and the talk turns to their journeys, there is usually an argument put forward by the older ones that there was a time in the past—fifty or sixty years ago, though some say less—when this planet was ripe for travel. Then, the world was innocent, undiscovered, and full of possibility. The argument runs as follows: In that period the going was good; it is no longer, because passports are now necessary, the White Fleet has ceased to cruise among the pretty islands of the Malay Archipelago, the great hotels have installed air-conditioning and removed the *punkahs,* and trains like the *Orient Express* are bare of luxury. These older travelers look upon the younger ones with real pity and seem to say, "Why bother to go?"

It is of course a ridiculous conceit to think that this enormous world has been exhausted of interest. There are plenty of simple trips (any travel agent can recommend a thousand) and there is enough that is remote and difficult to challenge a Shackleton, enough variety to puzzle Edward Lear and satisfy Mark Twain. There are still scarcely visited places, if you have the stomach and eyes for them, and there are exhilarating ways of reaching them. It is elderly and snobbish to dismiss present-day travel as somehow more feeble or less rewarding than in that other age; very likely Christopher Columbus reminisced in much the same way to his son Hernando. It is every traveler's wish to think of himself as Adam or Noah, to see his achievements as pure, unique and impossible for anyone else to recover. But for the bold and even the not-so-bold the going is still good, and as for the latter, there has never been a time when the faint-hearted could get so far.

What is unspoken in all these travelers' tales is that inexplicable wish to visit capital cities. A very pleasant man said to me recently, "How do you manage to meet all these amazing people? I've been all the places you have, but nothing happened to me." He gave me as proof a description of some terrible days he had spent in Bangkok and Kuala Lumpur. I challenged him. How had he gotten from one place to the other? He had flown, he said, and seemed surprised that I had wondered at that. I stated the obvious, that the real interest for me was neither of these cities but rather what lay between them, the long feathery tail of Thailand where the train occasionally winds along the Gulf of Siam and sends a sea-breeze through the compartment; the "bathroom" on this train, *The International Express,* with its tall stone water jars; the easily-met Thais, Chinese, Malays, homeward-bound Australians—all of them calmed by the movement of the train; the jungly frontier at Padang Besar, the shop-houses of Butterworth and the sight of Penang Island, the long trip through the ravaged tin-mining district of Ipoh, and the climb across the lower escarpment of the Cameron Highlands, and finally arrival at the strangest-looking railway station in the world, Kuala Lumpur's, with its minarets and its light-blue Arabian domes. The cities that connect this interesting railway are not exciting places—Bangkok is gasoline alley and a proliferation of mismatched temples and brothels that you first take for supermarkets. K.L. is rather small but recently fairly prosperous. The hotels in one are indistinguishable from the hotels in the other. This is not a sneer—every traveler needs a good hotel to convalesce in before setting out again.

After the journey the arrival cannot but seem an anti-climax. It is travel that matters, and the fact is that the airplane is not a mode of travel but a way of being transferred; from airport to airport there is little in between—ragged clouds like old bridal veils, and then a blue immensity of space, and just before landing, a country below that is an irregular and unmarked map, green and brown, stained with settlements. One learns to dread the excitements of the airplane, since most airplane excitements spell disaster for the passenger—the hi-jack, the burnt-out engine, the lunatic in economy, the puking child or the bore strapped beside you. No one needs more evidence that airplanes are at best very tedious capsules; there is a world of difference between travel and transfer.

Home on the Rails

The advantages of rail travel are well-known—you don't need to be Lucius Beebe to appreciate them. The train is the answer to motion sickness; it allows eating in peace, the post-prandial stroll, the close study of landscape and a choice of travel companions. Planes require that people sleep upright, making even a first-class passenger look like a tramp snoozing in a doorway; you can be horizontal in a train in your own bedroom. I have spoken at length in my travel book *The Great Railway Bazaar* of the pleasures of rail travel, but recently another occurred to me. The train is the only vehicle that permits the traveler access to all his luggage. In a car it's in the trunk, in a plane or bus it is hidden in the underbelly; on a train it travels with you, suitcase, valise, messkit, library, parcels; and the headache of keeping it together is relieved by the knowledge that at any moment you can root around, change your socks, find another book, verify that you haven't forgotten your tennis racket, set out your bottles and invite that corker in the next carriage over for a drink. What a comfort to be among all your belongings!

It is like being home, it has all those consolations, except that you are on the move. For this reason the train passenger is calm, he is game, he is good company; he knows he will arrive refreshed, and though time has no real importance in railway travel I think I should say that when I traveled from London to Tokyo and back on over thirty trains, just a few years ago, every one of them left the station the minute it was supposed to and most arrived on time as well.

My love of trains is non-technical. I am not a train-buff, though I can tell the difference between a steam locomotive and a diesel engine, and I know a good berth the morning after. The train-buff is a hobbyist; the real lover of trains is a traveler. I would go anywhere on a train, anywhere at all, and I have little interest in countries where there are no tracks, such as Laos, Chad, Afghanistan, or Western Samoa. On the other hand, I find it a great comfort to know that Mexico is full of railways, Corsica has a beauty, and Vietnam is toiling to rebuild the line from Saigon to Hanoi; there are enough railways in the world to fill a whole lifetime with travel—could anyone wish for more? I know of no thrill greater in travel than boarding a sleeping-car at night and knowing that I am to spend several days in it.

It was in such a mood that in 1973, in London's gray drizzle, I boarded a train for Paris to join the *Orient Express* and all the others that would take me to Tokyo via Ceylon and Singapore. Many people have asked me how I thought of it, how I planned it. It was simple. I had finished a book, I needed new sights, a journey, all of Asia. I knew I wanted to take trains, and so I got maps of Europe and Asia and traced a line along the railways—which were shown as black threads—a task no more demanding than the child's game of follow-the-dots. When I was done I had a picture of my journey, a parabola that took in most of Asia. My publisher was enthusiastic, and for the first time in my life I received an advance of money on an unwritten book. I spent the money before I reached Peshawar, and financed the rest of the trip by lecturing to Bengalis and Thais—wherever a railway junction happened to be near an American consulate (there was a particularly bullet-riddled station in Hue, and a university, too). I had left London with two tickets—one from London to Istanbul, the other from

Yokohama to Moscow. The rest I bought as I needed them, and in four months of travel I never made a hotel reservation in advance.

The going was good; it still is, and I am sure it will always be. Before I set out I looked around for a guide to the railways of the world but found only jingoistic turn-of-the-century handbooks about projected lines. *Cook's Continental Timetable* got me as far as Turkey; after that I was on my own. This Fodor Guide has been long overdue, and at last we can see—as the first European cartographers suggested four hundred years ago—the true size of the world: it is much larger and more complicated than any airline official would care to admit, and only the rankest jackass would call it a global village. Everyone knows that you can catch a plane from Boston to Central America, but isn't it a relief to know that you can board a train at South Station and after nine trains be at the Guatemalan border next week at the earliest?

FACTS AT YOUR FINGERTIPS

 WHY TAKE THE TRAIN? When pro-train and anti-train people get together, they invariably work up a big head of steam over the same argument: why, say the plane buffs, would anyone in his right mind want to spend all those hours or days cooped up in a train when a plane will get you where you're going so much faster at basically the same price?

Good question. Who *are* all those people who ride the trains?

Early in the formation of Amtrak, the giant corporation that took over most U.S. railroads in 1970 in an attempt to put them back on the right track, a government market study covering the income, tastes and travel habits of people who were riding the trains regularly at the time between Washington, D.C., and New York, revealed that the average family income of the typical railroad passenger was close to $15,000. The officials were flabbergasted. They, like most public transit "experts" were under the impression that the average train rider made about $3,000 to $5,000 a year. Nothing, apparently, could have been further from the truth.

A more recent survey proved equally interesting. It was taken in the Mid West, where a majority of passengers travel long range via USARail passes, and revealed that the primary reason 49 percent of the passengers surveyed were traveling by train was for "pleasure." That means they weren't out to beat traffic, save money or afraid to fly. It means they simply enjoyed traveling by train. They enjoyed moving at a leisurely, relaxed pace, seeing up close a land they obviously felt close to.

Needless to say, there are practical advantages for taking the train as well. As a promotional jingle for the fine Southern Railway System, one of the few independently-owned railroads left in the U.S., puts it:

> An experienced traveler we know,
> Chooses train as the best way to go;
> He gets lots of rest
> Arrives feeling his best
> With no worries about fog, sleet or snow.

Frequently, pure logistics give the edge to train travel. A college student, for instance, traveling from Montpelier, Vermont, to Washington, D.C., would have a number of alternatives to chose from: a Greyhound bus with layovers and changes in Albany and New York, $32.40; a bus to Burlington, Vermont, then fly to Washington with a change of planes at Albany, $58.02; an Air New England commuter flight from Montpelier to New York, then a jet shuttle to Washington, $67.64; the train from Montpelier to Washington, $27 coach; $56.50 for a roomette. To fly from Montpelier, it would be necessary to get up at 5:45 A.M.,then change terminals in New York to make the connecting flight to Washington. By train, one could board the Montrealer at 10:12 the night before, sleep on the train and arrive in Washington at 11 A.M. the next day, the same time, in fact, the plane would arrive. Clearly, the train makes more sense.

Since the very advent of air travel, the railroad's advantage of making downtown-to-downtown stops has clearly stood out. Many cities were actually built—grew up—around train stations, particularly in the western part of the United States. Airports were generally an afterthought, often plunked down in the middle of nowhere. Twenty years ago, according to a recent travel report, 90 percent of the door-to-door time for an average plane trip was spent in the air. Today, with getting to and from the airport and waiting, it's 50 percent. As the cost of travel continues to escalate, the expenses involved in getting to and from the airport are also increasing appreciably. With tip and tolls included, a taxi from midtown Manhattan to Kennedy Airport can average about $18. The airfare to Boston is $35. An Amtrak coach ticket, New York to Boston, is $16.50.

In Europe, where airfare is generally higher than it is in the United States and train fares are considerably lower, centrally located train stations have long been vital to the city complex—the big Bahnhofs of Germany, for instance. Arrive at the train station in Frankfort and you'll find a tourist office in the main concourse where visitors receive a wealth of free goodies—maps, souvenirs, discount tickets and a friendly face to send you off in the right direction. Outside, Kaiserstrasse is the nerve center of Frankfort, about ten minutes away from the city's best known hotel, the Frankfurter Hof, and the main shopping area beyond it, passing along the way startlingly pretty girls, full of health and strong strides and laughter, with high cheekbones and cropped blonde hair. Forty-five minutes from Frankfurt by train is lofty, romantic Heidelberg, with its long tradition of student life, good times and rousing song. A reserve-seat, round-trip, first-class ticket costs about $10. From Paris, numerous day trips are available by train to the countless "must see" destinations beyond the city—from the Gare Montparnasse station for Chartres with its famous cathedral, the Gare de l'Est station for Champagne, from the Gare de Lyon station for Fountainbleau and to hundreds of other famous excursion points. The traveler in Italy can take the new super express from Rome to Florence in one-and-a-half hours, emerge from the station across the street from the Cathedral of Florence with its famous Giotto bell tower and find himself immediately in the center of one of the most historically dazzling cities on earth. He'll also find himself in the middle of the city's main tourist shopping area, stalls set up along narrow, winding streets where Michelangelo once walked. Belguim has the densest railway network in continental Europe—anywhere in that country can be reached by train from Brussels within two hours—and trains in tiny Holland are so frequent that timetables are hardly necessary: at least twice every hour of the day from any station to any other.

Because homes and apartments are small, Europeans entertain frequently at restaurants and sidewalk cafes and they roam wide boulevards. Students study in the parks. Cities somehow seem more designed for human habitation there than in other parts of the world and the train stations reflect this feeling. Instead of eyesores, they are marvels of construction and convenience.

Fear of flying accounts for a small, though highly celebrated, number of train travelers. There are those who find it amusing that people are afraid to fly. Yet for the thousands of white-knuckled men and women who go into cataclysmic trauma at the mere thought of boarding a plane, there is nothing at all funny about their dedication to train travel. After all, they reason, if something happens to the train at least it's on the ground. Also, except perhaps for some fictional late-night capers on television, no train has yet been hijacked.

 PLANNING YOUR TRIP. Years ago, the fellow taking an extended train trip was always pictured in cartoon proportions as someone with a befuddled look on his face clutching an unwieldy ribbon of railroad tickets. All that's changed. Today, a computerized reservation system makes it possible to book accommodations and issue tickets within seconds. Tickets now are the coupon type similar to those used by airlines and come in the same convenient kind of ticket envelope. (In fact, many of the railroad's newest innovations have been borrowed from its chief competitor, the airlines.) Railroads generally accept all major credit cards, something they rarely did before. Travel agents can sell railroad tickets now and they give rail passengers full V.I.P. treatment, mainly because they receive a 10 percent commission on train tickets as compared to the 7 percent on airline ticket sales. (In Mexico, travel agents receive no commissions at all on rail tickets and are likely to tell you to come back some other manana if you want to buy one.) Amtrak and the Canadian National Railroad recently agreed to allow rail travelers from either Canada or the United States to purchase tickets from either company, making across-the-border trips that much easier.

Railroad timetables still require a Master's Degree in advanced logic to decipher, but with patience and 20-20 vision you'll find them quite informative. Amtrak's 64-page national timetable, covering non-Amtrak routes as well, lists 75 trains and the cities they serve by name. They can be obtained free at any Amtrak station, sales office or on the trains. Symbols designate the type of equipment, whether dome, Amfleet, turboliner, metroliner, diesel or electric, and the type of service and accommodations provided—dining car, lounge, sleeping cars, baggage and such—and whether or not reservations are required. Reservations are always required for sleeping cars and quite often, especially on longer runs, for coaches as well. Other data include sample fares, connecting bus service, connecting Canadian and Mexican rail service at the borders, track conditions (where delays can be anticipated due to repair work) and, most importantly, instructions on how to read the symbols.

When planning your trip, you might particularly note sleeping facilities listed for each train. Accommodations shown for the *Lake Shore Limited,* running from New York to Chicago, for example, include bedrooms, roomettes, slumber coaches and coaches. Cheapest always is the coach. That's because you've got to sit up all night in your seat. If you're a five-foot-tall cheer leader who can curl up like a kitten and sleep anywhere, you're in luck. But if you're a six-foot-two cowboy who likes to stretch out, a reclining seat, foot-rest, a pillow with a paper towel case over it and even a thoughtfully provided blanket won't do the trick. "Coaching it," in any event, is easier over western routes where track tends to be smoother and there aren't as many short, jerky stops to pull you out of your dreams.

The best economy buy is the slumber coach, less roomy than a roomette but providing bed and toilet in single and double rooms at about one-third the price. Not all trains have slumber coaches, in fact very few do, so if you're bargain hunting, you might check to see if your train offers them. For anyone traveling alone, a roomette is best. It's a little like camping out in a sardine can, but it offers privacy, a toilet and a fold-away bed that you can operate yourself in case you want an afternoon nap or just want to lounge around in bed all day, Sunday-style. For a couple, a bedroom is best. It has two beds, usually one on top of the other. For a family of four, a double connecting bedroom, or bedroom suite as they're called, is best. It provides two bathrooms, so there won't be any jam-ups in the morning.

In Europe, because of the wide variety of railroads, national and privately owned companies, you're apt to find more ingenious and sometimes more exotic sleeping arrangements—as many as three bunks stacked one on top of the other. "Couchettes" are popular, coach compartment seats that can be flattened out at night to sleep four to six. The conductor provides a pillow and blanket and of course you keep your clothes on. A standard $6 fee is charged all over Europe for "couchette" service in both first and second class compartments. In Russia and in many of the Eastern European countries, when you book sleeping accommodations you'll frequently find yourself sharing a room with somebody of the opposite sex. No one seems to mind much.

For U.S.A.: If you have questions not covered in the timetables, check with your travel agent or call your locally listed Amtrak number or any of the following for reservations and information:

IF YOU ARE CALLING AN 800-NUMBER
... please remember all 800-numbers (in some areas 1-800) are toll-free, long-distance numbers. Consult the local telephone directory for the proper way to place toll-free calls.

Albuquerque, NM .. 800- 421-8320	New Orleans, LA .. 800- 874-2800
Baltimore, MD 800- 523–5700	New York, NY .... (212) 736-4545
Boston, MA 800- 523-5720	Oklahoma City, OK 800- 421-8320
Champ.-Urb., IL 800- 972-9147	Omaha, NE 800- 421-8320
Chicago, IL .... (312) 786-1333	Orlando, FL 800- 342-2520
Cincinnati, OH 800- 621-0317	Philadelphia, PA .. (215) 824-1600
Denver, CO............ 800- 421-8320	Phoenix, AZ 800- 421-8320
Detroit, MI 800- 621-0353	Pittsburgh, PA 800- 562-5380
EL Paso, TX 800- 421-8320	Portland, OR 800- 421-8320
Fargo, ND.............. 800- 421-8320	Richmond, VA........ 800- 523-5720
Fort Lauderdale, FL 800- 342-2520	Sacramento, CA 800- 648-3850
Fort Worth, TX...... 800- 421-8320	San Antonio, TX 800- 421-8320
Harrisburg, PA 800- 562-5360	San Diego, CA 800- 648-3850
Houston, TX 800- 421-8320	San Francisco, CA .. 800- 648-3850
Indianapolis, IN...... 800- 621-0353	Savannah, GA 800- 874-2800
Jacksonville, FL .... (904) 731-1600	Seattle, WA 800- 421-8320
Kansas City, MO 800- 621-0317	Springfield, IL 800- 972-9147
Los Angeles, CA .. (213) 624-0171	St. Louis, MO 800- 621-0317
Louisville, KY 800- 874-2775	St. Petersburg, FL .. 800- 342-2520
Memphis, TN 800- 874-2800	Spokane, WA.......... 800- 421-8320
Miami, FL 800- 342-2520	Tampa, FL 800- 342-2520
Milwaukee, WI 800- 621-0353	Tucson, AZ 800- 421-8320
Minneapolis, MN.... 800- 621-0317	Vancouver, BC .... (604) 681-4418
Montgomery, AL 800- 874-2800	Washington, DC 800- 523-5720
Nashville, TN 800- 874-2800	W. Palm Beach, FL 800- 342-2520

For information about routes, facilities and services of train in *Europe,* again contact your travel agent or write to the following:

AUSTRIA
Österreichische Bundesbahnen, A-1010 WIEN, Elisabethstrasse 9.

BELGIUM
Société Nationale des Chemins de fer Belges, 1070 BRUXELLES, Rue de France 85.

DENMARK
Danish State Railways, Solvgade 40, DK 1349 KOBENHAVN K.

EIRE
Coras Iompair Eireann, Heuston Station, DUBLIN 8.

FINLAND
Valtionrautatiet, 00100 HELSINKI 10, Vilhonkatu 13.

FRANCE

Société Nationale des Chemins de fer Francais, 75 PARIS IXe, 88 Rue St Lazare.

GERMANY (Federal Republic)
Deutsche Bundesbahn, Friedrich-Ebert-Anlage 43-45, 6000 FRANK-FURT (MAIN) 1.

GREAT BRITAIN
British Rail, 222 Marylebone Road, LONDON NW1 6JJ.

ITALY
Ferrovie dello Stato, ROMA, Piazza della Croce Rossa 1.

NETHERLANDS
Nederlandse Spoorwegen, Moreelsepark, UTRECHT.

NORWAY
Norges Statsbaner, OSLO 1, Storgaten 33.

PORTUGAL
Caminhos de ferro Portugueses, LISBOA 2, Calcada do Duque 20.

SPAIN
RENFE, Plaza de los Sagrados Corazones 7, MADRID 16.

SWEDEN
Statens Järnvägar, S-105 50 STOCKHOLM.

SWITZERLAND
Schweizerische Bundesbahnen, CH-3000 BERN, Hochschulstrasse 6.

For information and addresses of railroads in Canada, Mexico and elsewhere in the world outside the U.S.A. and Europe, see specially designated sections elsewhere in this book.

WHAT WILL IT COST? Recently, the market research chief at Amtrak went to his computers, fed into them various figures on passenger miles traveled, ticket costs and other related data and came up with the figure of 5.7 cents per mile as the average cost of traveling by rail today in the United States. He points out that the figure tends to vary in different parts of the country—it's slightly cheaper per mile to travel in the West than in the East—and USARail passes and other discounting policies shade the final figure somewhat, but, in all, the fare boils down to 5.7 cents per mile.

A general gauge for the cost of traveling by coach would fall somewhere between the price of a bus ticket and an economy class airline ticket. Bus fare from Chicago to Los Angeles, for example, is $99.10. Economy plane fare is $153. Train coach fare is $110; a roomette is $182.50. Neither the train nor the bus fare include meals and beverages, which are complimentary on the plane.

Some other sample rail fares:	Coach	Roomette
Boston to Indianapolis	$64.50	$112.00
Seattle to Los Angeles	$71.00	$126.00
Chicago to New Orleans	$47.50	$90.00

A bedroom usually costs about a third again as much as a roomette. The roomette indicated above between Chicago and Los Angeles is $182.50. A room would be $297 if occupied by one person. For a couple on the family plan it would be $352.

An adult passenger traveling from Washington to Atlanta on the Southern Railway System's crack Southern Crescent faces an even wider range of accommodations and prices: coach $44.25; roomette $58.05; bedroom $67.40; bedroom suite $85.90; drawing room $89.22; master bedroom $130.90. (The latter has the only shower available on any passenger train in North America.)

These fares all represent a relatively new pricing structure that incorporates "first class" charges into the overall cost of the ticket. The practice of charging higher first-class rail fares to passengers using parlor car or sleeping car accommodations goes back to the days when such "luxury" service on passenger trains was provided by Pullman and other private companies. The railroad, selling only *transportation,* charged higher per mile fares to passengers in the Pullman cars than it charged passengers in its own higher capacity coach cars. Today, passengers are no longer charged the extra first-class tariff for parlor car and sleeping car accommodations, but prices for such have been raised proportionately to absorb the difference. The price is the same in the end, only the terms have been changed. The premium, high-speed Metroliner serving the Northeast Corridor between Washington and New York is the one exception. It still maintains a distinction between Metrocoach and Metroclub rail fares.

In Europe, first- and second-class differentials are strictly adhered to in train accommodations, even in coach seating. First-class seats are reserved. Second-class seats generally aren't. Thrifty Europeans frequently buy the unreserved second-class seats and then sit in any empty first-class seat they happen to see. As a result, every time the train pulls into the station a wild game of musical chairs ensues as reserve-seat ticket holders come aboard to claim their seats and everybody else, bag and baggage, goes scampering off to find other empty spaces.

In what has become almost the standard mode for merchandising anything in America from orange juice to magazine subscriptions, today's traveler can be nothing but dazzled by the incredible array of bonus and bargain discount plans available when he rides the rails. As with any other business transaction seen in the harsh light of the cashier, such programs are designed to bolster sagging business, be it during off hours, off seasons or off on some forgotten railroad, and to attract new passengers. That's fine. Anything that costs less these days can't be all bad.

U.S.A.'s Family Plan. Traveling only on Mondays through Thursdays and Saturdays, the Family Plan provides a 25 percent discount on first-class or coach fares for a husband or wife and/or children 12 through 21 who are traveling with one full fare, and a 62.5 percent reduction for kids from two through 11. Children under two travel free. You can't travel "Family Plan" on Fridays or Sundays.

Excursion Rates. Excursion fares are part of a promotional campaign to encourage rider-ship on segments of routes, or at off-peak hours of the day, when passenger loads are light and there is plenty of space on the train. Discounts range from 25-31 percent of the regular round-trip coach fare and tickets are limited to 30 days after the first date of travel. Savings are substantial. For example, passengers between all points on the New Orleans-El Paso segment of the Sunset Limited's route are eligible for a 25 percent discount when using the 30-day round-trip excursion rate. Sample fares include: New Orleans-El Paso $110, a saving of $36; New Orleans-Houston, $38.50, a saving of $12.50; New Orleans-San Antonio, $55, a saving of $18; and Houston-San Antonio $23.50, a saving of $7.50. Use is restricted: anytime except between noon and 6 P.M. on Friday, Sundays and special holidays is okay. Excursion rates do not apply to Metroliners. Other excursion routes include New York-Buffalo; Norfolk/Newport News-Chicago; Boston/Springfield-Washington; Nashville-Florida; Seattle-Portland; San Francisco/Oakland-Bakersfield; Dallas-Laredo; Springfield-St. Louis; Chicago-Quincy; Memphis-New Orleans; Chicago-Dubuque; and Truckee (California)-Reno/Sparks. Excursion routes change frequently, so inquire about them when you plan your trip.

Off-Season Excursions. An example: off-season coach excursion fares include Montreal to Florida and New York to Florida runs during the period of September 8 through December 17. The round-trip $109 New York-Florida and the $144 Montreal-Florida fares represent $43 and $54 savings respectively over the regular coach fares. The reduced rate can also be used on intermediate points along both routes. During the same periods, a one-way discount between Chicago and Florida trims $26.30 off the regular $88 fare. Discounts apply to coach travel only and stopovers are not permitted. These off-season excursion rates also change frequently, so again inquire when planning your trip, especially when traveling to a high-season/low-season resort destination.

Group Rates. Amtrak offers a 25 percent discount for all groups of 15 or more passengers traveling round-trip in coach. Groups of 15 or more are also allowed to purchase one-way tickets at a 15 percent reduction, a travel incentive particularly aimed at groups traveling by intermodal means, air-rail, rail-cruise and such.

Tour Packages. Literally thousands of tour packages are now being offered to interesting places around the country (and Canada and Mexico as well), organized both by the railroad companies and independent agencies and tour group packagers. These include escorted and unescorted tours either exclusively by rail or rail combined with air, bus or cruise travel. Savings are generally quite substantial.

Typical is a "Rail, Road and City Adventures" tour that allows a family or a party of four to choose from 222 U.S. vacation destinations for as little as $8.75 a day each (plus rail fares), a program sponsored jointly by Amtrak, Holiday Inn and Hertz. The tour offers a stay at a Holiday Inn with accommodations ample for four, plus a full day with unlimited mileage in a Hertz Pinto, Dart or similar automobile. The price is the same for one, two, three or four traveling together—$34.95 a day in most cities; $35.95 at West Coast destinations ($9 a day each for a party of four), and $36.95 ($9.25 each for four) in the East from New England through Virginia. Rail fares are extra, but Family Plan, excursion rates and USARail passes can all be applied.

Escorted tours generally depart on a weekly basis and range in duration from a few days to several weeks. Assuming double occupancy in hotels, rates usually run about $50 to $70 a day and are all inclusive with such "extras" tossed in as welcoming cocktail parties and farewell dinners.

Amtour, one of the nation's largest packagers of railroad tours, offers 42 "Stopover" and "Short Stay" tours in the Western part of the United States. The one-night to four-or-more-night packages range in price from $16 (each, double) for a simple stopover in Santa Barbara to $152 for a San Francisco vacation. Tours include Berkeley, San Jose (with Marriott's Great America), San Simeon Castle, Santa Barbara, San Diego, Disneyland, Portland, Seattle and Mt. Rainier National Park. (Amtrak's Pacific International, linking Seattle and Vancouver, may be used in conjunction with Vancouver-Victoria and "Royal Hudson Steam Train" tours in British Columbia.) Tour folders available from Amtrak travel agents or the Amtrak Travel Center, P.O. Box 262, Addison, IL 60101.

USARail Pass. One of the biggest and most successful innovations in American rail travel, the *USARail Pass* was initiated in 1975, originally for the exclusive use of visitors from abroad. The following year it was introduced on an experimental basis for American citizens as well (and those of Canada and Mexico) and was a resounding success. It was extended and re-extended and now seems to be here to stay. Since its introduction, USARail Pass rates have fluxuated almost as much as the Mexican peso. Its lowest recent prices: $165 for 14 days; $220 for 21 days;

$275 for 30 days, plus tax. Half price for children two through 11. Higher on-season rates usually prevail in the summer. The pass is good for unlimited coach travel on all Southern Railway and Amtrak trains, except Metroliners, a network of 25,000 miles, and may be upgraded when sleeping accommodations are available by paying the difference between the coach and premium fare. Travel must begin within 15 days of purchase. The pass itself cannot be used for boarding, but may be presented in exchange for tickets at any station in 484 cities and towns in the U.S., as well as in some areas of eastern and western Canada. They are not transferable; holders are required to sign the purchased tickets in the presence of a conductor and the signature must match the signature on the ticket. Passes can be paid for by cash, check or some credit cards.

Eurailpass. If you plan to do a lot of traveling by rail in Europe, a *Eurailpass,* granddaddy of all railroad bargains, is a must. This is a convenient, all-inclusive ticket that can save you money on over 100,000 miles of railroads and railroad-operated buses, ferries, river and lake steamers, hydrofoils, and some Mediterranean crossings in 13 countries of western Europe (excluding the United Kingdom, Ireland and Greece). It provides the holder with unlimited travel at rates of: 15 days for $170; 21 days for $210; 1 month for $260; 2 months for $350; 3 months for $420; and second-class student (up to age 25) fare of two months for $230. Children under 12 go for half fare, under 4 go free. These prices cover first-class passage for the Trans Europe Express and other services. Available only to those who live outside of Europe or North Africa, the pass must be bought from an authorized agent before you leave for Europe. Apply through your travel agent; or the general agents for North America: French National Railroads, Eurailpass Division, 610 Fifth Avenue, New York, N.Y. 10020; or through the German Federal Railroad, 630 Fifth Avenue, New York, N.Y. 10020 and 45 Richmond Street, W., Toronto, Ontario M5H 1Z2 Canada. To get full value from your pass, be sure not to have it date-stamped until you actually use it for the first time.

Excellent value as the Eurailpass is it should be remembered that it is essentially for those who plan to do a lot of traveling. If you only want to make say two or three journeys it is best to purchase the tickets as required. In some countries if you travel a certain distance on a return trip or circular trip basis and stay a minimum length of time (generally just a few days) you can get reductions on the standard fares. For example in France if you travel more than 1500 kms. and spend five days or more in the country you get a 20T reduction on the normal fare.

Britrail Pass. In Great Britain (England, Scotland and Wales only), you can purchase a *Britrailpass,* which again allows you unlimited rail (and associated ferryboat and bus) travel for certain periods. For second-class travel, the cost for 7 days is $60; for 14 days, $90; for 21 days, $120; and for one month, $145. For first-class travel, the cost for 8 days is $80; for 15 days, $115; for 21 days, $145; and for one month, $165. *Note:* prices likely to rise.

In addition to these, young people (ages 14-22) can also obtain *Britrail Youth Passes,* which cost $50 for 7 days, $80 for 14 days, and $120 for one month, all for unlimited mileage in second class.

Apply to BritRail Travel International Ltd, 270 Madison Ave., New York, N.Y. 10016; or 510 West Sixth Street, Los Angeles, Calif.; or U.K. Building, 409 Granville Street, Vancouver 2, B.C.; or 55 Eglinton Avenue East, Toronto 4, Ontario, Canada. *Please note that these British arrangements are subject to review.*

Young people with a desire to travel extensively in Europe by rail should purchase an *Inter-Rail Card.* This is available to anyone under 21 years of age and the holder is entitled to unlimited second-class rail travel (along with connecting ferry and in certain cases bus services) in no fewer than 18 countries in western and central Europe plus Morocco. The card also allows half-fare travel on all rail services in the U.K. and Ireland and on the Sealink ferries connecting the British Isles with the continent. The Inter-Rail Card is valid for one calender month and can be purchased at most mainline stations, rail ticket agencies and travel agents. You must show evidence of age on purchase and the card is NOT transferable.

Britrail has honed its famous "Britainshrinker" tours of the English countryside down to a fine science. Taking advantage of British Rail's high speed trains, these extremely low-priced tours (especially now with the fractured British pound) give visitors a quick trip to a town outside London in the early morning. There, a special chartered bus is boarded and a guide shows off a picturesque corner of England. After a leisurely day of visiting towns and stately homes, there's another fast trip back to London. Lunch and admission fees are included. Typical is the "King Arthur's England" tour, leaving Paddington Station every Tuesday and Thursday at 8:30 A.M. for Glastonbury. There's a check-in point and uniformed hostess at the station. The specially trained guide sorts out King Arthur fact from fiction during the train journey. Glastonbury Abbey where King Arthur is buried, the Vale of Avalon, the Chalice Well and other Arthurian associations are visited. After lunch, Wells and the 18th century city of Bath. The train arrives back at Paddington Station at 6:26 P.M., in time for evening festivities. Price: $24.

Another tour covers Bath and Stonehenge, $27. There's one to Canterbury and Dover, $21; Stratford-on-Avon, Warwick Castle and Coventry Cathedral, $22; York and Harewood House, $31; Oxford and the Cotswolds, $22; Brighton and Arundel Castle, $22; Cambridge and the Suffolk Villages, $19.

Details available from: BritRail Travel International, 270 Madison Avenue, N.Y., N.Y., 10016; 510 West Six Street, Los Angeles, CA, 90014; 333 North Michigan Avenue, Chicago, IL, 60601; and 76 Arlington Street, Boston, MA 02116.

 GETTING THERE. Traveling by train in Europe, of course, first requires getting there, the cost obviously a major consideration in planning your trip. Transatlantic air fares vary considerably. Transatlantic airfares have been approved for the upcoming European tourist season. To insure the best value for the travel dollar, *Air France* has prepared the following guidelines to this year's tariffs.

There are now 11 types of scheduled fares between New York and Paris. With seasonal variations, this makes 24 possible roundtrip prices ranging from $350 to $1,564. The price ranges given below represent the low and high season rates.

Concorde $1,564 (New York) $1,654 (Washington). 1976 marked the beginning of the supersonic era—the opportunity for every traveler to experience SST flight on a regularly scheduled basis. The Concorde fare, which is the subsonic first class plus a 20% surcharge, permits this unique travel experience that cuts travel time to Europe in half. (Note: New York service subject to gov't. approval.)

First Class $1,302. Provides maximum service and convenience, with no limitations on time of travel or number of stopovers. The only fare with no seasonal variations, it is especially attractive during heavy traffic periods when the other fares go up.

Economy Class. $692–866. Advantageous for the independent traveler seeking maximum flexibility with no limitations on stopovers or time of travel.

14-21 Day Excursion. $588–681. For the independent traveler with a two to three week vacation, who wants no group land programs plus the flexibility of up to five stopovers. Its small seasonal variation makes it especially attractive during high fare summer months.

22-45 Day Excursion. $451–541. The best price for the independent traveler who doesn't want to be tied down to a fixed program. Offers a price break to those who can plan a three to six week stay in Europe and require no stopovers.

APEX. $350–446. Lowest available North Atlantic airfare for a passenger who desires the services and guaranteed departures of a scheduled carrier and is willing to meet the conditions typical of charter flights including: a. full payment two months in advance; b. no changes in reservations; c. no stopovers; d. a 22-45 day stay.

YOUTH. $457–508. For ages 12 through 21, it is ideal for young people wishing to stay abroad for more than six weeks. Reservations not accepted more than five days prior to departure. No stopovers.

7-8 Day GIT (Group Inclusive Tour). $400–426. The most popular fare for short visits to Europe, valid during most of the year (Sept 16-May 22). Allows one stopover and requires simultaneous purchase of between $70 and $90 minimum land arrangements (hotel, rental car, sightseeing, etc.). Available to groups of ten formed by the airline.

14-21 Day GIT. $420–521. The original group vacationer's fare combines year round low group airfare with prepackaged land programs at discounted rates. Allows three group stopovers and requires $120 minimum land arrangements.

Affinity. $410–519. Previously offered the advantage of charter group rates to members of recognized organizations, requiring 40 or more passengers in a group, but new Civil Aeronautics Board (CAB) ruling now makes low-cost flights available to just about anyone. Charter operators and travel agents are now allowed to organize round-trip flights for individuals without requiring membership in sponsoring organizations. You still have to buy your ticket in advance, however. A minimum of 45 days advance purchase is required for destinations in nine European countries; 30 days suffice for all other countries. Charter-flight travelers to the nine European countries are required to stay at least a week; other destinations carry no layover requirements.

Incentive. $410. Similar to above but requires five-to-15 day stay and is available only from September 1 through May 31.

 BY SHIP. Transatlantic tourists who prefer a leisurely sea crossing to frenetic air travel are finding this form of transportation harder to arrange. The elegant liners, with their aura of romance and luxury, that once sailed the North Atlantic on regular runs are rapidly taking to more profitable cruise schedules, or being scrapped altogether. At this writing, the only big company with fairly regular crossings is the *Cunard Line* from New York to Southampton or Cherbourg.

Two smaller shipping lines with sailings from Montreal are *Polish Ocean Lines,* calling at Southampton or London, then on to Rotterdam and Gdynia; and the *Baltic Steamship Co.,* which also sails from New York and calls at Le Havre, Bremerhaven and London (Tilbury), going on to Leningrad (June–Oct.). Both have modern, air-conditioned and stabilized ships.

Fares. When you travel by sea, your transportation cost is an elastic if not actually elusive quantity. In addition to tipping, which adds from $15–50 to your expenses, depending on class, you are almost certain to spend an equivalent amount on incidentals during your days aboard.

Fares vary according to route and season, and roundtrip usually saves you 5 percent. The basic one-way transatlantic fare ranges from about $900 first class, $515 tourist, in season, to $760 and $430 respectively, thrift season. Enquire from your travel agent, as fares vary according to the shipping line and port of entry, and also will be subject to change due to international currency adjustments.

Children under 1 year old not occupying a separate berth are carried for $40 in first class and $20 in cabin or tourist class. Children from 1 to 12 travel at half the adult fare, but have full adult baggage allowance.

Transatlantic passengers who embark or disembark at a French port pay a port tax of 25 frs. in addition to the tourist or first class fares.

 ON THE TRAIN. Taking your first lengthy train trip can be as awesome an experience as anything else you do for the first time. Suddenly all your preconceived ideas about train travel seem to have been formed by watching late-night movies on television and are probably as outdated as June Allyson's hairdo.

There are some basic rules. First, you've got to get to the train on time. Trains may leave late for a variety of reasons, but they rarely leave early. If you have more baggage than you can comfortably handle, free porter (Red Cap) service is available at most American stations (a 35-cent tip per bag is customary) and a majority of U.S. stations now have free baggage carts as well. In most foreign countries, there is a standard charge (see individual chapters). If you have a compartment and, say, only two pieces of luggage, you may want to keep the bags with you for convenience. If you have a great caravan of bags, you can check three pieces through to your destination free of charge. The weight limitation is set at 150 pounds for checked baggage, but unlike airlines where weight factors are understandably important, you won't be hassled if you're a few pounds over. As a rule, you can stuff as much baggage as you can handle in your compartment. The sleeping car attendant, on station at the front of each sleeping car, will help you. If you're too crowded, he'll even store some of the bags in an unused compartment for you, and, as with any other extra bits of personal service, you're expected to tip extra at the appropriate time. (See section on tipping.) If you do check baggage through, be sure not to include anything you'll need during your trip, toilet articles and such; if you're traveling in a foreign country, especially not your passport. Be alert, particularly in the larger cities such as New York, Chicago or Detroit, to "freelance" porters who will offer to carry your bags for you and then demand a ridiculous fee, if indeed your bags don't disappear completely.

If you're traveling coach and arrive at the train station just as the train is pulling out—or if you get there early and lines are jammed up at the ticket counters—you can buy your ticket from the conductor once you're aboard. A service fee of 25 cents is charged. You can also buy parlor car and sleeping car tickets or upgrade your coach ticket once you're on train, but since space is always "reserved," you're taking a bit of a gamble by counting on it.

Crossing the country by train takes three nights over most routes. You can figure one night from the East Coast to Chicago by way of the *Broadway Limited* or the *Lake Shore Limited*, then two nights to the West Coast on any number of trains that travel through that scenic part of the country.

Your compartment, be it slumbercoach, roomette or bedroom, will be small and will seem even smaller the longer you're in it. Roomette #3 in car # 1401 on the Lake Shore Limited from New York City to Chicago, for example, is more or less standard. It has an outside curtain that zips to the floor for privacy; it also has a sliding door that locks. It has a toilet and wash basin. The latter folds into the wall when not in use. The toilet has a heavy vinyl-upholstered cover so it can also be used as a spare seat. The bed folds away into the wall and there is a large, rather stiff and not particularly comfortable upholstered chair. When the bed, made up in advance, is released from the wall—a simple turn of a handle does this—the bed comes down over the chair which folds flat and over the toilet. Be sure not to position the bed until you're sure you won't have to use the toilet again, otherwise you've got to reverse the whole process. If you have to do this, make sure the bed is firmly latched back into the wall. Otherwise it may fall on your head.

The compartments are actually ingenious in design. When the bed is down, two large wall mirrors, depending on your outlook, will either make the room look larger or make it look more crowded. Also, when the bed is down, the sink is automatically locked into the wall. There is a closet with hangers for your clothes and a compartment on top for your shoes. A bedside tray holds your change, watch and personal items. Rooms are automatically heated or cooled via an individal control switch above the bed. There is a fan above and a reading light. Wall speakers for piped-in music and radio broadcasts are forever silent now; the rickety-split of the moving trains played havoc with the sensitive mechanism and the service, though pleasant, proved too costly to maintain.

Rooms are designated by letters—A, B, C, etc. and roomettes by numbers. Experienced rail travelers always request the higher numbers and the lower letters, thus assuring space as close as possible to the center of the car, away from the vibration of the wheels. Your sleeping car attendant will make up your bed for you or, as indicated previously, you can easily do so yourself. If you don't want to be disturbed after you're in bed, you should wait until the conductor pulls your ticket before retiring. Otherwise, as soon as you get settled in, he'll come banging on your door. (Abroad, Passport Control at the border points goes through this same irritating ritual.) Tell your porter when you want to be awakened and he'll be there with a cheerful knock on your door, and coffee and juice if you request it.

American trains travel through four time zones, so you should set your watch ahead or back if a time change is indicated on your timetable. But don't worry if you don't. No one has yet been known to suffer a severe case of train lag!

The romantic clickey-clack of the train as it rolls steadily on through the night lulls some people right off to sleep like babies in their cradles. It drives other people right up the wall. If you find yourself heading into a creaky night of total insomnia, what with the strange surroundings and being jostled about, you might try reversing your direction. If you're sleeping north to south, then change around to the other direction, south to north. It may work. The porter will wonder what you're doing with your feet in the pillow when he comes by to wake you up in the morning, but at least you'll have had a good night's sleep.

Bedrooms are considerably more comfortable than roomettes, simply because they're roomier. They also feature a self-contained bathroom with a sink and toilet. After several days on a train, you'll find that such miner features as these can make a major difference in your sense of pride and well being. You'll also make other discoveries. If you ask your porter, he'll bring you a little portable table that can be attached securely to your wall and used for writing, reading, working or drinking. If you know your neighbors, the porter can also fold up the dividing partition between the two bedrooms and you can have a party.

 DINING ON WHEELS. In the heyday of railroading, a line's reputation rose and fell on the quality of its dining car service and the skill of its chefs. But we live in a hurried age where opulent dining has given way to fast-food chains and specialty restaurants that are more gimmicky than grand. And so, too, have railroads been forced into a more practical and realistic means of feeding passengers and keeping the majority of them happy. The food is still good—on some trains excellent—and the service is traditional, but, alas, most meals come from microwave ovens now and glittering crystal has been replaced by plastic.

LUNCH/DINNER

Cranberry Juice Cocktail
*

Mexican Cole Slaw
(NOTE: Price of entree includes Appetizer, Salad, Roll and Butter,

Dessert and Beverage)
Beef Burgundy
Buttered Noodles—Peas with Sweet Peppers
$3.35

*

Breast of Cornish Hen
Cordon Bleu
Wild Rice Combination—Peas and Carrots
$4.65

*

Veal Parmigiana
Rice Pilaff—Cut Green Beans
$3.25

*

Roll and Butter

*

Light Cream Cheese Cake

*

Coffee, Tea or Milk
Enjoy a bottle of wine with your meal . . .
Imported Mateus Rose, Split $1.00

The above menu is one featured recently on an Amfleet train running between Boston and Washington. Meals are picked up in the Amcafe car and taken to the passenger's seat; the new trains feature traybacks. Drinks, standardized throughout all of Amtrak now, are priced as follows: cocktails and cordials $1.50; beer and ale .75; premium beer (imported) .90; wine (½ bottle) $2.00; soft drinks .40.

Dining car service on long distance trains, discussed elsewhere in the individual section on trains, is more elaborate. Table d'hote dinners range from $3 for "fluffy three-egg omelettes" to $3.95 for chicken cacciatore, to $6.95 for a sirloin steak. The evening menu might include a chef's salad for $2.95, a beefburger deluxe with trimmings, $1.85, and steak sandwich for $4.25. Dining car as well as snack bar service is available for coach passengers.

If given 24-hours' notice, Amtrak can supply a variety of kosher meals in almost any area of the country. Such lunches and dinners currently feature beef jardiniere, roast boneless breast of chicken and filet of sole almondine. Breakfasts offer a Spanish omelette or Nova Scotia salmon omelette. Cost of a kosher meal, served with the rabbinical seal unbroken and with kosher eating utensils, ranges from $3.50 to $4.25.

Passengers requiring salt-free, low calorie or other special diets should consult the maitre d' in the dining car. Such food can be prepared to special request— broiled instead of fried, or without seasoning or butter. Most long-distance trains carry a limited supply of baby foods, but to be safe a mother should bring along her own supply. Baby foods and bottles can be heated in the galley.

For dieters, most Amtrak luncheon and dinner menus feature a "Waistliner Special."

In Europe, where dining is still more of a fine art than a practical necessity, railroad meal service runs the gamut from elegant dining cars to self-service buffet aboard France's Gril-Express, as choice and as elaborate a selection as any land-based cafeteria. On the "Radio Train" in Southern Ireland, meals and refreshments are served to passengers at their tables as they listen to commentaries on the passing scene. Computerized check-out equipment helps give Swedish buffet car diners quick, efficient service.

Many stations, particularly those in Europe, sell box lunches and snacks at departure points and at stops along the way. Haggling out the window over the price of a salami sandwich is a common sight. You can also bring your own. If you do decide to store food in your compartment, it's wise to keep the food well secured in air-tight containers or wrappers. Rodents and roaches are not unknown to trains, particularly some of the older models still in service. Drinking water on trains abroad can often be a problem, so you might consider bringing a ration of your own. Also, when traveling through a variety of different countries, remember to bring sufficient currency along for each country; frequently on a train you'll have trouble converting your "foreign" money, especially for smaller meal purchases. One fellow with only U.S. greenbacks in his pocket got so hungry on the famed Orient Express going through Yugoslavia that he had to trade a pair of shoes for three jelly doughnuts!

 TRAVELING WITH CHILDREN. Robert Benchley once wrote, "There are only two ways to travel. One is first class. The other is with children."

Mr. Benchley obviously never watched kids on a train, or he might have tempered his comment. Children love trains (didn't you when you were small?). For a youngster, sleeping overnight in a compartment—climbing up the bunk ladder and fidgeting with all the buttons and switches—is as much fun as a trip to Disneyland or camping out on top of Old Smoky. In the coaches, little girls make endless visits to the bathroom and stay forever, and young Casey Joneses inch their way toward the engineer's compartment, full of awe and wonder. It's a great trip at a marvelous age. Children under 2 travel free in North America, under 4 in Europe. From 2 to 11, they go half fare on Amtrak, and its Family Plan even betters that.

Unescorted children 8 through 11 may travel on Amtrak trains provided the parent or guardian fills out an application specifying such information as the name and address of the person putting the child on the train and the name and adress of the person meeting the child at the destination. The application also requires a signature on the following acknowledgement: "It is understood that this minor is capable of making this trip alone, has been informed of schedule, has sufficient funds for meals and other incidentals, and will cooperate with any instructions given by Amtrak or carrier(s) personnel."

Traveling in unfamiliar surroundings can be traumatic for adults, much less children, so parents should exercise all due precautions when sending a child on a train alone. Look for the kindly lady, preferably someone traveling with a child the same age, who might be getting off at the same stop. Ask her to keep an eye on your little one. Also be sure to inform the conductor that the child is traveling unescorted and inform him where the child should get off. Train stations, for whatever reason, seem to attract derelicts and perverts, so if a child has to travel alone it's best done in daylight hours. Unaccompanied children are charged full adult fares.

When traveling in foreign lands, children, even babies, needn't be a special problem. Most hotels, unless a special cot or crib is requested, do not charge for a child who sleeps in the same room as parents. The majority of first-class hotels abroad offer bonded baby-sitting service. It's either free, in which case a tip is anticipated, or the charge can go as high as three or four dollars an hour.

Denmark has an extensive and extremely well run baby-sitting service geared for travelers. In essence, it consists of numerous hotels set up exclusively for groups of children of various ages. Trained, English-speaking nurses look after the youngsters from infants to twelve-year-olds, serving them meals and tucking them in for afternoon or evening naps. Cost, with pick-up and delivery of the child, is $12 to $15 a day, with reductions for two or more children within the same family. Baby carriages can also be rented in Copenhagen for about 70 cents a day. Most European trains, Canadian trains, Mexican trains and some U.S. trains offer kids coloring books, souvenirs, cut-outs, paper hats and the like to keep them amused and entertained. And there's always the scenery.

 TRAVELING WITH PETS. Planning to take your cat, dog, trained monkey or boa constrictor along? Amtrak realizes that some passengers like to travel with their pets, so it has special arrangements for transporting them. It prefers that all pets travel in the baggage car. (Guide dogs, however, are always allowed to travel with their masters.) Pets should be placed in a well-ventilated crate or cage and checked as baggage. There is a small fee for this service. (Suitable containers in three different sizes are sold at the baggage department of over 40 Amtrak stations and range in price from $15 to $30.)

 TRAIN ETIQUETTE. You may as well face it. There is just no way to pour coffee on a moving train without spilling it. That's what those little paper doilies are for that separate your cup and saucer. Etiquette on a train, like etiquette anywhere else, is based on consideration and common sense. When you're escorting a lady (or elderly person) through a train, you always precede her so you can open those heavy doors. Once you've entered the dining car, the maitre d' takes over to escort her to a table.

The purchase of your train ticket entitles you only to the space specified on it. Don't fill the adjoining seat or the car platform with your possessions. If you have too much baggage to be contained in the overhead rack or other space provided, you should check it through on the baggage car. An introduction to your seat mate isn't required, nor should it be offered. If you feel sociable, make sure your seat mate prefers conversation to reading or just watching the scenery roll by before you launch into the story of your life. If you find that your neighbor enjoys talking as much as you do, confine your conversation to impersonal matters; you needn't explain how your first wife ran off with the drummer from the American Legion Club.

Your ticket doesn't entitle you to the personal services of the train's personnel. You're expected to tip for special assistance, and you should always *request* service and not order it.

In the dining car, the informal rules of dining prevail, just as they do when eating on a plane. In other words, you don't have to peel your apple with a silver knife on a saucer and eat it with a fork. You can just pick it up and eat it. Similarly, you don't have to dress for dinner, although on longer trips it's often fun to do so. Whether you're traveling alone or as a couple, you'll invariably be seated with strangers at a table for four. Even if there's only one person seated in an otherwise empty dining car, you'll still be seated at that table. It's as though all dining car personnel took their training at Club Mediterranee where such is the standard practice in order to "break the ice" for newcomers. You're expected to be reasonably polite and friendly to your table companions, but not overbearing. You don't have to pick up a newly-found acquaintance's tab just because he or she is at your table or next to you in the club car—not even if you suggested that the two of you dine at the same time. On a long trip, this could set an expensive precedent. Let the other person order directly or fill out an order slip, which is the way it's usually done on trains.

Because of the increased public awareness of smoking in public places, railroad companies are quite specific as to where you can and cannot smoke. The areas are clearly designated. Smoking is permitted in lounge cars and sleeping cars. Smoking is *not* permitted in dining cars or in coaches except in places specifically set aside and so identified—in certain coach, lounge, bar, grill and restroom areas.

If you're sharing a bedroom, be considerate. Don't leave your things spread out all over the place. The rooms are small and become congested quickly. When beds are made up and in place, there is only room for one of you to get dressed or undressed at a time. So either stay in bed or remain in the club car until the other party is up and dressed or settled in for the night. The walls between train compartments are thin, so don't sing "La Boheme" at four in the morning.

On the new Amfleet trains, the toilets in the coach cars are coed now, all the more reason to clean up, as the sign says, after you use them. It's impossible for train crews to keep the restrooms tidied up at all times.

When traveling abroad, you'll make no serious breaches of etiquette if you keep in mind at all times that you're a "guest" in a foreign land. If you're not arrogant and overbearing, if you don't behave as though everybody is trying to steal your money, if you're not given to making smug comparisons or vulgar, ostentatious displays, then they'll accept you as you are—and maybe even like you.

 TIPPING. Tipping—derived from the now almost forgotten phrase, "To Insure Promptness"—has long been traditional for the first-class passenger given good service in sleeping cars and in full-service diners. Budget-minded coach travelers need not tip at all. Redcap baggage service is free at all Amtrak stations and carts are available at most stations for those who prefer to handle their own luggage. Of course, it is the passenger's prerogative to tip baggage porters if he wishes, in which case 35 cents a bag is appropriate. If they do something extra, such as hail a cab, give them 50 cents.

Sleeping car attendants should normally get $1 a night. This is given as you leave the train. You might also tip a little something when you board the train, most certainly if you plan to do a lot of entertaining in your room. If you put the porter through a lot of extra work, pulling down the room dividers every morning and setting them up again at night, racing off into one station after another to buy newspapers, then certainly reward him for his extra work.

Waiters in dining cars get 15–20 percent of the total bill; the maitre d', perhaps $1 when you're being seated for the first time and another after your last meal in the dining car, more if you've put him through such little chores as chilling your private supply of wine or keeping your frozen fish on ice.

Amtrak service representatives, conductors and anyone else in uniform are never tipped.

Tipping in foreign countries tends to be more prevalent but often less extravagant than in the United States. The appropriate amounts vary from country to country. If you're not sure what's expected, ask a native or hotel desk clerk or travel agent. Tip in the currency of the country you happen to be in; it'll probably save you money in the long run and will be more appreciated by the recipient. When in doubt, tip just a little. It's better to tip too little than too much.

 HOW TO GO? When you have decided where you want to go, your next step is to consult a good travel agent. If you haven't one, the *American Society of Travel Agents,* 360 Lexington Ave., New York 10017, or the *Association of British Travel Agents,* 50–57 Newman St., London W1P 4AH, will advise you. Whether you select *Maupintour Associates, Havas, American Express, Cook's,* or a smaller organization is a matter of preference. They all have branch offices or correspondents in the larger European cities. There are good reasons why you should engage an agent.

Travel abroad today, although it is steadily becoming easier and more comfortable, is also growing more complex in its details. As the choice of things to do, places to visit, ways of getting there, increases, so does the problem of *knowing* about all these questions. A reputable, experienced travel agent is a specialist in details, and because of his importance to the success of your trip, you should inquire in your community as to which organization has the finest reputation.

If you wish your agent to book you on a package tour, reserve your transportation and even your first overnight hotel, his services should cost you nothing.

If, on the other hand, you wish him to plan for you an individual itinerary and make all arrangements down to hotel reservations and transfers to and from rail and air terminals, you are drawing upon his skill and knowledge of travel as well as asking him to shoulder a great mass of detail and correspondence. His commissions from carriers won't come close to covering his expenses, and thus he will make a service charge on the total cost of your planned itinerary. This charge may amount to 10 or 15 percent but it will more than likely *save* you money on balance. A good travel agent can help you avoid costly mistakes due to inexperience. He can help you take advantage of special reductions in rail fares and the like that you would not otherwise know about. Most important, he can save you *time* by making it unnecessary to waste precious days abroad trying to get tickets and reservations. Thanks to his work, you are able to see and do more.

There are four principal ways of traveling: (1) The *group tour,* in which you travel with others, following a prearranged itinerary hitting all the high spots, and paying a single all-inclusive price that covers everything—transportation, meals, lodging, sightseeing tours, taxis, guides. And here your travel agent can book you with a *special interest group,* thus you needn't spend a high proportion of your tour trotting round museums if you would much rather be wandering round botanical gardens or pot-holing, and you will be among people with similar interests. (2) The *prearranged individual tour,* following a set itinerary planned for you by the travel agent, with all costs paid in advance. (3) The *individual tour* where you work out the itinerary for yourself, according to your own interests, but have your agent make transportation and hotel reservations, transfers, sightseeing plans. (4) The *free lance tour,* in which you pay as you go, change your mind if you want to, and do your own planning. You'll still find a travel agent handy to make your initial transport reservation and book you for any special event where long advance booking is essential.

SPECIAL INTEREST TOURS. More and more, special interest tours are gaining in popularity, especially among younger travelers who, imbued with high conscience and a sense of duty, feel that travel should be purposeful, and among others who plan to roam Europe often and with a more intimate view of life abroad than the old-fashioned bird's-eye tour. Travel agencies in the U.S., Britain and France offer a staggering variety of special interest tours, ranging from the most luxurious chateau-gourmet trips in Rolls-Royces through rugged archeological work camps in little-known regions of France.

Airlines (*TWA, Air France, British Airways,* etc.) also work closely with travel agents in setting up package tours. Your own hometown clubs: Rotary, Lions, ski, stamp-collecting, bird-watching, book-binding, law, medicine, etc., are often active in arranging special interest tours for their members.

If you are looking for a special interest tour, begin by contacting your hometown travel agent. If he is too limited, write, in America, to the American Society of Travel Agents; in Britain, to the Association of British Travel Agents. For addresses, see "How to Go," earlier in this section.

WHAT TO TAKE? The first principle is to travel light, and fortunately for the present-day traveler this is possible due to the availability of strong, lightweight and drip-dry, crease-resistant fabrics for clothing. If you plan to fly, you have a real incentive to stay below the first-class transatlantic limit of 66 pounds and economy limit of 44 pounds; each pound overweight costs extra money. Many of the crack international express trains and almost all buses also put limits on the weight (usually 55 pounds) or bulk of your baggage.

Even if you're traveling by ship, resist the temptation to take more than two suitcases per person, or to select luggage larger than you can carry alone. Porters are increasingly scarce in these days of European prosperity, and you will face delays every time you change trains (or hotels) or go through customs. Motorists need to be frugal, too. You should limit your luggage to what can be locked in the trunk or boot of your car when you make daytime stops. At night, everything should be removed to your hotel room, and your car locked.

Almost inevitably you will find yourself accumulating gifts, souvenirs, extra clothing, picture books, etc., on your travels. A good holdall for these is a collapsible suitcase that can be packed in your ordinary luggage on the outward journey. An alternative is to mail books and printed matter back home.

Major purchases such as furniture, sets of china, and the like have to be shipped specially, of course. Before you do this, however, consider the pros and cons carefully. Unless you deal with a thoroughly reliable and experienced store, you run the risk that either the goods you ordered won't be sent at all or else will be so poorly packed that they are damaged in transit, two alternatives that you are largely helpless to remedy after your return home. Assuming that you are dealing with a reputable firm, insist on finding out exactly what the shipping charges will amount to. In many cases, shipments such as these are handed over to customs brokers and freight forwarders in your country whose charges may be in addition to what you have already paid. Americans in particular sometimes find themselves having to pay $30 to $50 in supplement charges such as these on shipments whose value may actually be little more. Parcel post, of course, is the cheapest and most satisfactory means of sending items whose weight and size are not too great. Make sure, too, that your shipment is insured and that the proper customs documents are attached.

Travelers can arrange with one of the travel credit organizations for a European charge account that enables you to sign for hotel and restaurant bills, car rentals, purchases, and so forth, and pay the resulting total at one time on a monthly bill. This is particularly advantageous for businessmen traveling on an expense account or on business trips whose cost is deductible for income tax. Offering this service are the *American Express,* with branches in all major cities, *The Diners Club,* 10 Columbus Circle, New York, or 214 Oxford St., London, W.1, Hilton's *Carte Blanche, Eurocard International,* and many others.

Holders of American Express credit cards can cash up to $500 at one time (only $50 in currency, the rest in travelers checks of your choice) upon presentation of their Amexco card, a personal check and passport. This transaction can be repeated in 3 weeks. British travelers can cash cheques abroad for up to £30 each transaction on production of a Barclaycard or one of the other bank cheque cards participating in the scheme.

CLOTHING. If you are wisely limiting yourself to two average-size suitcases it's obvious that your clothes must be carefully selected. The first considerations are the season of the year and the regions you plan to visit. Paris can be sizzling in summer and chilly in winter, although neither extreme will likely be as great as transatlantic visitors might be inclined to expect. Both men and women will feel less conspicuous if they avoid the sportier kind of clothing in Paris and other major cities. At Mediterranean and Atlantic beach resorts, especially along the Riviera, dress in summer is as casual as anywhere in the world—and more elegant.

Women. More basic is the problem of versatility, particularly for women, so you need to select outfits that can be combined in different ways. You can usually accomplish this by mixing skirts and pants outfits with blouses, sweaters and accessories.

Dresses made of materials that resist crushing are practical and easy to care for. Knit wear and silk shantung (and, in cool weather, perhaps, synthetic fibers) are ideal for this purpose. Bare-shoulder models should have jackets for cool evenings or less formal occasions. Several cocktail dresses should be included if you're traveling first class on a ship or move in dressy circles; otherwise you can get by with a dressier suit or a dress with jacket.

Practical, low-heeled shoes may be less flattering than dainty pumps, but they're better suited for wet weather, cobbled streets, and long hours on your feet. A pair of soft slippers may be a lifesaver during long flights or train trips, and you will need evening slippers. A folding umbrella and raincoat that doubles as a sports coat are essential in rainy Europe.

Handbags can be another problem. It may not be wise to select a model big enough to hold your passport, travelers checks, sunglasses, tickets, cosmetics, and other necessities—something really outsize may literally seem like a millstone dangling from your shoulder after you've carried it day after day for weeks or months. More to the point is the handbag with enough interior pockets (at least one with a zipper closing for your money) to keep things in some kind of order. Something with a positive fastening is protection against pickpockets (who seem to be more active than ever these days). Don't forget an evening bag unless you plan to buy one on your travels.

Men. Men's clothing problems are less complex. A dark business suit is adequate for most functions unless you travel first class by ship or expect to visit ultrachic nightclubs and the like, so formal outfits can be left at home. A lightweight suit, a sport coat, and two or three pairs of slacks that can be mixed with the sport coat will complete your outer wardrobe, except for a light overcoat/raincoat that you'll likely prefer to carry over your arm. The synthetic fibers are ideal for these garments because of their strength and resistance to wrinkles.

Wash-yourself shirts of dacron, orlon, etc., are marvelous conveniences when you're traveling light or making many one-night stops. The same considerations apply to socks, underwear, and pajamas. A lightweight dressing gown is useful for excursions to and from the bathtub. Handkerchiefs and neckties are good buys in France, so take the minimum and supplement your supplies with local purchases.

PASSPORTS. It is best to give obtaining a passport priority in your plans. **U.S. residents** must apply in person to the U.S. Passport Agency in New York, Chicago, Boston, Miami, New Orleans, San Francisco, Los Angeles, Philadelphia, Seattle, Washington, D.C., or the local County Courthouse. In some areas selected post offices are also able to handle passport applications. Take with you your birth certificate (or certified copy), 2 identical photographs 2½ in. square (full face, taken within the past 6 months); $13, or $10 if applying by mail, and proof of identity such as driver's license, etc.

If a non-citizen, you need a Treasury Sailing Permit Form 1040D, certifying that all Federal taxes have been paid. You will have to present a blue or green alien registration card, travel tickets, most recently filed Form 1040, W2 forms for the most recent full year, most recent payroll stubs—and maybe more, so check. To return to the United States, you need a re-entry permit only if you are planning to stay outside the U.S. more than one year. Apply for it at least six weeks before departure in person at the nearest office of the Immigration and Naturalization Service, or by mail to the Immigration and Naturalization Service, Washington,

D.C. Or, six weeks before leaving, inquire whether an Alien Registration Card (green card) would suffice in your case.

British subjects: apply for passports on special forms obtainable from your travel agency or from the main post office in your town. The application should be sent to the Passport Office in your area (as indicated on the guidance form) or taken personally to your nearest main post office. Apply at least 3 weeks before the passport is required. The regional Passport Offices are located in London, Liverpool, Peterborough, Glasgow, Newport (Mon.), and Belfast. The application must be countersigned by your bank manager, or by a solicitor, barrister, doctor, clergyman or Justice of the Peace who knows you personally. You will need two photos. Fee £6.

British Visitor's Passport. This simplified form of passport has advantages for the once-in-a-while tourist to France and most European countries. Valid for one year and not renewable, it costs £3. Application must be made in person at an Employment Exchange and two passport photographs are required.

Canadian citizens entering the United Kingdom must have a valid passport, application forms for which may be obtained at any post office; these are to be sent to the Canadian Passport Office at 40 Bank Street, Ottawa, together with a remittance of $10.

VISAS. Not required for nationals of the United States, Canada, United Kingdom and most countries of the British Commonwealth for a stay of less than three months. If that period is about to expire and you wish to stay longer, go to the Prefecture of Police, and make application for a *carte de sejour.* The prefecture in Paris is located on the Ile de la Cité, near Notre-Dame.

HEALTH CERTIFICATES. Not required in Western Europe, but necessary in most other parts of the world. Neither the U.S. nor Canada requires a certificate of smallpox vaccination on re-entry, unless coming from area where infection recently reported, so if you're going anyplace except Western Europe, in our opinion, you'd be wise to have it. The simplest way is to be vaccinated before you leave. Have your doctor fill in the standard form which comes with your passport, or obtain one from a steamship company, airline, or travel agent. Take the form with you to present on re-entering.

 MEDICAL TREATMENT. The *I.A.M.A.T.* (International Assoc. for Medical Assistance to Travellers) offers you a list of approved English-speaking doctors who have had postgraduate training in the U.S., Canada or Gt. Britain. Membership is free; the scheme is world-wide with many European countries participating. An office call costs about $8, though subject to change. Hotel and night calls, of course, higher. For information apply in the U.S. to Suite 5620, 350 Fifth Ave., New York 10001; in Canada, 1268 St. Clair Ave. W., Toronto M6E 1B9.

Europ Assistance Ltd. offers unlimited help to its members. There are two plans: one for travelers using tours or making their own trip arrangements, the second for motorists taking their cars abroad. Multilingual personnel staff a 24-hour, seven-days-a-week telephone service which brings the aid of a network of medical and other advisors to assist in any emergency. Special medical insurance is part of the plan. Basic prices: £2 per person, £6 for a vehicle, £2 for caravan or trailer. Write to Europ Assistance Ltd., 269 High St., Croydon, Surrey CRO 1QH, England, for details.

Free Medical Care (or reduced cost treatment) for *British* residents is available in many European countries, but documentation is necessary in most cases: obtain from your local office of the Department of Health and Social Security, Form CMI, at least one month before leaving Britain. Fill this in and return it, when you will get Form E111 to take with you. In France, for instance, major surgery and childbirth may be free, but you pay doctors on the spot and reclaim 10 and 90 % of the cost by taking Form E111 to the local Caisse Primaire de Securité Sociale (address from the town hall). Names of English-speaking doctors can be obtained from the local tourist office or the British Counsel.

 CUSTOMS RETURNING HOME. If you propose to take on your holiday any *foreign-made* articles, such as cameras, binoculars, expensive timepieces and the like, it is wise to put with your travel documents the receipt from the retailer or some other evidence that the item was bought in your home country. If you bought the article on a previous holiday abroad and have already paid duty on it, carry with you the receipt for this. Otherwise, on returning home, you may be charged duty (for Britishers, VAT as well).

U.S. Customs. At this writing, Americans who are out of the United States at least 48 hours and have claimed no exemption during the previous 31 days are entitled to bring in duty-free up to $100 worth of bona fide gifts or items for their own personal use. Under legislation passed in 1965, the duty-free purchases are now based on the retail value (previously on the wholesale), so keep your receipts. Also, all items purchased must accompany the passenger on his return: it will therefore simplify matters at customs control if you can pack all purchases in one holdall. Every member of a family is entitled to this same exemption, regardless of age, and their exemptions can be pooled.

The $100 exemption includes one quart of wine or liquor (none at all if your passport indicates you are from a "dry" state or if you are under 21 years old). Duty on anything above this is, *per bottle* (1/5 gallon): brandy or liquor, $2–3; champagne, 90¢, wine 11¢.

Only one bottle of perfume that is trademarked in the United States (Caron, Lanvin, Guerlain, Patou, Chanel, etc.) may be brought in. Other perfumes are limited by the weight or value. The specialized houses will give you the complete list, as will the Customs Service of the American Embassy in Paris.

Antiques are defined as articles 100 years old, or over, and are duty-free. You may be asked to supply proof of age.

Do not bring home foreign meats, fruits, plants, soil, or other agricultural items when you return to the United States. To do so will delay you at the port of entry. It is illegal to bring in foreign agricultural items without permission, because they can spread destructive plant or animal pests and diseases. Limitations on foods vary greatly according to the product, origin, and degree of processing involved. Ask for U.S. Dept. of Agriculture pamphlet No. 1083 "Traveler's Tips on Bringing Food, Plant and Animal Products into the United States" for details. Write to: "Quarantines", U.S. Dept. of Agriculture, Washington, D.C. 20250.

Small gifts may be mailed to friends (but not more than one package to one address). There should be a written notation on the packages, "Unsolicited Gift, value under $10". Duty-free packages, however, cannot include perfumes, tobacco or liquor.

If your purchases exceed your exemption, list the items that are subject to the highest rates of duty under your exemption and pay duty on the items with the lowest rates. Any articles you fail to declare cannot later be claimed under your exemption. To facilitate the actual customs examination it's convenient to pack all your purchases in one suitcase.

American rates of customs duty may change, therefore it is best to check the regulations with the American Embassy before or during your visit. In Paris—tel. ANJ. 74-60, ask for Customs Service (in Hotel Talleyrand, 2 Rue St.-Florentin).

DEVALUATION—REVALUATION—INFLATION

The rising and falling of the dollar and devaluation and revaluation in most European countries, with consequent rising taxes and costs throughout and possible inflationary trends to come, make accurate budgeting long in advance an impossibility. Prices mentioned throughout this title are indicative only of costs at time of going to press. Check with a travel agent before your trip.

Travelers checks are the best way to safeguard travel funds. They are sold by various banks and companies in terms of American and Canadian dollars and pound sterling. You can also buy traveler's checks in the currency of the countries you plan to visit. American Express, Barclay's Bank, Thos. Cook and a number of foreign exchange houses (Perera, Deak) offer such services. There is a fee, of course, but you'll find them easier to exchange and you'll frequently save on the exchange rate. If you prefer to buy the checks in your own currency, most universally accepted are those of American Express, while those issued by CitiBank of New York and Bank of America are also widely used.

Best known and most easily exchanged British travelers checks are those issued by Thos. Cook & Son and these banks: Barclays, National Westminister, Lloyds, and Midland.

For last minute buys, the shops at Orly, Roissy, Le Bourget and other duty-free airports offer for some articles (watches, cameras, scarves, jewelry, clothes, etc.) a higher discount than in Paris for payments made in travelers checks. Returning American tourists can replenish their supply of liquor, liqueurs, champagne, wines and perfumes. Purchases can be carried on board *after* baggage has been weighed.

BALANCED BUDGETS AND JUDGMENTS

Despite scare stories in the press of skyrocketing prices, it is still quite easy to visit Europe without losing your shirt. Many of the panicky reports have been biased, probably unconsciously, with the writer comparing deluxe establishments on the Continent with moderately-priced hotels or restaurants at home, which is unfair both to the potential traveler and the country concerned. In expensive countries like France, you don't have to go to the deluxe hotels and restaurants to sleep and eat well. Try first class or moderate instead. You'll learn much more about the country itself, and meet its top-ranking citizens on their home ground. Americans having to economize a bit for the first time can take lessons from the British, who learned to do this many years ago and have come to like the new way of traveling—seeing the off-beat places, avoiding the tourist traps and immersing themselves in local color.

Planning to buy a car in Europe? Make sure foreign-made models meet new U.S. safety and air-pollution standards: Write (for free comprehensive booklets on the subject) to "Buying a Foreign Car," Public Affairs, Environmental Protection Agency, Washington, D.C., 20406. Another booklet, "Federal Motor Vehicle Safety Standards," is available from the Office of Standards Enforcement, National Highway Safety Administration, U.S. Department of Transportation, 200 Mamaroneck Ave., White Plains, N.Y., 10601.

British Customs. There is now a two-tier allowance for duty-free goods brought into the U.K., due to Britain's Common Market membership. *Note:* The Customs and Excise Board warn that it is not advisable to mix the two allowances.

If you return from an EEC country (Belgium, Denmark, France, W. Germany, Holland, Eire, Italy, Luxembourg) and goods were bought in one of those countries, duty-free allowances are:

300 cigarettes (or 150 cigarillos, or 75 cigars, or 400 gr. tobacco); 1.5 liters of strong spirits (or 3 liters of other spirits or fortified wines), plus 3 liters of still table wine; 75 gr. perfume and .375 liter toilet water; gifts to the value of £50.

If you return from a country outside the EEC *or if the goods were bought in a duty-free shop on ship, plane or at airport,* the allowances are less:

200 cigarettes (or 100 cigarillos, or 50 cigars, or 250 gr. tobacco); 1 liter of strong spirits (or 2 liters of other spirits or fortified wines), plus 2 liters of still table wine; 50 gr. perfume and .25 liter toilet water; gifts to the value of £10.

Canadian Customs. In addition to personal effects, the following articles may be brought into Canada duty-free: a maximum of 50 cigars, 200 cigarettes, 2 pounds of tobacco and 40 ounces of liquor, provided these are declared to customs on arrival. The regulations are strictly enforced, so check on what your allowances are and make sure you have kept receipts for whatever you bought abroad.

TRAVEL THE WORLD OF LINDBLAD

The ne plus ultra
from Lindblad Travel...
ARTS & CIVILIZATIONS TOURS

For those precious holiday weeks abroad, why not the very best? Unhurried schedules. Small, congenial groups. The finest hotels and restaurants en route. And, most important, the services of two professional escorts: an expert lecturer-guide to illuminate your sightseeing and a Lindblad courier to see to your needs and comfort.
This year's Arts & Civilizations Tours® include:

Asia Minor—Turkey's fabled coast from Istanbul to Tarsus, then inland to Cappadocia and Ankara. June 4, Sept. 17, Oct. 8.

The Road to Compostela—retracing the medieval pilgrimage route from Paris to Santiago, via the Pyrenees, Castile, and Galicia. June 11, July 23, Sept. 3.

Etruscan Places—an adventure in archeology through the incomparable Tuscan hill country of Italy. April 29, June 24, Sept. 23.

Joan of Arc's France—following the Maid's footsteps from her birthplace in Domremy to her execution site in Rouen, via the Loire Valley and Reims. June 10, July 1, Sept. 16.

Asian Dances, Dramas, Deities—an in-depth investigation into the arts, crafts, traditions, and philosophies of Japan, Java, Bali, and Thailand. Our lecturer-guide is the well-known writer and authority on Asian culture, Faubion Bowers. April 23, Oct. 8, Nov. 5.

Please write for our brochure or give us the name of your Travel Agent.

LINDBLAD TRAVEL, INC.
Dept. NYAC
133 East 55th Street, New York, N.Y. 10022, 751-2300 or toll-free 800-223-9700.

NORTH AMERICA

Americana Rail Cruises®

Fully Escorted ...All inclusive

From California to Nova Scotia, from the Rockies to Acapulco—16 to 25 days. Your tour director takes care of everything! Stop & stay at America's famous hotels & resorts...Canada's Jasper Park Lodge and Banff Springs Hotel ... Jackson Lake Lodge in the Tetons...St. Francis in San Francisco...the Las Vegas Hilton. In-depth sightseeing included throughout. Leave your train for a day or more...tour an area or relax at a resort before your train moves on.

Canadian Rockies • Northwest
16, 22 or 25 days . . . Seattle, Victoria, Vancouver, Jasper, Lake Louise, Banff plus Glacier, Yellowstone and the Tetons.

Canada...East and West
17 or 20 days . . . Montreal to the Canadian Rockies with Jasper, Banff, Glacier Park, Gaspe, Nova Scotia, Prince Edward Island.

California • The West • Parks
16, 21 or 22 days . . . California, Pacific Coast to Colorado Rockies and Salt Lake City plus Grand Canyon, Zion, Bryce, Yosemite and Las Vegas.

Canyonlands • Navajolands
17 days . . . From the Colorado Rockies to Monument Valley with Mesa Verde, famous "Durango" Railway, Sante Fe and Denver.

Mexico • Deep South
22 days . . . New Orleans, Bellingrath Gardens. Houston, San Antonio, Acapulco. Mexico City, Taxco. Cuernavaca.

Mississippi Queen Cruise
16 days . . . 7 days cruising The Mississippi River on the new luxury steamboat Mississippi Queen plus 8-days visiting the Deep South in-depth.

- All Tours fully escorted
- First-class rail — including sleeping cars
- Luxury hotels and resorts
- Most meals included
- All sightseeing
- All-inclusive rate
- April thru November departures from N.Y., Newark, Phila. and Chicago

For brochure. see your Travel Agent or mail coupon

FOUR WINDS TRAVEL, INC., Dept. R974
175 Fifth Ave., N.Y., N.Y. 10010, Tel.: (212) 777-0260
Please send me your 36 page Americana Rail Cruises brochure.

Name
Address
City_____ State_____ Zip_____

Four Winds®

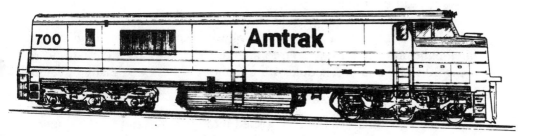

UNITED STATES OF AMERICA

There's a toot left in the old railroad industry after all.

Not long ago, any American even near the age of 30 understandably grew up thinking trains had gone the way of the covered wagon. Service was deplorable, equipment was falling apart, roadbeds were crumbling away and most train stations looked like evacuated war zone relics. The trains themselves were museum pieces, and the people who ran them, like the people who rode them, were old and crotchety.

Suddenly, however, the trains are back. Business isn't exactly booming as yet, but steady, impressive gains are being made. Conductors are smiling again. Equipment has been updated. Service has improved. Tickets and reservations are being dispatched with airline-like efficiency. There's a crackle in the air. Travelers are regaining confidence in a mode of transportation that has long been maligned, neglected and misused. The railroad is no longer the runaway car it once was, careening down that steep-graded incline toward oblivion. It's back and it's here to stay.

As incredible as it may seem, there was once a time when the fastest way to get from New York to Chicago was to board the *Twentieth Century Limited*. The New York Central took such pride in its crack train that whenever it headed west, crews fired the fireboxes of standby locomotives all along the route, ready to take over instantly in case the Limited's locomotive broke down. There were other great trains, of course. The prestigious *Overland Limited* was as elegant as any of the finest trains in Europe, complete with champagne breakfasts, Oriental rugs and fresh-cut flowers every day.

In 1924, eight out of every ten Americans who traveled from city to city did so by train. In the Thirties, the luxury of train travel was equated only to the splendor of ocean travel and prized dining car recipes were closely guarded secrets. The big metal giants in all their burly attire, flaunting their stacks, domes and rivets, belching steam and roaring smoke and fire, were the symbol of a young, sprawling nation on the move. It was a grand era. When the trains went by, kids stood along the tracks waving and throwing kisses instead of stones.

In the early Forties, the arrival of film stars at New York's Grand Central Terminal was as much a part of the Hollywood mystique as the glittering klieg-light premieres they came to attend. Coast-to-coast flights still took some 20 to 24 hours; schedules were tenuous at best; and many travelers felt that if God really intended man to fly, he would have never invented the Pullman.

When Frank Sinatra's train whooshed into New York upon the singer's triumphant return from his first Hollywood assignment, thousands of hysterical bobby-soxers were on hand to greet him. (The press agents had worked overtime.) Sinatra, who now owns his own jet, is still a train man. Recently, accompanied by a retinue of friends and a well-stocked supply of champagne and imported vodka, he made the two-day journey from San Bernadino to Chicago in a plush private sleeping car attached to the *Southwest Limited* (formerly the *Super Chief*). The "age of the automobile" after World War II sent passenger train travel screeching into the red. Stagnation set in. The lines deteriorated rapidly. Losses were in the hundreds of millions. One dreary series of bankruptcies, takeovers and mergers followed another. By 1969, the railroad's share of public transit passengers had dropped to 20 percent; half were traveling by bus and the airlines carried the rest. The railroad had gone so long without a spruceup or improvement of any kind that the average passenger car in service at the time was 19 years old. Tracks were turning to rust. The once raucous giant was reduced to a mere shadow, a stone age colossus struggling for survival in a quagmire-world of advanced speed and technology. Characteristically, as noted one critic, railroad men from around the United States celebrated the moon landing by gathering at Promotory Point, Utah, to reenact the driving of the Golden Spike that heralded the completion of the first transcontinental track 100 years earlier.

All the experts knew what was wrong with the railroads, but nobody knew quite how to tell them—a rigid, time-honored seniority system that went back to the stovepipe-hat days of Lincoln (when most top railroad officials were recruited from the ranks of the Civil War brass), gross mismanagement, a stifling of new ideas, and a stubborn aversion to change.

Canada *seemed* to have the answer. Its nationalized railroad was wooing travelers by the thousands away from airlines and highways with fast new trains and snappy, first-rate service, including bistro-style club cars with live entertainment, baby-sitting service and free morning coffee. But it proved not to be the answer. In the summer of 1969, the Canadian National Railroad announced it was losing between $40 and $50 million a year and made one more request to the government to cut back service.

Meanwhile, Penn Central, created early in the merger movement by the marriage of the New York Central and Pennsylvania Railroads, two of the nation's biggest lines, introduced (with government assistance) the Metroliner, a sleek, low-slung, electric-powered train capable of speeds up to 160 mph. It was put into service between Washington and New York, trimming an hour off the time it took conventional trains to make the same run. It was well received, with its bright pumpkin-colored interiors, tweed carpeting, on-board telephones and pleasant young coach and snack-bar attendants dressed in smartly styled uniforms. During its first year of operation it carried 700,000 passengers, representing a high 70 percent of its capacity seating, and, with its virtual door-to-door downtown deliveries, it challenged air shuttle service between the two cities for the first time. (Eastern Airline's shuttle, after years of steady 3 to 15 percent annual passenger increases, showed only .04 percent increase that year.)

But, the Metroliner, a first-rate train, was operating on a third-rate track, one it shared with freight trains, commuter and conventional trains. Excessive battering quickly deteriorates track, loosening joints, hammering rail ends and pounding down ballast. The run also included 28 slow-speed grade crossings and more than 200 bridges, many of them constructed before 1895. The Metroliner never even approached its top cruising potential. Along stretches of particularly worn track, the train shook so violently at times that terrified passengers all but jumped off.

The Metroliner project cost $55 million, but it was only the tip of the Penn Central's financial iceberg. The following year the line filed for bankruptcy. It was a staggering blow to the industry, and Congress, after years of study, argument and debate, approved the Rail Passenger Service Act of 1970, creating the National Rail Passenger Corporation, otherwise known as Amtrak.

Enter Amtrak

A quasi-private, quasi-public corporation, Amtrak was formed to take over the nation's dilapidated passenger trains—then running at over $500 million a year in the red—and provide passenger service linking major cities where it was not feasible for private companies to do so. Beginning May 1, 1971, it contracted with the railways to operate express trains over 23,000 route miles serving 440 cities and towns. (New routing has since increased this to 26,000 miles and 484 stations.)

Along with Penn Central, twelve other railroads signed contracts with Amtrak: Atchison, Topeka and Santa Fe; Burlington Northern; Baltimore and Ohio-Chesapeake and Ohio; Chicago, Milwaukee, St. Paul and Pacific; Gulf, Mobile and Ohio; Illinois Central; Louisville and Nashville; Missouri Pacific; Richmond, Fredericksburg and Potomac; Seaboard Coast Line; Northern Pacific; and Union Pacific. (Three lines—the Denver & Rio Grande Western, the Chicago, Rock Island & Pacific, and the Southern— chose not to sign and are still, by law, operating passenger service independently today.)

Thus Amtrak was launched, with the government playing angel. The plan was unique. Amtrak would generate income from its rail passenger service and also have access to public funds for expenses it couldn't meet. The fledgling corporation's original profile was a low one. Employees for the most part were still attached to the railroads, so an Amtrak passenger might actually make a reservation, buy a ticket, check luggage and complete his journey without ever coming in contact with an Amtrak representative.

The system began with 186 long-distance trains, pared down from the 400 then in operation. Inertia had set in so firmly that manufacturers had stopped making passenger equipment. Amtrak had money to spend but there were no new intercity cars available. It scoured the country for the best of what was already in use and came up with about 2,000 Art Deco museum pieces (at approximately $14,000 each) that had to be overhauled and refurbished. It also put in an order for 150 new locomotives (a type that could also be used for freight in the event Amtrak was dissolved). New equipment in service when Amtrak got underway consisted of the electrically-powered Metroliners between New York and Washington—their frequency now doubled to 14 daily runs each way—and a smaller version of Canada's TurboTrain, this operated between New York and Boston.

Almost with Amtrak's inception, the downward trend in rail passenger ridership reversed itself and began to climb upward. In 1972, Amtrak's first full year of operation, ridership increased about 11 percent. During that year Amtrak sold 3 billion passenger miles of travel. All Amtrak tickets could be purchased with credit cards and through travel agents. A public relations blitz got underway to announce, in Amtrak's words, that "tracks are back," using lapel pins, buttons, bumper stickers and even colorful airline-type "flight" bags (rail bags?) to carry the message. The following year, the passenger-miles-sold figure climbed to 3.8 billion, an increase of 25.2 percent, and Amtrak did what anyone might do at the first taste of success, it went on a buying spree.

In August, 1973, Amtrak took advantage of foreign railroad technology and leased two five-car turbine trains that had been built for the French National Railroad. Each five-car turbotrain set includes a power car at each end, so it's never necessary to turn the train around. The trains proved their worth, and the following June Amtrak purchased the two already under lease and ordered an additional four trains. (In July, 1974, it ordered another seven Turboliners to be built under license by Rohr Industries of California. They were delivered in mid-1976 and put into service on New York State's Empire Line.)

Meanwhile, Amtrak successfully romanced American manufacturers back into the passenger car-building business with a 1973 order for 57 non-powered, locomotive-hauled cars from the Budd Company in Philadelphia. Similiar in design to the Metroliners, 250 Budd-built cars now comprise Amtrak's celebrated "Amfleet" service, with another 250 on order, a total expenditure of $206.3 million. Designed primarily for regional corridor service, they are capable of long-distance operation as well and come in a variety of types including coach, coach-snack car, first class and sit-down dining service. They have already proved to be crowd pleasers.

In addition, 235 Amtrak-designed bi-level cars are being manufactured by the Pullman-Standard Company for 1977 long-distance service over Amtrak's western routes. These will provide coach seats, sleeping compartments and dining facilities. Upstairs diners will enjoy a much smoother ride. The new cars, in fact, with their stairways, double-levels, generous lounge and dining areas, will provide a train more spacious and varied than ever before possible. Improved air-cushioned suspension systems will make for a smoother ride, and sound-absorbing materials will isolate passengers from exterior noise while softening the sounds inside.

"These," in the words of Amtrak's president Paul H. Reistrup, "will make up the finest trains in service anywhere in the world."

Track and roadbeds are being replaced at a stepped-up pace. Previously the process of repair was so slow it would have taken 120 years for all tracks to be renewed. Main line tracks are now generally being replaced with continuous "welded" rail, the gandy dancer's delight, rail laid in 1,440-foot lengths and fused together for easier maintenance and a far smoother ride. Normal rails, accounting for the train's romantic clickety-clack sound, are 39 feet long and are held together by joint bars that require constant inspection and tightening.

Old stations are being repaired and new ones are being built as additional routes and cities are added. In its five-year history, Amtrak has renovated in some degree over 400 stations and built new ones in Cincinnati, Jacksonville, Roanoke, Richmond, Bluefield, Port Huron, Catlettsburg and Worcester. They are modest by comparison to the huge stations left over from the "golden age" of railroading, but they are attractive, easier and less expensive to maintain and they meet the quick come-and-go needs of the modern traveler.

The Future

Amtrak's main showcase is the northeast corridor between Washington and Boston, properties and rail rights of which were purchased in April, 1976, from Conrail, a merged group of northeast railroads, for $87 million. Over $500,000,000 has been earmarked for improvements on this span within the next five to ten years, primarily to reduce the Washington-New York time to two hours and New York-Boston to two-and-a-half. The problem until now has not been achieving high speeds but maintaining them.

When Japan built its New Tokaido Line, it literally built a whole new railroad. The Tokaido trains speed along track specifically built for its needs. The so called "Bullet" trains run a straight-arrow course from Tokyo to Osaka every 15 minutes, each way, averaging 102 mph over the 320-mile span. North America has no such tailored tracks. Work is currently underway, however, from one end of the northeast corridor to the other—road beds, tracks, stations, bridges and grade crossings. (The American motorist is notorious for his daredevil-bullfighter tactics at grade crossings, inspiring the need for an automatic failsafe system to keep him at bay.)

Eventually the corridor, with almost exclusive Amfleet and Metroliner service, will be extended to include the heavily populated areas around Richmond, Virginia. Other corridors will be extended or joined to long-distance trains to form a modern, efficient rail passenger service throughout the country. Amtrak envisions an intermodel station system for metropolitan areas whereby passengers could step out of their homes, take a bus or subway to the station, continue via train to any point in the country, exit at another intermodel station and continue via bus or subway to their precise destinations. At the current rate of population growth (one child is born every ten seconds in the U.S.), our urban population will have added at least 60 million more people by the year 2000. Such a system would be essential in restoring balance to the nation's overall transportation complex.

Improvements within the trains are also apparent. Food and beverage quality has improved; regional dishes are being served in many areas. Prices are reasonable. A standard breakfast of eggs, juice, coffee, ham, bacon or sausage and toast is $2.50; a complete chicken dinner on some trains is $2.75. Porters, coach car attendants, dining and club car attendants are more attentive and efficient. ("A noticeable increase in the consideration with which Amtrak and railroad employees handle the public" was a corporate mandate in the formation of Amtrak.) Attractively uniformed passenger service representatives and bilingual service representatives can be found at most major stations ready to help passengers with any number of problems, from rerouting after a missed train, hotel reservations or even placing a free long distance phone call when a train has been delayed and somebody's waiting.

Of course, not all of today's rail passenger news is Amtrak's. While Canada's railway system continues to lose about $167 million a year, and further cutbacks and route slashes are scheduled, passengers still enjoy quality service in uncrowded comfort. Last year only a third of all available railway seating was sold. Daily Canadian Pacific all-stainless-steel scenic dome trains set out from Montreal, Toronto and Vancouver on a three-day transcontinental run that's considered among the most scenically picturesque in the world. *The Canadian* includes skyline coaches with reclining lounge-style chairs, spacious dome cars serving cocktails and snacks, dining car and sleeping accommodations ranging from berths to three-passenger drawing rooms. A sound system for announcements or music may be switched on or off in all rooms. The Canadian National's government-owned coast-to-coast train, called *The Super Continental* has a full range of sleeping facilities, plus "Dayniter" cars for those who want a bit more luxury than standard coaches but who don't require full sleeping accommodations. These have recliner seats, lush carpeting, window curtains and blinds, indirect and floor level lighting as well as individual reading lights. Canadian National also operates an auto-carrying program allowing passengers to ship cars ahead as cargo, or, during summer months, ship them on the same train.

Autotrains are almost old hat in the U.S. For the past five years, Auto-Train Corp., a private firm, has offered car-carrying service from the Washington, D.C., area to the vicinity of Orlando. Thus passengers can avoid the highway hassle, ride a comfortable coach or sleeper to Florida and have their car with them when they get there. Amtrak and Auto-Train have agreed to cooperate on some services.

The Southern Railway, the last major private line to continue its own passenger operation, still runs the prestigious *Southern Crescent* from Washington to Atlanta daily and to New Orleans three times a week, a page torn from yesterday's timetable—white linen tablecloths, heavy silver service and fresh flowers in the dining cars—the only U.S. train offering a master bedroom with a shower. Elsewhere, a resurgence of old-time steam trains whistle around the bend, from Vermont's Steam Train Expedition to the California Western out of Fort Bragg. Many of the old trains were recruited as Bicentennial projects but are remaining on for extended, if not permanent, runs, much to the delight of wide-eyed youngsters and nostalgia buffs alike.

And so, phoenix-like from the ashes of financial ruin, a new rail passenger industry emerges. Considering the state of our overcrowded airports and congested highways, the continuing energy crisis and the high cost of fuel and airfares, its future seems not only assured but vital. But the cost has been brutal. Lost somehow in the plastic-cup world of advanced technology, with all its shortcuts, is the pride, glamour, romance, and pampered luxury of yesterday.

AMTRAK

Formed in 1971 to help solve the structural and financial woes of America's troubled railroads, Amtrak (the National Passenger Railroad Corporation) runs most railroad passenger service throughout the country. It has virtually replaced all conventional daytime equipment in the Northeast Corridor between Boston and Washington with its wide array of brand-new stainless steel Amfleet passenger cars. It has introduced them also in the Midwest, in the Detroit and Chicago areas, and in the Pacific Northwest between Seattle and Portland. These showcase trains also run four times daily each way between Los Angeles and San Diego with intermediate stops at Fullerton (for Disneyland), Santa Ana, San Juan Capistrano, San Clemente, Oceanside and Del Mar. The cars have improved suspension and sound-proofing, including use of carpet on floors, walls and even ceilings, and reliable, electric-powered air conditioning and humidity controls. Other improvements are individual reading lights, pull-down seat trays for eating or writing, a public address system and automatic sliding doors.

Coast To Coast

Several Amtrak trains make daily connecting cross-country runs from New York and/or Washington, changing in Chicago and continuing on for Los Angeles (via the *Southwest Limited*), San Francisco (via the *San Francisco Zephyr*) and Seattle (via the *Empire Builder*). Transcontinental sleeping car service to Los Angeles is offered on the Southern Railway's *Southern Crescent* and Amtrak's *Sunset Limited*, and via Kansas City on the *National Limited* and the *Southwest Limited*.

THE BROADWAY LIMITED, New York/Washington - Chicago. As famous and celebrated as its name—long a favorite of stage and film stars, authors and business tycoons—The *Broadway Limited* was totally refurbished by Amtrak, with sleeping car service, bedrooms, roomettes and low-cost mini-rooms called "slumbercoaches." Complimentary wake-up coffee and orange juice are served in lounge car (6–9:30 A.M.) or, on request, in rooms. Trains leave New York and Washington in the late afternoon, become one in Harrisburg, and continue on through picturesque Pennsylvania Dutch country, arriving at Chicago's Union Station the next morning. On route, ten minutes past Altoona, Pa., the train rounds the 180-degree Horseshoe Curve, giving passengers a panoramic view of their own train, a popular attraction for the late-night crowd in the lounge car. Departs Chicago eastbound at 3:30 P.M.

New York section stops at Newark and Trenton, then passes through but does not stop at Philadelphia, Paoli and Lancaster enroute to Harrisburg. Washington section makes stops in these cities, as well as Capital Beltway, Baltimore and Wilmington. After Harrisburg, train stops at Altoona, Pittsburgh, Canton, Crestline, Lima, Fort Wayne, Valparaiso, Gary and Chicago.

THE LAKE SHORE LIMITED, New York/Boston - Chicago. On October 31, 1975, Amtrak restored passenger service over the famous "water-level route" linking Boston, with a special section from New York, with Albany, Buffalo, Cleveland and Toledo, carrying an average of 300 people per day in each direction over what is considered one of the most magnificent and historical rail routes in all America. Boston-Chicago passenger service had been discontinued in the 1950's. Totally refurbished Lake Shore Limited features lounge and economical Slumbercoach service, as well as rooms and roomettes, lounge and complete dining and beverage service. Reservations are required in coaches except for local travel between New York and Albany. The Lake Shore Limited leaves New York City in the early evening, travels up the scenic Hudson River, then joins through Boston cars at Albany. While most Amtrak trains leave New York from Penn Station, note that the Lake Shore Limited leaves from Grand Central. It arrives at Chicago's Union Station the following mid-afternoon. (Since both the Broadway Limited and the Lake Shore Limited depart from New York at about the same time, Chicago-bound New York passengers will find the Broadway train about five hours faster. The Lake Shore Limited, however, will give passengers making cross-country connections out of Chicago a shorter wait.) The Boston portion of the Lake Shore Limited leaves from Boston's South Station at mid-afternoon. Train leaves Chicago eastbond at 2:15 P.M.

New York section stops at Croton-Harmon, Poughkeepsie, Rhinecliff, Hudson and Albany-Rensselaer. Boston portion stops at Back Bay, Framingham, Worcester, Springfield, Pittsfield and Albany-Rensselaer for the New York connection. On continuation, stops are Utica, Syracuse, Rochester, Buffalo, Erie, Cleveland, Elyria, Toledo, Elkhart, South Bend and Chicago.

THE JAMES WHITCOMB RILEY, Washington/Newport News - Cincinnati - Chicago. Named after the "Little Orphan Annie Came To Our House"-poet,

James Whitcomb Riley. This train leaves Washington and Newport News stations in the late afternoon, becoming one in Charlottesville, and continues on through charming Virginia countryside into the West Virginia night. It arrives in Chicago the following mid-afternoon. (Eastbound departures at 2:35 P.M.) Coach passengers may have complimentary use of pillows and blankets on request. Complete dining and bar service from Washington to Chicago. This train, though a bit seedy, has a definite touch of Southern appeal.

Train goes to Chicago, making intermittent stops at Clifton Forge, White Sulphur Springs, Hinton, Tri-State Station, Ky., South Portsmouth, Ky., Cincinnati, Richmond, Muncie (private bus line operates motor coach service between Muncie and Indianapolis), Peru and Lafayette.

THE MOUNTAINEER, Norfolk - Chicago. The *Mountaineer* provides daily service between Norfolk, Roanoke, Cincinnati and Chicago. This all-reserved train features complete dining and beverage service, sleeping car accommodations, and complimentary pillows and blankets on request in the coaches. It leaves Norfolk early afternoon and arrives in Chicago by mid-afternoon the following day, passing through some of Indiana's most interesting countryside. (In fact, both the *James Whitcomb Riley* and the *Mountaineer,* which follow identical routes between Catlettsburg, Ky., and Chicago, offer a striking tapestry of some of the most fascinating scenery America has to offer.) Chicago departures east are at 2:35 P.M. The *Mountaineer* stops briefly in Suffolk, Virginia, the world's best known peanut-producing market before Plains, Georgia won that honor.

The Mountaineer also stops at Petersburg, Nottoway County Station, Farmville, Lynchburg, Bedford, Roanoke, Christiansburg, Narrows, Bluefield, Welch, Williamson, Tri-State Station, Ky., Cincinnati, Richmond, Muncie (private bus line operates between Muncie and Indianapolis), Peru, Lafayette and Chicago.

SOUTHWEST LIMITED, Chicago - Los Angeles. When Amtrak took this Ritz of the rails over in the spring of 1974, it retained for a time its world renowned name, *The Super Chief,* but Santa Fe officials later withdrew permission to use the name. Thus, only the menu notation "meals served in the tradition of the Super Chief" give a hint of its famous past, when so many film celebrities "Chiefed" in from the Coast in the 30's and 40's with their retinue of press and attendants. It's still the same fine train—double-deck coaches with reclining chaise-longue seats on the top level, and restrooms, storage areas and even a hideaway coffee nook downstairs. The high level, wide-aisled coaches, plus two dome-top observation lounges, provide a spectacular view of some of America's most exciting country. Kansas City. Dodge City. The Santa Fe Trail. Flagstaff. Cimarron. Taos. Albuquerque. Gallup. The Mojave Desert. At night the lights dim and the sky is ablaze with stars. For dining, there are three restaurants: a gigantic 72-seat dining car for coach passengers, smaller deluxe restaurant for sleeping-car passengers (used only at peak travel times), the Kachina Coffee Shop plus the famous "Turquoise Room" for private dinners of up to 12 people. The all-reserved *Southwest Limited* leaves Chicago daily at 6:30 P.M. and arrives in Los Angeles, 2,200 miles away, two mornings later; daily Los Angeles departures for Chicago leave at 7:30 P.M. Smooth roadbeds provide a gentle rocking motion at night which will get you to either destination well rested. The train in both directions makes an afternoon stop in Las Vegas. Everybody goes neck-craning for a look at the famous Las Vegas Strip—and is disappointed. The stop is not the famous Las Vegas, Nevada, but Las Vegas, New Mexico, the view of which, at least from the train, is nothing less than dismal.

The Southwest Limited also stops at Joliet, Streator, Chillicothe, Galesburg, IL.; Fort Madison, IA.; Kansas City, MO.; Emporia, KS, Newton, Hutchison, Dodge

City, Garden City, KS.; Lamar, CO; La Junta, Trinidad, CO; Raton, NM; Lamy, Albuquerque; Gallop, NM.; Winslow, Flagstaff, AZ.; Kingman, Needles, CA.; Barstow, San Bernardino, Pomona, Pasadena.

THE SAN FRANCISCO ZEPHYR, Chicago - Oakland/San Francisco. Another of America's great scenic trains, the *San Francisco Zephyr* travels through the Rockies between Chicago and San Francisco, a 2,420-mile run that follows the "Overland Trail" of explorers and pioneers. Full range accommodations are available on this all-reserved train, including leg-rest coach seats, roomettes, bedrooms and bedroom suites. Full dining and beverage service and dome-car lounge. Train leaves daily from Chicago in the afternoon and arrives in Oakland two days later, where passengers make a trainside transfer to a connecting bus for a scenic 30-minute drive across the Bay Bridge to San Francisco. Eastbound passengers leave San Francisco's Transbay Terminal by bus to the Oakland station at 10:25 A.M. During the first three hours, eastbound, the train averages only 37 miles an hour passing through many famous Mother Lode settlements as it begins climb to the highest track point in the Sierra Nevadas, 7,018 feet, with stunning mountain peaks rising up 3,000 feet higher. There is a quick stop virtually in downtown Reno, Nevada, but not long enough to investigate the famous gambling casinos and nightclubs in the immediate vacinity.

The San Francisco Zephyr makes westbound stops at Aurora, Galesburg, Monmouth, IL.; Burlington, IA.; Mt. Pleasant, Ottumwa, Osceola, Creston, IA; Omaha, NE.; Lincoln, Hastings, Holdrege, McCook, NE.; Akron, CO.; Fort Morgan, Denver, Greeley, CO.; Cheyenne, WY.; Laramie, Rawlins, Rock Springs, Green River, Evanston, WY.; Ogden, UT.; Elko, NV.; Carlin, Winnemucca, Sparks, Reno, Truckee, CA.; Sacramento, Martinez and Oakland.

THE EMPIRE BUILDER, Chicago - Seattle (Via Havre). On everybody's list of favorite trains, the *Empire Builder* is old (it was the first train ordered in this country for post-World War II delivery), but has been comfortably spruced up for its daily long-distance haul from Chicago to Seattle, 2,289 miles, passing through three different time zones. This all-reserved train has wide-view coach and dome cars, sleepers with roomettes, and bedrooms. The dining car is noted for its fine cuisine, local fish specialties when available, fried chicken, roast beef. A huge breakfast of juice, hotcakes, sausage and plenty of hot coffee, is $2.60. Leaves Chicago 3:30 P.M.; departs Seattle eastbound 2:30 P.M. Passes through land explored by Lewis and Clark, Glacier National Park (early evening westbound, early morning going east), Sitting Bull country, the Great Plains of North Dakota. Train stops for 20 minutes at Harve, Montana, to change crews. It's time enough for passengers to grab a cold beer in a cowboy bar near the tracks and swap stories with local wranglers.

The Empire Builder makes stops at Glenview, IL; Milwaukee, WI; Columbus (with bus connections to and from Madison), the Wisconsin Dells, La Crosse, Winona, MN; Minneapolis, Willmar, Morris, Breckenridge, MN; Fargo, ND; Grand Forks, Devils Lake, Rugby, Minot, Stanley, Williston, ND.; Wolf Point, MT; Glasgow, Malta, Havre, Shelby, Cut Bank, Browning, Glacier Park Sta.; Belton, Whitefish, Libby, MT.; Standpoint, ID.; Spokane, Pasco, Yakima, Ellensburg, East Auburn (with connecting bus service to and from Tacoma) and Seattle.

THE NORTH COAST HIAWATHA, Chicago - Seattle (Via Billings). Formerly the *North Coast Limited,* renamed the *North Coast Hiawatha* when acquired by Amtrak, this popular all-reserved train with "Lounge in the Sky" dome car, complete dining, beverage, coach and sleeping car service, leaves Chicago in the late morning and arrives in Seattle, 2,229 miles away, two mornings later. Eastbound departures leave Seattle at 9:15 P.M. Daily departures in each direction are made only in the summer (June 15 thru Sept 8). The rest of the year, it runs daily between Chicago and Minneapolis only, with tri-weekly departures between Minneapolis (Monday, Wednesday and Saturday) and Seattle (Wednesday, Friday and Sunday). The *Hiawatha* travels through eye-popping northwest country along the Lewis and Clark Trail and along the Yellowstone and Clark Fork Rivers. It makes a 15-minute pit stop at Billings, Montana, named after Frederick Billings, former president of Northern Pacific Railroad.

The North Coast Hiawatha makes same stops as the Empire Builder above until Minneapolis, plus Portage, Tomah and Red Wing, then continues on with stops at St. Cloud, Staples, Detroit Lakes, MN.; Fargo, ND.; Valley City, Jamestown, Bismarck, Mandan, Dickinson, ND.; Glendive, MT.; Miles City, Forsyth, Billings, Livingston, MT (for Yellowstone National Park); Bozeman, Butte, Deer Lodge, Missoula, Paradise, MT; Sandpoint, ID.; Spokane, Ephrata, Wenatchee, Everett, Edmonds and Seattle.

THE NATIONAL LIMITED, New York/Washington - Kansas City (Los Angeles). Through sleeping car service from New York to Los Angeles is available with a bit of rail magic here. The sleeping car makes the regular New York to Kansas City run, lays over for eight hours (5 hours on the eastbound run) and is then attached to the Southwest Limited for its trip to Los Angeles. Passengers can remain in the car (if conceivably they want to) or go off on their own for a famous Kansas City steak dinner or a night on the town. (The layover is from 6 P.M. until 2:10 A.M.) The *National Limited* to Kansas City from New York and Washington leaves both points at about noon and join in Harrisburg. (Except for Tuesday, Thursday, Saturday and Sunday, coach passengers from Washington must make an across-the-platform transfer in North Philadelphia; alternate days on the return trip.) The daily return trip from Kansas City departs at 11 A.M., picking up that eastbound sleeper from Los Angeles. Schedules for the *National Limited* have been somewhat slower than those previously operated due to repairs on deteriorated track. This all-reserve train features all the usual comfortable long-range passenger services except for a dome-top observation car.

Leaving New York's Penn Station, the National Limited stops at Newark, Trenton, North Philadelphia, Paoli, Lancaster, Harrisburg, Lewistown, Huntingdon, Tyrone, Altoona, Johnstown, Latrobe, Greensburg, Pittsburgh, Columbus, Dayton, Richmond, Indianapolis, Terre Haute, Effingham, St. Louis, Kirkwood, Jefferson City, Sedalia, Warrensburg and Kansas City.

THE SUNSET LIMITED, (New York) New Orleans - Los Angeles. Another great train in the old-time tradition, the *Sunset Limited* leaves New Orleans at 1 P.M. on Monday, Wednesday and Friday, arrives in Los Angeles early morning two days later. Through sleeping car service is available from New York and Washington via an assist from the Southern Railway's *Southern Crescent.* The sleeping car lays over in New Orleans' combined Union Station bus and train terminal, acting as an overnight hotel. Mid-morning, it's attached to the *Sunset Limited* in time for its California departure. Moving out through colorful, moody bayou country with its cypress and Spanish moss, the train travels through five states, 2,033 miles, on its route to the West Coast. At Paisano, Texas, it scales mountains reaching a height of 5,074 feet and at Salton Sea, California, it dips to 231 feet below sea level, an altitude variation of over a mile. About 50 miles west of Del Rio, Texas, the *Sunset Limited* crosses the Pecos River over the 1,390-foot-long Pecos River High Bridge, 321 feet above the water, at a point not far from where the last spike was driven completing the country's second transcontinental railroad. Excellent equipment all the way. No dome car, but fine wide-window coach, dining and lounge-car scenery across Texas, New Mexico and on into the Arizona sunset, where giant saguaros have stood tall since before the time of Cortez. Eastbound departures from Los Angeles, Sunday, Tuesday and Friday, at 9 P.M. (Passengers traveling between all points on the New Orleans-El Paso segment of this route are now eligible for a 30-day round-trip coach excursion fare of 25 per cent off the regular coach fare.)

Leaving New Orleans, the Sunset Limited stops at Schriever, New Iberia, Lafayette, Lake Charles, LA.; Beaumont, TX.; Houston, San Antonio, Del Rio, Sanderson, Alpine, El Paso, Deming, NM.; Lordsburg, Benson, AZ; Tucson, Phoenix, Yuma, Indio, CA.; Pomona, and Los Angeles.

AMTRAK TRAINS EASTERN - THE NORTHEAST

This is Amtrak's national showcase, the routes between Boston and Washington, undisputedly the busiest stretch of passenger railroading in the country. It was the first area to receive the new 85-foot-long all-stainless steel "Amfleet" cars, "Amcafe" cars offering hot meals or snacks and, more recently, the popular "Amlounge" cars containing a food and beverage counter as well as an adjacent lounge and eating area containing eight tables. Thus, a passenger can either socialize in the lounge at mealtimes or return to the privacy of his seat with its drop-down food tray. (During Amfleet's first three months of operation, Amtrak spent $1.1 million advertising it, more than one-fifth of its total $5.8 million 1976 ad budget.) Amtrak's acquisition of ConRail properties in the Northeast Corridor gave it the go ahead it needed to spruce up the line, repairing tracks and building new train stations or improving the old ones, including a $750,000 clean-up of New York's Penn Station.

AN AMFLEET GLOSSARY

Amcoach

Chair car seating, two seats on each side of the aisle. Because of track-mounting, capacities can range from a low of 52 seats for long-distance trains to a high of 84 seats for short runs.

Amcafe

Food service car, with a special food and beverage unit located in the center of the car. Passengers take their food to their seats and use the fold-down trays built into the seats.

Amclub

The Amfleet "parlor car". Basically an Amcafe, but with wider seats in the first-class section, arranged in a 2-and-1 configuration. The Amclub section seats 18.

Amlounge

Also basically an Amcafe, but with eight tables, seating 32 people, in one end of the car. Passengers can eat at the tables after purchasing food at the service unit.

Sleek, jetliner-styled, high-speed (and higher priced for the passenger) Metroliners also operate in this corridor between Washington and New York. Metroliners generally operate as four-car trains, two coaches, a lounge and snack-bar car. The club car has one-to-one swivel seats. The snack-bar car is similar to the Amcafe cars. The all-reserved Metroliners make the New York-Washington run in a flat three hours; Amfleet takes 3 hours and 55 minutes.

The first Metroliner leaves Washington for New York at 6 A.M. Monday to Friday and there are departures every hour on the hour after that until 7 P.M. (8 P.M. Friday and Sunday), with frequent weekend runs as well. Hourly New York departures begin at 6:30 A.M.

Metroliner stops between Washington and New York include Capital Beltway Station, Baltimore, Wilmington, Philadelphia and Newark. (There are frequent variations in stops during peak hours and on weekends and evenings, so check timetable.)

THE MINUTE MAN, THE SOUTHERN CRESCENT, THE STATESMAN, SENATOR, MERCHANT'S LIMITED AND THE NIGHT OWL, all offer daily Washington-to-Boston service.

The *Minute Man,* the *Senator* and *Merchant's Limited* are Amfleet trains, the latter named after the most famous train ever to run in the Northeast Corridor. It was a favorite of Boston bankers, brokers and politicians who liked to travel into New York on it after the working day. Women rarely rode the trains at that time except in private staterooms. The Merchant's Limited, with its brass and fine upholstery, was the last all-parlor car to operate in America.

The *Night Owl,* which leaves Boston at 10:30 P.M. and arrives in Washington at 8:30 A.M., and vice versa, offers sleeping car service.

Numerous other trains make limited runs along the Northeast Corridor, New York to Boston, Washington to New York, Springfield to Washington, and such, including Amfleet's *Bicentennial* between Boston and Philadelphia. An inland route between Springfield and Hartford connect these cities with Corridor trains at New Haven. Amtrak offers an off-peak coach excursion discount of 25% for round-trip travel on Boston/Springfield and Washington lines, except on Metroliners.

Station stops between New York and Washington same as Metroliner above. Boston-New York stops are Boston Back Bay, Route 128 MA., Providence, Kingston, Westerly, Mystic, New London, Old Saybrook, New Haven, Bridgeport, Stamford and Rye. Stops between Springfield and New Haven: Thompsonville, CT., Windsor Locks, Windsor, Hartford, Berlin, Meriden and Wallingford.

THE MONTREALER, Washington - New York - Montreal. Here's another one

of those trains that seems to be a favorite with everybody. During prohibition it was known as "The Bootlegger." After partying in Montreal, thirsty Americans invariably tried to bring booze back with them past sharp-eyed border guards. Today it's something of a single's bar on wheels, especially during the ski season when the snow crowd uses it to reach Vermont ski destinations such as Brattleboro, White River Junction and Waterbury (for Stowe). It's an overnight trip both ways, but nobody except the most dedicated ski buffs, who need their rest, ever seems to sleep. The bar car, officially named "Le Pub," is a lively little bistro with a rinky-tink piano. Meals in the counter-style dining car feature standard fare plus a regional specialty, New England scrod, at $2.35. The Montrealer leaves Washington in the early evening. After a brief pause in New York (reservations are required from New York on), it continues to New Haven where it turns north for Springfield, Hartford, Vermont and Canada. It crosses the Canadian border at about 8:30 A.M. and that's when Canadian customs officials come aboard to roust you out of bed. On the return trip, the train leaves Montreal's Central Station at 6:10 P.M. and arrives in New York City the next morning at the bewitching hour of 6:35. The Montrealer is a slow, bumpy train, but it's a fun train because the people who ride it seem to be people who like people.

The Montrealer makes all major Northeast Corridor station stops between Washington and New Haven, continuing with stops at Meriden, Berlin, Hartford, Springfield, Northampton, Brattleboro, Bellows Falls, White River Junction, Montpelier Junction, Waterbury, Essex Junction, St. Albans, and Montreal.

THE ADIRONDACK, New York - Montreal. Put into service in the fall of 1974 as a second daily train to Montreal, the *Adirondack* leaves New York's *Grand Central Station* at 10 A.M. for a scenic daylight run along the Hudson River through Albany. En route, it passes spectacular mountain and lake country and the sites of Dutch, British, French and American colonial history, reaching Montreal in the evening. It doesn't have "Le Pub," but it does have full dining, beverage and lounge service. A dome car is put on at Rensselaer. It makes the New York-Montreal run in far better time than the all-night Montrealer, partly because it is 60 miles shorter and partly because of the latter's poor stretches of track through Massachusettes and Vermont.

Between New York and Montreal, the Adirondack makes stops at Croton-Harmon, Poughkeepsie, Rhinecliff, Hudson, Albany-Rensselaer, Watervliet, Mechanicville, Saratoga Springs, Fort Edward, Whitehall, Fort Ticonderoga, Westport, Plattsburgh, Rouses Point, Lacolle, PQ and Montreal West.

EMPIRE SERVICE. Amtrak services upstate New York with seven trains daily in each direction. These include the *Adirondack,* mentioned above, and two other through trains, the *Lake Shore Limited* and *The Niagara Rainbow* (formerly the *Empire State Express*) which goes to Buffalo (where there is connecting train service to Toronto and connecting bus service to Niagara Falls) and continues on to Detroit. Of the others, all unreserved coaches with light meals and refreshment service, the *Washington Irving* and *The Dewitt Clinton* (which becomes *The Henry Hudson* on the return trip) terminate in Albany; the *Salt City Express* terminates in Syracuse and *The Water Level Express* terminates in Buffalo. Departures in both directions are spaced conveniently throughout the day, roughly every two hours. All Empire Service trains leave New York City from Grand Central Station, the only Amtrak trains now that don't leave there from Penn Station. New Amfleet equipment and Rohr-built turboliners are scheduled to replace all existing Empire Service trains in the near future.

NEW YORK - HARRISBURG. Completing Amtrak's service in the Northeast is an array of daily commuter-like streamlined electric trains running frequently between New York, Philadelphia, Lancaster and Harrisburg, making innumerable stops.

Other Eastern Trains
THE BLUE RIDGE, Washington - Cumberland. The Chesapeake and Ohio Canal, the Shennandoah and Potomac Rivers, historic Harper's Ferry and the scenic Blue Ridge are all part of this unique Amfleet special's 146-mile run between the nation's capital and Cumberland, Maryland. During the week, it acts as something of a commuter train, arriving in Washington at 8:30 A.M. from Cumberland and leaving again in the early evening. On weekends, it reverses its schedule, offering the Washington crowd an escape to the mountains or a day at Harper's Ferry, returning again in the evening. The colorful, old three-car train was recently replaced with new Amfleet cars, including an Amcafe car for light meals and refreshments. The trip takes about three hours.

Blue Ridge station stops between Washington and Cumberland are Silver Spring, MD., Rockville, Gaithersburg, Brunswick, Harper's Ferry, Martinsburg and Hancock.

The Florida Fleet
Up from the sand bogs only a few decades ago, Florida is now perhaps the world's number one resort—thanks to supersalesmanship and supersunshine, orange juice, press agents, bikinis and gutsy speculation.

In 1976, the state earned $8.8 billion in tourism dollars, more than even any nation except our own. Amtrak has a whole fleet of trains taking winter-weary travelers from the North to the promised land of sunshine and fun, Miami Beach, Tampa, Saint Pete and Disney World.

THE SILVER METEOR, New York - Miami. Finest of the Florida fleet, the mighty *Meteor* streaks out of New York every afternoon at 3:50 and arrives in Miami the next day in time for its passengers to have a late afternoon dip. It was once known as a swinging party train—free champagne punch, orange juice, coffee, games (bingo, keno and horse racing via a closed-circuit TV system), movies, a live fashion show, afternoon tea and a $1-per-drink Happy Hour. But like many well-intended celebrations, the party went sour. The TV sets rattled out of focus, the movie projectors needed constant repair and fights broke out during the Happy Hour. The entertainment was subsequently discontinued, but the orange juice and coffee is still free (from 6 to 9:30 in the morning) and dining car service both with a snack car and full dining car is considered to be the best in the East. Travelers to Florida pass through Washington in time to see the city dazzlingly lit; returning passengers see it at daybreak. The all-reserved *Silver Meteor* has full coach, sleeping and lounge car service. It departs Miami northbound daily at 9:05 A.M.

The Silver Meteor makes major corridor stops between New York and Washington, then continues on with station stops at Alexandria, Richmond, Petersburg, Va., Rocky Mount, N.C., Wilson, Fayetteville, Florence, S.C., Charleston, Yemassee, Savannah, Thalmann, Jacksonville, Waldo, Ocala, Wildwood, Winter Haven, Sebring, West Palm Beach, Deerfield Beach, Ft. Lauderdale, Hollywood, Miami (Miami Beach).

THE CHAMPION, New York - St. Petersburg. The *Champion* is much the same train as The Silver Meteor above. In fact, it's actually attached from New York to Jacksonville except at peak travel times. At Jacksonville, it switches routes, veering inland to Orlando and Walt Disney World, Tampa and St. Petersburg. It has the same services as *The Meteor,* plus economical Slumbercoaches. Returning, it leaves St. Petersburg at 9:20 A.M. to meet up again with the Meteor at Jacksonville for the return to New York.

Between Jacksonville and St. Petersburg, the Champion makes station stops at Palatka, DeLand (for Daytona Beach), Sanford, Winter Park, Orlando, Kissimmee, Lakeland, Tampa, Clearwater, St. Petersburg.

THE SILVER STAR, New York - St. Petersburg/Miami. More of the same. The all-reserved *Silver Star* leaves New York City at 9:35 in the morning, daily, follows along the "corridor," then past Washington via the Columbia, South Carolina, inland route for Kissimmee (Walt Disney World) where it splits, one section traveling via Lakeland and Tampa to St. Petersburg, the other going along the coastal route to Miami, arriving there in the early afternoon. The *Silver Star* has complete dining and beverage service, lounge service and sleeping cars. Departures north from Miami and from St. Petersburg are in the early afternoon.

THE FLORIDIAN, Chicago - St. Petersburg/Miami. The *Floridian* is a daily, all-reserved train, with a choice of coach and private accommodations, that journeys from Chicago's Union Station through the heartland of America and then swings southeast into the historic South. At Jacksonville it splits; both sections continue on to Walt Disney World and then one section goes to St. Petersburg, the other to Miami. Despite a few miles of rough Penn Central track, the Floridian is a smooth, comfortable train. It leaves Chicago at 8:30 A.M. for a two-day, one-night trip. It has full dining, beverage and lounge service, including a dome recreation car with reading materials and comfortable lounge chairs. Departures from Miami and St. Petersburg are in the evening.

Between Chicago and Jacksonville, the Floridian makes station stops at Logansport, Lafayette, Indianapolis, Bloomington, Louisville, Bowling Green, Nashville, Decatur, Birmingham, Montgomery, Dothan, AL., Thomasville, GA., Valdosta and Waycross, Ga.

THE COLONIAL, New York - Newport News. This run, inaugurated June 15, 1976, marks the first time a regularly scheduled train connects the Northeast with Williamsburg and Newport News—a boon to vacationers traveling to Colonial Williamsburg and to the Nearby Busch Garden theme park "The Old Country." The Colonial, a new Amfleet train, departs New York daily at noon, and Washington at 4:35 P.M., arriving in Williamsburg at 8:30 P.M. and at Newport News 40 minutes later. Return departures from Newport News are at mid-afternoon. Amcafe and Amlounge light meals and beverage service.

Along with regular "corridor" station stops between New York and Washington, the Colonial also stops at Alexandria, Quantico, Fredericksburg, Richmond, Williamsburg and Newport News.

THE PALMETTO, New York - Savannah. The *Palmetto* is the first all new Amfleet train put into service over a medium distance route (828 miles). Beginning in June, 1976, it supplements Amtrak's existing New York-Savannah service on the overnight Silver Star and Silver Meteor/Champion. The Palmetto has "Amclub" and "Amlounge" food and beverage service. It leaves New York at 8 A.M. and arrives in Savannah at 11:50 P.M., daily. It departs Savannah at 6:50 A.M.

The Palmetto makes all major "corridor" stops between New York and Washington, and continues with station stops at Alexandria, Quantico, Fredericksburg, Richmond, Petersburg, Rocky Mount, Dillon, Florence, Kingstree, Charleston, Yemassee and Savannah.

Midwest Amtrak Trains

Chicago—the Midwest—is the hub of American railroading. "Hog butcher for the world, Tool Maker, Stacker of Wheat, Player with Railroads and the Nation's Freight handler," wrote poet Carl Sandburg. Trains out of Chicago opened the West to commerce and business, and today Chicago is still a major transportation center, with the world's largest concentration of rail, truck and air transportation. Amtrak's huge Union Station serves virtually all major routes and destinations in the U.S.

THE PANAMA LIMITED, Chicago - New Orleans. From Chicago's jackhammer pace to languid New Orleans, the *Panama Limited* moves through America's heartland, gliding along a cross section of cities, towns, fertile farmlands, industrial areas and historic waterways, following the jazz and blues route of American music. The train takes its name from the Panama Canal. When the Canal was being built, prior to World War I, New Orleans was the gateway to South America, and many of the train's early riders were workers and engineers heading for the Canal Zone, many never to return. Under the Illinois Central's banner, the *Panama Limited* was noted for its grand epicurian meals. Anyone who finished the "King's Dinner" repast received a certificate and lapel pin celebrating his gourmet venture. Today, the *Panama Limited* still serves fine meals in its diner (sans the certificate and pin). Sleeping accommodations include roomettes, double bedrooms, and bedroom suites. At last report, there were delays on this train due to extensive track repairs. The *Panama Limited,* an all-reserved train, leaves Chicago daily at 6:10 P.M. and arrives in New Orleans at noon the following day. Coach passengers on the Memphis-New Orleans segment are eligible for a 30-day round-trip excursion rate, good between any two points south of, and including Memphis, at 25 per cent less than the regular round-trip fare. The Panama Limited departs New Orleans northbound at 4:30 P.M.

Between Chicago and New Orleans, the Panama Limited makes station stops at Homewood, Kankakee, Rantoul, Champaign-Urbana, Mattoon, Effingham, Centralia, Carbondale, Cairo, Fulton, Dyersburg, Memphis, Batesville, Grenada, Winona, Durant, Canton, Jackson, Hazelhurst, Brookhaven, McComb and Hammond.

Two daily Amfleet trains follow the initial route of the *Panama Limited* in and out of Chicago. The *Illini* acts suspiciously like a commuter train. It leaves the twin cities of Champaign and Urbana—they share the main campus of the University of Illinois—at 7 A.M., arriving in Chicago about two-and-a-half hours later. It departs Chicago for the return trip at 4:20, making all intermediate stops both ways. The *Shawnee,* which has an Amcafe car serving light meals and beverages (the Illini doesn't), leaves Chicago at 8:40 A.M. and arrives in Carbondale, home of Southern Illinois University, at 2:30 in the afternoon. It departs for Chicago again two hours later, making all stops.

TURBOLINER SERVICE, Chicago - Milwaukee; Chicago - Detroit; Chicago - Port Huron. Fast and convenient service on the Chicago-Milwaukee corridor is operated by Amtrak's Turboliners, big, streamlined, five-car, 120-mph trains with a power car at each end (so the trains never have to be turned around). Each power car has twin turbines for faster breaking and acceleration. When the train reaches cruising speed, one of the turbines can be idled, thus guaranteeing backup power for the train. The Turboliners offer comfortable, stretch-out, unreserved coach seating, light meals and beverage service. Through trains, *The North Coast Hiawatha* and *The Empire Builder* also cover the Chicago-Milwaukee corridor. Arrivals and departures are made regularly throughout the day, roughly every two hours.

Station stops between Chicago and Milwaukee are Glenview and Sturtevent. (Trackside bus connections available for Green Bay.)

Turboliner service also operates daily between Chicago and Detroit, with unreserved coach seating, light meals and beverage service. The Turboliner leaves Chicago at 1:40 P.M. and arrives in Detroit at 8:20 in the evening. Return departures leave Detroit at about noon.

Station stops between Chicago and Detroit are Niles, MI., Kalamazoo, Battle Creek, Albion, Jackson, Chelsea, Ann Arbor and Ypsilanti.

Turboliner service between Chicago and Port Huron also features unreserved coach seating, light meals and beverage service. The train, *The Blue Water Limited,* leaves Chicago daily at 3:25 P.M., and arrives in Port Huron at 11:30 P.M. Return departures leave Port Huron at 5:45 A.M., arriving in Chicago at noon.

Station stops between Chicago and Port Huron are Niles, Kalamazoo, Battle Creek, East Lansing, Durand, Flint and Lapeer.

The Chicago-Detroit corridor is also served daily by two Amfleet trains, *The Wolverine,* leaving Chicago in the early morning and arriving in Detroit at 2:15 P.M., and the afternoon departing *The Saint Clair,* which gets into Detroit at 10:30 P.M. Return schedules are approximately reversed. Amclub and Amcafe service are available on both trains, as well as unreserved coach seating.

THE ANN RUTLEDGE, THE STATE HOUSE, THE ABRAHAM LINCOLN, Chicago - St. Louis. The *State House* and the *Ann Rutledge* are two Amfleet trains that leave Chicago daily at 5:45 P.M. and 8:10 A.M. respectively, arriving at 11:30

P.M. and 1:30 P.M. in St. Louis. The *State House* leaves St. Louis at 4:20 A.M. and arrives in Chicago in time for the business day. The *Ann Rutledge* leaves St. Louis at 4: P.M. and arrives in Chicago about five hours later. Amclub and Amcafe service are available on both trains, along with unreserved coach seating. The *Abraham Lincoln* runs daily (except Saturday) from the Windy City to St. Louis, leaving in the afternoon and arriving at 9:35 P.M. It runs a daily (except Sunday) return to Chicago, leaving St. Louis in the early morning and arriving in Chicago at about noon. An older, refurbished train, it features complete dining and beverage service and a parlor car. The scenery is rich midwest farmland.

Station stops between Chicago and St. Louis are Joliet, Pontiac, Bloomington, Lincoln, Springfield, Carlinville and Alton.

THE ILLINOIS ZEPHYR, Chicago - Quincy. This is a daily train that leaves Quincy at 5:45 A.M. (7:30 on Sunday), arriving in Chicago in 4 hours and 45 minutes. It makes the return out of Chicago at 6 P.M. Unreserved coach seating and light lunch and beverage service.

Between Chicago and Quincy, the Illinois Zephyr stops at La Grange Road, Aurora, Plano, Mendota, Princeton, Kewanee, Galesburg and Macomb.

THE BLACK HAWK, Chicago - Dubuque. Completing the almost perfect hub of rail routes in and out of Chicago, *The Black Hawk* leaves Dubuque at 5:55 A.M. heading toward the Chicago work day, arriving at 10:10 A.M., Monday through Friday. It departs Chicago again at 5:15 P.M. On weekends, it leaves Dubuque at a leasurely 7:30 A.M., arriving in Chicago in time for lunch and a theater matinee. Unreserved coach seating, snack and beverage service. Thirty-day round-trip excursion rates available for all points on this line.

Station stops between Chicago and Dubuque are Elmhurst, Rockford, Freeport, Warren, Galena, and East Dubuque.

THE LONE STAR, Chicago - Dallas/Houston. Big, roomy, high-level coaches and a scenic view of America's rolling prairies where wild herds of buffalo roamed and Commanches and Kiowas once chanted their ageless hunting songs are the main features of this luxury train that crosses the middle of America, 1,369 miles, in little more than 24 hours. It has complete dining and beverage service, lounge service, roomettes, bedrooms, and bedroom suites. *The Lone Star,* and it is truly a "star", leaves Chicago every day at 4:30 P.M. and arrives in Houston at 7:25 the following night. On its return, it departs Houston at 7:30 A.M. and makes Chicago by mid-morning the next day.

Between Chicago and Houston, the Lone star makes station stops at Joliet, Streator, Chillicothe, Galesburg, Fort Madison, La Plata, Marceline, Topeka, Emporia, Newton, Wichita, Arkansas City, Ponca City, Perry, Guthrie, Oklahoma City, Norman, Purcell, Pauls Valley, Ardmore, Gainesville, Fort Worth (with a direct leg to Dallas), Cleburne, McGregor, Temple and Brenham.

THE INTER-AMERICAN, Chicago - Laredo. Put into service in March, 1974, connecting the midwest and Laredo, Texas, gateway to Mexico, for the first time, the *Inter-American* now runs daily between Chicago and Fort Worth and three times weekly between Fort Worth and Laredo (Monday, Thursday and Friday), arriving at 6:15 P.M. It departs Laredo, northbound, at 10:55 A.M. Sunday, Tuesday and Friday. The scenery, most of it through the Texas daylight hours in both directions, is bleak—vast expanses of nothingness; dry, inhospitable land that seems to roll on forever. But the service is quick and attentive, the lounge-car crowd amiable Westerners. The train has complete dining car service and sleeping cars. For those continuing on by rail into Mexico, taxi service is available from

Laredo to the National Railroads of Mexico station in Nuevo Laredo, about a mile away. The Inter-American is scheduled to get into Laredo at 6:15 in the evening and the Nuevo Laredo NdeM train leaves at 7:10. Good luck is needed to make the connection!

Station stops between St. Louis and Laredo are Poplar Bluff, Walnut Ridge, Newport, Little Rock, Malvern, Texarkana, Marshall, TX., Longview, Dallas, Fort Worth, Cleburne, McGregor, Temple, Taylor, Austin, San Marcos and San Antonio.

Amtrak Western Trains

THE COAST STARLIGHT, Seattle - Los Angeles. Amtrak is justly proud of this superstar train that pounds gloriously down the sun-dappled Pacific Coast, using track of five different railroads to give travelers "through" daily train service from Seattle to Los Angeles. The *Coast Starlight* leaves Seattle at 11:50 A.M. It gets into Oakland (where the San Francisco bus awaits) at 8:25 the next morning and arrives in Los Angeles at 7 that evening. On the return trip the *Coast Starlight* leaves Los Angeles at 10 A.M., Oakland at 8:30 P.M., and arrives in Seattle, Washington, at 5:20 P.M. the following day. On its journey, the train takes a coastal route much of the way, climbing up snow-covered mountain valleys and flirting recklessly with the blue Pacific for a pure, foamy 113 miles, from San Luis Obispo to just above L.A., and then up again over sky-high bridges. This is another of those once-party trains (with hostesses, games and movies) that has grown more conservative in the last couple of years. (With rare exception, organized "Fun" on trains seems to be about as successful as organized fun on a Greyhound bus!) But the scenery more than compensates. When you book reservations on this train, remember to request space on the starboard, or water side (especially when you have sleeping accommodations and can only see out of one side of the train), otherwise you might be viewing used car lots instead of pink, white, and baby-blue marinas. The train offers a choice of comfortable, reclining coach seats, or private roomette, or bedroom accommodations. It has a recreation lounge car and Coast Starlight Dining Room with complete dining and beverage service (including California wines). Trainside connections at both ends, north to Vancouver, British Columbia, and south to San Diego.

Station stops between Seattle and Los Angeles are Tacoma, Centralia, Kelso-Longview, Vancouver, WA.; Portland, OR., Salem, Eugene, Klamath Falls, Dunsmuir, Redding, Orland, Davis, Oakland (with bus connections to San Francisco), San Jose, Salinas, San Luis Obispo, Santa Barbara, Oxnard and Glendale.

THE SAN JOAQUIN, Oakland/San Francisco-Fresno-Bakersfield (Los Angeles). Operating since early 1974, The *San Joaquin* runs daily between Oakland and Bakersfield, with bus connections trackside at each end for San Francisco and Los Angeles. The *San Joaquin* leaves Oakland at 9:30 A.M. and arrives in Bakersfield at 4:05 P.M. It leaves Bakersfield northbound at 11:25 A.M., arriving in Oakland at 6 P.M. It traverses some of California's richest farmland, offering complete dining and beverage service.

Station stops between Oakland and Bakersfield are Martinez, Stockton, Riverbank, Merced (with bus connections to Yosemite), Fresno (for Yosemite, Sequoia and Kings Canyon National Parks), Hanford and Wasco.

THE PACIFIC INTERNATIONAL, Seattle - Vancouver. Light meals and drinks are served on this daily unreserved Amfleet coach train leaving Seattle at 6:15 in the evening and arriving in Vancouver, British Columbia, at 11 the same night. Return departures from Vancouver are at 6:50 P.M., arriving in Seattle at 11:20, with *Coast Starlight* connections south 30 minutes later.

Station stops between Seattle and Vancouver are Edmonds, Everett, Mt. Vernon-Burlington, Bellingham, Blaine, WA., and New Westminster.

THE MOUNT RAINIER, THE PUGET SOUND, Portland - Seattle. Two trains daily between Seattle and Portland. The *Mount Rainier* leaves Seattle in the early evening, the *Puget Sound* at 8:30 A.M. They arrive in Portland about 4 hours later. Both return on the same schedule. Unreserved coach seating, light meals and beverages. Both now have Amfleet equipment.

Station stops between Seattle and Portland are the same as the Coast Starlight above.

THE SAN DIEGANS, Los Angeles - San Diego. The first area outside the Northeast Corridor to be thoroughly "Amfleet-ed" was this busy 128-mile run between Los Angeles and San Diego, via Disney Land, San Clemente and Del Mar Raceway. Four trains daily in each direction complete the distance in about two-and-a-half hours. The trains leave Los Angeles at 8:30 and 10:30 in the morning and at 4:10 and 8:20 P.M. San Diego departures are at 7 A.M. and 1, and at 5 and 8:20 P.M. The route is picturesque, most of it skirting the blue waters of the Southern California coast. Groups of school kids with identifying name tags around their necks climb aboard in the morning, off for a day at Disney Land or for a tour of the San Diego zoo, all giggles and squeals. Everybody strains for a glimpse of the Nixon compound at San Clemente, but it's not visible from the train. Light meals and beverage service is available on all the trains, but if you're in a romantic mood, a lunch basket and a picnic on the beach somewhere along the way might be fun.

Station stops between Los Angeles and San Diego are Fullerton, Santa Ana, San Juan Capistrano, San Clemente, Oceanside and Del Mar.

INDEPENDENT (NON-AMTRAK) TRAINS

Southern Railway

When Amtrak was formed in 1971, a number of American railroads chose to continue their own passenger service, along with lucrative freight operations. Of these few railroads, Southern Railway is the largest and best known people-mover. Its famed *Southern Crescent* ranks with the best trains in North America.

SOUTHERN CRESCENT, Washington - New Orleans. A vigorous "be kind to passengers" employee-incentive program (Operation Southern Hospitality) keeps the traditional hospitality of the South perking on this train, one of the most comfortable anywhere. It even smells clean, and it should. Each car gets a $35,000 refurbishing job every three years. Green-and-gold diesels buffed like jade, aluminum cars shined. Luxurious reclining seats in tweed-like finish, roomettes, bedrooms, and the only American train today offering the almost lost luxury of a master stateroom with a shower. (It costs little more than double a roomette fare.) A dome car is added for the Atlanta-New Orleans portion, a daylight tour of the Southern heartland in both directions. In the immaculate dining car, where absorbent doilies stand guard between saucer and cup, a single red rose on each table, hominy grits and well-cooked strips of fatback are served with "The Old Southern Special Breakfast," and the New Orleans coffee has a tinge of chicory. Dinner is a la carte, except for the sizzling sirloin (steak, two vegetables, salad, dessert, rolls, and beverage, $6.75). The *Southern Crescent* leaves Washington daily in the early evenings and arrives in Atlanta the next morning. It continues on to New Orleans three times a week (Sunday, Tuesday and Thursday). In cooperation with Amtrak it carries a through sleeper car from Boston, which lays over in New

Orleans for a night acting as a hotel on rails for California-bound, or California-returning, passengers. It leaves New Orleans for Atlanta on Monday, Wednesday and Friday at 7 A.M.

Main station stops between Washington and New Orleans are Alexandria, Charlottesville, Lynchburg, Danville, Greensboro, Salisbury, Charlotte, Greenville, Atlanta, Birmingham, Tuscaloosa, and Meridan.

Denver & Rio Grande Western Railroad

THE RIO GRANDE ZEPHYR, Denver - Salt Lake City. The *Rio Grande Zephyr* —train # 17—is the last passenger train of the historic Denver & Rio Grande Western Railroad save one. The other is the summer tourist excursion train, the steam-powered *Silverton,* a pioneer narrow-gauge train operating in the San Juan Mountains of Southwestern Colorado. Ironically, its future seems assured, but the *Rio Grande Zephyr* runs on financially perilous track. It's an exceptional train and a spectacular trip, nonetheless, a spellbinder in the grand tradition of western railroading. It loops high through the Colorado Rockies where towering cliffs rise above as it meanders along the banks of Big Red. At Moffat Tunnel, a six-mile-long cavity at a more than 9,000-foot-high altitude, the engineer traditionally toots the whistle as the *Rio Grande Zephyr* crosses the Continental Divide. The train is old, made up of cars from the former *California Zephyr* ("Butch" Cassidy and the Sundance Kid once robbed the line's payroll), but they hardly show their quarter century of service. The observation-bar-lounge car has four private bedroom-drawing rooms for daytime occupancy. Food served in the elegant old dining car is excellent. Perhaps to remind us of our own bygone era, martinis and Bloody Marys are still only $1. Along with its dining and lounge car, the *Rio Grande Zephyr* generally runs with four Vista Dome coach cars, but during busy holiday seasons may carry as many as eight or nine. The Zephyr leaves Denver on its 570-mile trip at 7:30 A.M. on Monday, Thursday and Saturday, arriving in Salt Lake City at 9:30 P.M., with limousine connections to Ogden. It leaves Salt Lake City at 6:50 A.M. on Tuesday, Friday and Sunday. Family fare discounts are available.

Station stops between Denver and Salt Lake City are Granby, Bond, Glenwood Springs, Rifle, Grand Junction, Thompson, Green River, Price, Helper and Provo.

The Rock Island Line

THE PEORIA ROCKET, THE ROCK ISLAND ROCKET. The Peoria train leaves Chicago at 6:15 P.M., arriving in Peoria at 10:40 P.M. The Rock Island train, for which the line is named, leaves Rock Island at 6:45 A.M. and arrives in Chicago at 11:15 A.M. Both are daily trains.

Station stops between Chicago and Peoria are Englewood, Blue Island, Joliet, Morris, Ottawa, LaSalle-Peru, Bureau, Henry and Chillicothe.

Station stops between Chicago and Rock Island are the same as above until and including Peru, then continuing on to Sheffield, Genesco and Rock Island.

The Georgia Railroad

This consists solely of a coach car attached to a regular freight train traveling between Atlanta and Augusta, a four-and-a-half hour trip, 171 miles from railroad yard to railroad yard. The one-way fare is about $6 and the schedule is extremely flexible, a factor that doesn't seem to discourage its small band of regular passengers and a surprisingly large number of visiting train buffs who enjoy the ambience of it all.

Alaska Railroads
ALASKA RAILROAD, Anchorage - Fairbanks. The *Alaska Railroad,* operated by the U.S. Department of Transportation, serves as a passenger train between Anchorage and Fairbanks, a stunning, 356-mile run where, in the wintertime, the train occasionally slows down to nudge a moose off the tracks. The *Alaska Railroad* runs daily during the summer, with bi-weekly service from September through May. The train passes Mt. McKinley National Park (four hours from Fairbanks; eight from Anchorage). Coaches, complete dining facilities and observation-lounge car.

WHITE PASS AND YUKON, Skagway - White Horse. This train runs in search of a definition. It's a passenger train that travels between Skagway, half ghost town, half frontier museum, across the Alaska panhandle, over the northwest corner of British Columbia and on into White Horse in the Yukon Territory. It's the same route used by sourdough prospectors back in 1898 when Skagway was the rip-roaring takeoff point for the Klondike gold rush. It's the same train, in fact, a narrow-gauge pioneer railroad with plush-upholstered reversible seats, a potbellied stove to keep everybody warm and an ancient water cooler where tiny cornucopia cups are dispensed with awesome frequency to an endless line of thirsty youngsters. The White Pass and Yukon is also a work train, with a small-scale cargo operation, and it's an auto-train. You can ship your car or medium-sized camper or trailer and two people the entire 365-mile route for $193, an all-you-both-can-eat lunch included at the Lake Bennett station stop. And it's an excursion train, ferrying camera-clicking tourists along the White Pass Trail to Klondike country at Bennett on one-day, round-trip outings ($29, with the all-you-can-eat prospector's lunch). It's as exciting as it is corny. Waterfalls, roaring rivers, and lakes as still as a forgotten poem. Dead Horse Gulch. Inspiration Point. With comfortable A.M. departures in both directions.

AUTO-TRAINS

Lorton (near Washington) - Sanford (near Orlando) and Louisville - Sanford. This privately-owned ferry on wheels had its initial run December 6, 1971, and was at the time as revolutionary a concept for American railroads as the formation of Amtrak just seven months earlier. Cheerful, big, dome-topped coaches, roomy sleeping cars, and up to 20 enclosed rail-going automobile carriers. So you're going to Florida? Your car goes on the back of the train, you climb into a comfortable coach or private sleeping compartment and, in essence, you leave the driving to Auto-Train. Auto-Train first began service between Lorton, Virginia (near Washington, D.C.), and Sanford, Florida (in the vicinity of Orlando). Because passengers arrived and departed in and with their own transportation a major downtown metropolitan departure point wasn't necessary. Since then, the highly successful operation has opened a new route between Louisville, Ky., and Sanford. Obviously, Auto-Train was conceived to service the traffic-choked Disney World complex, now considered to be the world's number one tourist attraction, and at times it actually seems as though it might have been inspired by the fantasy master himself. The train exteriors are brilliant white, with bright purple and red trim. Personnel, both at the ticket counters and on-board attendants, mostly pretty young girls in the Disney Land mold, wear snappy, eye-catching uniforms, and it's rumored that if one is ever caught not smiling she's fired on the spot. Fares are all-inclusive, except for drinks; when the train's rolling there's so much going on that you almost need a program to keep track of it all—movies in two buffet dining cars, The Lemon Tree and the Purple Plum, games, supervised entertainment for the kids, a boutique (selling newspapers, magazines, souvenirs and sunglasses). In a bi-level entertainment car known as "The Whistle Stop Club," a guitarist-singer is featured in the Starlight Lounge above, soft, cozy lighting in the cocktail bar below.

The nitty-gritty: service between Lorton and Sanford and between Louisville and Sanford is daily in both directions. Either route takes less than 24 hours. There are no intermediate stops and you must accompany your car (you can't ship it independently). Basic fare including car or station wagon (no buses, campers or house trailers) and one or two occupants is $212 between Lorton and Sanford, and $225 between Louisville and Sanford. For each additional passenger, regardless of age, limited to the capacity of the automobile, an additional $28 is charged from Lorton, $25 from Louisville. That's for coach, with blankets and pillows provided at night. Add $45 for two passengers, $60 for three and $75 for four if you plan to book sleeping accommodations on the train. Dinner and breakfast are included, as is lunch on the longer Louisville run.

COMMUTER TRAINS

When asked several years ago at a news conference why New York state paid $250 million to put the battered, rundown Long Island Railroad back on its feet, then-Governor Nelson Rockfeller replied: "We made a survey and found that we would have had to build 24 lanes of highways through New York City to handle the commuters who depend on the railroad." And so it goes in New York with the Long Island Railroad, the Staten Island Rapid Transit, the Hudson Line, Harlem Line, New Haven Line, the Erie-Lackawanna Railroad, and in Chicago with the Chicago and Northwestern and other commuter lines, and in most other major metropolitan areas of the country—Boston, Philadelphia, Washington, Pittsburgh, Cleveland, Detroit and San Francisco—where daily commuter trains perform a valid, invaluable service.

MAJOR U.S. TRAIN STATIONS

The oldest train station in America is in Thompsonville, Maine. Now a railroad museum, it predates the Baltimore and Ohio stations at Mount Clare and Ellicott City, Maryland, both built in the 1830s and long believed to be the oldest in the country, by 35 years. It was originally a cookhouse and servants' quarters of the "Montpelier" estate, home of Revolutionary War general Henry Knox. By the time the first railroad came through, the Knox & Lincoln Railroad (later absorbed by the Maine Central), 1894, the splendid estate had deteriorated. The original mansion was torn down and the old cookhouse—the tracks went right past it—was converted to a train station. It served as such for over a century. Railroad stations have come a long way since then, through the "golden age" of railroads when stations were as ornate and cavernous as cathedrals, and then through a long period of decline and neglect. Stations, like the trains they serve, are now undergoing a tremendous improvement program. In 1976, Amtrak emphasized its station work along the route of the *Lake Shore Limited* between Chicago and Boston, and committed funds to build new stations in Cleveland, Ohio, and Worcester, Massachusetts, and to improve eight other stations along the route. Amtrak also cooperated in a comprehensive project sponsored by both the Department of Commerce and the Department of Transportation, in conjunction with local governments, to renovate ten stations in the Northeast corridor. In other areas, Amtrak began to improve nine stations in a joint project with New York, twenty-one stations in cooperation with Illinois, and explore a similar program with Connecticut. New stations were completed in Richmond and Roanoke, Virginia; Bluefield, West Virginia; and Catlettsburg, Kentucky. In the nation's railroad hub at Chicago, it opened a new passenger lounge and baggage facility in Union Station. Amtrak now owns some 130 railroad stations of its own as result of property conveyances from bankrupt Northeast railways. Largest are Amtrak's two busiest stations, former Penn Central properties, in New York and Philadelphia.

ALBANY, NEW YORK (pop. 114,873). *Amtrak Station,* East Street, 12143. Located two miles from downtown area. Ticket office hours are from 6:30 A.M. to 11 P.M. Waiting room hours: 7 A.M. to midnight. Services include snack bar and vending machines, pay phones, newsstand, taxi stand and public bus service, storage lockers, free (unattended) parking lot adjacent to terminal. Eight miles from Country airport by connecting limo, $2.
Phone Numbers (area code 518)
Ticket Office: 462–3823
Hotels (within 2 mile vicinity): Sheraton-Inn—Wellington—434–4141

ALBUQUERQUE, NEW MEXICO (pop. 350,000). *Albuquerque Station,* 314 First Street, S.W., 87101. Designed in Spanish-style architecture, located downtown, near Highway 66 and 85 Intersection, about a mile from picturesque, ancient Spanish plaza. Pay parking lot. Red Cap and hand carts available. Services include snack bar and vending machines, four pay phones, taxi stands and public bus service. Sunport Airport 15 minutes away, $1.50 by limo. Local Indians frequently meet "through" trains at station stop to sell handcrafted silver and turquoise jewelry.
Phone Numbers (area code 505)
Ticket Office: 263–8006
Hotels (within four to 8 blocks): Hilton—243–4421, Desert Inn—243–1773, Gaslight Motel—247–0416, Quality Inn—247–1501

BALTIMORE, MARYLAND (pop. 905,759). *Pennsylvania Station,* 1515 N. Charles Street, 21201. One mile from the center of town and all spruced up is the old Baltimore passenger station which recently underwent a $369,440 renovation by Amtrak, part of a larger effort involving the City of Baltimore and the Federal Railroad Administration which also contributed substantial sums for general cleanup and painting of the station, as well as site improvements and landscaping. Remodeling of the concourse area for use as a passenger lounge, rebuilding and expansion of the ticket counter and office areas, installation of modern ticketing equipment, and a baggage conveyor check-in system; new restrooms; a new security and surveillance system were all part of the extensive overhaul. Station handles 75,000 passengers a month. Ticket office hours from 6:15 A.M. to 11:15 P.M. Waiting room hours: 5 A.M. to 1 A.M. Services include snack bar, vending machine, cocktail lounge, restaurant (7 A.M. to 2 A.M., closed weekends), newsstand, travel aid desk, taxi stand, public bus service, commuter train connections, Red Cap, storage lockers, direct phone service for Avis, Hertz and Airways Rentacars, escalators and elevators to covered platform. Parking lot on Lanvale Street, $2.15 for 24 hrs. Baltimore/Washington International Airport 10 minutes south by taxi.
Baltimore is the birthplace of the American railroad, the Baltimore and Ohio line. The world's largest collection of historic railroad equipment and memorabilia is on display at the B & O Transportation Museum located at Mt. Clare Station, at West Pratt and Poppleton Streets.
Phone Numbers (area code 301)

Ticket Office: (800) 523–5700

Hotels: Baltimore Hilton—752–1100, Holiday Inn—685–3500

BIRMINGHAM, ALABAMA (pop. 300,901). *Birmingham Station,* 1819 Morris Ave., 35203. Half-mile from center of town. Ticket office hours are from 10 A.M. to 6 P.M. Waiting room hours: 10 A.M. to 6 P.M. Services include free (unattended) parking lot, pay phones, taxi stand and public bus service, Red Caps, hand carts and storage lockers. No food service. Five miles to Municipal Airport by taxi, $4.30; by limo, $2.25.

Southern Crescent also services Birmingham, but uses Southern Railway Station, 2617 7th Avenue, North (phone: 800/ 874–2800), about a mile from main station. No shuttles; taxis required.

Phone Numbers (area code 205)

Ticket Office: 324–3033

Hotels (within mile of station): Center Motor Inn—324–0601, Holiday Inn Downtown—323–8931, Parliamont House—323–7211, Francis Hotel Lodge—871–0343, Holiday Inn Civic Ctr.—328–6320

BOSTON, MASSACHUSETTES (pop. 641,071). *Back Bay Station,* 145 Dartmouth Street, 02116. Small station serving Back Bay residential area of Boston, an architectural museum reflecting building fashions of the late 19th century, and the next to last stop on the Boston end of the Northeast Corridor. When acquired by Amtrak, it received little more than a new coat of paint and a bright, new sign with the Amtrak logo. Station is located opposite Prudential Building. Ticket office hours are from 6:30 A.M. to 7:30 P.M. Waiting room open 24 hours. Pay parking lot, snack bar, phones, taxi stand and public bus and commuter train connections. Red Cap service is available. Transportation to Logan Airport, three miles east by taxi, $3.50; by limo, $1.50.

Phone Numbers (area code 617)

Ticket Office: 536–5933

Hotels (within mile of station): Colonnade Motel—261–2800, Ritz Carlton—536–5700, Lenox Hotel/Motor Inn—536–5300, Statler Hilton—426–2000, Copley Plaza—267–5300

South Station, Atlantic Ave. and Summer St., 02210. Boston's main station is currently undergoing a massive face-lifting. Amtrak has appropriated $96,000 to improve passenger facilities and commissary space and the city of Boston diverted an additional $750,000 of federal redevelopment funds to tear down a section of the station and redo it as part of its downtown redevelopment program. No train station ever needed it more. In the February, 1976, issue of locally published *Boston Magazine,* authors Anne Bernays and Justin Kaplan described it thusly: "Some of this initial elation evaporates the instant we enter South Station. It looks like a movie set for a city under siege, maybe during the Crimean War. Abandoned, grungy shops, lighting by Edgar Allen Poe, pools of dirty water, people looking so discouraged they might be waiting for a train to transport them to a labor camp. The main station clock has no hands—but why face up to the implications? The whole place looks as if somebody forgot to tell the Boston end that the trains were still running. . . . Passengers huddled against an unfinished cement wall, trying to avoid the wet blasts that sweep in every time the platform gate is opened." Anyway, all that's being fixed up. Ticket office and waiting room in the new, improved Boston South Station are open 24 hours. Station is adjacent to South Postal Annex and Stone and Webster Building. Numerous private parking lots in the immediate vicinity. Cocktail lounge (closes at 11 P.M.). Red Cap service, hand carts available, storage lockers, pay phones, taxi stand, public bus and commuter train connections. Bank service 8:30 A.M. to 2:30 P.M. No food service at present. Logan Airport two miles northwest, by taxi $4; no limo service available from station.

Phone Numbers (area code 617)
Ticket Office: 482–6830
Hotels (within two miles): Lenox Hotel—536–5300, Sheraton-Boston—236–2100

BUFFALO, NEW YORK (pop. 426,768). *Amtrak Station,* Memorial & Paderewski Drive, 14212. Station is located four miles from the center of town, with directions on how to get to it posted on highway signs on all major roads. Lots of track renovation here in preparation for new Turbo-Train service on the New York-Albany-Buffalo "Empire Service" route and general station improvements. Ticket office and waiting room open 24 hours. Parking lot adjacent to station, $1. Restaurant (6:30 A.M. to 6 P.M.; closed weekends). Snack bar, baggage carts, storage lockers, pay phones, taxi stand and public bus service. Buffalo International Airport, nine miles east by taxi, $5; no limo.

Phone Numbers (area code 716)
Ticket Office: 856–6568
Hotels (within two miles): Holiday Inn—886–2121, Lafayette—852–5470, Statler Hilton—856–1000

CHICAGO, ILLINOIS (pop. 3,336,957). *Union Station,* 210 S. Canal Street, 60606. Busiest train station in the western U.S.A., serving the hub of American railroading, including all Amtrak trains in and out of the city, is located west of Sears Building, between Jackson and Adams. One of the most modern stations in the country (old concourse was torn down in 1925 and huge office building was erected over terminal's air rights, with the totally refurbished station below), including a new $1.5 million Amtrak passenger lounge and baggage facility. Station is so big that on rainy days industrious Chicagoans line up at the Lost and Found office to see if anyone's turned in a plain black umbrella, and it's yet to run out of umbrellas! Ticket office is open from 6:30 A.M. to 10:30 P.M.; waiting room, 24 hours. Numerous parking facilities outside the station and a variety of eating places inside—snack bar, restaurant (7 A.M. to 10:30 P.M.), cocktail lounge and vending machines. (Fashionable travelers crossing the country in the late 30's and 40's always used waiting time between Super Chief and 20th Century Limited connections to "dine at the Pump Room," still a chic move today.) Many good restaurants are located within blocks of the station, and the Chicago skyline alone, with the soaring Sears Tower dominating the immediate area, is worth the walk. The station's lower level shopping arcade is a swirl of activity—an attractive Salvation Army band playing jazz arrangements sophisticated enough to win a spot at the Playboy Club—everything from a gourmet shop offering frozen packets of "the world's best chili" to souvenir stands hawking Henry Winkler posters. Red Cap service available, baggage carts and storage lockers, phones, newsstand, travel aid desk, taxi stands, public bus and commuter train connections. O'Hare International Airport, 19 miles northwest by taxi, $10; by limo, $3.15. Midway Airport is 10 miles southwest by taxi, $5; by limo $2.50.

The Rock Island Line's two daily "Rocket" trains are the only inter-city Chicago trains that don't use Union Station. They terminate at La Salle Street Station (CRI&P), 139 West Van Buren Street, 60605 (phone: 435–7850).

Phone Numbers (area code 312)
Ticket Office: 443–8634
Hotels (within one mile): Palmer House—726–7500, Conrad Hilton—922–4400, LaSalle—372–0700, Ramada Inn—427–6969

CINCINNATI, OHIO (pop. 452,524). *Amtrak Station,* 1901 River Road, 45204. Small, functional station built in 1972 by Amtrak, some distance from the huge ghost of Cincinnati terminal that was once among the most opulent in the country but, is no longer in use. Amtrak station, now undergoing enlargement, is located about one mile from downtown at River Road and Evans, with a free parking lot next door. Ticket office and waiting room hours are from 6 A.M. to midnight. No food service except vending machines. Hand carts for baggage, storage lockers, and taxi service. Greater Cincinnati Airport is 17 miles south, by taxi, $10.50; by limo, $2.75. Auto rental companies, especially Budget, will pick up and deliver at station (except Sunday).

Phone Numbers (Area code 513)
Ticket Office: 921-4127
Hotels (within two miles): Netherland Hilton—621-3800, Holiday Inn—241-8660, Stouffer's Inn—721-8600.

CLEVELAND, OHIO (pop. 750,903). *Amtrak Station,* 200 East Memorial Shoreway, 44114. This beautiful, new downtown lakefront station, with convenient curbside baggage check-in and pick-up facilities, is the first new passenger station to be built in the city since the Cleveland Union Terminal opened in 1930. More than $1 million was spent on the building, parking lot, platforms, landscaping and related work. Since the *Lake Shore Limited* was put into service, close to 5,000 passengers a month board or debark Amtrak trains in Cleveland. The 5,700-square-foot structure has a capacity of 150 people. Ticket office and waiting room hours are from 6:30 A.M. to midnight. Hand carts are available for baggage. Other services include phones, taxi stand, and shuttle bus from station to town center. No food service at present. Cleveland Hopkins Airport is 12 miles west by taxi, $10; no limo.

Phone Numbers (Area code 216)
Ticket Office: 696-5115
Hotels: Sheraton Cleveland (11½) miles)—861-8000, Holiday Inn (3 miles)—695-5175.

DALLAS, TEXAS (pop. 844,401). *Dallas Transportation Center,* 400 South Houston Street, 75201. This large downtown station holds its own in a principally airline-orientated city. Ticket office hours are from 6 A.M. to 6 P.M. on Monday, Wednesday, Thursday and Saturday, and 10:30 P.M. on Tuesday, Friday and Sunday when *The Inter-American* comes pounding through from Laredo. Waiting room open 24 hours. Hand carts are available for baggage. Pay phones, vending machines, taxi stand, public bus service and travel aid desk. Free parking when meeting train, paid parking when leaving car. Dallas/Fort Worth Regional Airport, 20 miles northwest by taxi, $15 each passenger; by bus $2.50. Love Field now utilized by Southwest Airlines only, 7 miles north by meter taxi.

Phone Numbers (Area code 214)
Ticket Office: 653-1101
Hotels (within two miles): Dallas Marriott—748-8551, Fairmont—748-5454, Holiday Inn—748-9951, Statler Hilton—747-2011.

DENVER, COLORADO (pop. 500,000). *Union Station,* 17th and Wynkoop Streets, 80202. Huge midtown train station serves this beautiful mile-high city on the edge of the Great Plains. Ticket counter, opposite station platform entrance, is open from 6:30 A.M. to 6:30 P.M. Waiting room is open from 6:30 A.M. to 9 P.M. Tuesday, Friday and Sunday, and until 7 P.M. all other days. Red Cap, baggage carts and storage lockers available. A restaurant opens at 6:30 A.M. and closes after lunch at 2 P.M. Station also has snack bar, as well as souvenir shop, newsstand, pay phones and public bus service. Denver Metro Transit bus #40 stops in front of station and goes to downtown area and Trailways and Greyhound bus terminals (exact fare required: 25 cents mornings until mid-afternoon, 35 cents all other times). Stapleton International Airport seven miles east by taxi, $5.35; by limo, $1.75.

Phone Numbers (Area code 303)
Ticket Office: 534–2812
Hotels (within one mile): Brown Palace—825–3111, Cosmopolitan—623–2181, Denver Hilton—893–3333.

DETROIT, MICHIGAN (pop. 1,500,000). *Detroit Train Station,* 2405 West Vernor, 48216. Currently getting a facelift. Amtrak and the State of Michigan are spending a combined $500,000-plus to put this aging catacomb into top working order. New ticket office and baggage facilities; new, relocated rest rooms; renovation and painting of the passenger lounge, subway entrance and stairs; sandblasting of the exterior; and a repaved parking lot adjacent to the station are all under way. The Chicago-Detroit corridor is Amtrak's fastest-growing route. An average of 22,752 passengers a month use the Detroit station, which is located five blocks west of Tiger Station at Vernor and Michigan Avenue. Parking lot charges $1 per day. Metropolitan Airport 23 miles southwest by taxi, $15; by limo, $3.50. Detroit City Airport 5 miles northeast by taxi, $7. Avis, Hertz, National, Airways and Budget Rentacar have downtown offices which close at 5 P.M. Several at airport remain open through evening. Station ticket office is open from 6:30 A.M. to 11 P.M. Waiting room is open 24 hours, with police permit required after midnight. Snack bar and vending machine. All-night restaurant half block from station. Pay phones, taxi, public bus service, Red Cap, baggage carts, storage lockers, and wheelchairs.

Phone Numbers (Area code 313)
Ticket Office: 965–0314
Hotels (within two miles): Holiday Inn-Downtown—965–0171, Howard Johnson—965–1050, Pontchartrain Hotel—965–0200, Sheraton-Cadillac—961–8000.

FORT WORTH, TEXAS (pop. 393,476). *Fort Worth Station,* 1501 Jones Street, 76102. Small, functional mid-town station serves this cattle-rich city 30 miles east of Dallas. Ticket office and waiting room hours are from 7 A.M. to 11 P.M., Tuesday, Friday and Sunday, and until 5:30 P.M. all other days. Snack bar, vending machine, baggage carts, storage lockers, phones, newsstand, and public bus service. Free parking lot. Dallas-Fort Worth Regional Airport, 20 miles northeast by taxi, $15 each passenger; by limo, $3. Tri-weekly Amtrak *Inter-American* connects Fort Worth and Dallas, as does daily *Lone Star.* Modern four-lane superhighway and frequent bus service.

Phone Numbers (Area code 817)
Ticket Office: 332–2931
Hotels (within 4 blocks): Downtown Motel—336–2011, Sheraton-Ft. Worth—332–3151, Hilton Inn—335–7000.

HARRISBURG, PENNSYLVANIA (pop. 68,061). *Amtrak Station,* 4th and Chestnut Sts., 17101. This midtown terminal is junction point for New York and Washington portions of *Broadway Limited* and *National Limited* trains. Ticket office and waiting room open 24 hours. Restaurant opens 6 A.M., closes 9:45 P.M. Vending machines, Red Cap, baggage carts, travel aid desk, newsstand, pay phones, taxi stand and connecting bus and commuter trains. Harrisburg International Airport is 9 miles south by meter taxi; by limo, $2.

Phone Numbers (Area code 717)

Ticket Office: 236–7902

Hotels (within 4 blocks): Holiday Inn—234–5021, Nationwide Inn—233–1611.

HARTFORD, CONNECTICUT (pop. 158,017). *Hartford Station,* Union Place, 06103. Small, mid-town station in Connecticut's capital city, home of 37 major insurance firms, is open 24 hours (ticket offices and waiting room). Located in vicinity of lovely Bushnell Park and State Capitol. No food service available, nor assistance for baggage (if you can't lift your own bags, you'd better make friends on the train). Station has phones, taxi stand and public bus service. Meter parking in street in front of station. Bradley Field Airport 17 miles north by meter taxi; limo, $1.75.

Phone Numbers (Area code 203)
Ticket Office: 525–9504
Hotels (one block): Harford Hilton—249–5611, Holiday Inn—549–2400, Hotel Sonesta—278–2000.

HOUSTON, TEXAS (pop. 1,232,802). *Houston Station,* 902 Washington Ave., 77002. Station, located next to the Houston Post Office, is so small it's hardly there, but cheerful, open atmosphere. No formal food service but enough vending machines to be reminiscent of New York's Automat, dispensing coffee, sandwiches, soft drinks and candy. Ticket office and waiting room hours are from 6:15 A.M. to 11:15 P.M. Free parking lot next to station. Phones, newsstand, baggage carts, taxi stand and public bus service. Continental Airport 20 miles north (40 to 60 minute drive) by meter cab; limo, $3.50.

Phone Numbers (Area code 713)
Ticket and Paging: 226–5923
Hotels (within one mile): Continental House—225–1781, Rice Hotel—227–2111, Downtowner—228–0911.

INDIANAPOLIS, INDIANA (pop. 744,624). *Indianapolis Station,* 39 Jackson Place, 46225. Centrally located station with ticket office and waiting room open from 6 A.M. to midnight. No food service or baggage assistance. Storage lockers are available, also phone and public bus system. Municipal Airport is five miles southwest by meter cab; limo $2.50.

Phone Numbers (Area code 317)
Ticket Office and Paging: 269–6728
Hotels (within 1 to 7 blocks): Atkinson—639–5611, Hilton—635–2000, Holiday Inn—638–3311.

JACKSONVILLE, FLORIDA (pop. 528,865). *Amtrak Clifford Lane Station,* 3570 Clifford Lane, 32209. Located about 6 miles from the center of town, off U.S. Highway #1 (to Clifford Lane), this is the Florida Fleet's main junction point for Amtrak trains switching routes to either Miami or St. Petersburg. Also a pit stop of sorts, a maintenance station for light repairs. Ticket office and waiting room open 24 hours. Free parking lot next to station. No formal food service, but numerous vending machines and 24 hour microwave oven for warming light snacks and sandwiches. Red Cap, baggage carts, and storage lockers available. Pay phones, newsstand, and taxi stand. Jacksonville International Airport is 15 miles away, by taxi only, approximately $10.50. Greyhound Terminal open 24 hours, 10 N. Pearl St., by taxi only, about $5.

Phone Numbers (Area code 904)
Ticket Office: 768–1553/4

Hotels (3 to 6 miles): Jacksonville Hilton—398–3561, Robert Meyer Hotel—355–4411, Holiday Inn—764–7511, Econo-Travel—786–2794.

KANSAS CITY, MISSOURI (pop. 507,087). *Union Station,* 30 West Pershing Road, 64108. Located about a mile from the center of town at Main Street and Pershing Road, this is a remnant of the more grandiose days of American train stations—a cathedral-like sweep of open space to ceilings eight stories high, a French Renaissance cupcake built in 1914 at a cost of $50 million. A "Pretty Boy" Floyd shoot-out with cops in front of the station in an attempt to free prisoner Frank Nash, who was being transported, left Nash and four policemen dead. The station was once the nation's third busiest, with 160 passenger trains coming through daily. Today only the *Lone Star,* the *National Limited* and the *Southwest Limited* come calling. Ticket office and waiting room open 24 hours. Parking lot next to station, $1.25 a day. Red Cap service, hand carts, and storage lockers available. Snack bar, vending machine and restaurant. Theater-supper club, landmark, in southeast corner of station. Pay phones, newsstand, travel aid desk, taxi stand and public bus service. Frequent bus service to town (until 11 P.M.); fare is 45 cents. Taxis are about $2. Bus #56 marked "Country Club" goes to station from downtown. Limo to Kansas City Airport is $3. Station is just one block from fabulous Crown Center (hotel, shops, restaurants, etc.) and is across street from the impressive Liberty Memorial.
Phone Numbers (Area code 816)
Ticket Office: 421–3622/3
Hotels (1 block): Crown Center—474–4400
Hotels (1 mile): Continental—421–6040, Holiday Inn—221–8800, Downtowner—471–0080, Prom-Sheraton—842–6090.

LOS ANGELES, CALIFORNIA (pop. 6,960,733). *Union Passenger Terminal,* 800 N. Alameda St., 90012. Beautiful, old station built in the 1930's in mission-style architecture with soaring clock tower, Spanish arches, desert-beige exterior, ringed with towering palm trees. Well maintained and efficiently run, its cheerful personnel seem to take pride in having one of the finest stations anywhere, with its shaded-plaza waiting areas outside, and pleasant, spotless waiting room indoors. Amfleet connections here for San Diego, buses to Disney Land and points north and south and a steady stream of star-calibre trains coming and going—the *Southwest Limited* and the *Coast Starlight* among them. Ticket office and waiting room open from 6 A.M. to 10 P.M. Red Cap service, hand carts, and storage lockers available. Station has snack bar and vending machines, but if you have any time at all, dash across Alameda to Olivera Street, the old Mexican section of Los Angeles, and feast on green corn tamales, enchiladas, frijoles, and warm flour tortillas, all washed down with a cold bottle of Carte Blanca, and then browse in the endless sprawl of colorful handicraft shops. You may never make it back to the train station! Pay parking lot, pay phones, newsstand, taxi, and public bus service available. Courtesy phones for hotels and car rentals. Local bus schedule at information services desk. Los Angeles International Airport 17 miles (45 to 60 minutes) southwest by limo, $1.25.
Phone Numbers (Area code 213)
Ticket Office: 683–6873
Hotels (spread out): Alexandria Hotel—626–7484, Biltmore—624–1011, Holiday Inn—748–1291, L. A. Hilton—629–1980.

MIAMI, FLORIDA (pop. 334,859). *Amtrak Station,* 2206 N.W. 7th Ave., 33127. Small, well-run functional station about one mile from downtown, 69th Street exit off I-95, south on 7th Avenue, with ticket office and waiting room open from 7:30 A.M. to 7 P.M. Free parking lot adjacent to station. Red Cap, hand carts, and storage lockers available. Vending machines. Pay phones, taxi stand, public bus service. Biscayne Bay separates Miami from Miami Beach, but frequent bus service is available across the causeway. Miami International Airport is 5 miles southeast by taxi, $6.50; no limo service.

Phone Numbers (Area code 305)

Ticket Office: 324–4121

Hotels (within 4 miles): Columbus Hotel—373–4411, Holiday Inn—324–0800, Howard Johnson—358–3080.

MILWAUKEE, WISCONSIN (pop. 717,090). *Milwaukee Station,* 433 St. Paul Avenue, 53203. Located on Paul Avenue, between 4th and 5th, downtown, station is open from 6:30 A.M. to 9 P.M. for ticket sales; waiting room same, except until midnight on Sunday. Free parking lot across the street from station. Red Cap service and storage lockers. Restaurant open from 6:30 A.M. until 4 P.M. Newsstand, pay phones, taxi stands and public bus service. General Mitchell Airport is 6 miles south by limo, $1.40. Greyhound Terminal four blocks away.

Phone Numbers (Area code 414)

Ticket Office: 271–0840

Hotels (within 3 miles): Holiday Inn-Mid—344–7000, Downtowner—273–2950, Marc Plaza (3 blks)—271–7250.

MINNEAPOLIS, MINNESOTA (pop. 434,400). *Minneapolis Station,* 2 Hennepin Ave., 55401. Financial complications have stalled plans for an elaborate station here to serve the Minneapolis-St. Paul area. Meanwhile, this architectural antique, just off the Mississippi, off First and Hennepin, bustles with efficiency nonetheless. Ticket office is open from 6 A.M. to 11:30 P.M.; waiting room, 6 A.M. to 11:15 P.M. Red Cap service is available, but no storage lockers or hand carts. Baggage office located on main floor near door to street. Vending machines (no formal food service), pay phones, taxi stand, public bus service. Free parking lot next to station. Minneapolis-St. Paul Airport 10 miles northwest by meter taxi; limo, $2.

Phone Numbers (Area code 612)

Ticket Office: 336–1621

Hotels (within 1 mile): Curtis Hotel—333–5144, Hyatt Mtr Lodge—335–9311, Holiday Inn—332–0371.

NASHVILLE, TENNESSEE (pop. 447,877). *Nashville Station,* 10th and Broadway, 37203. Brand new $140,000 passenger station stands in bright contrast to dilapidated Louisville & Nashville Terminal (I-265 to Broadway East exit), in the heart of the country music capital. It's located at the north end of the L&N freight and baggage building, immediately east of the main station building. It fairly glistens—suspended modernistic ceiling, vinyl floor covering, pendant lighting, formica-topped ticket counter and all new tiling in the johns. Ticket office and waiting room open 9:30 A.M. to 6:30 P.M. No formal food service but a number of vending machines inside the station and several good restaurants outside. Red Cap service is available, and storage lockers. Greyhound and Trailways bus station is two blocks away. Sheraton Motor Hotel in same block as station. Metropolitan Airport 8 miles northwest by taxi, $3; by limo, $1.75.

Phone Numbers (Area code 615)

Ticket Office: 255–7381

Hotels (within mile): Golden Eagle—254–1401, Sheraton Mtr Hotel—383–1147, Ramada Inn—244–6130, Holiday Inn (3 mls)—254–1921.

NEW HAVEN, CONNECTICUT (pop. 137,707). *Amtrak Station,* Union Ave., 06511. Main junction for Northeast Corridor and Empire Service trains, this station is located off Route 95 at Intersection 91. Due to be completely overhauled. Ticket office open from 6 A.M. to 11 P.M.; waiting room open 24 hours. No formal food service, but vending machines dispensing soft drinks, coffee, and sandwiches. Small neighborhood bar "up the hill." Red Cap service available, but no hand carts or storage lockers. Newsstand, phones, taxi stand and public bus service as well as commuter train connections. Tweed-New Haven Airport 4 miles northwest by taxi, $5; by limo, $3.60.

Phone Numbers (Area code 203)
Ticket Office: 497–2414
Hotels (within mile): Holiday Inn—777–6221, Taft—787–1121, Sheraton-Park—772–1700.

NEW LONDON, CONNECTICUT (pop. 31,630). *Union Station,* Foot of State Street, 06320. Complete restoration of this station, the first and most ambitious of eight Northeast Corridor restorations planned by Amtrak, was a major victory for concerned group of local citizens anxious to preserve the city's architectural heritage. The 90-year-old landmark, designed by Henry Hobson Richardson, the Frank Lloyd Wright of his day, was built at a time when New London rivaled Newport as the ultimate in seaside elegance. Overlooking the Thames River, the red-brick structure was a classic of 19th century design. Over the years, it fell into a state of decay and was literally on the verge of falling down—paint peeling everywhere and chunks of plaster falling on the heads of startled passengers. It was a hangout for derelicts. The station stood suspended under the wrecker's ball for almost 15 years as various proposals were offered as to what to do with it. The solution came when Anderson-Notter Associates of Boston, an architectural firm, with the help of a local group called The Union Station Trust, convinced Amtrak to rent part of the station for $45,000 a year. Then, with lease in hand, they persuaded the city's Redevelopment Agency to sell the station to them for $11,-400, the cost of the land alone. Since then, more than $700,000 has been spent on restoration and the citizens group has received a Society of American Travel Writers Conservation Award. The station, its heritage preserved, now features a wood-paneled ticket and baggage area, a mezzanine restaurant and an airy stairwell down to a granite-lined waiting room. Ticket office open from 6 A.M. to 11 P.M.; waiting room open 24 hours. Red Cap. Newsstand, restaurant, phones, taxi stand, public bus service, as well as commuter train connections. Block Island Ferry landing is adjacent to the station. Numerous small restaurants and cocktail bars in the immediate area, including the *Crocker House,* a favorite haunt of playwright Eugene O'Neill, whose boyhood home in New London has been preserved as a public museum and library by the Eugene O'Neill Memorial Theater Center of nearby Waterford.

Phone Numbers (Area code 203)
Ticket Office: 442–5813
Hotels (within 3 miles): Holiday Inn—442–0631, Lamplighter—422–7227.

NEW ORLEANS, LOUISIANA (pop. 627,525). *Union Passenger Terminal,* 1001 Loyola Avenue, 70113. Huge, modern downtown terminal near the Superdome (I-10, Downtown Exit: Loyola) serves both buses and the trains of both Amtrak and Southern Railway. Ticket office is open from 6 A.M. to 10 P.M.; waiting room open 24 hours. Meter parking in front of station. Full range of services: cocktail lounge until 10 P.M., all-night restaurant, snack bar, vending machines, newsstand, souvenir counters, taxi stand, public bus service, and even private shower rooms (50 cents). No baggage carts and limited Red Cap service, but plenty of Southern gentlemen. Famous French Quarter is within walking distance: walk down Loyola to Canal, turn right for several blocks to Bourbon and Royal and see New Orleans at its most glittering. If you're short on funds, combined YMCA-YWCA is located four blocks from station. Moisant International Airport is 20 miles northwest by taxi, $10; by limo, $3.75.

Phone Numbers (Area code 504)
Ticket Office: 586–0027
Hotels (within 2 miles): Fairmont Roosevelt—529–7111, Pontchartrain—524–0581, Marie Antoinette—522–0801, Royal Orleans—529–5333.

NEW YORK, NEW YORK (pop. 7,867,760). *Grand Central Station,* East 42nd and Park Ave., 10017. Fate of this Beaux Arts landmark has been in the high courts for over two years, whether to tear it down to build an office skyscraper in its place, a project planned by a British investment builder, or, perhaps even worse, to leave it standing and build the skyscraper on top of it. The Committee to Save Grand Central, operating out of a storefront headquarters in the adjacent Biltmore Hotel for more than a year, wants it preserved just as it is. Through public contributions, the sale of books, literature and related material pertaining to the station ("Save Grand Central" T-shirts—$5), the committee has mustered enough legal clout and influential support to keep the battle raging. Jackie Onassis, a strong supporter of the movement to save the station, recently flicked the switch lighting the heroic statue of the Olympian god Mercury atop the station for the first time since the building was completed in 1913. Grand Central Terminal was designated a landmark in 1967. In January 1975 the designation was removed, but was reinstated in December of that year when the Appellate Division of State Supreme Court voted 3 to 2 to overturn the decision. Penn Central, Grand Central's owner, is now appealing that decision, the outcome of which may not be known for years. Meanwhile, the station, handling only commuter train traffic now, as well as Amtrak's limited number of Empire Service trains to and from upstate New York, remains one of the busiest, most impressive and best known in the nation. (Remember that old radio show? "Grand Central Station—crossroads of a million private lives.")

A service directory posted in the 42nd Street waiting room lists, along with the station's general facilities, two bakeries, five banks, an Off-Track Betting parlor, three book stores, seven candy shops, a clothing repair service, locksmith, nine snack-bars, two *Cobb's Club Car* cocktail lounges, the *Suburbanite Tap Room, Childs' Pancake House* and the *Oyster Bar.* The latter, closed for a number of years and recently re-opened, is world-renowned for its shellfish stews and pan roasts. The Oyster Bar and its gleaming equipment are themselves a tourist attraction, around which extends dining space for hundreds under a tile ceiling. The pure simplicity and beauty of the station's interior design has been totally obscured by advertising displays, among them gigantic Kodak transparencies, the largest in the world. They've been changed of late from scenes of children and cuddly puppydogs to more timely topics, such as Viking photos of the Martian dunes. The station's ceiling, 116 feet high, is hung from steel trusses. Few of the thousands of commuters who walk beneath it daily realize that above is located the posh Vanderbilt Tennis Club, and any given day might find Johnny Carson or Robert Redford playing here. The station's main newsstand (there are four others), located off the 42nd Street entrance, is conceivably the largest volume newsstand in the world. For years, New York-based publishers have gauged the success or failure of new magazines by how many are sold here, and how quickly. On Wednesdays, the Committee to Save Grand Central conducts free walking tours of the station beginning at 12:30 at the Committee's Biltmore headquarters. In one hour, the noontime stroller can view a 300-foot zodiac painting, an acoustical "whisper chamber," a wealth of Beaux Arts sculpture, Italian marble halls and other fascinating exhibits.

From the aesthetic to the practical: Grand Central's ticket office and waiting room is open from 7 A.M. to 11 P.M. Red Cap service, storage lockers, but no hand carts. Baggage office is located near Track 34. Authorized Red Caps wear identification tags as well as their familiar caps. Avoid rip-off artists who plague both Grand Central and Penn Station, offering to carry bags and then demanding exorbitant payment, figuring an out-of-towner would rather pay than risk a scene. Subways, buses, taxis, commuter trains, all available at Grand Central. Subway shuttle service to Times Square. Port Authority Bus Terminal for all major bus lines is about a mile away. Avis, open 24 hours, located three blocks from station at 217 East 43rd. Budget, closing at 6 P.M., is four blocks away at 330 East 44th Street. Kennedy Airport is 15 miles northeast by taxi, about $15; by limo, $4.25. Carey Airport Limousines dispatch point is across 42nd Street entrance, at 42nd and Park. LaGuardia is eight miles northwest by taxi, about $10; by limo, $3.25.

Phone Numbers (Area code 212)
Ticket Office: 340–2766
Hotels (adjacent): Biltmore—687–7000, Roosevelt—686–6384
Hotels (within 5 blocks): Algonquin—687–4400, Waldorf-Astoria—353–3000, Barclay—755–5900, Belmont—755–1200, Lexington—755–4400, Roger Smith—755–1400.

Pennsylvania Station, 8th Ave., West 31st to 33rd Sts., 10001. Until 1966, for over 55 years the great hulk of the old Pennsylvania Station stood on this site. Now, new "Penn Station" sprawls out below street level, serving all but a handful of Amtrak trains, Long Island commuter trains, Penn Central trains to New Jersey and four Metropolitan Transit Authority subway lines. In all, 750 trains are scheduled daily. Above the station now looms new Madison Square Garden and a sprawl of office complexes, a fate many concerned preservationists feel might also befall Grand Central Station (see above). Since assuming control of Penn Station from the former Penn Central railroad last April, Amtrak has spent $750,000 on station improvements, including extensive repairs, cleanup operations, the installation of a new Amtrak passenger lounge and an air conditioning system overhaul. Map and information guide to Penn Station facilities available free at information desk. Ticket office (with 23 ticket windows) open from 6 A.M. to 11:30 P.M.; waiting room and Amtrak Lounge, reserved for Amtrak passengers only (complimentary coffee or tea always available, and modestly priced drinks) are open 24 hours. Parking garage at 1 Penn Plaza. Red Cap service and storage lockers available. Baggage office located near Track #5, upper concourse. A wide variety of shops, stores, cocktail lounges, snack bars and restaurants located on main concourse and lower level.

Many restaurants and bars in immediate vicinity of station, or nearby, including such homey, hearty, old-fashioned spots as *Paddy's Clam House,* 215 W. 34th St.; *Solowey's,* 431 Seventh Ave., big with garment-center gourmets. Several *Horn & Hardarts* in area, but more cafeteria now than automat. Statler-Hilton, formerly Hotel Pennsylvania, is half block from station. Glenn Miller wrote tune called "PE 6-5000" here, still the hotel's number today. All major rentacar firms have agencies adjacent to station, on 31st. All major bus lines at Port Authority Bus Terminal, about 10 blocks from station. Limos and taxis to Kennedy and LaGuardia Airports same as Grand Central (above).

Train buffs note; book store on main concourse has special section on steam train and railroad books, mostly discount prices, train photos and postcards.
Phone Numbers (Area code 212)
Ticket Office: 239–6343
Hotels (across street): Statler-Hilton—PE 6–5000.

NEWARK, NEW JERSEY (pop. 382,417). *Pennsylvania Station,* Raymond Plaza West, 07102. This dilapidated, 41-year-old nightmare, serving Amtrak, Jersey Central, PATH and Penn Central Commuter trains, was recently acquired by Amtrak and plans are in the designing stage for a much needed structural and cosmetic repair. Meanwhile, ticket office and waiting room are open 24 hours. Red Cap service available, plus hand carts and storage lockers. Restaurant, snack bar and vending machines. Also has newsstand, taxi stand and public bus service. International Airport is three miles north by taxi, $3.25; no limo. Downtowner Inn half block from station.
Phone Numbers (Area code 201)
Ticket Office: 643–4501
Hotels (within 2 miles): Downtowner Inn—622–5000, Holiday Inn—643–4200, Howard Johnson's—824–4000.

NORFOLK, VIRGINIA (pop. 750,000). *Norfolk Station,* 2200 Redgate Ave., 23507. Located four miles from downtown, with ticket office and waiting room open from 10 A.M. to 7 P.M. Station is five miles south of Norfolk Naval Station on Hampton Blvd., turn right on Redgate Ave., one mile to station. Red Cap service available, plus hand carts, storage lockers. Baggage desk located at ticket counter. Newsstand. Taxi stand. Regional Airport is eight miles west by taxi, $6; limo, $3.
Phone Numbers (Area code 804)
Ticket Office: 622–9528
Hotels (within 6 miles): Sheraton Inn—420–9292, Holiday Inn—464–9351.

ORLANDO, FLORIDA (pop. 99,006). *Orlando Station,* 1400 Sligh Blvd., 32806. Handsome, cheery, whitewashed building in Spanish-style architecture, serving Florida's largest inland city, is the rail gateway to Disney World. Station is located one mile from downtown (take Gore to Sligh Blvd., south two blocks). Ticket office and waiting room open from 6:15 A.M. to 10:15 P.M. Free parking. Red Cap and hand carts available, but no storage lockers. Vending machines; no formal food service. Amtrak trains met by special shuttle service to Disney World: Florida Limousine Service provides transfer between Orlando station and major hotels in the Orlando and Disney World area. Rate is $4.75 per adult; children 3–12, $2.50; toddlers free. Hendon Airport is three miles west by limo, $2.50.
Phone Numbers (Area code 305)
Ticket Office: 425–9411
Hotels (within 1 mile): Kahler Motor Inn—843–3220
Hotels (within 15 miles): Travelodge—828–2424, Johnny Unitas-Sheraton—859–2711.

PHILADELPHIA, PENNSYLVANIA (pop. 1,948,609). *30th Street Station,* 30th and Market Sts., 19104. Another klunker scheduled for revamping under Amtrak's $1.6 billion facilities improvement program (with an assist from the Federal Rail Reorganization Act), station is located across from the U.S. Post Office just off Schuylkill Expressway. Ticket office and waiting room open 24 hours. Paid parking north of station. Food services include snack bar, vending machines, and a cocktail lounge that closes at 7 in the evening. Red Cap service available, plus hand carts and storage lockers. Baggage office is located at northeast corner of station's 29th Street side. Station has travel aid desk, banking service from 8:30 A.M. to 4 P.M., newsstand, taxi stand, public bus service, commuter train and subway connections. Hertz and Avis agency in station. Philadelphia International Airport is 7 miles southwest by airport bus, $1; limo, $2.40.
Phone Numbers (Area code 215)
Ticket Office: 387–5911

Hotels (within 1 mile): Holiday Inn—561-7500, Penn Center Inn—568-3300, Warwick Hotel—753-3800.

PROVIDENCE, RHODE ISLAND (pop. 179,213). *Amtrak Station,* Railroad Terrace, 02903. More improvements due for this quaint old downtown station in Rhode Island's capital city. (Atwells Avenue Exit from I-95, turn right, 2 blocks.) Ticket office open 6:30 A.M. to 7:30 P.M.; waiting room 5:30 to 12:30 P.M. Pay parking lot across the street from station. Hand carts, storage lockers, but no Red Cap service. Vending machines; no formal food service. Taxi stand, public bus service and commuter train connections. Green State Airport is nine miles north by limo, $1.75.
Phone Numbers (Area code 401)
Ticket Office: 331-1735
Hotels (within 6 miles): Colonial Hilton—467-8800
Hotels (3 blocks away): Holiday Inn—831-3900.

ROCHESTER, NEW YORK (pop. 296,233). *Rochester Station,* 320 Central Avenue, 14605. This midtown station has served New York's third largest city since January 19, 1914, and is scheduled to be torn down sometime in 1977 to make room for a modern passenger facility to be constructed on the same site. (During the construction flux, a temporary modular facility will serve in its place.) The new station construction will be a joint effort by Amtrak, the City of Rochester and the State of New York. Meanwhile, ticket office and waiting room are open 24 hours. Free parking lot next to station. Storage lockers, but no Red Cap service or hand carts. No formal food service. Vending machines aplenty, including even one for newspapers. Taxi stand and public bus service.
Phone Numbers (Area code 716)
Ticket Office: 454-2894
Hotels (within 1 mile): Downtowner—232-3600, Holiday Inn DTN—546-6400, Flagship—546-3300.

ST. LOUIS, MISSOURI (pop. 622,236). *Union Station,* 1820 Market Street, 63103. Located one mile from downtown, this marvelous old station with its soaring clock tower was built in 1894, covering 11 acres. In its heyday it was one of the busiest stations in the country; now only a few long-haul trains call here. Station is located across the street from Aloe Plaza with its beautiful lighted fountain and imposing bronze figures, dedicated to the "Meeting of the Waters," the place nearby where the Mississippi and Missouri Rivers meet. Ticket office is open from 6:30 A.M. to 6 P.M.; waiting room, 24 hours. Red Cap service available, plus hand carts and storage lockers. Baggage office is located at the ticket counter. No food service except vending machines. Taxi and public bus service.
Phone Numbers (Area code 314)
Ticket Office: 231-0061
Hotel (3 blocks away): Holiday Inn—231-3232
Hotels (within two miles): Bel-Air East—621-7900, Stouffers Riverfront Inn—241-9500.

SAN DIEGO, CALIFORNIA (pop. 696,769). *Santa Fe Station,* 1050 Kettner Blvd., 92101. Amtrak's modern Amfleet trains arrive and depart here four times a day on their 128-mile-run to Los Angeles and back. Ticket office is open from 6 A.M. to 6:30 P.M.; waiting room, from 6 A.M. to 11:30 P.M. Parking lot next door to station, $1 for 24 hours. Red Cap service available, hand carts, and storage lockers. Baggage office is located next to ticket office. Services include snack bar, newsstand, taxis, public buses, including direct bus service from station to Tijuana,

Mexico. Lindbergh International Airport is three miles southeast by taxi, $1.10; by bus, 35 cents.

Phone Numbers (Area code 714)
Ticket Office: 239–9021
Hotels (within 1 mile): Holiday Inn—239–6171, Travelodge—233–0398, Royal Inn/Wharf—232–6391.

SAN FRANCISCO, CALIFORNIA (pop. 715,674). *Amtrak Travel Center,* Transbay Terminal, Mission St., 94105. Eastbound or arriving Amtrak passengers from eastern cities all depart from or terminate their trips in Oakland, so San Francisco visitors must shuttle back and forth over the scenic Bay Bridge to get where they're going. Greyhound and Trailways share same terminal. Amtrak information and ticket counter is to the right of the main concourse and directional signs point the way. Ticket office is open from early morning to 11:30 at night; waiting room is always open. There's Red Cap service, but no hand carts or storage lockers. (When shuttling to or from Oakland, bags are handled, put on or off the bus, by Amtrak employees.) Plenty to eat here—snack bars, vending machines, cocktail lounge and a restaurant that's open from 6 A.M. until 4 P.M. Newsstand, taxi stand and public bus service. San Francisco International Airport is 15 miles north by taxi, $15; by limo, $1.25.

Phone Numbers (Area code 415)
Ticket Counter: 556–8287
Hotels (within 3 miles): Fairmont—772–5000, Del Webb—863–7100, St. Francis—397–7000.

SAVANNAH, GEORGIA (pop. 118,349). *Savannah Station,* 2611 Seaboard Coastline Drive, 31401. Handsome, old station located four miles from downtown is not quite as busy as it used to be since the advent of Disney World and the diversion of train routes to that area, bypassing their former Savannah junction point. Ticket office and waiting room open 24 hours, nonetheless. Red Cap, hand carts, storage lockers available. Vending machines for simple snacks, no other food services. Free parking lot adjacent to station. Taxi stand, but no bus service. Travis Field 8 miles southeast by taxi, $5; limo, $2.

Tourists visiting Savannah now have a central facility with parking from which they can venture into the community. The Chamber of Commerce raised $200,000 from area businesses to restore the old Central of Georgia Railroad Station. The station, built in 1860, was donated to the city by the Southern Railway System. The city in turn made it available as a visitors' center.

Phone Numbers (Area code 912) Ticket Office: 234–2611
Hotels (within 4 miles): Desoto Inn—232–0171, Holiday Inn—236–1355, Downtowner—233–3531.

SEATTLE, WASHINGTON (pop. 530,831). *Amtrak Station,* 303 East Jackson St., 98104. *Empire Builder's* termination point on its run from Chicago, and a key junction point for trains to Canada and the *Coast Starlight,* this big, modern well-run station is centrally located, next door to the Kingdome Stadium. Ticket office is open from 7 A.M. to 6:30; waiting room, 7 A.M. to 9:30. Pay parking lot in front of station. Red Cap, hand carts and storage lockers available. Snack bar, vending machines, newsstand, taxi stand and frequent buses (the signs are well posted) into city center. Direct phone for car rental. Seattle/Tacoma International Airport is 14 miles south by limo, $2. Bus #19 from station passes bus terminal.

Phone Numbers (Area code 206)
Ticket Office: 624–4831

Hotels (within 1 mile): University Tower—634–2000, Roosevelt Motor—624–1400, Olympic—682–7700, Washington Plaza—624–5955.

SYRACUSE, NEW YORK (pop. 197,208). *Amtrak Station,* East Syracuse/Manlius Center, 13075. Serving industrial city of Syracuse in upstate New York, station is located three miles from downtown area. Ticket office and waiting room open 24 hours. Limited services. Vending machine, no food service. Taxi, public bus. Hancock Field seven miles south by meter taxi; limo, $2.
Phone Numbers (Area code 315)
Ticket Office: 463–1135
Hotels (within 5 miles): Dinkler Motor Inn—472–6961, Hotel Syracuse—422–5121, Holiday Inn Dtn—474–7251.

TOLEDO, OHIO (pop. 383,318). *Central Union Station,* 415 Emerald Avenue, 43697. This modest downtown station is located on Emerald near Summit and Broadway. Ticket office and waiting room open from 8 A.M. to 11 P.M. Hand carts for baggage, no Red Caps or storage lockers. Baggage office located at ticket counter. Snack bar, newsstand, taxi, public bus service. Free parking lot adjacent to station.
Phone Numbers (Area code 419)
Ticket Office: 246–0159
Hotels (within 4 miles): Ramada Inn—836–1361, Holiday Inn—243–8860, Sheraton—535–7070.

TRENTON, NEW JERSEY (pop. 104,638). *Amtrak Station,* 72 S. Clinton St., 08609. A lot of work has been done on this station, and it is in pretty good shape. Ticket office is open from 6 A.M. until 11 P.M.; waiting room open 24 hours. Meter parking adjacent to station. Trenton is primarily a commuter stop, so no facilities for baggage assistance. Snack bar, vending machine, restaurant and cocktail lounge (open until early evening).
Phone Numbers (Area code 215)
Ticket Office: 596–1764
Hotels (within 1 mile): Holiday Inn—989–7100, Imperial 400—392–7166, Howard Johnson's—896–1100.

WASHINGTON, D.C. (pop. 756,510). *Union Station,* 50 Massachusetts Ave., 20002. Handsome, historic station a few blocks north of the Capitol, offering arriving visitors a breath-taking sweep of fountains, parks, trees, grassy slopes surmounted by the gleaming dome of the Capitol Building itself. Washington is Amtrak's headquarters and no station is more appropriate than this one as a showcase for Amtrak's phenomenal accomplishments over the last two or three years. Station has undergone tremendous renovation recently, primarily to make way for a National Visitor Center, officially dedicated in July, 1976, with numerous Washington dignitaries on hand, including the Secretary of the Interior and the Director of the National Park Service under whose administration the center is maintained. Ticket office and waiting room at Union Station are open 24 hours. Parking ramp at 400 N. Capitol Street, open 24 hours daily; entrance to parking on "E" Street, rates 95 cents per hour, $3.50 all day, with free shuttle bus to station. Red Caps, baggage carts, and storage lockers available. No formal food service. Vending machines. Newsstand. Taxistand and public bus and commuter train connections. National Airport is 3 miles south, (25 minutes) by taxi, $3.50; limo, $1.75. Dulles Airport is 26 miles west by limo (55–70 minutes), $3.50.
Phone Numbers (Area code 202)
Ticket Office: 484–7874

Hotel (within 2 blocks): Hyatt Regency—737-1234
Hotels (within 2 miles): Hotel Washington—638-5900, Quality Inn—638-1616, Quality Inn N.E.—832-3200.

WILMINGTON, DELAWARE (pop. 80,386). *Wilmington Station,* Front & French Streets, 19801. Midtown location. Ticket office open 6:10 A.M. to 10:30 P.M.; Waiting room, 5 A.M. to 1 A.M. Parking lot located half block from station, $2 for 12 hours. Red Cap service available, and storage lockers. Snack bar, newsstand, taxi stand, public bus service and commuter train connections. Greater Wilmington Airport 6 miles southeast by taxi, $5.50; by limo, $1.75. Philadelphia International located 20 miles northeast by taxi, $34; by limo, $5.85.
Phone Numbers (Area code 302)
Ticket Office: 655-7123
Hotels (within 6 miles): El Capitan Hotel—655-6111, Hotel DuPont—655-8121, Holiday Inn—478-2222.

NOSTALGIC TRAINS

Nothing clouds an old railroad buff's eyes (or puts a cinder in them) faster than the husky cough of a full-throttled steam train chewing rail. Ironically, the tremendous resurgence of old-fashioned locomotives with their antique coach cars rattling along behind is as much a phenomenon of the young as it is a sentimental journey for old-timers. A kind of discontent with the way things are in America today has brought new respect for the days of our country's birth and development. The Concorde Jet roars overhead and suddenly our obsession with speed seems to have gotten out of hand.

More than 100 steam trains are now in operation around the country. They range from commercial theme-park attractions such as those at Disney Land and Knott's Berry Farm to more ambitious undertakings—immaculately polished engines with jewel-like fittings, train depots, round houses, miles of well-tended track and roadbed, and enough care and dedication to make even the most determined antique automobile buff look callous by comparison. Many of the steam-train operations were Bicentennial projects that stayed on and prospered. Others grew out of community restoration projects. What eases the eyesore of a run-down section of town faster and more profitably than restoring it to its natural historical proportions—and then charging admission?

At present there are an estimated 30,000 miles of abandoned railroad rights and deteriorating track in the U.S. Illinois Prairie Patch, a 40-mile nature and recreation trail running west of Chicago, was once the Chicago, Aurora and Elgin Railway. Abandoned railroad rights of way offer communities around the nation a largely untapped potential for recreation. Nature trails along abandoned railroad beds is one approach. Restoring the track and putting a working steam train into operation is another.

Do the Gods of Iron approve? Apparently, and for practical as well as nostaglic reasons. In Deadwood City, South Dakota, a $500,000 steam train project, scheduled for completion early in 1978, will link a huge

parking area outside of Deadwood with the center of town—the first intra-
city steam commuter railroad to be built in this country since the late 1880s.
The 24-gauge railroad will keep automobiles out of the city where there
is almost no parking, and will serve as a tourist attraction as well.

The Deadwood City project is in the highly capable hands of Norman
K. Sandley, a foremost expert on narrow-gauge steam trains and operating
head of the Sandley Light Railway Equipment Works at Wisconsin Dells,
Wisconsin, the only such firm of its kind in the country. Obviously enjoying
a boom in business, Sandley, who wears bowler hats and carries a furled
umbrella on dress occasions, also produced the steam railroad at Brookfield
Zoo in Wisconsin, at the All-American Park in Quincy, Illinois, and the one
at the Milwaukee Zoo, as well as for other parks, zoos, municipalities and
private estates throughout the country. A former Chicago and North Western Railroad engineer, Sandley is convinced that narrow-gauge railways
and steam transport will be used more and more as fuel prices continue to
soar and fuel shortages increase.

Steam has been reborn outside the U.S. as well—on the five-and-one-
half-percent grades of the incredible "Devil's Nose" in Ecuador; Brazil's
two-and-one-half-foot gauge VFCO Railway with its tiny outside-frame
Baldwins and their cap stacks, polished brass and brightly painted smoke
boxes; the Resistencia woodburners of Argentina; the Royal Hudson—
Steam Locomotive 2680—north out of Vancouver; and the White Pass and
Yukon through Klondike gold country.

The Freedom Train

It is not surprising that the American Freedom Train, a Bicentennial
highlight, was hauled across the country on its two-year, 20,000-mile journey from Wilmington, Delaware, following the original transcontinental
railroad route, by a massive 425-ton locomotive. By the end of 1976, more
than eight million people were transported along the 10-car display train's
moving walkways viewing documents, art treasures and memorabilia. Because a large part of our nation's past achievements were due to railroads,
much of the American Freedom Train's display proved to be a sensory blitz
for the railroad enthusiast. Included were the silver spade used by Charles
Carroll, a signer of the Declaration of Independence, at the ground-break-
ing ceremony for the B&O Railroad in 1828; a replica of the golden spike
used at the ceremony linking east and west at Promontory Summit, Utah,
in 1869; models of such historic trains as the 1863 civil war version which
hauled President Lincoln to his first inauguration, and to his funeral; the
whistle from the "John Bull" locomotive, circa 1850, the first locomotive
on the Camden and Amboy Raolroad, a predecessor to the Penn Central;
a model of "The Arabian," an 1834 engine nearly eight feet high and
nicknamed "grasshopper" because of its long, spindly connecting rods;
and, in sharp contrast to all those, a model of the Linear Induction Vehicle,
an engine capable of propelling high speed futuristic trains along a single
rail.

The American Freedom Train, dream-come-true of New York commodity broker Ross Rowland, was a non-profit enterprise. The project was given a financial boost at first by four corporations which donated $1 million each and was largely self-supporting after that (a $2 adult admission was charged). Rowland, a rail buff who had the idea of touring the country with the train, spent over $200,000 of his own money to purchase and restore the locomotive used to pull it.

Steam and Museums

Most steam trains operate in the summertime. Some, such as those in New England, are most popular during the fall foliage season for their splashy displays of rich, autumn colors. Still others, when the tourists have gone, serve as ski trains in winter.

Numerous museums around the country are devoted either totally or in part to railroads and their place in America's heritage. Most impressive is the California State Railroad Museum, a massive project currently under construction along the banks of the Sacramento River in Old Sacramento, California, devoted to the growth and development of the railroad in the West, particularly in California. Its primary purpose is to house the collection donated to California by the Railway and Locomotive Historical Society, as well as to entertain and enlighten the public to a century of railroad development. Designed in size and scope as a virtual world's fair of railroading, the $9-million undertaking even has "Future World" characteristics. According to the original concept by Barry Howard Associates of Scarsdale, New York, "Within the museum, the visitor is led through introductory graphics to a well appointed space where he is invited to sit in a plush vintage coach seat. All around him are artifacts and images drawn from the history of railroading which are animated and colorful. Warning lights blink, signals are raised and lowered, wheels and gears turn.

"All of this is accompanied by a symphony of railroad sounds and classic railroad music. At a point in this continuing program of sound and sight, attention will be drawn to a live host or hostess who will emerge within the visual sculpture to officially greet the visitors. The staff person will use an informal and brief script to explain to the visitor the nature of the experience which he is about to have as well as other information relevant to his visit. As the welcome comes to a close, the sound and light dims and the visitor becomes aware that he is moving ever so slightly.

"In a matter of moments, the visitor finds himself removed from the highly illuminated space into which he was conducted and into a darkened area. He is now confronted with a montage of images which move, fade and reappear in an exciting series of vignettes which begin to suggest the growth of California and the Railroad. At times the images are 'still' produced from daguerreotypes and wet plate photographs documenting scenes and incidents relevant to Western history. At times the images will be excerpts from famous motion picture films which feature railroading and/or early California society. From time to time also, the images will include classic documents, graphics and other archival evidence of Western progress reaching from the mid-19th to the mid-20th century. The sound accompanying this visual montage will combine material from existing sound-tracks with music and effects, scored to amplify and expand the visual experience.

"Toward the end of this presentation, the host's voice once again is imposed on the visitor's experience. The narrator reinforces the visitor's impressions achieved in this portion of the show and suggests in dramatic fashion that all of these incidents and all of this history had its beginning right here almost at the very spot where the visitor now finds himself. As the narrator continues, the visitor is once again aware that he is in motion. Now, from the intimate environment of many screens the visitor finds himself conveyed into a vast space which seems to go on forever. When the visitor reaches his appointed position in this new space, his final intro- ductory experience begins. In big sound and in vast visual images, the panorama of the railroad unfolds. The story begins with the arrival of Theodore Judah in the fledgling community of Sacramento, traces the beginning of the Sacramento Valley Railroad, the fight for Federal support of the Trans-Continental Railroad, the incorporation and evolution of the Central Pacific and its historic race to Promontory, the maturation of the State of California as the railroad reduced its isolation and encouraged its ties with the East, the dominance of the many standard and narrow gauge railways throughout the successive periods of mining and industrial growth in California and Nevada, the rise and pre-eminence of the Southern Rail- way, and the conversion of railroads from steam to diesel.

"In the final scenes, the drama portrays the changing environment of California in the post World War II years, and footnotes the incredibly successful story with the fact that even today, the Southern Pacific remains one of the few profitable railroads in the nation. As the presentation con- cludes, and the lights come up, the visitor is once again returned to his starting position where he is invited to leave his seat and follow the path onward through the Museum."

Of the many buildings comprising the California State Railroad Museum, between which narrow-gauge steam trains will ferry visitors, a reconstruct- ed Passenger Station is already opened to the public; it was formally dedi- cated on September 25, 1976. The main structure, the museum's 70,000-square-foot "History Building," is scheduled for completion by the end of 1977.

Meanwhile, numerous other railroad museums and steam train expedi- tions around the country vie for visitors' attention.

ARIZONA. *Arizona Pioneers' Historical Society,* directly across the street from the main Park Avenue entrance to the University of Arizona campus in Tucson, contains extensive research material and early pioneer relics pertaining to Arizona, including an impressive collection of railroad memorabilia. An early steam locomotive in front of the building was moved to safer display quarters at Tucson's Himmel Park several years ago after mischievous fraternity students, as an annual prank, persisted in moving it during the night to a nearby coed dormitory and leaving it on the girls' front walk. Open 9–5 Monday through Friday, until noon Saturday. Admission is free. Also located in Tucson is the studio of famed Western primitive artist *Gene "Shorty" Thorn* (3301 North Mountain Avenue) whose best known and most reproduced painting is "Yuma Bound," a train moving horizontally across the entire center of the canvas, an orange and pink sunset above blending with the tan and cream colors of the desert below, a wisp of grey smoke moving parallel along the forward length of the cars. (By appointment: 602–622–8621.)

CALIFORNIA. California has the greatest concentration of steam trains in the U.S., among them the popular steam-powered people-movers at Disney Land and Knott's Berry Farm. *California Western Railroad* operates its regular bright yellow diesel passenger trains, called "Skunks," through dense redwood forests on the 41-mile route between Fort Bragg (on the coast midway between Eureka and San Francisco) to Willits, as well as a daily steam train for tourists called "The Super Skunk." The name comes from the odors of its nineteenth century cargo—fish and lumber—combined with its smoke and coal fumes. The route, much of it accessible only by train, includes 32 bridges, several tunnels and some of the lushest scenery in Northern California.

The Roaring Camp and Big Trees Narrow-Gauge Railroad at Felton, just north of Santa Cruz, still heads old-fashioned excursion passenger trains up the steepest railroad grades in the West. En route, the train crosses spectacular bridges over redwood canyons and, at Spring Canyon, one trestle loops over another in one of the most dramatic of railroad engineering feats: Corkscrew Loop. At its Roaring Camp base, passengers can tour a period village where Chuckwagon Bar-B-Q meals are available on weekends. There's an 1880 general store. Saturday night "moonlight steam train parties" are held for groups of 100 or more during the regular June through October season. The two-hour train trips are conducted off-season as well. Admission: $3.90 for adults; $1.95 for kids three to fifteen; toddlers free.

Other California lines include: *The Klamath and Hoppow Valley R.R.* through the redwood forests of Northern California; the *Camino, Cable and Northern R.R.,* Sundays only, through pear orchards and wooded glades; the *Alton and Pacific R.R.,* just south of Eureka; and the *Tahoe, Trout Creek and Pacific R.R.* out of South Lake Tahoe.

The Laws Railroad Museum in Sierra County, an old 1883 rail depot and narrow-gauge railway, was in use until 1960 and is now an historic railroad museum containing a five-room station agent's house, a hand-operated gallows-type turntable used when Laws was the northern terminus of the Southern Pacific, water tower, pump house, loading bunkers, branding irons, old farm equipment, mining exhibits, period antiques and a Western movie set. Season: Year round, 10–4, admission free. Located 5 miles northeast of Bishop on U.S. 6.

COLORADO. Colorado also has a considerable number of old-time trains. The *Denver and Rio Grande's* summer excursion train, "The Silverton," is easily the most famous. A genuine bit of history, the train runs between Durango and Silverton, a 47-mile run past deserted mining camps and over narrow canyon ledges. The three-foot gauge originally reached Silverton in 1882, the fastest growing mining camp in the towering San Juan mountains at the time. An amazing feat of construction was accomplished when the line was completed in only nine months and five days, in treacherous terrain and deplorable weather. In 1967, the line became a Registered National Historic Landmark and the following year it was designated a National Historic Civil Engineering Landmark. Today's adventurous traveler can experience pioneer Rocky Mountain railroading as it really was, reliving the exciting days before the turn of the century when the narrow-gauge route up the Animas river represented the very ultimate in modern transportation. It is not uncommon for reservations to be made a year or two in advance for this popular train run. Tickets are $10.25 each for adults; $6.25 for children under 11; and free for those not occupying seats, five or under. In Durango, passengers can arrange for a tour that includes the train ride and visits to Mesa Verde National Park and Ouray's "Million Dollar Mile" Road. Groups may book private railroad cars ($350 a day) that are hooked onto the Silverton for a day's outing. They contain ice box, stove, tables and circa 1882 interiors. According to the advertising spiel, the Silverton puts you "in another century, ready to relive the frontier days of railroading in the Rockies. With the chuff-chuff of the engine and clickety-clack of the wheels you're quickly out of the station and on your way to a wilderness only rails can reach."

Another train, the *Cumbres & Toltec Scenic Railroad,* operates on the only other surviving portion of track along the old 1,200-mile mountain route that the Denver & Rio Grande was forced to build when the Santa Fe beat it to Raton Pass. It runs for 64 miles between Antonito, Colorado, and Chama, New Mexico, through a series of Western postcards—soaring cliffs, plunging canyons, feisty rivers and moody ghost towns. The train runs weekends from June 14 through October as well as on Tuesday and Wednesday through July and August. Adults $15; children under 11, $5.

Other trains in Colorado include the *Colorado Central Narrow Gauge Railway,* a summer weekends-only operation 35 miles outside of Denver; *The Cripple Creek & Victor Narrow Gauge,* on the side of Pike's Peak, a daily four-mile run; the *High Country Railroad* out of Golden, operating daily during the summer; and the *Georgetown Loop Railroad* at Silver Plume, 50 miles west of Denver, operating daily from August through September. All are limited-run railroads that charge from $1.50 to $2 for adults, and half that for children.

The Colorado Railroad Museum at Golden—it operates the High Country Railroad—contains an extensive collection of Colorado-orientated trains and railroading memorabilia, including engines, cars, early records and the oldest narrow-gauge locomotive in Colorado (built by Baldwin, 1881). Housed in an 1881-style railroad station, the museum is at 17155 West 44th Ave., 2 miles east on Colorado 58. Open 9–5, daily; adults $1.25; children, 50 cents; families $2.95.

CONNECTICUT. *The Valley Railroad* is an old-time steam train that runs between Essex and Chester where at the Deep River Station it connects with the Silver Star excursion river boat. The schedule is daily during the summer and on weekends and holidays for most of the rest of the year, with Santa Claus riding all trains during December. Train uses tracks of a former New Haven Branch line. Roundtrip, Essex to Chester (about one hour) is $2.50 for adults; $1.50 for children. With the boat ride it's $4.75 for adults; $3 for children. The Essex Depot is a century-old affair with gift and souvenir shops and an authentic 1915 Grill Car Restaurant.

Branford Electric Railway and Trolley Museum in East Haven has more than 90 electric cars, locomotives and street cars on display. Offers 20-minute rides during summer in trolleys dating back to 1906. Museum is located off Connecticut Turnpike Exit 51. Adults $1.50; children, 75 cents.

DELAWARE. Delaware's only steam railroad is the *Wilmington and Western,* a four-coach train operating between Price's Corner (3 miles southwest of Wilmington) and Mt. Cuba, along the Red Clay Valley and some of Delaware's finest scenery. Gift shop, caboose parties, flea market and occasional "Billy The Kid"-style holdups. Adults, $2.25; kids $1.

FLORIDA. *The Gold Coast Railroad* in Fort Lauderdale provides a half-hour steam train trip along the Perimeter Road area near the airport, its contrast with jet planes coming and going its most memorable function. Museum car, the armored *Ferdinand Magellan,* was used by Presidents Roosevelt, Truman and Eisenhower and contains many railroad mementos of those years. Operates Sundays 1–5 P.M. Admission: $2; kids $1; toddlers under 5 free.

GEORGIA. *Stone Mountain Scenic Railroad* offers a five-mile excursion around Stone Mountain (in about 25 minutes) with locomotives of Civil War vintage. *Okefenokee Heritage Center* is a new federally-funded attraction at Waycross, the town so-named because it grew up around the point where two railroad lines crossed. Displays include a complete train with steam locomotive, coal tender, freight car, baggage car, passenger coach, and caboose. An actual depot moved from Hoboken, Georgia, contains a gift shop and restaurant. The Center is located on a 20-acre tract of pine woodlands called Winona Park, north of Waycross off U.S. 1.
Georgia Peach Special is the April-through-October steam train operation of the Southern Railway, partly a public relations activity to promote good will and partly a revenue-producing function of the railroad. The day-long train trips are generally sponsored by local chapters of the National Railroad Historical Society who fill it up to its 570-seat capacity with members and friends. The trains are pulled by a variety of locomotives including #4501, the Grand Old Lady of Steam, built in 1911. Included are air-conditioned coaches, an open-air gondola car and commissary. W. Graham Clayton, Jr., president of Southern Railway and a long-time railroad aficionado, frequently joins the groups on their day-long outings.
Savannah has a $200,000 restored *Central of Georgia* Railroad Station which is used as a visitors' center. The station, built in 1860, was donated to the city by the Southern Railway System. Savannah visitors are encouraged to use the visitors' center for parking while venturing into town by foot to alleviate traffic congestion.

HAWAII. *The Lahaina-Kaanapali & Pacific Railroad* is Hawaii's only passenger train. The authentically reconstructed 1890 sugar cane train with its brightly painted engine travels a narrow-gauge track between Lahaina and Kaanapali on the island of Maui in a style reminiscent of a bygone era. Depots have also been reconstructed in exacting detail. Free railroad bus transports passengers between depot and town. A jitney to and from the depot via the various resort hotels costs 50 cents. Train operates daily. Adults, $2; children $1. Sightseeing excursions are available with a connecting boat trip.

ILLINOIS. *Illinois Railway Museum,* located in Union, about 25 miles south of Lake Geneva, is one of the world's largest operating museums, with 46 acres of outdoor displays—over 100 steam engines, streetcars, inter-urban cars, elevated railway cars, steam railroad coaches and trolleys. In all, the museum has more than a mile of exhibits. Several trains operated on demonstration track. Adults $.75; children, $.40; parking free.
Historic Pullman Foundation maintains a period community in Chicago developed by George Pullman. Many of the buildings owned by the former railroad tycoon are preserved and daily tours are conducted from The Hotel Florence (11111 South Forrestville Avenue) Monday-Friday at 1:30, and on the first Sunday of the month—May through October—from the Historic Pullman Center at 614 East 113th Street at 1:30 P.M. Donations $1 for adults; $.50 for children.

MAINE. *Montpelier,* a state historical museum, in Thomaston includes a reproduction of the 1795 home of General Henry Knox, Revolutionary War hero and first U.S. Secretary of War, as well as the oldest railroad depot in America, the home's former cookhouse. It was converted to a station for the Knox and Lincoln Railroad in 1894. Rail buffs point out that the care and recognition the building receives today was made possible through the railroad's utilization of the station for more than a century. Otherwise, it might never have survived. Museum is open summers only, 10–5, with a nominal charge for admission.

The *Seashore Trolley Museum* in Kennebunkport has the nation's oldest and largest collection of electric railway trains.

MARYLAND. One of the world's largest collections of historic railroad equipment and memorabilia is on dispaly at Baltimore's *B & O Transportation Museum* located at Mt. Clare Station, the birthplace of American Railroading, built in 1830. The most spectacular exhibits are the antique locomotives, ranging in size from the tiny Tom Thumb of 1829 to the Iron Mule of 1945, elegant passenger coaches and freight cars. The Chessie System, Inc. (modern day successor to the old B&O and C&O Railroads) recently reopened the museum, which is situated in a complex of three historic buildings at 901 W. Pratt Street. The Museum is a repository for literally thousands of items associated with railroading around the world. The central and largest structure of the Museum group is an old passenger car roundhouse where the world's most famous locomotives have been arranged in historical sequence. Most striking is a railroad clock collection covering an entire wall, all of them accurate enough to set one's digital. The museum is open Wednesdays through Sundays, 10–4. Admission is $1.50 for adults; $.75 for children.

The *Baltimore Steetcar Museum* houses delightful trolleycar relics, including a horse-drawn car, Gay Nineties railrider and an open-air summer car, which can be boarded for nostalgic rides.

MASSACHUSETTS. The *Edaville Railroad* in South Carver once journeyed as far as Maine, but is now limited to a nostalgic 5-and-a-half-mile run through cranberry bogs near Cape Cod. Antique carousel and horse-drawn trolley car rides are also available. Two museums house steam trains, fire engines, antique cars, guns and the like. Open daily during the summer, Sundays and holidays during spring and fall. Admission: adults, $2.40; children, $1.20. Includes train ride and museum.

MICHIGAN. The Henry Ford Museum in Dearborn offers a quiet, 20-minute ride over a two-and-a-half mile loop of railroad via the *Greenfield Village Railroad*—period coaches and vintage locomotives. The Ford Museum occupies 14 acres, with numerous exhibits devoted to railroads. Museum and village admission $2.50 each for adults; $1 for children 6–14; under six free.

MISSOURI. *National Museum of Transport* in St. Louis (3015 Barretts Station Road) has a wide variety of steam locomotives, railway cars, city transit conveyances from horse cars to buses and antique automobiles. Open daily 10–5. Admission: $2 for adults; children (admitted only in the company of adults) $.75; under 5, free.

NEW HAMPSHIRE. *Mount Washington Cog Railway.* Allow at least three hours for this breath-halter, from the base station (6 miles east of U.S. 302) up 6,288-foot-high Mount Washington with grades as steep as 37 percent. A cog rail set between regular tracks provides traction needed for the intensive climb. Check locally for schedules and prices.

NEW JERSEY. Four oldtime railroads make New Jersey a railroad buff's dream. The *Morris County Central Railroad* at Newfoundland has a vintage 1907 locomotive pulling period coaches and guarantees a "James Gang" holdup on every ride. Youngsters (and adults, too, if they want to get into the act) are given wads of play money when boarding, and are deprived of it soon enough when the shooting begins. Train operates daily during the summer; adults, $2.50; kids half price.

The *Black River & Western* (between Flemington, Ringoes and Lambertville) operates out of a restored 1854 station and shuttles to the re-creation of a small-town business center of the 1890's in Flemington. One-hour round trip is $2 for adults; $1 for kids. When the train isn't hauling tourists it hauls freight.

The *Pine Creek Railroad* in Farmingdale is a 36-inch gauge steam train that runs for about a mile through a restored 19th century iron-making community ($.50 for adults; kids free) and the *Whippany Toonerville Railroad* is a standard-gauge steam train that runs a nine-mile, 45-minute round trip from the Morristown and Erie Railroad Station at Whippany. Adults, $2.50; kids $1.25.

NEW MEXICO. *Chumbres & Toltec Scenic Railroad* at Chama offers day-long, 64-mile outings to Antonio, Colorado, aboard an historic narrow-gauge steam train. Route crisscrosses over the Colorado-New Mexico border 11 times while passing through magnificent mountain terrain, backwoods country, and over the 10,000-foot-high Cumbres Pass across the Continental Divide. Train travels in alternate directions every other day. Rail trip is one way, with return by bus. From late May through mid-October. Adults $14; children under 12, $5. Fare includes return bus ticket. Warm clothes advised because of altitude.

NORTH CAROLINA. With a name like *"Tweetsie Railraod,"* this three-foot-gauge steam train out of Blowing Rock (daily June through October) can't take itself too seriously. The name comes from the "sweet" sound its whistle makes on the train's three-mile loop around Magic Mountain. It's all part of a Western theme park operation, complete with a "Gold Mine in the Sky," chair lift up Magic Mountain, Indian raids, and outlaw hold ups. If all that sounds like too much on the nerves, there's also a picnic area on the grounds. Adults, $3.50; kids, $2.50; under 4 free.

OREGON. The *Galloping Goose* runs past lumber camps between Cottage Grove, (near Eugene) and the Bohemia Lumber Plant, a 34-mile, two-hour trip on the Oregon Pacific and Eastern Railway. One locomotive, circa 1915, was part of the McCloud River RR, and another, 10 years younger, pulled coaches for the Magna Arizona. Trip begins and terminates at Village Green Station, adjacent to Railtown, U.S.A., where antique steam locomotives, coaches and extensive memorabilia exhibits are on display. Operated mid-May through September. Adults, $4.90; kids, $3.35; under 5 free.

PENNSYLVANIA. The *New Hope and Ivyland Railroad,* standard-gauge steam train, departs from a restored depot in New Hope, along the Delaware River, for a 14-mile, 75-minute round trip. Assorted weekend runs. Adults, $2.50; children, $1.25.

The *Strasburg Railroad* (Lancaster County) runs through beautiful Pennsylvania Dutch country on a 9-mile, round trip every half hour daily through July and August. Equipment includes 1905 Camelback locomotive, open platform observation cars, bright yellow coaches, some of which were featured in the "Hello, Dolly!" film with Barbra Streisand. The Strasburg is one of the oldest and busiest steam trains in the country. Ride terminates across the highway from the *Railroad*

Museum of Pennsylvania with its collection of 35 locomotives, freight and passenger cars dating back to 1875, and audiovisual displays. Train ride is $1.75 for adults; $.75 for children; toddlers free. Additional fee for museum. Strasburg, the city, was at one time the largest center for the construction of railroad cars (it was 7th on a top-secret German list of American cities to be bombed during World War II), and boasts the world-famous Horseshoe Curve, at one time one of the seven engineering wonders of the world. It is the home of Terrance Clark and some of the other most knowledgeable railroad buffs in the country.

SOUTH DAKOTA. The *Black Hills Railroad* has an 1880 engine which steams between Custer and Hill City, a 16-mile run with 3 percent grades, through some of the state's most magnificent scenery, including Crazy Horse Memorial, and grazing herds of buffalo. Train has open and closed cars. Adults, $5; kids, $2.50; under 6 free. Operates only during summer.

TEXAS. The Bicentennial debut of the refurbished *Texas State Railroad* as a state park between Rusk and Palestine gave East Texas one of its brightest new tourist attractions. The Texas Parks and Wildlife Department acquired jurisdiction of the railroad in 1972. The right-of-way contains 110 acres over a distance of 25 miles. Convict crews from Ellis and Eastham Prison Farms spent four 10-hour days a week (at fifty cents a day) building fences, clearing underbrush, replacing ties and adding new ballast to raise the roadbed crown. Twenty-eight trestles were restored to serviceable condition, the longest a 1,115-foot span over the Neches River. Four "iron horse" steam locomotives alternately pull rebuilt and refurbished period coaches on a 25-mile depot-to-depot run. Passenger cars contain period-piece chandeliers; one serves as an ice cream parlor-coach. The round trip takes three hours. Adults, $5.75 round trip; children, $3.25; under 2 free. Recreational campground sites are also available here with trailer hookups for water, electricity and sewerage.

The *Pioneer Town and Pacific Railroad* is part of a reconstructed Western town of the 1880's in Wimberley. The locomotive, a half-scale replica of an 1873 wood-burning Union Pacific engine built from the original plans, pulls three cars and a caboose.

Other Texas railroad relics include an antique coach car at the *Pate Museum of Transportation* on U.S. Highway 377, midway between Fort Worth and Cressen; *Texas & Pacific Engine #610,* in Fort Worth, last remaining survivor of the powerful 600 series, which saw service with the American Freedom Train on its tour through Texas; and the Jay Gould private railroad car, *"Atlanta,"* the goddess of speed, located in downtown Jefferson. Built in the early 1890's, this "palace on wheels" reflects Jay Gould's love of luxury. This flamboyant millionaire prided himself on having the finest of private railroad cars. He always took his doctor along; he carried a cow and a farmer in the baggage car ahead; and he took a special baker along to keep a fresh supply of ladyfingers at all times. Other trains got out of the way when his train came along.

The *Harrison County Historical Society* in Marshall, Texas, also has considerable railroad memorabilia on display including a cancelled check from the Texas & Pacific to Jay Gould for $333,752.32, dated 1904, and a crumb tray from the private parlor car of the line's president; as does the *San Antonio Museum of Transportation* located at HemisFair Plaza in the center of town.

UTAH. More than one hundred years ago, the Central Pacific and Union Pacific railroads steamed slowly together at *Promontory Point,* joining East and West in the first transcontinental railroad. In a joyous ceremony, railroad officials drove a final golden spike in a laurelwood tie, symbol of victory—and union. The area is now a national historic site, and re-enactments of the "Driving of the Golden Spike" are held four times daily during the summer and once a year in a gala anniversary ceremony on May 10. *Golden Spike Empire,* one of Utah's eight tourism promotion regions, is named for this historic event, and the area contains scores of railroad related points of interest.

The *Corinne Railroad Museum,* operated by the Sons of the Utah Pioneers, offers a fine collection of railroad equipment, historic buildings, artifacts, photographs and paintings. Located in the center of historic Corrine, the museum is open daily, 9–5, through the spring and summer months.

Lucin Cut-Off is on the national registry of engineering achievements. On March 8, 1904, the original Central Pacific (now the Southern Pacific) main line through Promontory Summit was replaced by a wooden trestle 12 miles long across the Great Salt Lake., one of railroad engineering's most ambitious projects. Replaced in 1959 by a $54 million rock causeway, it is still used occasionally. Both the original cut-off and its successor can be seen by passengers on Amtrak trains.

Currently under restoration is the *Union Depot* at Ogden, since 1869 one of the best known and busiest rail centers in the West. It was here at "Junction City," as Ogden was known, that the Union Pacific, the Southern Pacific and the Denver & Rio Grande met. In the late 1930's over 100 passenger trains a day used the depot. It was designated a national historic site in 1973. When restoration is completed, Union Depot will serve as the National Railroad Hall of Fame museum and will continue in its role as a working Amtrak station.

The *Heber Creeper,* operated by the Wasath Mountain Railroad out of Heber City, takes almost four hours to "creep" through 18 miles of rugged mountain terrain just east of Salt Lake City. The Creeper offers two departures daily from either end of the line—Heber City or Bridal Veil Falls. The train is pulled by one of three steam locomotives in the Creeper stable. Passengers have a choice of open-air observation car or air-conditioned coaches. Each train has a refreshment car with soft drinks, snacks and souvenirs. Lunch is served in the dining car on the 11 A.M. train and dinner on the weekend night train. The original "Heber Creeper" was part of the Eastern Utah Railroad Company. Adults $5; children, $2.50; under 2 free. Operates only during the summer.

VERMONT. Vermont's *Bicentennial Steam Expedition,* a dark green steam locomotive emblazoned with gold letters and coupled to eight rebuilt Tuscany red passenger cars, carried travelers on a regular daily schedule between Bellows Falls and Burlington from July to mid-August, and between Burlington and Bennington from mid-August through the fall foliage season during 1976, and will do so again in the summer of 1977. It is hoped this service can be continued in future years.

Tourists see the Green Mountain state in a leisurely way, much as their grandparents did. Along both routes the train travels through spectacular scenery, and stops at each of seven stations twice a day—once northbound and once southbound—allowing passengers to detrain for a few hours, or even a few days, at a typical Vermont village or town for a visit to local museums, antique and craft shops, country inns and restaurants. Its speed averages only 25 miles an hour, affording passengers an unhurried look at the pastoral countryside and a journey through Revolutionary history. The train's locomotive is named "The Spirit of Ethan Allen," in honor of the state's foremost patriot. A number of Vermont hotels and inns offer transfer service from and to both Amtrak and Bicentennial Steam Excursion terminals as well as package tour rates in connection with the trip. (Both Bellows Falls and Burlington/Essex Junction are served by Amtrak's The Montrealer.) Aboard the train, a pleasant contrast is provided between the veteran railroad men manning the steam engines and the youthful crew of host and hostesses, mostly college students or recent graduates from Vermont colleges. The railwaymen—a retired engineer, fireman, conductor and trainman—represent over 200 years of railroad experience. An extra attraction on the train is a shop stocked with rail-oriented gift items—books, engineers' caps and bandanas, railway insignia. A sandwich bar is called "The Great Train Robbery." Passengers buy individual slices of ham, cheese, roast beef, or whatever, and "build" their own sandwiches. Drinks are available, both hard and soft.

Passengers on the Bellows Falls-Burlington run board or get off at *Steamtown, U.S.A.,* a transportation museum featuring perhaps the largest collection of locomotives and coaches from America's past. Steamtown, founded by F. Nelson Blout as the realization of a boyhood dream, began operation in 1961 and has grown steadily to become the foremost steamtrain exposition in the nation, including nostalgic train rides along the Connecticut River and the Williams River and periodic "steam ups" when as many as six locomotives all fire up at the same time. Steamtown admission is $5.50 for adults; $2.95 for chuldren; under 3½ free. Contact Steamtown USA, Bellows Falls, Vermont 05201 (802) 463-3937 for information. Tickets for the Bicentennial Steam Expedition are $15.75 for the full run and half that for children (under 5 free), with proportionate rates for limited station to station runs.

The *Shelburne Museum* in Shelburne, Vermont, 35 reconstructed buildings sprawled over 100 acres, seven miles south of Burlington on U.S.-7, also has considerable memorabilia and displays on American railroading, including a railroad station of the Victorian period, railroad train shed and a number of historic engines. Adults $4; children $2; under 6 free.

VIRGINIA. *Liberty Limited,* a cooperative project of nonprofit railroad historical organizations in the Washington, D.C. area, sponsors antique steam locomotive excursions on weekends to three towns in Virginia—Front Royal, Charlottesville and Calverton. The trips all start at Union Station in Alexandria, Va. Train includes both open-window and air-conditioned coaches, observation cars and a luggage car equipped with power for recording enthusiasts. Food service is available. Depending on destination, fares range from $17.50 to $12.50 for adults and from $14 to $10 for children. Advance reservations required. Contact: Liberty Limited, P.O. Box 456, Laurel, Md., 20810.

WASHINGTON. The depot of the *Puget Sound and Snoqualmie Railroad,* just outside of Seattle, has a collection of old steam engines, some of which make short runs on abandoned railroad grades.

WEST VIRGINIA. Steep grades and switchbacks are part of the *Cass Scenic Railway* route 22 miles from Cass to the top of Bald Knob, through former logging country. Shorter rides also available.

WISCONSIN. *National Railroad Museum* is located at 2285 South Broadway. Excellent collection of standard and miniature-gauge steam trains, cars and coaches. Daily 9:30–5. Adults $1.50; children $.75; under 5 free. Includes ride on steam train over a mile-long loop of rail. Steam train rides also available at the *Brookfield Zoo,* over 24"-gauge track for 30 minutes, about two-and-one-half miles (Adults $1; children $.60, and at the *Milwaukee Zoo* on a 15"-gauge installation. Track runs a mile-and-a-half and the cost is 50 cents for adults, twenty-five cents for children.

CANADIAN-U.S. BORDER

Perhaps the greatest symbol of peace in today's churning world of conflict is an imaginary line that runs across North America from the Atlantic to the Pacific—the border between the U.S. and Canada.

Major passenger train gateways into Canada from the U.S. include: Vancouver, served by Amtrak's *Pacific International;* Detroit (ground passenger vehicles cross the bridge to Windsor); Buffalo (railcar service to Toronto); and Montreal (via the daily *Montrealer* and *Adirondack* from New York).

The 5,000-mile span is the longest unfortified border in the world. Canada established itself as a Dominion 109 years ago, giving birth to a country second in size only to the U.S.S.R. Any unfriendly power in control of Canada would spell grave danger to the U.S. If enemy planes attacked this country they would most likely do so over Canada's northern polar route. Thus, when a smiling Canadian border guard waves a U.S. citizen in his automobile across the border in Toronto, Kingston, Winnipeg, Vancouver, Victoria or any of the 465 official border crossings—or "outports," as they're called—it is far more meaningful than just a pleasant gesture.

During informal talks in Washington in 1976, Canadian Prime Minister Pierre Trudeau presented then-President Ford with a book of scenic photos taken along the boundary. The Canadian-U.S. border doesn't divide but rather "brings us together," he said. The book is titled "Between Friends."

Any traveler who has visited a country where surly customs inspectors pick and poke their way through baggage like gourmets sampling suspicious meatballs will appreciate the ease with which one may enter Canada. A U.S. citizen of permanent residence is required only to show proof of identity—social security card, driver's license or voter's registration card. While passports and birth certificates are excellent forms of identification, they are not required, as they are in most other countries.

Usual restrictions on alcohol and tobacco prevail (50 cigars, 200 cigarettes, two pounds of tobacco and 40 ounces of alcohol for each adult). However, anyone driving a car with U.S. plates who's reasonably respectable-looking will generally be waved right through. If an individual is stopped, the Canadian customs officer usually asks the nature of the visit and how long a visitor intends to stay in Canada. Automobile inspections tend to be quick, visual ones. Long-haired hippie types hiding behind purple-tinted glasses and smoking cigarettes of questionable content may be searched more thoroughly.

Although the border symbolizes a long record of unbroken peace between the two nations, there have been some sticky moments. One was a Great Lakes fishing rights dispute that resulted in naval artillery being bandied about. The dispute was settled by the Rush-Bagot disarmament agreement of 1817, but it was not really until the Treaty of Washington in 1871 that the Canadians felt secure enough to let their fortifications along the Great Lakes fall into decay.

Another crisis came in 1838 when heavy-fisted Canadian and Maine lumbermen got into a row over lumber rights along the Aroostook River. The State of Maine called out her militia and New Brunswick did likewise. Nervous troops faced each other across the river, but the battle failed to occur when high-ranking negotiators settled the conflict.

The most serious strain came during the 1920's when U.S. prohibition of alcoholic liquors struck Canadians as silly and great quantities of "imported" Scotch whiskey began pouring across the border from the north. Both the big thirst and the squabble between government law enforcement agencies ended with the repeal of prohibition in 1933.

Such disputes, and the recent hard feelings fostered by Canada's harborage of U.S. draft-evaders during the Vietnam conflict, tend to be little more than lovers' quarrels. The U.S. and Canada share not only the world's longest unfortified border but also a common language, heritage and culture. The tie, never more apparent than during the United States' Bicentennial year, remains a strong one.

CANADA

Railroad development has been associated with the course of Canadian history since a group of British colonies first combined to form the Dominion of Canada in 1867. Four years later, the colony of British Columbia made the construction of a transcontinental rail link a condition for joining the confederation. The linking of the Atlantic and Pacific oceans with a thin line of track thus became an obsession of the country's founding fathers, who were convinced that the railway would become the single most unifying force in Canada. It took 14 years to bridge the country with rail. Today, two coast-to-coast train networks whisk passengers through 4,000 miles of changing topography in less than four days and three nights.

In a country where trains played so vital a role throughout history, it is not surprising that many Canadians were outspokenly irate when Canadian Transport Minister Otto Lang in 1976 outlined plans to drastically reorganize routes of the government-owned Canadian National Railroad and the privately owned but partly subsidized CP Rail. His proposal included a single trancontinental service that would eliminate present duplications. Canada's railroads have been running at a loss of $167 million a year; and in 1976 it exceeded $200 million for the first time; 55 percent of the trains carry fewer than 47 persons and 20 percent carry ten passengers or less. At the present rate of deterioration, the railroads, he said, would be losing over $400 million a year by 1980.

The Toronto *Daily Star* replied in an angry editorial: "What this all means, of course, is that the Canadian government is getting ready to destroy not only 'obviously unneeded local services' but also some of the longest, oldest and, yes, most romantic passenger routes in the country."

The program, as outlined by Mr. Lang, is scheduled to be completed by 1978. Meanwhile, the government remains committed to a promise made earlier to provide $100 million over a five-year period, beginning in 1977, for the purchase of new commuter equipment.

Coast To Coast

Canadian National (VIA CN) and Canadian Pacific (CP Rail) trains wind their way through the wooded valleys of the Canadian Shield, vast prairie grasslands, and western mountain forests. The 3,000-mile distance from the Montreal headquarters of both lines to Vancouver can be covered without changing trains.

THE CANADIAN, Montreal/Toronto - Vancouver. CP Rail's stainless steel dome train leaves daily in each direction and takes roughly three full days. Westbound departures leave Montreal and Toronto in the morning (connecting at Sudbury). Montreal reservations address is: CP Rail Passenger Reservations, Windsor Station, Montreal, Quebec. From Toronto, reservations may be made through CP Rail Passenger Reservations, Union Station, Toronto, Ontario. The Canadian, which takes a more southerly route than its Canadian National counterpart, is one of the finest anywhere. Its elegant dining car holds 48 people at one seating; private cubicles at either end are divided from the main dining area by glass partitions etched with Canadian bird scenes. There is usually a choice of three main dishes: ham steak ($3.95), omelet with Canadian (what else?) bacon ($3.40), plus such specialties as rib steak ($8.50) or breaded pork chops ($4.15). Service is impeccable. The train seems to be a favorite of Japanese tourists. Scenery is spectacular, including the dazzling summer and winter resort of Banff, like a toy village nestled among towering mountains. Thunder Bay. Winnipeg. Regina. Calgary. Canada's prairie flatlands are called "the breadbasket of the world," where tiers of giant grain elevators punctuate fields of golden wheat. Arrow-straight roads lead monotonously off into the distance. Banff is served by an enormous railway-operated hotel, castle-like in its splendor. The journey into British Columbia follows the turbulent, historic Fraser River, first discovered in 1805. The 5,000-mile-long Trans-Canada Highway is within hailing distance in many places. Finally Vancouver, Canada's "gateway to the Orient," and site of the second largest Chinatown in North America. Basic fare between Montreal and Vancouver is $139 for reclining lounge-type chairs that can be reserved at no extra charge; roomette is $229 in the off-season and $278 from June 1 through September 15; bedroom is $352 during the off-season and $457 from June 1 through September 15. A public address system providing music and announcements about points of interest along the way may be turned on or off by passengers in their room. Sleeping car attendants respond promptly to the summons of a bedside buzzer. Departures eastbound from Vancouver are at 5:45 P.M. Reservation office address is: CP Rail's Passenger Reservation Service, 601 West Cordova St., Vancouver, B.C. CP Rail connects Montreal and Quebec City with other major towns in Quebec Province, as well as Saint John, New Brunswick. There are other services as well.

THE SUPER CONTINENTAL, Montreal/Toronto - Vancouver. CN recently unveiled a new name and color scheme for all its passenger trains. The name VIA and the bold blue and yellow color scheme stand for a renewed dynamism in CN passenger train services.

VIA CN's Super Continental leaves daily from Montreal and Toronto, joining at Capreol, just north of Sudbury, for its 2,914-mile run through Winnipeg, Saskatoon, Edmonton and Jasper to Vancouver. Montreal reservation address is: VIA CN Rail Travel Bureau, Central Station Concourse, Montreal, Quebec. From Toronto, reservations may be made through the VIA CN Service Center, Union Station, Toronto, Ontario. Westbound departures leave Montreal and Toronto in the late evening and take roughly three full days. A deluxe hotel-on-wheels, the air-conditioned Super Continental has a wide choice of accommodations—from reclining coach seats through upper and lower berths, compact, efficient roomettes to single and double bedrooms. A VIA CN exclusive is the Dayniter car which provides deluxe coach type accommodation for daytime and overnight comfort. Sceneramic Dome cars are operated between Winnipeg and Vancouver, allowing an even more dramatic view of the majestic scenery. For children, there's a supervised play hour in the morning with story books and coloring books available. And for the adults, Bingo games in the dining car after dinner provide a change of pace. VIA CN's Car-Go-Rail plan even lets you have the use of your own car at destination.

The Super Continental takes the high road across Canada, through the wild northern Ontario lake country, across the prairies and swinging up west of Winnipeg to Saskatoon and Edmonton. As it enters the Canadian Rockies following the Yellowhead Pass, the train passes through Jasper National Park, location of one of the world's great mountain resorts, CN's Jasper Park Lodge, a mini-village of chalets nestled around a crystal clear mountain lake. Then on, through the mountains and down the Fraser River valley to Vancouver, arriving there in the morning. VIA CN's Passenger Service Center in Vancouver is at 1150 Station Street. VIA CN's fares are quite a bit less than Canadian Pacific's, ranging from $90 to $124, depending on the time of travel. And there's a 7 to 30 day return fare of $136.40.

Turbotrains

VIA CN Turbotrains speed twice daily between Montreal and Toronto. On April 22, 1976, a VIA CN Turbo set a new Canadian rail speed record of 140 m.p.h. near Morrisburg, Ontario, on a press run. Its pendulum-like suspension permits cars to bank on curves and allows a 30 per cent faster speed on curves, with maximum passenger comfort. The Turbos cruise comfortably at 95 m.p.h. Passengers can choose Turboclub or Turbocoach service. In Turboclub, passengers can try at-the-seat meal service, with such delicacies as cornish hen, filet mignon and Arctic char amandine on the rotating menu. Turbocoach passengers can either go to the cafe for hot and cold snacks or use the service wagon which rolls through the coach aisles. At each end of the VIA CN Turbos there are dome cars which provide a different look at the scenery flashing past and, in the forward car, an opportunity to watch the enginemen at work. The Turbos are painted a striking yellow with dark blue accent markings and the VIA name.

Rail Excursions

VIA CN offers a wide variety of tours and excursions covering most parts of Canada. In addition, there are several special interest tours and steam excursions available.

THE EXPLORERS' TOUR. One of VIA CN's most unusual Maple Leaf Package Tours is a six-day Explorer's Tour from Winnepeg to Churchill. The tour is a complete vacation package; but the city of Winnipeg has so much to offer that some "explorers" may want to linger following their visit to the sub-Arctic. The excursion train leaves Winnipeg every Sunday afternoon from June 12 to September 11. Package price ranges from $399 to $475 per person. Regular CN accommodations, from upper berth to drawing room, are offered on the train and tour fare includes all meals on and off the train, cafe-lounge car priviliges, sightseeing trips, hotel room at Flin Flon and gratuities. The tour starts late Sunday afternoon. The first overnight ride goes to Thompson, a modern city that stands on what, only 15 years ago, was forest atop the fabulous ore deposit, now mined by the International

Nickel Company. The train reaches Churchill on Hudson Bay Tuesday morning. A tour bus takes passengers to see the historic port and to Cape Merry from where Fort Prince of Wales, built in 1770, can be seen on the opposite bank of the Churchill River, a mile away. After a day and a half at Churchill, the next stop is The Pas for an overnight stay and a visit to the Little Northern Museum, with its collection of northern objects and artifacts associated with the Indians and early trading days. Next morning, a bus goes to the mining community of Flin Flon, 94 miles away, for an overnight stop. The group returns to The Pas the following day after lunch at Cranberry Portage, and the train returns to Winnipeg early Saturday morning.

THE POLAR BEAR EXPRESS. The Polar Bear Express, operated by Ontario Northland Rail Services, takes passengers on a thrilling ride down the Arctic watershed on a one-day return trip from Cochrane, Ontario, 460 miles north of Toronto.

THE ROYAL HUDSON. The 80-mile round trip to Squamish from North Vancouver follows the eastern shore of Howe Sound, and the train is pulled by Steam Locomotive No. 2860. The scenic route is bordered by water on one side and towering mountain peaks on the other. Steam locomotive No. 2860, of the Royal Hudson class, pulls the train.

TORONTO-NIAGARA FALLS. A 94-foot long mainline locomotive built in 1944, Number 6060 spent about a dozen years in retirement at Jasper National Park. Completely refurbished and put into first class working order, Number 6060 now runs out of Toronto on Wednesdays and Saturdays, bound for Niagara Falls. While excursion passengers enjoy the sights at Niagara, Number 6060 plies a side trip from Niagara to Yager for the benefit of other visitors to the area, returning her excursion passengers to Toronto the same evening.

The excursion covers territory roamed by the fur traders of 300 years ago. Line's end is Moosonee, more than 100 miles beyond the nearest paved road. All along its run, the Express stops to let hunters off and Indian trappers on, or stops for animals camped on the tracks. Lumberjacks, missionaries, miners and geologists are among its regular travelers. Moosonee, population 1,000, one of the last frontier towns, is on the banks of the Moose River, about 15 miles from the salt water of James Bay.

Moose Factory, a short canoe ride from Moosonee, is the site of the second Hudson's Bay Company trading post, built in 1673. The post is still in operation and some of the buildings date back to the early 18th century. The Anglican Church in Moosonee has a beaded moosehide altar cloth, Cree-language prayer books and wooden plugs in the floor. If the tidewaters of James Bay get too high in the spring, parishioners just pull the plugs. The water bubbles up and keeps the church from floating away. After six hours in the Moosonee district, the train heads back toward Cochrane, 186 miles to the south. Free parking is available adjacent to the Cochrane station and there are several hotels in Cochrane for visitors wishing to stay on.

Steam Locomotive No. 2860 went into service from Montreal to Vancouver in 1939. She went through 25 crews without breakdowns during the 3,100-mile trip and earned the right for Canadian Pacific Railroad Hudson locomotives to carry the designation "royal." No. 2860 plied the main CP lines until the mid-50s when she was replaced by diesels. She survived dangerously close to the scrap heap for years until rescued by the British Columbia government and put back in service for tourists. In the 30s, this "steam locomotive fit for a king" was considered the ultimate in power and beauty. Many old railwaymen consider the Royal Hudson the best steam locomotive ever built. It weighs 657,000 pounds with its tender and is driven by six 75-inch driving wheels. Its nine coaches, baggage car, observation car and club car all bear names seen along the main line of British Columbia Railways; names like Sundance, Lone Butte, Brandywine Falls and Lillooet. The trip to Squamish is the longest daily scheduled steam passenger trip in North America.

CAPE BRETON STEAM RAILWAY. Two steam locomotives, one built in England and the other in the United States, take visitors on a 10-mile run from the mining town of Glace Bay, Nova Scotia, to the little fishing village of Port Morien. Repton, No. 926, was built in Britain in 1934 and in its day was considered the most powerful of its type in Europe. It is an engine of the famous Schools Class and was built for express trains. Today, it is the only British steam engine in service in North America. Old 42, a Mogul Class locomotive built at Schenectady, N.Y., in 1899, was close to the scrap heap when it was restored in 1973, in the Glace Bay roundhouse. It had seen many years of service on the Sydney and Louisbourg Railway before its temporary retirement. The vintage locomotives pull a coach built in 1881, one of the oldest still in operation in the world. It includes a kitchen with a coal-burning range and a room with a brass bed. Among the more interesting cars on the train are a former Great Western corridor coach and two beautifully decorated vintage lounge cars complete with bars. The train is operated by retired railwaymen of the old Sydney and Louisbourg Railway. At Glace Bay, a city of 24,000, the *Miner's Museum* displays equipment of early mining days. The museum is in an old railway station which also serves as an information center and houses an old-time company store and gift shop.

THE WAKEFIELD EXCURSION. Ottawa is the starting point of the Wakefield Steam Locomotive Excursion, a 25-mile ride through Canada's capital city and along the Gatineau River to Wakefield. The trip is advertised as "a typical branch-line passenger train ride of 50-or-so years ago, complete with the sight, sounds and smells inseparable from a steam-hauled train." It is reminiscent of the old picnic specials of the turn of the century when families would board a train on Sunday, with their lunch baskets and parasols, and return in the evening. The train is pulled by No. 1201 of the G-5 Class of locomotives built in Montreal in 1944, the last steam locomotives built in Canada. The Light Pacific locomotive weighs 208 tons. Its official maximum speed is 70 m.p.h. but it has been clocked at more than 90. On the Wakefield run, however, the maximum speed allowed is 25 m.p.h.

The Wakefield train sets out from the *National Museum of Science and Technology*. The station agent stamps all tickets in a station that is an exact replica of one built about 1910. The train puffs its way through Ottawa, over the Ottawa River, through Hull, Quebec, and then up the Gatineau River to its destination. The historic river still carries logs for pulp mills on the Ottawa River. Sailboats and cosy cottages can be seen along the route. At the end of the line, passengers can watch the locomotives being turned around manually on a turntable, or they can visit the old Wakefield grist mill on the Lapeche River, now being restored. There is ample time for a picnic in the riverside park and a nearby bakery sells fresh oven-baked bread and pastries. The engineer sounds the whistle 10 minutes before the trip back to the Museum of Science and Technology, home of an interesting collection of steam locomotives and coaches.

RAILROAD STATIONS

UNION STATION, OTTAWA, ONTARIO. Ottawa station is located on the southeastern outskirts of Ottawa, east of the Rideau River at Hurdman's Bridge near the access crosstown Queensway/Alta Vista Drive interchange, approximately two miles from downtown. VIA CN provides chartered bus service between the station and downtown Ottawa and Hull in conjunction with all CN train arrivals and departures.

CN CENTRAL STATION, MONTREAL, QUEBEC. The heart of this complex embraces 24 acres in the center of the metropolis. Linked to Central Station, and larger than New York's Rockefeller Center, is a mammoth complex known as Place Ville Marie. Near the northeast corner of the station is CN's own luxury Queen Elizabeth Hotel. It has 1,200 rooms and is operated by the Hilton, Canada, organization.

Immediately to the rear (south) is Place Bonaventure, an $80 million complex—one of the largest commercial centers in the world and, along with Place Ville Marie, one of the most famous projects in Quebec. To the south is another luxury hotel, the Chateau Champlain. An underground passageway connects the station to these major Montreal hotels as well as to shopping plazas and the city's metro rapid transit system. The station also connects with CN's headquarters and regional office buildings, well-known features of the Montreal skyline. All told, some 112,-000 people pass through the station daily. Located beneath its football field-size concourse, some 78 regular passenger trains leave and enter the station's 23 tracks daily. Fifty-two of them are commuter trains, which handle approximately 22,000 passengers a day.

Central Station boasts multiple facilities. Anything you might need is there. In addition to the bright general waiting room, there are ticket and sleeping car wickets; a travel bureau; information counter; traveler's aid facilities; ladies' washroom and waiting room; men's washroom; barber shop; shoeshine and repair service; several restaurants and lunch counters; newsstands; flower shop and kiosque; tourist bureau; brasserie; cocktail lounge; cheese shop; coin shop; souvenir shops; fruit and vegetable shops; doughnut shop; ladies' sundry facility; an epicurean shop for the gourmet; bank; drugstore; candy shops; book store; photographic supply outlet; radio and record shop; and two ice-cream parlors.

The post office occupies a large portion of the sub-track level used for handling inward and outward bound mail sacks. There are express facilities and a baggage room where incoming and outgoing heavy luggage is handled. Offices of Canadian and United States customs services are located here. In addition to these large facilities, the basement contains many offices for the transaction of purely interdepartmental railway business, garage facilities, express motor lorries and sleeping and dining car facilities.

Above the station concourse there are office floors connected with the concourse by elevators and stairways at the east and west ends of the building. These are offices of Canadian National Railways departments engaged in the operation of the station or of the train services using it.

UNION STATION, TORONTO, ONTARIO. Located on Front Street west in downtown Toronto, Union Station was opened in 1927 by the late Duke of Windsor, then Prince of Wales. The station is owned by Canadian National and CP Rail and operated by the Toronto Terminals Railway Company.

Union Station houses six restaurants, two of which are licensed, several gift shops, a drug store, cleaners and a liquor store. Passageways from the lower level of the station lead to Canadian Pacific's Royal York Hotel, Toronto Transit Commission's metropolitan subway system, and government of Ontario's commuter service, called GO Transit. More than 23,000 passengers ride GO Transit trains in and out of Union Station each day. A total of 120 passenger trains, 70 intercity and 50 GO Transit, are operated out of the station every 24 hours. More than

3,000 persons work in offices in the basement and on the four floors of Union Station. In addition to the Royal York, many other large hotels are located within walking distance of the station.

CN'S MONCTON STATION, NEW BRUNSWICK. The CN station in Moncton is located in the heart of the city and is served by Air Cab taxi service. There is also public bus transit service in Moncton with the nearest stop from the station less than a five-minute walk away on Main street. The building is a modern-style structure opened in 1963 as part of a development program for 25 acres of CN-owned land in downtown Moncton.

The single-story structure has waiting room space on two levels to accomodate 137 people. The nearest major hotel (approx. five minutes by cab) is CN's Hotel Beausejour which has more than 200 rooms. This facility has numerous excellent dining facilities to suit every taste, from its coffee shop to the Windjammer dining room noted for its haute cuisine. There are other excellent restaurants in the city, including CY's Seafood and a more recent addition, Poppa Joe's. Both are located within a 10 or 15 minute walk from the station. One of the most widely known entertainment outlets in the city is the Cloud 9 cabaret operated by Hotel Beausejour, located 20 stories atop an adjoining office tower.

CN'S HALIFAX STATION, NOVA SCOTIA. The CN station is located in the south end of the city on Halifax harbor, and was constructed back in the late 1920's. It is connected to CN's Hotel Nova Scotian, the largest convention hotel in Atlantic Canada. The hotel has an assortment of excellent dining facilities, including the famous L'Evangeline Room. The station is served by station cab and the city boasts an excellent transit system with several stops in close proximity to the station.

CN STATION, VANCOUVER, B.C.. CN Station Vancouver is located at Main Street and Terminal Avenue about one-and-one-half miles from downtown Vancouver. There is a small park in front of the station—Thornton Park—maintained by the Vancouver Parks Board. Two good steak houses are within walking distance, Kejacs and Station Street Warehouse. Both are licensed but do not have cocktail bars. A good Italian restaurant, Puccini's, is located about three city blocks away and has an interesting little cocktail lounge. Chinatown is about half a mile away, with a multitude of Chinese curio shops and restaurants. Gastown, a reconstructed part of early Vancouver with shops, bars, and restaurants, is about a mile away. Cara operates a fast-food cafeteria in the station.

There are no major hotels nearby, the closest being in downtown Vancouver, about one-and-one-half miles away. Pacific Stage Lines buses meet incoming and outgoing passenger trains for the convenience of passengers traveling to and from Vancouver Island points. These buses transfer passengers to the local bus depot about a mile away. Both Amtrak and CN use the Vancouver station.

The main floor consists of a concourse, ticket office, information booth, barber shop, baggage room. waiting room and baggage lockers. The upper two floors house CN administrative offices. There is sixty minute free parking for CN customers, but there is no nearby facility to store automobiles for passengers who wish to leave their autos here while on a trip.

CN STATION, WINNIPEG, MANITOBA. CN's station in Winnipeg is only a short block from Hotel Fort Garry and within walking distance of another six hotels. There is a free "dash" service (bus) around the downtown loop from 9 A.M. to 4 P.M. Monday through Friday, and both Hotel Fort Garry and the CN station are regular stops on its route.

Rather far from the station, but worth a special trip, is *La Vieille Gare* (The Old Station), a charming restaurant located in the former station. A railway car abuts the station, serving as a cocktail lounge. You'll find an excellent French menu, moderate prices, and good service.

SASKATOON STATION, SASKATCHEWAN. CN's passenger terminal in Saskatoon was opened in 1964. It is about four miles from downtown, and is served by public transit and taxi service. There is a restaurant in the station building. The one-story terminal is similar in size to the former downtown depot. With the contemporary design of the new station, the accent is on contrasting bright colors for the exterior and interior with extensive areas of glass for maximum use of natural light in the concourse. Viewing the site at a distance from either the north or south, the structure appears as two concrete buildings joined by another which is slightly higher and predominantly of glass construction.

The glass-enclosed concourse is flanked on the east side by baggage and ticket facilities and on the west by a restaurant, rendezvous areas and washrooms. A progressive feature is a self-service system for picking up checked baggage. Passengers coming off a train go to the baggage room to pick out their checked luggage from racks. Control is established at the exit point leading back into the concourse where a baggage staff member checks stubs. Incoming passenger luggage is processed in the usual manner over the baggage counter.

CN STATION, EDMONTON, ALBERTA. CN'S Edmonton station is located on the lower level of the 26-story CN building at 10004–104 Avenue. Opened in 1966, the building also houses a barber shop, coffee shop, newsstand and gift shop on the station level; a bank and gift shop on the mezzanine level; and a cafeteria, cocktail lounge and dining lounge on the 5th floor.

The three major Edmonton downtown hotels (Hotel Macdonald, Edmonton Plaza and Chateau Lacombe) are within five blocks of the station. A rapid transit station (due for completion in 1978) (underground) is now being contructed one block east of the station. The station is also served by Edmonton transit buses, and is only 2 blocks from the downtown shopping district. Taxis and private cars enter and leave the terminal by means of side ramps. They load and unload passengers and baggage under cover at the entrance to the terminal concourse. A redcap station is located adjacent to the driveway and a call button and telephone connect the redcaps with the taxi stand that serves the building.

The station concourse is laid out around a circular hub that houses ticket wickets and an information counter. Train arrival and departure times are shown on an illuminated panel on the wall of the hub as well as on three closed-circuit TV monitors placed in strategic locations. The station's public address system is connected to the fifth floor dining and lounge facilities.

CREDIT VALLEY RAILROAD. Sponsored by the Ontario Rail Association, the Credit Valley includes regularly scheduled excursions on seven miles of unused Canadian National track running from Georgetown to near Cheltenham, Ontario. Typical of Canadian branchline of the 1930s, railway headquarters are at Cheltenham Park in the Township of Chinguacousy. Here, the locomotive and cars of the Credit Valley Railway are serviced and stored during the operating season. A museum displays railway artifacts.

PINAFORE PARK. Located at St. Thomas in Southern Ontario, Pinafore Park operates two narrow-gauge steam locomotives. Built in 1926 at the Montreal Locomotive Works, they were used in Nova Scotia and Ontario until 1957. In 1961 they were brought to St. Thomas, where they have remained, being used short trips through a wooded area in the 90-acre park. The locomotives operate weekends from May to October, and passengers ride in two coaches, both originally open streetcars built before 1900. The larger of the two came from the Seaview Railway in Atlantic City; the smaller was built in 1897 by the Toronto Transportation Commission.

THE PRAIRIE DOG CENTRAL RAILROAD. Operated by the Vintage Locomotive Society in Winnipeg, Manitoba, the Prairie Dog Central Railroad is a standard-gauge steam train. It operates, thanks to Canadian National Railways, over the Cabot Subdivision from Charleswood, on the western outskirts of Winnipeg, to Headingly, a return distance of 15 miles. The train runs from June to the end of September, Sundays only, and the trip takes about one hour. Three coaches carry up to 150 passengers at a time. The locomotive, known as Old Number 3, was built in 1882 in Glasgow, Scotland, for The Canadian Pacific Railway. The coaches, complete with cinders, are of turn-of-the-century, all-wood construction. When necessary, they are stove heated. Light refreshments are available.

HERITAGE PARK. Located in Calgary, Alberta, Heritage Park goes back to the pioneer days of Canada's West. A reconstructed 60-acre prairie settlement, the park has a general store; a Volunteer Fire Hall; an elegant Calgary home of the late 1880s; St. Martin's Church, which opened in 1896; and the former Canadian Pacific Midnapore Railway Station, where visitors board a train for a one-mile circular trip around the park. The journey lasts less than 20 minutes. The engine was built for the CPR and pressed into first service at Ignace, Ontario in 1905 as No. 6144. It was donated to the park by Canmore Mines. One of the coaches is an old colonist car dating back to 1905, used by CPR to carry immigrants across the prairies to their new homes in the west.

The pride of Heritage Park, however, is certainly the Dunvegan business car. This car carried top rail officials to the driving of the last spike at Craigellachie, B.C. in 1885!

Midnapore Station was donated to Heritage Park by CPR. It was a typical class five station located in early years approximately 15 miles south of Calgary. As the story goes, at one time the area was known as Fish Creek, but villagers of Fish Creek were not enamoured with this rather commonplace name. The postmaster of the village received a letter from Midnapore in India, and thinking this a much more romantic sounding name, the village adopted the new name.

CALGARY. Near the Calgary Tourist Office stands No. 5934, one of 35 giant locomotives built for the Canadian Pacific Railway to challenge the roller coaster country that is the main line over the Rocky and Selkirk Mountains between Calgary and Revelstoke, B. C. Known to railroaders as the Selkirks, they were in service between 1929 and the early 1950s, when they bowed out to be replaced by diesels.

In their day, the Selkirks were the biggest locomotives in the British Commonwealth. The driving wheels measure five feet, three inches. From pilot to the back of the tender is a distance of 98 feet and the height is 15½ feet. Loaded weight of the engine in service was 447,000 pounds, and of the tender, 284,000 pounds. An oil burner, she carried 4,100 Imperial gallons of oil and 12,000 Imp. gallons of water to do her job over one of the world's most rugged stretches of railroad. This, the 5934, second last of the series, stands here, facing the mountains she was built to conquer, in tribute to that exciting era of steam railroading when Calgary was "the place where they put on the big engines."

ALBERTA PIONEER RAILWAYS ASSOCIATION. The only Northern Alberta Railways steam locomotive in existence is operated by the Alberta Pioneer Railways Association in Edmonton. Number 73 runs two daily excursions during Canadian long weekends, May through September. Admission to this two-city-block ride is free, but donations to the Association are welcomed. Since its founding in 1967 as a non-profit society, the Alberta Pioneer Railways Association has worked to preserve and operate historic railroad equipment. Two other steam locomotives, a diesel, plus combination coach-baggage cars, caboose, baggage car, steam crane and numerous freight cars comprise the main collection. Smaller pieces of rolling stock include a motor car, pump hand cars and velocipedes.

VICTORIA PACIFIC RAILROAD. The first private company to run steam locomotive excursions in Canada, the Victoria Pacific Railway, began operating in the summer of 1972. Passengers enjoy a five-mile journey along Canadian National tracks on the outskirts of Victoria, British Columbia. Tour runs from May to the first week in September, daily except Monday and Tuesday. The locomotive is a Mikado-type built in 1929, now owned by the West Coast Railway Association and leased to Victoria Pacific. Passenger cars include two former Canadian Pacific coaches built in 1930 and 1931 and one private business car built in 1890.

COWICHAN VALLEY RAILROAD. Just 36 miles from Victoria on Vancouver Island, and one mile outside Duncan, British Columbia, the Cowichan Valley Railroad operates narrow-gauge steam trains on weekends, May through September. A one-and-a-half mile loop runs through a forested area of the Cowichan Valley Forest. There are three steam locomotives, and coaches are open platform steel.

FORT STEEL HISTORIC PARK. Situated in the southeastern part of British Columbia, about 50 miles north of the U.S. border, the park represents a turn-of-the-century pioneer settlement and has a 20-minute, two-and-a-half mile train ride through the grounds of the museum village. The standard-gauge 35-ton Dunrobin, 0-4-4T locomotive was built at the Atlas Works in Glasgow, Scotland, in 1895. Originally built for the private train of the Duke of Sutherland, it was retired to Kent, England, in 1950, but was kept in working order. In 1965, it was moved to Victoria and used by the British Columbia Government during Canada's 1967 centennial celebrations. Later that year it was moved to Fort Steel. Passengers ride weekends, May and June, and daily July to early September, in a saloon coach and British Railways standard passenger car.

For more specific information about Canadian railroads write:

Newfoundland & Labrador Tourist
  Development Office,
Confederation Building,
ST. JOHN'S, Newfoundland

Department of Tourist Development,
Prince Edward Travel Bureau,
CHARLOTTETOWN, Prince Edward Island

Nova Scotia Travel Bureau,
5670 Spring Garden Road,
HALIFAX, Nova Scotia

Department of Natural Resources,
Travel and Tourist Development Branch,
796 Queen Street (P.O. Box 1030),
FREDERICTON, New Brunswick

Department of Tourism, Fish and Game,
Tourism Branch,
930 St. Foy Road,
QUEBEC, Quebec

Department of Tourism & Information,
185 Bloor Street East,
TORONTO 5, Ontario

Department of Tourism and Recreation,
408 Norquay Building,
401 York Avenue,
WINNIPEG 1, Manitoba

Tourist Development Branch,
Saskatchewan Industry Department,
Power Building,
REGINA, Saskatchewan

Alberta Government Travel Bureau,
1629 Centennial Building,
EDMONTON 15, Alberta

Department of Travel Industry,
VICTORIA, British Columbia

TRAVELARCTIC,
Tourist Development Section,
YELLOWKNIFE, Northwest Territories

Department of Travel and Information,
P.O. Box 2703,
WHITEHORSE, Yukon Territory

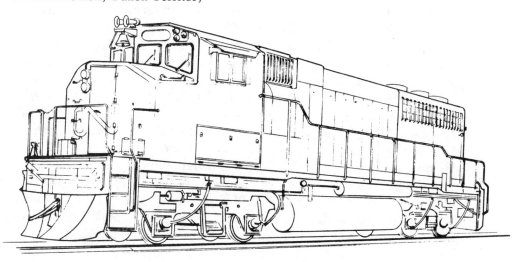

MEXICO

Trains in Mexico are incredibly old, intolerably slow, and, like everything else in that colorful confetti swirl South of the Border, infinitely charming and delightful. Bands of mariachis climb aboard at major station stops singing "Quando Caliente El Sol," and peddlers come up the aisles with buckets of ice-cold Carta Blanca and steaming green-corn tamales still fresh in their husks. Porters hustle about looking much like the comic Cantinflas, probably the best known and most beloved character in all of Latin America; the SARGARDOR, or porter's, typical costume has been his trademark for the past 40 years—pants on the verge of falling down, a battered felt hat, a faded, long-sleeved undershirt and a tattered vest treated with the utmost care and respect. The parlor car you're sitting in with the red plush-velvet seats and shiny brass trim might just be the very one that brought Pancho Villa north to Sonora for the first time, and who really cares if the train it's attached to left the Hermosillo station three hours late? (It left an hour early the day before.)

It goes without saying that if you're a stickler for hair-splitting schedules and crackling service, you'd better forget about train travel in Mexico. But if you want to see the country up close, enjoy its sunny conviviality at prices low enough to look like misprints, there's no better way than by train.

With few exceptions, all rail routes in Mexico are centered—coming and going—in Mexico City, and follow more often than not routes originally set down by the ancient Aztecs. Mexico City is the oldest city in the Western Hemisphere, and the largest. Major U.S. rail gateways into Mexico with connecting Amtrak service are Laredo, Texas (via the *Inter-American* from St. Louis) and El Paso (via the *Sunset Limited*). Other gateways, without connecting U.S. rail service, are Nogales (opposite Nogales, Arizona), Ojinaga (Presidio, Texas) and Mexicali (opposite Calexico, California). Service *through* Mexico is possible with a switch in Mexico City to the train for Tapachula (via Veracruz) which leaves Mexico City's Buenavista Central Station nightly at 8:42. From Tapachula, it's possible to make rail connections across the border in Guatemala, after a nightmare of stopovers and overnights, with the smaller-gauge International Railways of Central America for Guatemala City and points beyond. In other words, it's possible to hop on a train somewhere in Canada, pick up the *Southwest Limited* in Chicago, change at St. Louis for the *Inter-American* for Laredo and continue on across Mexico into Central America. Possible, but that's stretching one's affinity for train travel to the absolute limit! Even mariachi music loses its appeal after all that.

Mexico's more than 13,000 miles of railroad track are utilized by a number of different lines. The government-owned National Railways of Mexico (N de M) is the largest. Others are the Pacific Railroad, Chihuahua Pacific, Sonora-Baja California Railroad and the United Southeastern Railway. Through pullman service to Mexico City is available from all of the gateway cities. An express pullman from Mexicali to Mexico City makes the daily run in each direction in just over 44 hours. The regular Mexicali and Nogales pullman, joining at Benjamin Hill, is much slower. Amtrak's *Inter-American* just makes the Nuevo Laredo connection for the Mexico City-bound *Aztec Eagle,* providing the former is on time. (The trains connect conveniently northbound, however.) A series of planning conferences are also being held between Amtrak, National Railways of Mexico, U.S. and Mexican Customs and Immigrations officials for the purpose of establishing through-train service. U.S. passengers wishing to travel to the interior of Mexico by train must now de-train in Laredo, cross the border by Amtrak-provided bus or contract taxi and board the Mexican train in Nuevo Laredo. In its national timetable, Amtrak makes note of its desire for an international connection at Nuevo Laredo, but advises, "however, until track improvements are completed, this connection is not reliable."

Certain garages in both Laredo and El Paso specialize in storing tourist automobiles for an extended length of time at special rates.

Tours

Escorted tours into Mexico by rail, particularly from the Pacific Coast, are offered by a number of tour operators. Typical is Great Western Tours' 23-night rail package departing San Francisco and Los Angeles (passengers can also entrain in Phoenix, Tucson and El Paso). Accommodations include berths, roomettes, compartments and drawing rooms. A social hostess organizes fun and games. The firm uses its own private pullman cars and features its own dining service. En route to Mexico City, the train stops for sightseeing in Mazatlan, an overnight at the Camino Real in Guadalajara, plus visits to Lake Chapala, the pottery-making town of Tlaquepaque, and to Patzcuaro and Morelia. Three nights in Mexico City are spent at the Maria-Isabel-Sheraton, and so on, including nights in the tropics, Veracruz, and a visit to the Mayan pyramids at Chichen Itza and Uxmal in the

Yucatan. Rates, all-inclusive except for a few off-train meals, begin at $1,310. For information, contact: Great Western Tours, Sheraton Palace Hotel, San Francisco, Calif., 94105.

Another popular tour is Continental Trailways' "Railway in the Sky" 10-day bus and train excursion from El Paso, Texas, to Chihuahua, Mexico, where groups board the Chihuahua Pacific and cross the Sierra Madre Mountains through the "Grand Canyons" of Mexico, ending up in Los Mochis on the Pacific in one of the most unique railway rides anywhere. It includes traveling roller coaster style through 86 tunnels and across 39 trestles. From there, the tour goes north by bus to Hermosillo, Nogales, Tucson, and back to El Paso. The guided excursion includes a welcoming cocktail party in Mexico, seven meals, farewell dinner, hotels, transfers, tips and most admissions. Tour price per person from and back to El Paso is $427.50 for a single; $381.75 double. For information brochure, contact Continental Trailways.

From Nuevo Laredo

AZTEC EAGLE, is the fastest train from the border leaving Nuevo Laredo daily 7:10 P.M., arriving Mexico City the following night at 8:04. Return trip leaves Mexico City 8:10 A.M., arriving Nuevo Laredo 6:25 A.M., where, because of the early hour, passengers may stay on the train up to an additional hour. The *Aztec Eagle* consists mostly of vintage American pullman cars and has a dome observation car going back to the Chicago Railroad days with plush, red lining on the seats and everything inside but spittoons. Dining car service is excellent, and reasonable ($2 for a complete chicken dinner), but two Scotch and sodas will set you back $8. Here, as anywhere in Mexico, it is wise to avoid imported wines and liquors which are heavily taxed. When in Rome, drink tequila!

From Ciudad Juarez

EL FRONTERIZO leaves Ciudad Juarez daily at 7:10 P.M., arriving in Mexico City at 6:55 A.M. the second morning. Return leaves Mexico City at 7:50 in the evening and arrives in Cuidad Juarez at 5:35 A.M. the second morning, where, again because of the early arrival, passengers in sleeping cars may stay aboard until 7:15 A.M. Train is operated by the National Railways of Mexico, and, along with full sleeping facilities, it has dining car, observation lounge and unreserved coach seats. Passengers connecting from or with Amtrak's *Sunset Limited* at El Paso and Ciudad Juarez must make own arrangements for crossing the border, usually by taxi. However, the Mexican National Railroad passenger agents in Ciudad Juarez and El Paso are usually happy to give assistance with this—they are fully bilingual. Contact *A. Barraza S.,* Foreign Agent, Passenger Station, Cuidad Juarez, Chih. (Mexico) Tel 2–2557 (Cd. Juarez). Address: P.O. Box 2200, El Paso, Texas, for information and assistance.

Trains from Ciudad Juarez to Chihuahua leave daily at 5 P.M., arriving 4 hours later. Return train leaves Chihuahua at 8 A.M.

From Monterrey

EL REGIOMONTANO, an all-pullman train to Mexico City, departs daily at 6 P.M., arriving in the capital at 9 the next morning. Return trip departs Mexico City at 6 P.M. arriving Monterrey at 9 A.M. Train has dining car and observation lounge car.

From Nogales and Mexicali

PACIFIC RAILROAD has a daily pullman departure from Nogales at 5 P.M., with dining car, coaches and full sleeping facilities, which arrives in Mexico City at 8:47 A.M. the second day. Another train leaves Nogales daily at 7 A.M. and connects at Benjamin Hill with the *Sonora-Baja RR's* daily departures from Mexicali (8:45 the evening before) and together they arrive in Mexico City two mornings later. An express pullman also leaves Mexicali daily for Mexico City and makes the run in about 44 hours. On the return, Train 5 with through Mexicali pullman departs Mexico City for Guadalajara 8:30 P.M. each day, arriving 8:10 A.M. the next day, departing 9:10 A.M. on *Pacific Railroad,* arriving Benjamin Hill the following day. The train leaves Benjamin Hill at 7:40 A.M. to arrive in Mexicali at 12:35 (P.T.) that night. Nogales passengers depart Benjamin Hill 7:10 P.M., arriving in Nogales 9:35 A.M. (P.T.). There is also a noon departure north from Guadalajara, arriving in Nogales at 11:30 P.M. the following night and Mexicali 5:20 A.M. the morning after that. The regular Mexicali-Benjamin Hill pullman is antiquated, to say the least. There's no dining car and because the train frequently runs out of distilled water, it's best to bring your own supply along. No problem after making the Nogales train connection at Benjamin Hill or on the express.

General Information and Advice on Rail Travel

Reserve your pullman space as early as possible to the Mexican point of destination. Although there is no price reduction, buy a round-trip ticket immediately if you intend to return by rail. (Round trip is twice the one-way fare.) This saves later time standing in line in, for instance, the Mexico City railroad station, which is always busy. There are no family plan rail rates in Mexico.

Central Standard Time is observed throughout the entire system of Mexican National Railways.

Limit on round-trip tickets. Tickets purchased in Mexico have a limit of 30 days and are sold at double the one-way fare.

Adjustment of fares. Should any misunderstanding arise with conductors, train auditors, or ticket agents, pay the fare requested, request a receipt, and send it to *Sr O. Gutierrez de Velasco P.,* Chief Passenger Traffic Department, Mexican National Railways, Buenavista Grand Central Station, Mexico City 3, D.F.

Redemption of tickets. Unused or partly used tickets issued by the Mexican National Railways will be redeemed under existing tariff regulations. Communicate with *Sr. O. Gutierrez de Velasco P.,* Chief Passenger Traffic Department, at the address given above.

Loss of tickets. Passengers should guard against such loss, as railroads assume no responsibility.

Children. Under 5 years of age free when accompanied by parent or guardian; 5 years of age and under 12, half-fare; 12 and over full fare.

Stopovers. Permitted at any point en route on first-class local tickets but ticket clerk should be notified of intention at time of purchase, so he may endorse the tickets accordingly. A maximum of 15 days is allowed in connection with one-way but they should be validated in station at stopover point to enable holder to continue trip.

Air-conditioning. All pullman, deluxe *Autovia* equipment, dining cars, lounges and most reserved seat coaches are air-conditioned. Coaches generally are not.

Assignment of pullman space from stations other than those from which passengers board trains. When pullman accommodations are requested from a station that has no regularly assigned space for sale, or if such space has been sold out, corresponding rail and sleeping car fares will be assessed from point from which reservation is made.

Minimum ticket requirements for occupancy of space in sleeping cars: Seat—One adult ticket; Berth, upper or lower—One adult ticket each;

(One adult and one half-fare child can occupy a section—upper and lower—at no additional rail fare.)

Roomette—One adult ticket; Bedroom, single or double—Two adult tickets; Two bedrooms in suite—Four adult tickets; Drawing Room—Three adult tickets.

(Note: A section of upper and lower can be sold to one passenger at single occupancy rate by pullman conductor *on board* only.)

Checking of baggage. Mexican National Railways will handle checked baggage to any and all points on its system. When traveling southbound, passengers may check their baggage either at Nuevo Laredo or Ciudad Juarez. Baggage from points within Mexico should be checked northbound only to Nuevo Laredo and Ciudad Juarez. For the information of passengers into and out of Mexico through the El Paso-Ciudad Juarez gateway, the Southern Pacific has discontinued the handling of checked baggage on all its trains. The general passenger agents for Mexican National Railways at Nuevo Laredo and Ciudad Juarez will give assistance with baggage upon request. Customs inspection of all baggage, including that checked, is made before boarding. No checked baggage is accepted on the Ciudad Juarez—Chihuahua *Autovia.*

Baggage allowance. Free allowance of 110 pounds for each adult and 55 pounds for each half-fare child.

Definition of baggage. Personal wearing apparel, toilet articles except liquids, and other personal effects in actual use and necessary for the comfort and convenience of the passenger. The following must not be included in checked baggage: money, jewelry, negotiable papers and similar valuables, fragile or perishable articles, radios, phonographs, records, household goods.

Pullman hand baggage. Restricted to what can be conveniently placed in berth, bedroom, or seat occupied by passenger.

Parcel room facilities. At railroad terminals in Ciudad Juarez, Guadalajara, Mexico City (Buenavista station), Monterrey, Nuevo Laredo, and Veracruz, parcel room facilities are provided for the temporary storing of luggage, packages, etc. This is completely apart from the regular checking facilities for baggage to go on trains.

Dogs and other small pets can be transported in baggage cars (extra charge), provided you have proper veternarian's certificate attesting to anti-rabies vaccination.

Red Cap porter service. Available at stations in all larger cities. At the Buenavista Grand Central station in Mexico City, porter rates are approximately the following (proportionately more at northern border stations, less at other inland stations):

From 1 to 3 pieces, 4 pesos (32¢ U.S.) each service.

Four or 5 pieces, 6.50 pesos (52¢) each service.

For keeping special watch or guarding baggage, 2 pesos (16¢) each piece.

Wheelchair service from taxi to train or vice versa, including the transporting of hand baggage, 26 pesos ($2.08).

The Mexico City railroad terminal, known as the Buenavista Central Station, is modern, spacious, impressive. Bilingual clerks man the information bureau, tel: 547-1084, 547-1097, 547-6593. Reservations and requests for information may also be made by phone to Sr. J. Sanchez Mendes, Ass't Chief Passenger Traffic Dept., tel: 547-8972, who speaks English well. Ticket windows open 6:30 A.M. -9:30 P.M. daily. Downtown ticket office on Bolivar St. has been closed.

The Buenavista station has an upper-level restaurant bar with good food and service, a lower-level food counter with stools. Both are exceptionally clean and well maintained, the food simple and reasonably priced. A new service feature offered by the lower-level restaurant is a bountiful box lunch for about $1.50 (18.75 pesos). Both restaurants are open to 10 P.M. daily.

Important: The taxis serving the Buenavista station often try to charge more than the going service rate, although city authorities crack down on them periodically. Fare to any downtown hotel should be no more than 20 pesos, to a residential section 30, and to an outlying area 50. More often than not they will try to charge double these rates from both Mexicans and foreign visitors. Ask the rate *before* you get in the taxi. If the rate sounds too high and you're not too weary to argue, offer him the correct fare as stated above. If he wants your business, he'll finally agree. Memo: Night taxi rates are usually 10 pesos higher than during the day.

Mexican railroads pay no commission to travel agents on tickets or rail travel arrangements, so few agents keep on hand more than a small amount of rail information. This is a definite oversight on the railroad's part, as rail side trips out of Mexico City (and the spectacular Chihuahua-Pacific Railroad run over the high Sierras from Chihuahua) constitute one of the most delightful ways to see the Mexican countrysides. However, if offered a fee (15 percent of the fare), most travel agencies will obtain railroad tickets and provide the necessary information. Otherwise, it is necessary for travelers to obtain reservations and tickets at the railroad station itself. Most, if not all, railroad employees speak only Spanish. Because agent data is sparse, here are some additional railroad information offices in Mexico *(Mexican National Railways):*

Aguascalientes—Hotel Francia, Madero and Plaza Principal, tel: 5–60–80.

Chihuahua, Chih.—Hotel Presidente, corner Provincial del Norte Bank Bldg. and Juarez Ave., tel. 2–33–19.

Chihuahua. Chih.—Chihuahua Pacific RR, corner Mendez and 14th Sts.

Ciudad Juarez—Hotel San Carlos, Av. Juarez 126 Norte, tel: 2–7680, 2–7681.

Guadalajara—Colon Ave. corner of P. Sanchez St., tel: 13–62–87.

Leon, Gto.—Nuevo Hotel Condesa, Portal Bravo 14, tel: 3–1120.

Monterrey—Hotel Colonial, Hidalgo 475 Oriente, tel: 43–32–95.

Uruapan, Mich.—Hotel Mexico, Portal Matamoros 15, tel: 2–06–15.

Veracruz, Ver.—Hotel Imperial, tel: 2–70–03.

Address of the Buenavista Central Station *(Estacion Central de Buenavista)* in Mexico City is Insurgentes Norte, Mexico 3, D. F. From Continental Hotel—be sure you follow it north *(norte),* not south *(sur).* Information and passenger agent telephone numbers were previously given

Pacific Railroad has an office at the Central Administration Building, Av. Central 140 (near the Buenavista station), tel: 541–4134. Also, a passenger agent at Internacional 10, Nogales.

Sonora-Baja California Railway, Chihuahua-Pacific Railroad, United Yucatan Railroads have representatives in Mexico City at the Secretaria de Comunicaciones y Transportes, Xola and Av. Universidad, Wing H, 6th floor, tel: 519–6404, 530–7648.

Additional rail entry point from the U.S.

The *Chihuahua-Pacific Railroad* operates a tri-weekly diesel *Autovia* train from Ojinaga (across from Presidio, Texas) and a twice-weekly pullman to Chihuahua that make direct connections with its pullman or *Autovia* trip over the Sierras to Los Mochis. (See separate later section, *The Copper Canyon Route,* with suggested onward trips.) Entry via the Ojinaga gateway will allow a sightseeing stopover in Chihuahua, the center of Mexico's prime cattle-raising region, city of good steaks, and former home of General Pancho Villa, before continuing on to Los Mochis. Prices of through tickets given in above-mentioned section. *Autovia* schedule: Leave Ojinaga 4 P.M., arrive Chihuahua 8:05 P.M. Return: Leave Chihuahua 8:30 A.M., arrive Ojinaga 12:25 P.M.

The *Autovia* arrival time in Chihuahua makes a direct connection with pullman over the Sierras, or a one-night (or more for sightseeing purposes) layover in order to take the early morning departure of the picture-windowed *Autovia,* which makes one run daily through the Copper Canyon country.

For full information and folders write: *F. J. Saenz C.,* Gen. Traffic Mgr., Chihuahua-Pacific Railroad, Apartado 46, Chihuahua, Chih., Mexico, tel: 2-3867.

NOTE. All information given throughout this section is *subject to change without notice.*

Around Mexico By Train.

Mexico City is a perfect base from which to take side rail trips into provincial Mexico—the difference between this sophisticated megalopolis and the colonial cities such as Puebla, Guanajuato, and San Miguel Allende is akin to the difference between night and day. By rail you can take a giant step from the present into the fascinating past. All departures from Buenavista station, except as noted.

To Puebla. *Autovia* rail service to Puebla has been canceled.

To Guanajuato and San Miguel de Allende. The Mexican National Railways has discontinued service to Guanajuato and San Miguel de Allende. The rails are now used only by the various train tours originating at the U.S. border.

To Morelia, Patzcuaro, Uruapan. This route offers a morning and an evening departure. The former is definitely recommended to enjoy the beauty of pastoral Michoacan, the most charmingly scenic state in all Mexico.

Morelia is a favorite weekending city and Mexican National Railways runs a special Friday evening sleeper of 12 roomettes and 4 double bedrooms, returning to Mexico City Sundays.

To Veracruz. The overnight pullman is all right if you just want to reach Veracruz and have a good night's sleep along the way, but the best idea is the daylight trip departing Mexico City 7:34 A.M., allowing views of the highly scenic countrysides, including Mexico's highest volcano, the majestic Orizaba.

Unfortunately, the dining car has been taken off this run, so it's a good idea to buy one of the tasty box lunches for $1.50 on the lower level of the Buenavista railroad station before departure.

To Oaxaca. This is an overnight rail trip with no diner—again provide yourself with a box lunch. Roomettes and bedrooms.

To Guadalajara. An overnight fun trip on a deluxe pullman with diner and lounge car, depart Mexico City 8:30 P.M., arrive 8:10 A.M. Also 6:05 evening departure, arriving 7:38 A.M., and an all-coach, non-air-conditioned 7:08 A.M. departure arriving 9 P.M. Returns leave Guadalajara 6:45 and 8:55 P.M.. The all-coach train is 7:45 A.M. Guadalajara is a major rail center. There is also daily and tri-weekly service from Manzanillo plus the two trains a day from Nogales. The fastest trains from Mexico City and Manzanillo are the overnight expresses, which, in Manzanillo's case, is the tri-weekly carrier. The journey from Nogales takes either 26 or 34 hours, depending on which train you take.

Manzanillo is accessible by train, bus, and airline service. Train service is on the return portion of the Guadalajara run mentioned above.

To Merida, Yucatan. Daily pullman service is available to several of Mexico's most interesting southeast states—Veracruz, Tabasco, Campeche, and Yucatan, the heart of the ancient Maya civilizations. Stopovers can be made to visit the ruins at Palenque and go sightseeing in Campeche, but be sure to have your rail ticket issued in segments, i.e., Mexico City-Palenque, Palenque-Campeche, Campeche-

Merida. Good hotels in each site. From Merida be sure to take the sightseeing excursions to Uxmal and Chichen Itza.

This train departs the Buenavista station daily at 8:10 P.M., arriving Palenque 7:49 the next night, Campeche 5 A.M. the next morning, and Merida 8:35 A.M. Return train departs Merida 7:35 P.M., arriving Mexico City 9:15 A.M. the second morning.

A worthwhile side trip from Merida is to Isla Mujeres, the lovely tropical island lying in the Gulf. It's a 50-minute flight via a local feeder airline, or a pleasant drive by car on Highway 100 to Puerto Juarez and thence via ferry—5 a day, a 50-min. trip.

To Tapachula and Guatemala. From Veracruz a daily train departs 9:05 A.M. for Tapachula, Mexico's southernmost large city lying hard along the Guatemalan border. This is the same train that departs Mexico City 9:01 P.M. daily for Veracruz, carrying a through sleeper.

Many guidebooks tell you to take the train (after a stopover in Tapachula) on to Ciudad Hidalgo to cross the Guatemalan border to Ciudad Tecun Uman and make a connection with the *International Railways of Central America,* thence on to Guatemala City. On paper it looks simple; in actuality, it isn't recommended. The Tapachula-Ciudad Hidalgo train gets in 4:35 P.M., while the Central American train, which is narrow gauge, doesn't leave from across the border until 6 A.M. the next day. There is no adequate lodging in Ciudad Hidalgo, and the town across the border is worse—really out in the boondocks with unpaved streets, heat, dust, pigs, and other animals roaming at will. In addition, the railroad bridge crossing the border (which allows cars—one at a time) is over a mile long with a hefty toll charge.

Best to inquire at the *Loma Real Hotel* in Tapachula about bus or taxi service to the border at Ciudad Hidalgo—and even this is inconvenient because of the extremely early morning hour. Trying it is recommended only for the most adventuresome. The *Loma Real* personnel can also advise you about possible additional, improved service across the border in Guatemala.

In any event if you intend to visit Tapachula with a stopover in Veracruz, request your first-class rail ticket all the way through when purchasing it in Mexico City but advise the clerk of the stopover so he can endorse it accordingly.

Be sure, if you are going on into Guatemala, to have with you a smallpox vaccination certificate and a Guatemalan tourist card, which can be secured from the Embassy at Vallarta #1, 5th floor, Mexico City 4, D. F., tel: 546–4876.

The Bajio. Three trains a day go through San Juan del Rio and Queretaro on their way north. Tickets can be purchased at the Buenavista Station on Insurgentes Norte. There are no dining or club cars on the trains.

Oaxaca-Chiapas. Trains with pullman service leave every afternoon for Oaxaca, arriving the next morning. They are quite comfortable, but have no dining car. Palenque can also be reached by train.

Remote Campeche. Campache is 3½ hours from Merida via the daily Mexico City train that also passes through Palenque. To reach the latter from Villahermosa, you can take a bus or cab (200 pesos) to Teapa, 32 miles south, in time to board the 5:10 P.M. train for the 2½ hour ride.

The Yucatan. Mexico National Railways has joined with Yucatan's Unidos del Sureste to provide excellent, one-train, through service daily between Merida and Mexico City. Inexpensive pullman and dining-car service makes this 36-hour, 1,000-mile trip particularly attractive for the visitor who is not in a hurry. Merida is also connected by fast, self-propelled Autovia cars with Progreso; with Peto in the south, via Ticul; and with Compeche, three hours away via Becal and Calkini.

The Copper Canyon Route. The *Chihuahua-Pacific Railroad* is not long as most railroads go, but it has a well-deserved reputation of being the most scenic.

Originating in Ojinaga, across the Rio Grande from Presidio, Texas, it crosses the mighty Sierra Madres in the Mexican state of Chihuahua in a marvel of engineering skill that originally defeated a pair of American builders who started it. Mexican engineers finished the job.

This surprisingly little-known route provides one of the most exciting rail journeys the world has to offer, giving passengers a thrill a minute with its mile-high bridges and snaking, mountain-hugging rails. All trains stop at the summit to give a 20-minute view into distant Copper canyon. Those who have seen both term Mexico's canyons more spectacular than the Grand Canyon of the U.S.—and they are reputed to be four times as long.

The *Chihuahua-Pacific* has 86 tunnels—one almost a mile long—and 39 bridges, a true engineering masterpiece. Its tracks reach heights of over 8000 feet, it crosses the Continental Divide three times, and some of the canyons it "flies" over are more than a mile deep. On occasion one looks out the wide picture windows and sees nothing, feeling a distinct impression of flying through the air rather than riding safely on terra firma.

Passenger service extends from Ojinaga to Los Mochis in the Mexican state of Sinaloa, although the track goes on to the Pacific port of Topolobampo, this part is for cargo service only. The most scenic section lies between Chihuahua City and Los Mochis, about 410 miles of fascinating country—the rugged homeland of aborigine Indian tribes, including the Tarahumaras.

Two kinds of service link Ojinaga with Los Mochis, a distance of around 575 miles: 1) Italian-made *Fiat,* self-propelled diesel electric cars, in tandem, and 2) diesel-powered pullman trains. These offer buffet food service at passenger's seat.

The *Autovias* cover the Ojinaga-Chihuahua route Mon. and Wed., Sat. when demand warrants, and five times weekly from Chihuahua to Los Mochis. Ojinaga-Chihuahua time: 4 hrs.; Chihuahua-Los Mochis, 12 hrs. One-way Ojinaga-Chihuahua: reserved reclining seat, $5.85, chair coach, $4.85; one-way Chihuahua-Los Mochis: $10.92 reserved reclining seat, $9.05 regular coach seat.

Pullman trains traverse the full route from Ojinaga to Los Mochis twice a week (Tue-Fri) in 22 hrs., 16½ hrs. from Chihuahua. They stop 50 minutes in Chihuahua City en route. First-class fare Ojinaga-Los Mochis $13.32; roomette $13.50; bedroom $19.28, drawing room $36.63. First class fare Chihuahua-Los Mochis, $9.48. Occupation of a bedroom requires the purchase of two first-class tickets and a drawing room 3 tickets.

Cost for *shipping automobile* one-way Ojinaga-Los Mochis: $84 full freight charges per unit; from Chihuahua-Los Mochis, $68. Small automobiles such as Volkswagen, Renault, small Fiat and small Datsun are shipped at half these rates. Notice of intent to ship automobile must be given to *Chihuahua-Pacific Railroad Freight Office* at Chihuahua at least 2 days before intended departure date.

No checked baggage is handled on the *Autovias.* If desired, automobiles may be parked at lots in Presidio (Tex.) or at the depot parking lot in Ojinaga.

Autovia schedule over the Copper Canyon Route:

Mon-Tue-Thu-Fri-Sat	Sun-Tue-Wed-Fri-Sat
Lv. Chih. 8:00 A.M.	Lv. Mochis 8:00 A.M.
Ar. Mochis 8:20 P.M.	Ar. Chihuahua 8:40 P.M.

A luxury *Vistadome* train with a capacity of 160 passengers is operated on this run. It includes, besides the Vistadome car, two specially designed passenger coaches and an observation-dining car, drawn by a powerful diesel engine. The train leaves Chihuahua 8:20 A.M. every Monday, Thursday and Saturday, returning

Los Mochis to Chihuahua 7:20 A.M. each Tuesday, Friday and Sunday. One-way fare: $14.20, including tax.

Pullman schedules:

Lv. Ojinaga 3:00 P.M. CST Tue & Fri	Lv. Mochis 7:00 A.M. Mon & Thu
Ar. Chih. 9:00 P.M.	Ar. Chih. 12:50 A.M. Tue & Fri
Lv. Chih. 9:50 P.M.	Lv. Chih. 1:20 A.M.
Ar. Mochis 2:10 P.M. Wed & Sat	Ar. Ojinaga 6:20 A.M.

Those who would like to see the spectacular Copper Canyon country over again, in reverse, can return from Los Mochis to Chihuahua via the *Autovias* or the *Vistadome* train (better arrival time back in Chihuahua than the pullman), then make train connections on the Mexican National Railways into Mexico City.

Visitors who wish to go further into Mexico from Los Mochis but do not have their own car with them can rent a car or avail themselves of the excellent *Tres Estrellas de Oro* first class bus service into Mazatlan for a stopover, or on into Guadalajara which has a convenient overnight train connection into Mexico City. Feeder line air service by *Aeronaves del Oeste* is due for expansion.

For attractive folders in English on the Copper Canyon trip, schedules, and any late information, write: *Sr. F. J. Saenz C.* Chief, Traffic Dept. Chihuahua-Pacific RR, Apdo. Postal No. 46, Chihuahua, Chih., Mexico tel: 2-22-84 or 2-38-67.

Sr. Saenz is bilingual. Query him regarding the occasional rail tours out of the U.S. that incorporate the Copper Canyon trip in their itinerary. Wampler Tours, Berkeley, Calif., Midwest Travel Service, Oklahoma City, Okla., and Peck Rail Tours, Whittier, Calif. among them; your own travel agent may know of others.

Please note that all rates and schedules are subject to change without notice.

Copper Canyon Lodge. Located deep in the heart of the Tarahumara Indian country, about 15 miles from the Creel station of the Chihuahua-Pacific Railroad, the *Copper Canyon Lodge* is a unique hotel of 10 rooms with private baths, tile floors, hot and cold running water, heating, restaurant, and bar service. Management escorts informal tours to nearby Indian villages, waterfalls, warm-water springs, and mile-deep canyons. Horseback riding, rainbow trout fishing, and hunting available. Good for those who like to get away from the hustle and bustle of civilization.

For full information, rates, reservations, write via air mail to:

Copper Canyon Lodge	or
Apdo. No. 3	Santa Anita Hotel
Creel, Chihuahua, Mexico	Los Mochis, Sinaloa, Mexico

Hotel Divisadero. New and comfortable facility located at the highest point along the Chihuahua Pacific route from Chihuahua to Los Mochis. All the trains stop here for varying periods of time so passengers may enjoy the spectacular views and shop for Tarahumara Indian handicrafts and mementoes. Those who would like to stay over for a day to enjoy the scenery, the quiet, and the pure mountain air can continue their rail journey the next day. Rates: $34 U.S. double, full American Plan (3 meals). Reservations: Bolivar 303, Chihuahua, Chih., Mexico, tel: 2-33-62. By mail: PO Box 661, Chihuahua. Personnel speak English.

How To Request Sleeping Car Accommodations

Mexico's railroads regularly carry air-conditioned Pullman cars from Mexico-U.S. border points to Mexico City. Air-conditioned dining cars are also carried on through trains. To obtain pullman reservations, specify type of space desired (lower, roomette, bedroom, compartment) and direct your request to the passenger representative at the border gateway where you plan to enter the Republic of Mexico.

LAREDO

Mrs. Guadalupe Lopez
National Rys. of Mexico
P.O. Box 595
Laredo, Tex.

OW RR fare	$ 14.18
*OW Lower Berth	26.38
*OW Bedroom for 2	52.76

EL PASO

Mr. A. Barraza, Jr.
National Rys. of Mexico
P. O. Box 2200
El Paso, Texas 79951

OW RR fare	$ 22.08
*OW Lower berth	42.01
*OW Bedroom for 2	82.04

NOGALES

Mr. Francisco Hernandez
Ferrocarril del Pacificio
Calle Internacional No. 10
Nogales, Sonora - Mexico

OW RR fare	$ 24.51
*OW Roomette	57.74
*OW Bedroom for 2	96.49

For reservations from Mexicali (across Calexico), please address to Mr. J.M. Salgado, Traffic Manager, Sonora-Baja California Railway, U. Irigoyen & "F" Streets, Mexicali, B.C. - Mexico. One way rail fare $32.91, *roomette $72.65 and a *double bedroom $122.59. * Sleeping car fares shown include minimum railfare plus space charge.

For return Pullman space on the *National Railways of Mexico* and sleeping car reservations in the interior of the Republic, write to:

Mr. O. G. de Velasco, Chief
Passenger Traffic Department
National Railways of Mexico
Buenavista Central Station
Mexico 3, D. F. - Mexico Tel. 547–31–90

For information on the *Chihuahua al Pacifico* Railway, contact:

Mr. F. J. Saenz Colomo, T. M.
Ferrocarril Chihuahua al Pacifico

P. O. Box 46
Chihuahua, Chih. - Mexico Tel. 2-22-84

An interesting and convenient way to make the trip over the *Chihuahua al Pacifico* is to board the National Railways of Mexico Diesel Railcar leaving Ciudad Juarez daily at 5:00 P.M. to arrive at the city of Chihuahua 9:00 P.M. Spend the night in Chihuahua and leave the following morning (except Wednesdays and Sundays) at 7:00 A.M. on the Ch-P Diesel Railcar for an exciting all-day ride down to the Pacific, arriving at Los Mochis at 7:20 P.M. These are snack bar cars with picture windows. The NdeM fare from Ciudad Juarez to Chihuahua is $3.74 and the Ch-P fare from that point to Los Mochis comes to $14.20.

Fares are in approximate U.S. currency and for information only. Do not send money until your space has been confirmed.

Telephone number in Nuevo Laredo, Mex. 2-80-97. Telephone number in Ciudad Juarez 2-25-57.

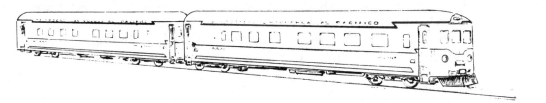

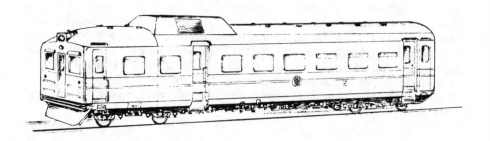

THE CARIBBEAN

Almost all major islands in the Caribbean and West Indies have small, narrow-gauge trains that are used for sugar cane harvesting, none of which takes passengers. Trinidad had passenger service out of Port of Spain at one time, but it was discontinued about nine years ago. The only surviving passenger railroads in the Caribbean are those in Jamaica and Cuba.

Jamaica—The Catadupa Choo-Choo

The Governor's Coach, or the Catadupa Choo-Choo, as it's more popularly known, consists of modern diesel coaches of the Jamaica Railway Corporation which leave Montego Bay daily at 9:30 A.M. for trips through Jamaica's colorful countryside. The train goes 40 miles into the interior, skirting sugar plantations, lush forests, vibrant villages and terminates at the Appleton rum distillery for a tour and sampling. Comfortable, spacious coaches are equipped with bar and kitchen. Many areas along the route are inaccessible by road. The train takes its nickname from one of the stops along the way, Catadupa, a tiny village famous for the colorful array of fabrics hanging on lines in the sun. The all-day excursion ends at about 5:30 P.M. when the Catadupa Choo-Choo chugs back into its two-story, curtain-windowed station at Montego Bay. Cost is $18.20 per person, including a picnic-style lunch, rum punches, an on-board calypso band and guide. Reservations for this popular, essentially tourist-oriented, run are required several days in advance and can be made through travel agents, hotel travel desks or Jamaica Tours in Montego Bay. Transfers between the train station and most Montego Bay hotels are included in the ticket.

Regular Service

A diesel train service runs between Montego Bay and Kingston and Kingston and Port Antonia every day in both directions. Fare to Montego Bay first class is about $3 (£1.67) one way; second class (all that's available) to Port Antonio, about $1 (56p) one way. The Kingston-Montego Bay train trip is a 4-½-hour kaleidoscope of the life and scenery of the Jamaican interior; from Kingston to Port Antonio - 3-½ hours.

Cuba

Rail information expected from Cuba was not received by press time.

SAVE MONEY!
BUY BEFORE YOU GO!

Railroads can offer lowest-cost travel per mile in Germany and the rest of Western Europe!
Plus outstanding comfort, convenience, dependability and frequency.

(1) EURAILPASS. Unlimited first-class travel in 13 countries: Austria, Belgium, Denmark, France, Germany, Holland, Italy, Luxembourg, Norway, Portugal, Spain, Sweden and Switzerland. More than 100,000 miles of track! Bargain passes for 15 or 21 days, 1, 2 and 3 months *must be purchased* before you go overseas.

(2) STUDENT-RAILPASS. Unlimited second-class rail travel in 13 above-listed countries at even lower rates for students under 26 years old at any North American educational institution. Pass *must be purchased* before you go overseas.

Get current rates, details and tickets for Eurailpass and Student-Railpass. And information on (1) special discounts for groups of ten or more in Germany, and (2) advantages of purchasing point-to-point tickets for European travel before you go overseas. SEE YOUR TRAVEL AGENT or contact: German Federal Railroad, 630 Fifth Ave., N.Y., N.Y. 10020, Phone: (212) 977-9300.

Germanrail
GERMAN FEDERAL RAILROAD

WESTERN EUROPE

Thomas Cook
International Timetable

A comprehensive schedule of European Rail Services and a condensed summary of principal rail service elsewhere in the world. Each Edition contains comprehensive information on rail travel, customs, currency, baggage, children, stations, charts, indexes, European shipping services, auto and sleeper trains, and much, much more.

Europe

North & South America
Africa & Middle East
India/Asia/Japan
Australia/New Zealand

Published monthly in London, each edition is imported by air by TRAVEL LIBRARY for sale in North America. Summer (June to September) and winter editions are generally available by the 6th of the month for which they are issued. Little change in consecutive issues during summer and winter. The issues from February to May contain an advance summer service supplement allowing users to plan summer itineraries before the complete summer Timetable is published in June. May issue contains summer services in Britain. Each issue approx. 580 pages, 9½" x 6¼" / 15 ounces. Price of $9.50 each includes Postage.

RAIL MAP OF EUROPE, by KUMMERLY + FREY, Switzerland. Full color, European Political map detailing all Main-Line and Secondary Rail Lines, Train-Ferry Services and Frontier Points. Very comprehensive. Measures 50" x 36". Folded to 9¼" x 5¼". (Scale 1"=40.6 Miles) 4½ Ounces. Price of $6.95 each includes Postage.

TRAVEL LIBRARY

Orders should be sent to:

TRAVEL LIBRARY
P.O. Box 249
Dept. F
La Canada, Calif. 91011

Thomas Cook International Timetable ...... **$9.50 each**
Rail Map of Europe .... **$6.95 each**
(Calif. residents please add sales tax. Prices include Postage.)

WESTERN EUROPE

By David D. Tennant

The author, travel correspondent for Thomson Regional Newspapers and travel editor of The Illustrated London News, *has been an ardent railway enthusiast all his life. Scots born—members of his family have been involved in railway management for four generations—he has traveled by train in many parts of the world including North America, Australia, South Africa, India, Malaysia and Europe, and is a supporter of several railway preservation societies.*

Throughout Europe today rail travel for business and pleasure is better placed than it has ever been to provide the public with a service that is second to none, though the over-all mileage of passenger-carrying track is considerably less than it was in the immediate post-war years. Many of the main lines have been completely re-built for today's high speeds and greater use. International co-operation in just about every aspect of railway management is more intensive than ever and is reflected in a highly efficient railway network. Increased electrification and other technical advances, such as the excellent turbo-trains operated by French Railways on a number of long distance routes, have resulted in higher speeds with averages of well over 80 m.p.h. being quite usual.

But even these high speeds are not the last word. The Italians have completed the first part of their very fast *direttissima* line which will link Rome and Florence. Even now, with only its southern half finished, it has knocked thirty minutes off the traveling time between the two cities. The French are also constructing a brand new, super high-speed railway between the suburbs of Paris and those of its second city, Lyon. In the U.K., British Railways High Speed Train (it travels at 125 m.p.h. over long stretches of route) now links London with both Bristol and South Wales and will be introduced also on the East Coast main line from London to Newcastle.

But comfort is just as important as speed, perhaps slightly more so to the leisure traveler. In the last few years there have been remarkable strides in this direction with all the railways of Europe progressively introducing new rolling stock for both day and night services. This new rolling stock offers comfort and spaciousness which a decade ago was restricted to the deluxe first class only trains. Under the UIC agreement second class coaches now have only three seats a side in compartments, as against four previously. Corridors are slightly wider allowing for easier access.

Air conditioning is becoming more common, mainly in first class but increasingly in second class also. Although not visually noticed by the average traveler the "behind the scenes" technical advances in coach design are of equal importance giving smoother and quieter riding all round. Multi-professional teams, including even psychologists and interior decorators, have been employed to make these new coaches more efficient and more attractive for the traveler.

These advances cannot be achieved in a short period, and you must not expect to find new coaches everywhere. However, in the course of thousands of miles of European rail travel each year, I am constantly impressed with the ever-rising standards, not only in first class (which is now quite luxurious in many cases) but also in second class.

Class Consciousness

The question of which class to choose is one that is often put to me, and the answer is both easy—and difficult. The easy part is "travel first when you can" for there is no doubt at all that it does give substantially more comfort, spaciousness, and generally a more relaxing atmosphere. But it is anything from 30% to 50% dearer than second class. Therefore, if economy is all important, then stick to second class. Where you want to economize but not sacrifice too many of life's comforts, then I would recommend traveling second class throughout Scandinavia, on the Benelux expresses in the Netherlands, Belgium and Luxembourg, on the TALGO, ELT and TAF trains in Spain, on "DC" trains in Germany, on the Transalpin express from Basle to Vienna (and also "TS" trains in Austria), on the fast inter-city expresses in Switzerland and on the turbo-trains and *Rapides* in France.

In the high summer season (and at peak traveling periods such as Christmas and Easter) second class travel is always very busy indeed, particularly on long-distance international trains. I advise first class travel then, if possible. It is also important to remember that in many European countries (but not all) supplementary fares are required for travel on certain express trains. The amount varies according to the distance traveled in most cases, and it is best to check this before departure. Holders of the full Eurailpass do not require to pay this extra supplement except on Trans Europ Expresses.

For Daytime Travel

One of the biggest advances in European rail travel had its beginnings 20 years ago when the first Trans Europ Expresses (known by their initials TEE) started operating, designed to give the business and holiday traveler the best available in rail travel. A success from the start this system now connects over 130 cities in no fewer than ten west European countries. Its smooth, stainless steel or cream and cerise coaches are now a familiar part of the European rail scene.

There are at present six different types of these trains in operation. But they all share certain characteristics—entirely first class, luxuriously equipped, full restaurant services (some with restaurant cars, others serving meals at every seat), fully air-conditioned and high speeds. Some travel entirely within one country such as the "Aquitaine" (Paris—Bordeaux) or the "Vesuvio" (Milan—Naples) while others connect two or more countries. The "Edelweiss" and "Iris", for example, link Brussels and Zurich serving Belgium, Luxembourg and France en route. One or two have secretarial services and telephone links.

All the TEE trains require a special supplementary fare which varies according to the distance traveled. However, this surcharge is comparatively modest when one considers the extras one gets. All are also day-time-only trains, their high speeds enabling them to connect cities far apart without the need for overnight travel.

However, the TEE system does not have a monopoly of European deluxe train travel, for many excellent international expresses operate all over the continent. In the U.K., where there are no TEE trains, all main line expresses have modern rolling stock with much of it now being air-conditioned.

For Overnight Travel

Even with the increase in train speeds there is still a wide variety of overnight expresses equipped with sleeping cars. The vast majority of these are of recent construction and design, offering the traveler a comfortable night's rest while he speeds to his destination.

Each sleeping compartment offers accommodation for one, two, or three people, the last being only in second class and special "tourist" cars. The majority of overnight trains carry both first and second sleeping cars. The beds are full size and each compartment has wash-hand basins with hot and cold running water. Toilets and washrooms are provided in each car. Showers have been installed in the newest ones on the German Federal Railway. On all the international expresses the sleeping car attendants are multi-lingual with English being almost the "lingua franca".

If you wish to travel overnight more cheaply, many trains (except in the U.K.) have "couchette" cars. These are more or less simple sleepers with blanket, pillow and small towel provided. In first class, each compartment takes four couchette passengers. In second class, six passengers. Couchettes are certainly more comfortable than sitting up overnight and in the newer coaches—and particularly in first class—they are excellent value for money. But if you require a degree of privacy then opt for a standard sleeper. Apart from the romantic appeal of overnight travel you can save on hotel bills by traveling overnight. Incidentally almost all sleeping car attendants will provide you with a cup of coffee or tea and many also now carry alcoholic refreshments as well.

Always make sleeping car and couchette reservations in advance, but sometimes one can get a last minute cancellation. The cost varies according to the class, the type of sleeper or couchette and the distance traveled. First class single occupancy of sleeper compartments is expensive. For two traveling together, the cost is more or less halved. There are no single sleepers in second class. On many routes where couchettes are used, a standard charge is made whether one is traveling first or second, but of course the appropriate first or second traveling ticket is required.

Meals on Wheels

Every railway system in Europe operates dining cars or refreshment cars of one kind or another. In addition to the standard and traditional dining cars (meals here are always expensive, being anything from £5 to £7 per head), there are buffet cars (which provide simpler meals from one third to one half the cost of a full dinner meal), self-service "grill" cars, mini bars and *vendes ambulantes*. The last is a traveling salesperson going through the train with a trolley selling sandwiches, coffee, soft drinks, beer and so on. This is the most economic way of having a meal en route. In some trains you can now get "pre-packed" cold meals at about the same price as on the cafeteria cars. These can be pre-booked or purchased at certain station buffets.

For formal meals in the dining car always book ahead—enquire about this as soon as you get on the train. In many cases you are given a "place card" and told what time the meal starts, or alternatively a dining car attendant comes along the train announcing the meal time.

At most stations, even quite small ones, all over the continent, there are good buffets (some have top-grade restaurants as well). At all main line stations, trolleys with food and drinks meet most trains. Payment is generally required in the currency of the country, although at frontier stations it has been my experience that they will take several currencies.

"The Union Internationale des Chemins de Fer (European Railway Union) issues a timetable with diagrammatic maps covering the main international routes in Europe. This is valid for the period June to September inclusive each year. In addition to the T.E.E. and other international and main line expresses it also gives details of the car train (Motorail) services both on the continent and in the U.K. The timetable which is called "Through Europe by Train" is in English as well as several other languages and is scheduled to be available free of charge from Centre de Publicite, UIC, Via Marsala 9, 1 001185, ROME, Italy from around the beginning of April onwards. In addition some international railway offices will have it available for distribution.

Scenic Routes

Many of Europe's top-line expresses pass through some of the continent's finest scenic areas in daylight. It is not possible to list all of these (there are around 200 all told), but we have selected a number which are particulary outstanding. In every case these trains complete all (or the major part) of their journey in the daytime during the summer holiday season, and operate all the year around unless otherwise stated. Those which are T.E.E.-operated are so marked. Each has a dining car and, where necessary, sleeping cars. All trains listed other than the T.E.E. services carry both first and second-class coaches. Some require supplementary fare for all or part of the way.

ARLBERG EXPRESS, Paris—Zurich—Innsbruck—Vienna. Leaves French capital in the evening, travels overnight to Switzerland. Goes through Swiss and Austrian Alps in daylight. Total traveling time 21 hours approx.

AURORA, Moscow—Leningrad. Fast (just over five hours) daylight train between Russia's two leading cities. Runs June 1st-September 27th. Reservation essential.

BLAUER ENZIAN (T.E.E.), Hamburg—Hannover—Munich. Through the heart of Germany. In summer, run is extended to Salzburg and Klagenfurt in Austria. Southbound route entirely in daylight. Total traveling time 7½ hours approx. (2½ hours more when extended to Austria).

CISALPIN (T.E.E.), Paris—Dijon—Lausanne—Milan—Venice (last named, summer months only). Leaves Paris at lunch time, arrives Milan mid-evening, Venice just after midnight. Total traveling time to Milan, 9 hours, to Venice under 12.

CORNISH RIVIERA, London—Exeter—Plymouth—Penzance. One of Britain's longest established expresses. Very scenic route, especially after Exeter. Connections for many resorts in Devon and Cornwall. Does not operate on Sundays. 5 ½ hours' travel.

EDELWEISS AND IRIS (T.E.E.), Brussels—Luxembourg—Strasbourg—Basel —Zurich. Twin trains which run twice daily in each direction linking four countries. Includes the attractive Ardennes country in south Belgium. Total traveling time approx. 7 hours.

FLYING SCOTSMAN, London—Newcastle-upon-Tyne—Edinburgh. Perhaps Britain's most famous train; rural scenery for much of way, passing many historic sites. Limited accommodation, reservations advisable. Nearly 400 miles in under 6 hours.

GLASGOW-MALLAIG. Twice daily (three times May to September), route is through the West Highlands and along the banks of Loch Lomond. One of the most scenic in Britain. Buffet car on all trains. About six leisurely hours for the 165 miles.

GOTTARDO (T.E.E.), Basel—Zurich—Lugano—Como—Milan. A very scenic route passing through the famous St. Gotthard tunnel. Southbound route always in daylight. Northbound terminates at Zurich but immediate connection for Basel. Total time approx. 4½ hours.

LE CATALAN (T.E.E.), Geneva—Chambery—Grenoble—Avignon—Narbonne—Perpignan—Barcelona. Only Talgo type train to operate outside Spain— very scenic route—overnight connections to/from Madrid at Barcelona. 10 hours trip Geneva—Barcelona.

LE MISTRAL (T.E.E.), Paris—Dijon—Lyon—Avignon—Marseille—Cannes—Nice. Perhaps the most luxurious train in Europe—secretarial services, boutique, beauty salon, speeds up to 100 m.p.h. Reservations advisable. Approx. 9 hours travel.

FOGUETE, Lisbon—Coimbra—Oporto. Three times daily express between Portugal's two major cities calling at the ancient University city of Coimbra en route. Travels through the heartland of the country. First class only. Reservation strongly advised.

MEDIOLANUM (T.E.E.), Munich—Innsbruck—Verona—Milan. Through the Tyrolean Alps and the famous Brenner Pass. Northbound route entirely in daylight throughout the year. Approx. 6 hours.

PELORITANO, Palermo—Messina—Salerno—Naples—Rome. Connects the Italian capital with the leading city in Sicily (through coaches also to Catania for Taormina). Runs beside the sea for much of the way. Limited accommodation. Reservation essential. Approx. 11 hours, including train ferry crossing of Straits of Messina.

RHEINGOLD (T.E.E.), Hook of Holland/Amsterdam—Dusseldorf—Cologne—Mainz—Mannheim—Basle. Runs up the Rhine Valley for much of its route. Through coaches go to Geneva via Lausanne, and to Milan via Lucerne and Lugano. Direct connections at Basle for Zurich.

RHONE-ISAR, Geneva—Berne—Zurich—Lindau—Munich. Through Switzerland and part of Bavaria by day most of the way. Dining car in Switzerland. About 9 hours for nearly 400 miles.

NORGEPILEN AND SVERIGEPILEN, Oslo—Stockholm. Twin trains connecting the two Scandinavian capitals—lake and woodland scenery most of the way. Approx. 6½ hours.

MARE NOSTRUM, Barcelona—Tarragona—Valencia—Alicante. Down much of Spain's Mediterranean coast and then inland; modern diesel unit train with buffet car all the way, daily in each direction. About 10½ hours for 350-mile journey.

TRANSALPIN, Basel—Zurich—Innsbruck—Salzburg—Linz—Vienna. One of the best trains in Europe for mountain scenery, most of which is in daylight throughout the year. Limited accommodation. Reservation essential. Approx. 10 hours.

TROLLTOG, Oslo—Bergen. A tourist special summer train (June-August) connecting the two Norwegian cities. Makes a lunch and photo-stop at Finse in the heart of the mountains. Also carries refreshment services. At other times use Bergen Express on same route. A "troll" is a sort of Norwegian fairy. Total time approx. 9 hours.

VESUVIO (T.E.E.), Milan—Bologna—Florence—Rome—Naples. A varied route from northern to southern Italy. Runs south in daylight all the way throughout the year, leaving Milan mid-morning and arriving in Naples late afternoon. Traveling time about 7½ hours.

City to City Expresses

In addition to the "scenic routes" mentioned above, there are also many excellent fast expresses connecting most of Europe's main cities, including those in Great Britain and Ireland. Here are a few that are of particular interest to the holiday traveler:

ABERDONIAN, London—York—Newcastle—Edinburgh—Dundee—Aberdeen. Daily restaurant car train linking the national capital with the "oil boom" city of Scotland. Total journey takes nine hours for the 535 miles. Also the "Night Aberdonian" on the same route with first- and second-class sleepers but not serving Newcastle.

BLUE TRAIN, Paris—Marseille—Cannes—Nice—Ventimiglia. One of the most famous trains on the continent—all sleeping car-dining cars—dining car all the way—overnight journey.

BRABANT (T.E.E.), Paris—Brussels. Non-stop (passports checked en route) between the two capitals—one of several similar expresses—very fast—2 hours 25 minutes.

NYMPHENBURG, Munich—Frankfurt—Wiesbaden—Bonn—Cologne—Dortmund—Hannover. One of Germany's "Inter-City" first-class-only expresses. Dining car throughout the entire journey. Takes just under nine hours for the 596 miles. Runs daily.

ENTERPRISE, Belfast—Dublin. Several-times-daily expresses connecting the two cities. One in the morning and one in the early evening each way are non-stop —buffet car on each one.

ETOILE DU NORD AND ILE DE FRANCE (T.E.E.), Amsterdam—Rotterdam—Antwerp—Brussels—Paris. Twin trains running in each direction—no stop at frontiers (passports checked on board). Five hours' travel.

FRECCIA DELLA LAGUNA, Rome—Florence—Bologna—Venice. Fastest rail service connecting these cities. Leave Rome at lunch time, arrive Venice for dinner. Runs daily. Reservation essential. Total time under 6 hours.

NIGHT FERRY, London—Paris/Brussels. Sleeping-car train. Leaves London for Dover, train crosses on ferry and then splits, one section for Paris, the other for Brussels—buffet car part of the way. Go to bed in London and wake up in Paris or Brussels.

PALATINO, Paris—Rome. Leaves each city in the early evening, arrives just after breakfast—sleeping cars all the way—dining car attached for dinner and breakfast. Inclusive tickets can cover journey, sleeper and meals.

ROYAL SCOT, London—Glasgow. A long-established daylight express running every day in the year. Less than 5 hours for the 400-mile journey.

PARSIFAL (T.E.E.), Paris—Cologne—Dortmund—Hamburg. A daylight express connecting several important cities. Also stops at Bremen. Total time 9½ hours.

PRINZ EUGEN (T.E.E.), Vienna—Nurnberg—Hannover—Bremen. Only T.E.E. go to the Austrian capital. Dining car all the way. Northbound route in daylight throughout most of the year. Takes about 10½ hours.

PUERTA DEL SOL, Paris—Madrid. Sleeping cars on this train go through all the way—day coach passengers change at frontier—dining car all the way. Fastest service between the two cities. Under 15 hours. Inclusive ticket can cover journey, sleeper and meals.

Car Trains

Parallel with the development of the vast network of fast motorways throughout much of western Europe, the various railway systems have built up a service of "car trains". These fall into two categories—day travel and night travel. In both cases the car travels with you on specially constructed wagons. By night you have the choice of ordinary coaches, couchette cars or full sleeping cars. By day there are both first and second class coaches. When timings are appropriate these trains carry a dining or buffet car or on some services "mini-bar" facilities.

Some of these trains are international connecting two or more centres while others run entirely within one country such as France and Germany, offers around 115 routes in Europe and about 25 in the U.K. Advance booking is advisable and essential in high season although in the offpeak periods places can often be found on the day of travel. Please note that most of these services run once or twice or in some cases three times a week. A very few offer daily services. All are in full swing in summer while many operate throughout the year. Bookings can be made through the appropriate railway offices in the U.S.A., Canada and Britain or from main travel agents. Last minute bookings are best made at the station of departure.

General Information

It is not possible to generalize with any degree of accuracy about cost of rail travel, as rates vary from country to country and according to the type of ticket issued. As a guide rule however, the farther you go, the cheaper the cost per mile becomes. It is more economic to book for long distances, then break your journey en route, than to buy individual tickets for each section of the journey. For example, if you bought a first-class ticket from London to Vienna, this would cost approx. £60 for the entire journey, including the North Sea ferry crossing. With this ticket, you could stop over, for example, in Amsterdam, Cologne, Frankfurt, Munich and Salzburg, all at no extra cost. But if you took individual tickets between each of these places, the total would be nearly £95. As you can see, there is a saving!

There are, however, certain restrictions on breaking your journey in some countries, and you should always enquire about these from a travel agent or main line railway station. Certain high-speed expresses such as all the T.E.E. trains require supplementary fares varying according to the distance traveled. But in no cases are these very high. All are clearly marked in the timetables and the supplementary tickets should be purchased before getting on the train, although in some cases this can be done after boarding.

Alas, with increased fares during the last two years the cost of first-class rail travel has gone up noticeably. This now is coming close to economy-class excursion return air fares on many routes and indeed in some cases first-class rail travel (on a return basis) is actually dearer than the equivalent economy air fare. It is however very much cheaper than first-class air travel (but then what is not?). As I stated earlier, second class fares are anything from 30% to 50% cheaper than first-class, but because of the big fare differential in different countries and on different types of tickets this is a wide generalization. Reservations are required on many trains and I would certainly advise it whenever possible, particularly during the busy periods. The amount is small, being between the equivalent of 65p. and £1 depending on the rate of exchange. Reservations can be made at main line stations and many travel agencies.

Concessions on fares are also given to children, the rates varying according to age and from one country to another. Roughly speaking, children under 3 (under 4 or 5 in some countries) travel free and those up to 10, 12, 14 or 15 (according to the country) for half price. On international tickets, travel is usually free under 4 and half rate between 4 and 11 years, inclusive.

The free baggage allowance again varies, but is always very substantial. You can send registered baggage on ahead of you even through international customs. We advise this if you are traveling a long distance by rail and have a lot to carry. Enquire at the station of departure.

In some cases, too, train tickets are interchangeable for bus travel over certain sectors. This also applies to some river steamer services, such as on the Rhine. With the last mentioned, for example, if you had a ticket from Dusseldorf to Frankfurt, you could sail on the Rhine for part of the way. Full information about interchanges (which, of course you must arrange in advance) can be got from the mainline stations and leading rail ticket agencies.

In all countries there are special cheap tickets for holiday travel. These sometimes involve using certain trains or traveling at certain times or going by certain routes. In other cases, they allow you unlimited travel within a certain period. Enquire locally on your arrival in the country.

Money-Saving Rail Passes

If you plan to do a lot of traveling around in western Europe, we suggest that you get a *Eurailpass*. This is a convenient, all-inclusive ticket that can save you money on over 100,000 miles of railroads and railroad-operated buses, ferries, river and lake steamers, hydrofoils, and some Mediterranean crossings in 13 countries of western Europe (excluding the United Kingdom, Ireland and Greece). It provides the holder with unlimited travel at rates of: 15 days for $145; 21 days for $180; 1 month for $220; 2 months for $300; 3 months for $360; and 2nd-class student (up to age 26) fare of 2 months for $195. Children under 12 go for half-fare, under 4 go free. These prices cover first-class passage for the Trans Europe Express and other services. Available only if you live outside Europe or North Africa. The pass must be bought from an authorized agent in the Western Hemisphere or Japan before you leave for Europe. Apply through your travel agent; or the general agents for North America: French National Railroads, Eurailpass Division, 610 Fifth Avenue, New York, N.Y. 10020; the German Federal Railroad, 630 Fifth Ave., New York 10020 and 45 Richmond Street, W., Toronto, Ontario M5H 1Z2, Canada. Also through the Italian and Swiss railways. To get full value from your pass, be sure not to have it date-stamped until you actually use it for the first time.

Excellent value as the Eurailpass is it should be remembered that it is essentially for those who plan to do a lot of traveling. If you only want to make say two or three journeys it is best to purchase the tickets as required. In some countries if you travel a certain distance on a return trip or circular trip basis and stay a minimum length of time (generally just a few days) you can get reductions on the standard fares. For example in France if you travel more than 1500 kms. and spend five days or more in the country you get a 20% reduction on the normal fare.

For travel in Great Britain (England, Scotland and Wales only), you can purchase a *Britrailpass,* which again allows you unlimited rail (and associated ferryboat and bus) travel for certain periods. For 2nd-class travel the cost for 7 days is $60, for 14 days $90, for 21 days $120, and for one month $145. For 1st-class travel, the cost for 7 days is $80, for 14 days $115, for 21 days $145 and for a month $165. Reduced rates for children.

In addition to these, young people (ages 14–22) can also obtain *Britrail Youth Passes,* which cost $50 for 7 days, $80 for 14 days, $95 for 21 days and $120 for one month, all for unlimited mileage in 2nd class.

All of these passes and coupons must be purchased in North America or Japan and are for Western Hemisphere and Japan residents only. Apply to BritRail Travel International Ltd., 270 Madison Ave., New York, N.Y. 10016; or 510 West Sixth Street, Los Angeles, Calif.; 333 N. Michigan Ave., Chicago Ill. 60601; 76 Arlington St., Boston, Mass. 02116; or U.K. Building, 409 Granville Street, Vancouver 2, B.C.; or 55 Eglinton Avenue East, Toronto 4, Ontario, Canada. *Please note that these British arrangements are subject to review.*

Young people with a desire to travel extensively in Europe by rail should purchase an *Inter-Rail Card.* This is available to anyone under 21 years of age and the holder is entitled to unlimited second-class rail travel (along with connecting ferry and in certain cases bus services) in no fewer than 18 countries in western and central Europe plus Morocco. The card also allows half-fare travel on all rail services in the U.K. and Ireland and on the Sealink ferries connecting the British Isles with the continent. The Inter-Rail Card is valid for one calender month and can be purchased at most mainline stations, rail ticket agencies and travel agents. You must show evidence of age on purchase and the card is NOT transferable.

A *Senior Citizen Pass,* entitling older travelers to discounts of from 1/3 to 1/2, is now offered by many West European countries, with others expected to follow suit; check with the country's tourist bureau. A passport-size photo is required for the card, which must be applied for in each individual country.

Most of the European railways issue free informative brochures about their networks. These can be obtained from the addresses given or from the appropriate national tourist offices. All, of course, also issue various timetables, some publishing special condensed tourist editions. These again can be got from the addresses given.

Alternatively, students of any age and young people up to the age of 21 wishing to purchase their tickets one at a time should contact *Transalpino,* 224 Shaftesbury Avenue, London WC2, where, upon proof of age or student status, rail travel can be booked from one to any other of 14 European countries at reductions of up to 50% on normal fares.

If you want to be really knowledgeable about train times in Europe (including Gt. Britain and Ireland), then you should purchase *Cook's Continental Timetable.* Packed with details and lots of information, it is issued monthly. It costs to the U.S.A. $9.50 per issue, surface post paid. This price is subject to revision. Order it from the U.S. sales agent, Travel Library, P.O. Box 249, La Canada, California 91011, from your nearest Thos. Cook/Wagons Lits office or direct from Publicity Dept. (Book Section), Thos. Cook & Son Ltd., 45 Berkeley Street, London, W1A 1EB, England. In Britain, the timetable is available from any Cook's branch for £1.50, including postage.

USEFUL ADDRESSES: Full information on rail services within the undermentioned countries can be got from the following addresses (in all other cases, contact the national tourist office of the country concerned):

Austrian Federal Railways, 545 Fifth Avenue, New York City 10017.

Belgian National Railroads, 720 Fifth Avenue, New York City 10019.

BritRail Travel International Inc., 270 Madison Avenue, New York City 10016

French National Railroads, 610 Fifth Avenue, New York City 10020.

German Federal Railroad, 630 Fifth Avenue, New York City, 10020

Irish Railways, 564 Fifth Avenue, New York, N.Y. 10036.

Italian State Railways, (CIT Travel Service, Inc. Official Pass. Agent), 500 Fifth Avenue, New York City 10036.

Netherlands Railways, 576 Fifth Avenue, New York City 10036.

Norwegian State Railways, 21 Cockspur St., London S.W.1.

Scandinavian Travel Bureau, Inc., 630 Fifth Avenue, New York, N.Y. 10020.

Swiss Federal Railways, 608 Fifth Avenue, New York City 10020.

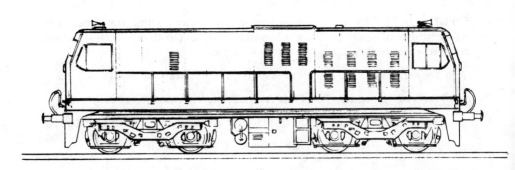

AUSTRIA

Along with Switzerland and, to a lesser extent Norway, the railways of Austria afford the traveler with some of the finest scenic routes in all of Europe. Indeed, it would be no exaggeration to say that around 95% of the Austrian railway runs through attractive and picturesque countryside, much of it quite dramatic. Add to this the fact that Austria is a European crossroads of rail traffic, that the Austrian railway system is remarkably extensive considering the mountainous nature of much of the country, that there is a good service and frequency of trains on almost all routes, and that generally the rolling stock is kept spotlessly clean and in excellent repair and you can easily see why rail travel in Austria has very much to offer the discriminating traveler.

The state owns the main system, called Austrian Federal Railways (or Osterreichische Bundesbahnen), with the initials OB on engines and rolling stock. This network is mainly standard gauge, with well over half its routes electrified, including all the main line services. Other routes are diesel hauled or diesel rail car operated. There are no steam hauled passenger trains in regular service on the OB system. The trunk routes are from the west (Switzerland) right across the country to Vienna and thence east into Hungary and Czechoslovakia. Coming from Switzerland through the Tyrol, at the town of Bischofshofen the line divides, one section going via Salzburg and Linz to Vienna, the other via Selzthal and Semmering to the capital. From Germany, via Munich, other trains run to Vienna and other Austrian cities.

There are four main north-south routes. The most westerly, from Munich, crosses into Austria and goes via Worgl and Innsbruck (capital of the Tyrol) to the Brenner Pass and thence into Italy. The second route goes south from Salzburg through Bischofshofen and the Tauern Tunnel to

Villach, where it divides, one section going into Italy and the other into Yugoslavia. The third north-south route goes from Linz via Selzthal to St. Michael. Here it divides, the easterly section going on to Graz (and thence by one line into Yugoslavia and by another into Hungary), the westerly section continuing to Klagenfurt and Villach. The fourth route goes south from Vienna to Bruck-an-der-Mur where it divides, one section going to Graz, the other to Klagenfurt and Villach.

In addition to the local trains (stopping at all stations and called Personnenzug), the Austrian trains are divided into the following groups. First the TEE (Trans Europ Express) services, all first class with supplement payable. Second the "Expresszug" (Ex in timetables) which are the international long distance expresses serving Austria. Third are the long distance express railcar services (including those connecting the main cities) called "Triebwagenschnellzug" or TS in the timetables. These are trains with both first and second class and either buffet or restaurant cars, very comfortable and popular. Reservations are strongly advised where possible. Fourth, there are the semi-fast railcar services called "Triebwageneilzug" (TE in the timetable) which call at more stations than the TS trains and are second class only. Fifth, there are the other express trains (locomotive hauled) called "Schnellzug" and shown by the letter "D" in the timetables. They have both first and second class and often have a restaurant car, buffet car or refreshment service. And sixth, there are the other semi-fast services called "Eilzug" with the letter "E" in the timetables.

On all Ex, TS and D trains within Austria there is small supplement payable unless your ticket has been purchased outside Austria.

The sleeping, restaurant and buffet car services (plus light refreshment trolleys) are operated by the Wagon-Lits Company, except on certain trains from and to West Germany, where the German DSG company is responsible.

In addition to the state system, there are a number of privately owned lines in various parts of the country. The main ones are the Achensee Railway (partly rack and pinion) from Jenbach to the Achensee in the Tyrol; the Graz-Kohlfach Railway; the Stern & Hafferl Light Railways (an electric network of short lines based mainly on Gmunden and Linz); the Styrian Provincial Railways with its headquarters, at Graz; the Vienna Local Railways linking the capital with the spa town of Baden; and the delightful Zillertal Railway which runs from Jenbach (on the main Innsbruck line) to Mayrhofen in the Tyrol. This last operates regular steam-hauled services. A number of these railways are narrow gauge.

Leading Trains

With such a wide selection, this text inevitably must be a sampling of what is available.

TRANSALPIN. (a TS train) is one of the finest. It connects Vienna with Switzerland (running through to Zurich and Basle) via Linz, Salzburg, Innsbruck and

Feldkirch (quick connection to Bregenz) before crossing into Switzerland. It has both first and second class and full dining car all the way. It leaves Vienna at 9:00 A.M. and reaches Feldkirch near the Swiss border at about 5:00 P.M. (Basle less than three hours later). Timings the other way are about an hour later. This train really gives one an almost literal "cross section" of Austria.

TS services link Vienna with the main cities, taking around two hours to Linz, three to three-and-a-half to Salzburg, five-and-a-half to Innsbruck, about seven to eight to Bregenz, and around four to Klagenfurt, with about thirty minutes more to Villach. All of these have either a dining or buffet car.

BODENSEE is another "cross country" train from Vienna (a TS service) via Linz, Salzburg and Innsbruck to Bregenz on the Bodensee (Lake Constance). This is a slightly slower service than the *Transalpin,* but does give you more time to appreciate the scenery, particularly in the Tyrol. It departs Vienna at 11:00 A.M. and arrives in Bregenz at about 7:40 P.M. The return journey operates at about 9:25 A.M. and reaches Vienna at 6:00 P.M. A dining car goes all the way with these trains.

ROMULUS is the fastest service connecting Vienna with Klagenfurt (for the Carinthian lakes area); it leaves the capital at 7:55 A.M. traveling via Bruck-an-der-Mur and reaching Klagenfurt just after midday, then going on to Venice and Rome. It has both first and second class and a buffet car. In the opposite direction it leaves Klagenfurt at about 6:05 A.M. reaching Vienna at 11:25 P.M.

Suggested Itineraries

Here again the permutations possible on the Austrian railway system are considerable and the following are only a few suggestions. For a "round Austria trip" with the possibility of stopovers in various places, try the following. Starting from Vienna, go to Linz, Salzburg, then via the direct through-Bavaria line to Innsbruck. From here one could make a day excursion to Bregenz and back (or stay overnight). From Innsbruck, return via Kitzbuhel, the Tauern Tunnel to Villach and Klagenfurt and thence via Bruck-an-er-Mur to Vienna. This could be done quite leisurely in a week allowing for various stopovers. For those with little time to spare, it *can* be done in two days - but this is not advisable. A three-day itinerary is more practical for a "quick look."

A three-day tour from Vienna could take you to Salzburg for one night, then south via the Tauern Tunnel route to Klagenfurt for a second night and thence back to Vienna. A good circular tour.

If you are based in Innsbruck, day trips by train are possible to the following: Kitzbuhel the famous winter sports (and summer) resort (about 1½ hours travel each way); Mayrhofen via Jenbach and the Zillerthal railway (a charming route), taking around 2½ hours including the steam/rail trip from Jenbach; Garmisch Partenkirchen in Bavaria, a scenic route (about 1½ hours each way); the Brenner Pass, which is only 35 minutes away; Bregenz on Lake Constance—a longer day trip with about four hours travel each way; and Salzburg, taking about 2½ hours each way by fastest services.

Tickets, Fares and Costs

Travel on Austrian railways is relatively cheaper than in Germany or Switzerland. Return tickets of various kinds or round trip tickets (based on distance and validity) save between 20% and 25% on single fares. If you plan to travel extensively within one of the provinces (e.g. Tyrol or Carinthia) there are "runabout" tickets available for limited periods but unlimited travel. You can also use these when the route overlaps into an adjacent province by paying a small extra surcharge.

For unlimited rail travel over the whole country, there is the "Austria Ticket." This is valid for eight or fifteen days, in both first and second class. It can start on any day in the year. In addition to travel by rail on both the state and privately-owned systems, you get unlimited trips on the steamers on Lake Constance and Lake Wolfgang, as well as on railway buses and cable cars. And it gives a 50% reduction on the Danube passenger ships between Vienna and Passau and on many cable cars and chairlifts. On top of that, you get free entry into Austria's eight gambling casinos.

These tickets can be purchased at any Austrian Airline office or through appointed travel agents both abroad and in Austria. They are also obtainable at many main line stations in Austria.

There is a special brochure (with booking form) on the "Austria Ticket" available from Austrian National Tourist Offices and Austrian Airlines offices.

Within Austria children under six travel free, those of six to fourteen ride for half-fare.

Miscellaneous Information

In Vienna there are three main stations - the West for routes to and from Linz, Salzburg etc. as well as to Budapest and beyond. The Sud station (sometimes called the Ost) serves the lines to Graz, Klagenfurt and Villach, thence to Yugoslavia and Italy as well as the routes to Bratislava in Czechoslovakia. The third and smallest of the main stations is the Franz Josef Bahnhof. This serves the line to Gmund and thence to Prague in Czechoslovakia.

Always check which station your train arrives or departs.

There is a good railway section in the Museum of Technology at 212 Mariahilferstrasse in Vienna.

The headquarters of the Austrian Federal Railways are at 9 Elizabethstrasse, Vienna 1. And those of the Federation of Private Railways (Fachverband der Schienenbahnen) at 13 Bauernmarkt, Vienna A1010.

Timetables are not issued free other than to travel agents, but can be purchased at all main line stations. And they are available for consultation, free of charge, at all stations, ticket agencies and Austrian National Tourist Offices.

BELGIUM

In 1926, the Societe Nationale des Chemins de Fer Belge (SNCB) celebrated its fiftieth anniversary of State ownership. It had been formed out of a number of variously owned (and quite efficient) standard-gauge rail routes, headed by the Etat Belge (a State railway) and the private line Nord Belge and including the prestigious Grand Central Railway of Belgium. At the same time, the densest network of steam tramways (known as "vicinals") in Europe was grouped under the heading Societe Nationale des Vicinales (SNCV).

SNCB is by far the largest undertaking in Belgium and the largest employer of labor in the country. It runs just under 3,000 miles of route and operates an intense passenger network, the majority of it under the wires. Some stations, notably Bruges and Antwerp Central, Namur and Liege, handle more than 500 passenger trains a day, while Brussels Central exceeds the thousand mark.

Belgium has only 11,750 square miles (about the size of Massachusetts and Connecticut together), but its population is close to ten million. Even so, the country manages to offer miles upon miles of rolling forested hills not unlike the Green Mountains of Vermont, and although linked to Holland as one of the "Low Countries," reaches heights in the Ardennes well in excess of 2,000 feet, with Botrange, at 2,400 feet, the "roof" of Belgium. Railways serve most parts of the country, and no town of any size is more than eight miles from a station. Along the forty miles of holiday coastline facing the southern North Sea, there is an electric *Vicinal* based on Ostend. In country areas, buses have largely taken over from Vicinales, and in a few regions, rural branch lines have lost passenger train service.

Brussels, capital of Belgium and of the European Common Market a major city with an expanding population now approaching two million, is the hub of SNCB. The previous terminals of Nord and Midi were made into through stations at the time of the World Fair of 1958 and a new station, Central, built underground, is now the city's most important.

TRAIN SERVICES IN BELGIUM

The fastest trains in Belgium run on the Ostend-Brussels-Namur-Arlon route from the coast to Luxembourg, and on the Aulnoye-Brussels-Antwerp line (part of the Paris-Amsterdam route). Another express service, though not so fast, is the Brussels-Liege-Aachen line which goes into Germany to Cologne.

An hourly electric service with standardised equipment takes 80 minutes for the 75 miles from Ostend to Brussels (Central) with stops at Bruges, Ghent, and Brussels Midi. From Brussels to Antwerp, 33½ miles, service is half-hourly, and for a brief period in 1946 carried the fastest trains in the world (taking half an hour), but now with stops at Malines and Brussels (Nord), the timings are standardised at 34 minutes.

Belgium did, in fact, rightly boast the fastest trains in the world in the 1936-37 period, taking over from the British Great Western Railway's *Cheltenham Flyer* and losing out in late 1937 to the Milwaukee Road's famed *Hiawatha*. The run was over the 26 miles from Bruges to Ghent, performed by streamlined *Atlantic* locomotives hauling five cars in 21 minutes. After electrification, heavier trains meant slightly slower speeds, and today's average is 24 minutes, the best taking 23 minutes.

The line from Brussels to the Grand Duchy of Luxembourg is electric all the way, crossing the unnoticed border at Arlon (no customs, no formalities) after a trip of 2 hours 3 minutes to 2 hours 17 minutes for the 127 miles, with stops at Namur and Jemelle. Semi-fasts call additionally at Ottignies and Marloie and Libramont. Service is hourly, with two hour gaps in the middle of the day.

Almost all international visitors to Belgium flying to the country ride SNCB at once, for their trains work the Melsbroek Airport link to downtown Brussels in place of limousines. The fare is 60 Belgian Francs (about U.S. $1.50) and time is 20 minutes. Standard electric trains are found all over Belgium, efficient but not distinguished, with first and second class but no diners. All buffet and dining service on Belgian Railways is provided by the Wagon-Lit Company (headquarterd in Brussels), but only on express trains passing through the country to foreign destinations or arriving from outside.

Numerous named trains enter Belgium or start from Ostend and Brussels. The prestigious Trans Europe Expresses (TEE) have nine units (out of their 35 total) passing through Belgium, four of them on the Brussels-Paris line. These are extra-fare, first class only, air-conditioned trains of great comfort, much used by business travelers. The four running to Paris, which take barely 2½ hours and beat jet planes on a center-to-center basis, are the *Rubens, Oiseau Blue, Brabant,* and *Memling.* The *Iris* starts from Brussels and runs to Basle, Switzerland, in 5½ hours. The *Edelweiss* starts from Brussels and reaches Strasbourg in 5½ hours, Zurich in seven.

Starting from Ostend in connection with the ships from Dover of the Regie Maritime Belge (taking 3½ hours for the crossing) are a battery of international trains. They include the *Ost-West Express* with through cars for Moscow, the *Ostend-Vienna Express,* the *Leningrad Express,* the *Nord Express* (for Copenhagen) and the *Tauern Express* for Yugoslavia.

At the lower end of the scale on Belgian Railways are non-electrified branch lines, where service is provided by diesel "autorails," clean, but not very comfortable. Most scenic line in Belgium is the 64-mile-long branch from Namur through Dinant to Bertrix, through the higher Ardennes and beside the Meuse. These are ordinary trains, every two hours, hauled by diesel locomotives. Steam traction was retired in Belgium in 1962.

Fares tend to be rather high, with one U.S. dollar buying 38 Belgian francs, which in turn buys about 25 kilomtres (15 miles) of ordinary second-class travel (not on the airport run).

MUSEUMS AND PRESERVED LINES

As yet no railway museum has been opened, despite a good collection of steam locomotives kept guarded and under lock and key at Louvain. It includes a Flamme Pacific and a world-beating streamlined Atlantic. There is a dispute as to the eventual location of a museum.

One of the world's finest tram museums is located at Schepdaal, six miles from Brussels. It contains more than 50 types, including four steam engines for the early Vicinales, also the Royal Tram of King Leopold II. It is open on Saturdays and Sundays, when some types are moved on 300 metres of track.

Two preserved lines are run by enthusiasts, one a Vicinal from Erezee in the Province of Belgian Luxembourg along the Valley of the Aine, the other a standard-gauge steam line from Nismes for 6 miles along the Viroin Valley. But both have a tendency to stop using their steam power during the shoulders of the tourist season and many visitors are disappointed. The Viroin Valley railway, restored in 1975, carries about 10,000 tourists a year and has five small industrial steam engines, often in bad repair. It also has a diesel pug which hauls some trains. The Aine tramway sometimes uses a tram converted to diesel. Try to check before going.

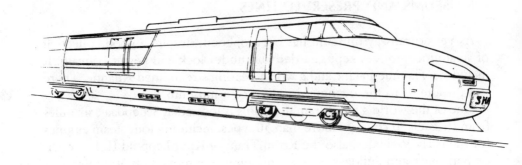

FRANCE

By Murray Hughes

French railways are famous, and the last ten years have seen them win even more renown for high speeds and technical achievements. Not for nothing are the names *Mistral, Aquitaine* and *Capitole,* recognized all over the world—these are the prestige trains of French National Railways (SNCF), and a showcase of the achievements of the French railway industry.

Since 1955, when two French electric locomotives broke the world speed record for rail traction by traveling at 205.6 m.p.h., a record which has not been exceeded since, SNCF has made steady progress in introducing high speeds on its day-in-day-out intercity services. Since 1965 the magic figure of 125 m.p.h. has been reserved for first-class clientele, but the present policy of *democratisation de la vitesse* is also allowing second-class passengers to benefit from high speeds.

The future holds even brighter promise. As this is written, sods are being cut for Europe's first 160 m.p.h. railway - between Paris and Lyon. The new line will be one of the first in a European network of high-speed routes that will revolutionize intercity travel in the 1980s and 1990s.

Geographically, the railways of France form a spider web shape, with Paris at the center and a number of routes radiating to the provinces. Administratively, the 22,000 mile network is divided into five *Reseaux,* each of which is subdivided into *Regions.* A number of subsidiary companies run various sections of the organization.

Financially, the SNCF chalks up a hefty deficit each year, but this appears to be accepted by the state because of the many advantages, such as low energy consumption, that rail transport has to offer. Passenger fares are strictly controlled and include several obligatory discount systems which tend to hinder SNCF's attempts to run on a commercial basis.

The fastest trains in France are the *Trans-Europ-Express* (TEE) services. TEEs are first class only and require payment of a supplement in addition to the first-class fare. In return, TEEs offer the quickest and most convenient schedules and all have restaurant and bar facilities, while some even carry a train secretary and telephone.

The next category is the *rapide,* which is a limited-stop intercity service offering a fast schedule. A handful of *rapides* are first class only with supplement, but most are two class with no supplement. Somewhat slower than the *rapide* are the *express* services. This category of train usually serves all major intermediate stations on main lines but is sometimes the fastest train over secondary and cross-country routes. Local and suburban trains do not usually have any special classification.

To allow sufficient time for slower freight services to travel between the main centers, passenger trains often run in flights. Day trains tend to be grouped to leave early in the morning and at midday, with overnight services leaving at various times throughout the evening. A glance at the destination indicators at one of the main Paris stations will confirm this.

Some of the best trains leave Paris at 6:45 A.M. The early departure allows a morning or midday arrival at provincial destinations and in some cases same-day return; consequently these trains are well patronized by businessmen and tend to have a high proportion of first-class accommodation.

There are relatively few cross-country routes as, in sharp contrast to West Germany, population centers are widely spread out. In the northeast an important freight artery serves the industrial areas bordering Belgium, Luxembourg and West Germany. In the center the most important east-west link is the route from Lyon to Nevers, Vierzon, Tours and Nantes, while further south are two routes between Lyons and Bordeaux. From the Italian border in the southeast corner at Ventimiglia, an important passenger route along the famous Cote d'Azur serves Nice, Cannes, Toulon and Marseille. This route continues around the coast through Narbonne and Perpignan to reach the Spanish frontier at Cerbere/Port Bou.

From Paris, international express services provide links with most other European countries and through carriages run as far afield as Copenhagen, Warsaw, and Moscow. On some routes there are special overnight trains formed exclusively of *couchette* and sleeping cars; the most well known of these are the *Palatino* to Florence and Rome and the *Puerta del Sol* to Madrid. To London, the *Night Ferry* makes a nightly journey via Dunkerque, where its sleeping-cars are shunted aboard a ferry to cross the English Channel.

Fast Intercity Timings
Substantial cuts in journey times made recently on many intercity routes are the result of the introduction of more powerful locomotives and improved rolling stock. With nearly every timetable change, more trains with

a top speed of 100 m.p.h. are added and service frequencies are stepped up. In September 1976, for example, the *Bourbonnais* line from Paris via Nevers to Clermont Ferrand underwent a major shake-up and five trains a day in each direction with a journey time of under four hours were introduced. There are now 11 two-class trains a day each way between Paris and Lille and between Paris and Bordeaux.

On the Bordeaux route to the *Landes* the improvements have been particularly spectacular. Two prestige TEE services, the *Aquitaine* and the *Etendard* now cover the 381 miles in 3 hours 50 minutes - an average speed of nearly 100 m.p.h. For those with smaller wallets, there are several two-class *rapides* offering excellent timings as well as a *tranche* of *express* trains serving intermediate stations.

Turbotrains

On selected routes, SNCF has introduced turbotrain services with astonishing success. The high power/weight ratio of a gas turbine in relation to a diesel engine prompted SNCF engineers to experiment with the application of aeronautical turbines to rail traction as long ago as 1966. Two years later, an initial batch of 10 turbotrains, called ETGs, was ordered and the first services began between Paris, Caen and Cherbourg in 1970. Since then a second generation turbo has been developed and many of these are now in service on serveral routes. Known as RTGs, these trains have proved extraordinarily successful - a fact borne out by the purchase of RTG's by Amtrak in the United States and by the State Railways in Iran. The first generation turbos now operate from Lyon and serve Grenoble, Valence, Geneva, and Chambery.

In France the popularity of RTGs on the Lyon-Nantes route caused SNCF to replace them in September 1976 with locomotive-hauled trains which have a more flexible capacity. More customers will undoubtedly continue to be attracted to this route, for the replacement trains are formed of brand-new Corail coaches.

New Coaches

These coaches, called Corail, are SNCF's equivalent to the Amcoach. The Corail is so called because of its coral-colored doors. It has a standard body design with various interior configurations - two-plus-one seating in first and two-plus-two in second class - and is destined to be the mainstay of intercity rolling stock for at least the next 20 years. Bogie and suspension design reflect the latest developments of railway technology. Air conditioning is standard in both classes; this may come as a surprise, but because of Europe's temperate climate, air conditioning has been regarded as a first-class luxury. Only now is the concomitant advantage of fixed windows, and therefore less dirt and noise penetration, becoming accepted as standard for both classes of travel.

The buoyancy of passenger journeys by rail in France during economic recession is quite remarkable; no other national railway system in Western

Europe recorded a rise in passenger traffic in 1975–76. Some of the most popular services are those which run to Alpine ski resorts during the winter and to the Cote d'Azur in the summer. Holiday travel by train in France is extremely popular and even first-class seats and sleeping berths are always well booked. *Couchette* coaches are relatively cheap for overnight travel. Second-class *couchettes* have six berths to a compartment and first-class have four.

There are still numerous passenger trains in France which do not offer the comfort and convenience of the latest rolling stock. Most common are the standardized UIC (International Union of Railways) coaches, many of which are equipped with various braking and electrical systems for international travel. Painted in green or grey-green livery these vehicles will remain in use for many years to come although they will be removed from *rapide* duties in the next few years as more Corail coaches are delivered.

More interesting are the coaches belonging to the former big five French railway companies. These can be recognised by their short length and odd window configurations. Even more intriguing is the variety of peculiar-shaped railcars which survive on country branches. Services on branch lines are not frequent and often seem excruciatingly slow, disturbing the peace two or three times a day at sleepy villages where old men wearing berets gaze into space from their street-front doorsteps. Many of the railcars with their elevated cabs and sloping front ends evoke the days of the first *Michelin* rubber-tired railcars of the inter-war period. However, their days are numbered, as SNCF is gradually replacing them with standardized 425 hp diesel multiple-units, square looking but efficient and reasonably comfortable.

Nearly all SNCF's main lines are electrified. Although electrified routes form only a little over a quarter of the total network length, they handle more than 75 per cent of the traffic.

The Future

SNCF's planned very-high-speed line between Paris and Lyons is probably the world's most exciting rail project. When the line opens in 1981-82, trains will run at 160 m.p.h., but the infrastructure has been designed for 185 m.p.h. Yet 160 m.p.h. will allow Lyons to be reached in just two hours. Similar in concept to Japan's Shinkansen network, the Paris-Sud-Est scheme, as it is known, will be relatively cheap to construct. It will be used exclusively for passenger services and all trains will have a very high performance standard, enabling them to climb gradients as steep as 3.5 per cent. By climbing hills instead of tunneling or cutting through them, many millions of francs will be saved.

The trains—which will be called TGVs *(Tres Grande Vitesse)*—will be compatible with existing lines and run over them as a matter of course. This eliminates the need for costly infrastructure in the built-up city areas of Paris and Lyons and gives the railway a decisive advantage over the *aero-*

train scheme once projected; the *aerotrain* test track can be seen from the SNCF main line near Orleans.

Compatibility of the TGVs offers other important advantages. Although new infrastructure will only be built over 236 miles between Paris and Lyons, the whole area of southeast France will benefit. Journey times from the capital will be slashed dramatically. Here are some examples of planned times from Paris to provincial centers: Marseilles 4 hours 43 minutes; Grenoble 3 hours 14 minutes; Montpellier 4 hours 37 minutes. Some trains will be equipped to run on Swiss power, and Lausanne will be 3 hours 29 minutes from Paris.

Design of the TGVs is based closely on a very-high-speed experimental turbotrain, Tgrool, which can still be seen running on tests; it has reached a maximum speed of 196 m.p.h. Each train will have two end power cars and eight intermediate trailers forming an articulated set. Two pre-production trains are under construction and should start running tests in mid-1978.

Famous Trains

LE MISTRAL. France's most famous train. Taking its name from the seasonal but violent wind that whistles down the Rhone valley in southeast France, *Le Mistral* runs daily each way between Paris and Nice (676 miles) at an average speed of 75 m.p.h. The train first ran in 1950 and during the 1950s and 1960s it was Europe's fastest train; in 1965 it became part of the TEE network.

The train is formed of center gangway and side corridor cars built specially for *Le Mistral* and its sister trains, *Le Lyonnais* and *Le Rhodanien*. A restaurant car is provided. At the center of the train is a bar car which features a boutique and ladies' and mens' hairdressing salons.

Le Mistral is well patronized by businessmen and holiday travelers and it is advisable to reserve seats well in advance of travel. *Le Rhodanien* is a train of identical stock which runs between Paris and Marseilles, and *Le Lyonnais* acts as a relief train, running about one hour ahead of *Le Mistral.*

The Marseilles line is limited to 100 m.p.h., so *Le Mistral* no longer holds the title of Europe's fastest train. This distinction is shared by SNCF's four 125 m.p.h. TEE trains: *L'Etendard* and the *Aquitaine* which runs between Paris and Bordeaux, and *Le Capitole* which is in fact two services—one each way in the morning and the evening between Paris and Toulouse.

The four trains all feature identical *Grand Confort* rolling stock designed especially for 125 m.p.h. The most distinctive feature of these cars is the inward curve of the bodysides towards the roof; this would allow the cars to be tilted when rounding curves at high speed, thus compensating for the unpleasant gravitational forces which passengers might otherwise experience. They are painted in a striking livery of alternate grey and red bands which matches the CC 6,500 locomotives. Car interiors are very similar to *Le Mistral.*

LE CAPITOLE has run at 125 m.p.h. since May 1967; so popular has the faster service been that trains are frequently duplicated and sometimes tripled.

Other fast trains which deserve mention are the Paris-Brussels TEEs which are extensively used by executives of European communities, and the *Stanislas* and *Kleber* between Paris and Strasbourg.

Day Trips

To sample a 125 m.p.h. service, one may take the morning *Capitole* from Paris (Austerlitz) as far as Limoges, where there is a ten-minute wait before returning on the Toulouse-Paris *Capitole* arriving back at Austerlitz at about 1:45 P.M.

Paris makes an ideal center for making shorter excursions to visit some of France's famous sights. SNCF operates a suburban network of nearly 600 miles which handles about 390 million passengers annually; intensive services operate throughout the day over most lines. The Palace and Gardens of Versailles are easily accessible from St. Lazare and gare de Lyons. Another day trip can be made to Chartres, where the famous cathedral merits a visit.

Some of the outer-suburban services from Paris have recently seen the introduction of double-deck coaches, and a pleasant trip can be made on a double-deck train to Rouen from St. Lazare; en route are many picturesque views of the Seine, with its many barges chugging busily to and from the coast. If you wish to travel on a railway opened in 1976, a rapid excursion to the new Roissy-Charles de Gaulle Airport is recommended.

Tickets and Fares

If extensive travel in Europe is planned, it is advisable to purchase a Eurailpass, but it should be noted that this must be obtained outside Europe. However, if travel only in France is intended, the following points should be borne in mind: the price of tickets is calculated on a distance-traveled basis; first class journeys cost about 50 per cent more than second class; supplements are payable in certain trains and selected trains are first-class only; reservation is sometimes compulsory and is in any case advisable for all long-distance, main line journeys. An ordinary return ticket to Lyons from Paris (318 miles) costs Frs 178.00 second class and Frs 268.00 first class, and a return ticket to Nice on the TEE *Le Mistral* costs Frs 554.00. For circular or return journeys over 932 miles, a *billet touristisque* can be purchased; this allows a reduction of 20 per cent compared with the normal fare, but the return journey can only be made after five days.

Details of prices and of all train timings are published in the SNCF *Indicateur Officiel,* obtainable from most station bookstalls and at selected bookshops and street kiosks. Alternatively, it may be consulted at major stations, where information offices are usually available. Tickets must be bought before travel and are obtainable from station ticket offices and SNCF agents. In the United States there are SNCF offices at New York, Chicago, Beverly Hills, and Miami, and in Canada in Montreal.

Sleeping Cars and Couchettes

Overnight journeys in sleeping cars tend to be expensive. Beds are available in several types of compartment: with first-class tickets in single or special (S or Sp) or in double (D) with two berths; with second-class tickets in two-berth (T2) or three-berth(T3). Not all trains offer all types of accommodation.

For those who don't mind sharing a compartment with strangers of both sexes, a cheaper way to travel in reasonable comfort is by *couchette.* In second-class, six-berth compartments are provided and in first-class, four-berth. A fixed charge of Frs 28.00 is payable, and in return the traveler is allocated a berth with pillow and blankets. It is, of course, possible to sit up overnight on most services.

Train and Station Catering

On supplementary fare services, there is nearly always a waiter-service restaurant car and sometimes a bar car as well; on selected trains, in-seat meal service is available. A three-course meal costs about Frs 50.00. On some *rapide* and many *express* services where the majority of passengers travel second class, self-service restaurant cars are provided. Known as *Gril-Express,* these cars provide hot and cold dishes at reasonable prices. On other trains, tray meals are available or sandwiches and snacks can be purchased from a refreshment trolley pushed from car to car by an attendant. It is called a minibar.

Station catering varies considerably and is often fairly expensive. If the traveler is prepared to hunt carefully in the adjoining streets, it is usually possible to find a restaurant where a fixed-price, three-course *menu touristique* is under Frs 25.00; always check the menu outside before entering.

Paris travel

Paris has six major main—line stations: *Gare St. Lazare,* for Normandy, Dieppe, Le Havre and Cherbourg; *Gare Montparnasse,* SNCF's showcase station, for Chartres, Le Mans, Rennes, Brest, Quimper and Nantes; *Gare d'Austerlitz,* for Orleans, Bordeaux, Limoges, Toulouse, Spain and Portugal; *Gare de Lyons,* for Lyons, Marseilles, Grenoble, the Cote d'Azur, Switzerland and Italy; *Gare de l'Est,* for Strasbourg, Basle, Luxembourg, southern Germany and Austria; and *Gare du Nord,* for Lille, the Channel Ports (England), Belgium, northern Germany, the Netherlands and Scandinavia.

SNCF operates an inter-station bus service between gare du Nord, gare de Lyons, gare d'Austerlitz, gare de l'Est and gare St. Lazare. Times should be verified before travel. Taxis are available at special taxi stands. Gare du Nord and gare de l'Est are within easy walking distance of each other, while gare de Lyons and gare d'Austerlitz are separated by a 10 minute walk across the river Seine.

For other inter-station travel, it is easiest and cheapest to use the metro, which offers both first and second class cars. First class cars, painted red, are in the center of trains. If several journeys are to be made, buy a *carnet* —a book of several tickets at a slightly reduced price. The metro operates from about 5:30 A.M. to 12:45 A.M. and a flat fare is charged for all journeys; no extra fare is payable if changes are made. Metro tickets are also available on buses operated by the Paris Transport Authority—RATP. Bus fares are, however, calculated according to distance traveled and several tickets may be needed for one journey. On the other hand, bus travel provides an excellent view of Paris sights.

To facilitate journeys within Paris, it is well worth buying a "Little Red Book"—the *Plan de Paris par Arrondissement.* Not only are all metro and bus routes shown on detailed maps, but there is also a street-by-street guide.

Museums and Preserved Railways

France's national railway museum is in Mulhouse; on display are about 35 steam locomotives and various items of rolling stock. Headquarters of the French Railway Museum Association is at 10 rue de la Bourse, 68056 Mulhouses.

There are several narrow-gauge steam tourist centers in France: one is the Tournon to Lamastre 20-mile meter-gauge railway near Lyons and another is a short, two-foot gauge line at Meyzieu, also near Lyons. There are about 20 other minor railways, including the railways of Corsica, and a number of rack systems in the Alps.

A useful source of information on French minor railways is *La Vie du Rail,* a magazine published at 11 rue de Milan, 75009 Paris.

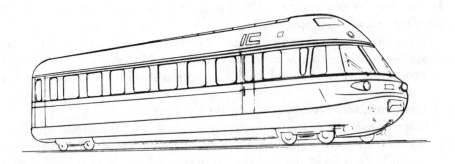

WEST GERMANY

Every two hours on weekdays one of German Federal Railway's (DB - for Deutsche Bundesbahn) red-and-cream *Intercity* trains slides into one of the specially reserved platforms at Hanover main station. Almost within seconds an identical train appears and glides quietly to a halt on the opposite side of the platform. Portly German businessmen and a few blonde secretaries walk from one train to the other; whistles shrill and the train doors close automatically. Two minutes later both trains have vanished.

DB's *Intercity* (IC) trains provide regular two-hour services allowing daytime journeys from one end of West Germany to the other. Cross-platform connections are made at five major interchanges: Hanover, Dortmund, Cologne, Mannheim and Wurzburg. Maintaining the connections requires split-second timing and slick operation. In normal circumstances, the trains do connect as planned, which helps to explain why DB enjoys an excellent reputation for punctuality and efficiency.

A look at the clocks and automatic departure indicators on each platform at a main station quickly confirms the punctuality. The efficiency is more suspect because DB loses a lot of money: in 1975 about DM10,000,000,- 000 was paid in subsidies. Plans for cutting the losses have been submitted to the Federal Government, which is now considering their implementation. It is, however, unlikely that drastic changes will be made before the end of 1977.

On the other hand, the traveler who uses DB certainly gains an impression of efficient operation. There is no doubt that operations are carefully planned down to the last detail, while the smart uniforms of railway officials enhance the atmosphere of military precision. DB is at the moment investing DM600 million in a computer network which should further improve operating efficiency.

Before 1939 the German rail network centered on Berlin. The *Reichsbahn* of that time had built up a number of high-speed daytime inter-city services worked by diesel railcars such as the famous "Fliegender Hamburger" between Hamburg and Berlin. Berlin acted as a magnet for traffic flows which moved predominantly east-west.

After World War II, all that had changed. Gone was the traffic to Berlin, while the capital of the new German Federal Republic in Bonn was a small town near Cologne. No single city stood out as a focal point.

When DB was set up in 1945, its first task was to rehabilitate the war-devastated network and reorganize the system to take into account the country's new shape. This has now largely been achieved, but congestion is still rife along the Rhine valley.

Today, in the north there are important movements to and from Scandinavia by the *Vogelfluglinie* (bird's flight line) through Puttgarten. This route and other lines in Schleswig-Holstein converge on Hamburg, known as *Das Tor zur Welt*—gateway to the world. From Hamburg, two routes run south, one keeping to the east across the Luneburg heath to Hannover, then serving Kassel, Frankfurt, Nuremberg and Munich, the other veering west to Bremen, the industrial area of the Ruhr and Cologne. From Cologne, a main line runs along either bank of the Rhine to Wiesbaden and Mainz, where services split to serve either Frankfurt or Mannheim and Heidelberg. The maze of lines in this area funnel into two main routes continuing southwards, one to Karlsruhe and Basle and the other to Stuttgart, Ulm, Augsburg and Munich. South of Munich, several lines give access to Switzerland and Austria.

DB features an extraordinary profusion of secondary and cross-country routes, many of which are rural branch lines that are hopelessly uneconomic to run. Cross-country routes running east-west are but a vestige of former routes to Berlin: in the north the east-west link runs from Belgium and Holland across the flat north German plain to Hannover, from which Braunschweig (Brunswick) and Wolfsburg (home of the Volkswagen) are reached before the border with East Germany—the German Democratic Republic. In the west there are numerous links from the Rhine valley to Belgium, Luxembourg and France, but these cater mainly to heavy industrial freight flows and passenger traffic is relatively low. To the east the links with East Germany see even sparser traffic, although the *Ostpolitik,* of the Brandt era, has eased rail communications to Berlin. In the southeast an important transit route runs from Nuremberg to Regensburg and Passau for Austria. Total length of DB's complex network, which should be carefully studied on a map, is about 18,000 miles.

Services

First-class-only Trans-Europ-Express (TEE) trains are slotted in with Inter City (IC) services to provide a regular two-hour service over four main routes. All these trains are able to run at 100 m.p.h., have air-conditioned cars, and offer dining and bar facilities. In the 1976-77 timetable, 55

TEE/IC trains had telephones and secretaries available for businessmen and executives. On IC trains, all but three of which are first class only, a supplement is payable. Connections are made at major intermediate stations with DC (D-City) services, for example, linking Braunschweig to the IC network at Hannover.

The normal fast trains are however the *D-Zug*, short for *Durchgangszug* and also referred to as *Schnellzug*. A small supplement is payable for *D-Zug* journeys of less than 50 miles. Many trains in the *D-Zug* category convey through cars to a variety of destinations, requiring frequent remarshalling and hindering the achievement of high average speeds. The large number of through cars is partly a result of the complex network structure. It is nearly always quicker to travel in an IC or TEE train, but even these only average 60 to 70 m.p.h. Another factor which restricts speeds is the large number of sharp curves, for example, along the Rhine.

Slower than the *D-Zug* is the *E-Zug (Eilzug)*. This is a semi-fast service running over medium distances and calling at most intermediate stations of importance; no supplement is payable. The slowest trains are *Nahverkehrszuge*, colloquially known as *Bummelzuge*, which happens to be easier to pronounce. They are to be found on nearly all lines, calling at all stations and catering to short journeys. First-class accommodation is not always provided.

Suburban Services

DB's train service in and around conurbations is characterised by the *S-Bahn*, a term which has gained almost worldwide recognition. Undoubtedly the most sophisticated *S-Bahn* is in Munich, where intensive regular-interval services are operated by three-car electric multiple-units. A similar operation is being set up in the Rhein-Ruhr conurbation—Essen, Dusseldorf, Dortmund, Duisburg, etc. Frankfurt (Main) will soon enjoy a similar standard of service, as *S-Bahn* construction is now nearing completion.

Sets of stainless steel coaches equipped for push-pull working are frequently used for suburban trains and 11 prototype coaches are being evaluated for future *S-Bahn* rolling stock requirements.

In Hamburg, the *S-Bahn* is closely linked to the underground *(U-Bahn)* and to buses and through tickets are available for all modes. Hamburg stands out as one of the very few cities in the world which can boast a truly integrated public transport network and this alone is sufficient reason for a visit.

Electrification

All main lines are electrified and many secondary routes such as the Black Forest line are now coming under wires. There are about 6,300 miles of route electrified. The electrification system is the same as that of Swiss Federal and Austrian Federal Railways and a number of Swiss and Austrian machines penetrate as far north as Munich, while German motive power reaches southeast to Vienna.

Electrification began in Germany during the 1920s in Bavaria and a substantial fleet of motive power had been built up by 1939. Much of this survives and can best be observed in the Munich area.

Motive power

Acquisition of new electric locomotives is one of DB's heaviest investment items and many main line passenger trains are now pulled by locomotives purchased since 1970. Most powerful of the passenger units are the streamlined Class 103 six-axle machines used principally to haul *Intercity* and TEE trains and painted in a matching red-and-cream livery. With an output of 6,200 kW, these locomotives feature a considerable degree of electronics, including a pre-selection speed control system. Maximum speed is 125 m.p.h. One locomotive of this type has been geared up for high-speed tests and has reached a maximum speed of 155 m.p.h.

Rolling stock

From 1975, all passenger rolling stock not due to be scrapped, as well as locomotives, is being painted in a new livery of turquoise and cream.

The air-conditioned cars used on IC/TEE trains give an excellent ride and the soundproofing and insulation are outstanding. Most *D-Zug* cars are of the side corridor type with six-seat compartments; the seats can be pulled out for overnight use. Second-class tends to be a little spartan, but is nevertheless reasonably comfortable. Technical design of the standard DB main line car won international approval in the 1950s and since then it has been built in large numbers, with later batches incorporating minor improvements. Passenger vehicles on DB total about 17,900. From 1977, selected international expresses through Germany will be equipped with the first of a new generation of 500 air-conditioned standard European passenger cars.

DB's local trains still feature six-wheeled coaches, although many of the six-wheel bodies have been fitted in pairs on rebuilt underframes and now appear as bogie vehicles. When traffic flows are intense at holiday periods or when Italy decides to have one of its frequent elections, many former *Reichsbahn* cars are brought out of mothballs to transport the *Gastarbeiter* —the so-called guest workers—to and from their respective homes in Italy, Yugoslavia, Spain and Turkey. The former *Reichsbahn* cars can usually be distinguished by their square windows and shorter length. *Reichsbahn* in the historical sense should not be confused with the present *Deutsche Reichsbahn* (DR) of East Germany.

The Rheingold

Germany's most famous train is undoubtedly the *Rheingold*. Once a true luxury express in the pre-war era of great trains, today it is a not particularly fast TEE service patronized by businessmen and identical to the IC trains except for the large number of through cars to and from different parts of Europe. Marshalling of these through cars provides convenience at the expense of faster journeys, but withdrawal of the facility would no doubt cause an outcry; the cars involved serve Hoek van Holland (for Harwich and London), Amsterdam; Hanover; Basle, Geneva and Chur in Switzerland; and Milan in Italy.

The route of the *Rheingold* provides one of Europe's most unforgettable rides. Starting from Holland, windmills and dykes are soon replaced by the industrial grey gloom of the Ruhr. All the more delightful, therefore, is the passenger's anticipation of the journey along the Rhine which he crosses at Cologne, glimpsing the famous cathedral. After passing through Bonn, there are several tempting glimpses of the river and it is only after Koblenz that the Rhine is joined. The twisting waters are furrowed by an extraordinary number of barges, interspersed by white Rhine steamers belonging to the Koln-Dusseldorfer Deutsche Rheinschiffahrt AG. Towering crags adorned by ruined castles loom out of the riverside slopes where vines and forest cultivation charm the eye. It is all too easy to imagine the Rhine maidens luring unsuspecting vessels on to rocks and into rapids. South of Mainz, the railway leaves the river and heads up the flat valley towards Basle, with tempting glimpses of the Black Forest in the distance. At Basle, the train is split into sections for its respective Swiss and Italian destinations and passengers can watch the Alps creeping nearer in the late afternoon.

Until 1976 the *Rheingold* of the post-1955 era carried a dome car affording excellent views of the scenery. Its outsized loading gauge was its downfall and passengers must now be content with seeking out an excursion with the glass train from Munich—the glass train is a railcar fitted with a glass roof and it enjoys tremendous popularity on beery outings in south Germany.

Excursions
There is no central point from which to make excursions to all parts of the country. Hamburg, Frankfurt, Cologne and Munich are all suitable as centers for visits to the surrounding areas, and the last-named is probably the best.

To the south of Munich some delightful rides can be made along branch lines serving charming Bavarian villages where flowers blossom from the many neat wooden balconies. Oberammergau, stage for the famous Passion Play every 10 years, is worth a visit—not least for the ancient two-axle steeple-cab locomotives used on the branch line. Berchtesgarten in the southwest corner is another place to aim for, while Mozart's beautiful Salzburg is just across the nearby border with Austria.

One outstanding ride best made from Cologne is along the Moselle valley from Koblenz to Trier. The vineyard covered hills provide a visual foretaste of the excellent wines to be found en route.

Tickets and timetables

Timings of DB's trains are published in the *Amtliches Kursbuch,* the official timetable. This is a hefty volume, and unless travel throughout Germany is intended it may be wiser to buy a *Regionalkursbuch* covering a particular geographical area. Information on tickets and times is available at all large stations and at DER travel agencies. DB has an office in the USA: German Federal Railroad, General Agency for North & Central America, 630 Fifth Avenue, Suite 1418, New York 10020.

Fares are published in the *Kursbuch* and are calculated on a distance traveled basis; a return ticket is usually cheaper than two singles. First class is about 60 per cent more expensive than second. 1977 will see introduction of the DB Tourist Card, which will be available for purchase outside West Germany only and valid for the entire DB network and on certain bus and coach services. The first-class Tourist Card will allow use of IC trains at no extra charge.

Inside Germany, various rover tickets *(Netzkarten* and *Bezirkskarten)* cover selected geographical areas. Special holiday tickets are available for midweek travel. In peak holiday periods, certain international trains may be restricted to cross-frontier travel and it may be compulsory to have a seat or berth reservation; it is advisable to check well before a journey.

Sleeping cars

Most sleeping cars are staffed by the Deutsche Schlaf-und Speisewagen Gesellschaft (DSG), although some trains have Wagons-Lits or Mitropa cars. Single, double and tourist (three) berths are available and the DSG supplement is usually slightly cheaper than the corresponding Wagons-Lits charge. A few cars are equipped with showers.

Liegewagen are cars similar to the French *couchette* vehicles and feature six-berth compartments. A pillow and blankets are provided in return for a relatively low supplement.

Catering

Dining car service is usually provided by DSG and full waiter service is standard in TEE and IC trains. At the appropriate times three or four course meals are served; but a wider range of dishes is available at other times. Full meals are not cheap, and some of the snacks offer a less expensive but equally sustaining alternative. Dining cars are also found on some long distance *D-Zug,* while buffet or trolley catering is available on others.

Station catering varies from the expensive restaurant to the platform trolley vending *Wurst* with a roll and mustard. Cafes and tea-rooms often abound in streets near main stations and frequently offer better value. Beer is a well-known german speciality and innumerable brews are on tap.

City transfers

In Munich the main station is flanked by the Starnberger and Holzkirche stations which both handle suburban services. The *S-Bahn* runs under the city center to the Ostbahnhof, and a loop passing through Munich-Sud also runs to Ost; this is used by main line trains. There is an *U-Bahn* and an extensive network of modern tram routes.

In Hamburg many trains to and from the south call at the main station before terminating at Hamburg Altona, which is the terminal for trains running to Denmark and Scandinavia, as well as Schleswig-Holstein. The *S-Bahn* and *U-Bahn* networks provide coverage of the city and surrounding areas and a major extension is underway to embrace the suburb of Hamburg-Harburg.

There is also an *U-Bahn* in Nuremberg and Stuttgart, but the distinctions between *U-Bahn, Stadtbahn* and tram services are becoming increasingly fine and it is correspondingly difficult to determine exactly what the various systems are. Some of the tram systems are superb and well worth visiting. The latest tram vehicles are suitable also for light rail operation and are known as *Stadtbahnwagen;* their modernity is helping to improve the already good image of West Germany's public transport. One tram company in Dusseldorf has for many years operated a service of articulated vehicles with the center section of each devoted to a bar/buffet, but rumor has it that this delightful and rare opportunity to sample rail catering will not last long.

Non-DB lines

There are over 175 minor railways in West Germany, many of them small industrial lines. Of the larger companies, two—the Osthannoversche Eisenbahn (OHE) and the Westfalische Landeseisenbahnen (WLE)—stand out, as they have both evolved successful operating methods with minimum staff. The WLE runs between Munster, Neubeckum and Belecke and the OHE has its headquarters in the quaint town of Celle.

Between Cologne and Bonn the Koln-Bonner Eisenbahnen (KBE) run regular interval services over two routes and extensions are planned to serve Cologne's city center.

Wuppertal is the home of the curious *Schwebebahn,* or overhead suspension railway. Opened in 1901, it has recently been equipped with new rolling stock. A ride along its 8-mile length is recommended.

A curiosity in the south of Germany is the Chiemseebahn at Prien. This is a short narrow-gauge line operated by a steam tram. It forms part of a transport chain dating from the last century involving paddle steamers and horse-drawn carriages on an island where there is a truly fantastic castle built by mad King Ludwig (Ludwig II of Bavaria). Also in Bavaria is the Zugspitzbahn, an electric rack railway up the highest mountain in West Germany.

For information on other lines, it is suggested that one of the following organizations be contacted: Bundesverband Deutscher Eisenbahnfreunde, 3 Hannover 1, Viethof 3, Postfach 1163; or Bundesverband Deutscher Eisenbahnen, Volksgarten 54a (5) Koln.

Museums

The Nuremberg Transport Museum has a large railway section and is located at Lessingstrabe 6. Among the exhibits are part of a car of the *Fliegender Hamburger,* a 4–6–4 steam locomotive which traveled at 125 m.p.h. in 1936 and a Bavarian 4–4–4 which attained 98 m.p.h. in 1907. Nuremberg is also the site of the first railway in Germany which ran to a place called Furth and, significantly, carried beer as its original freight consignment.

In Munich the Deutsches Museum has railway exhibits, including what is claimed to be the first usable electric locomotive in the world and a preserved Class S 3/6 Bavarian State Railways machine built by Maffei.

There is also a railway museum in Braunschweig at 3300 Heinrichstrabe 33.

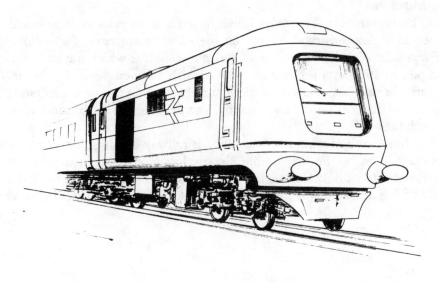

GREAT BRITAIN

By J.N. Slater

The author is Editor of The Railway Magazine, *London*

The British railway system is managed by British Railways Board from its headquarters in the former Great Central Hotel, opposite Marylebone Station in London. Physically, the railway system is of standard (4 ft. 8½ in.) track gauge though the "loading gauge," which limits the overall height and width of rolling stock, is considerably smaller than that of North American and Continental European railways, in spite of the common track gauge. This means that British trains are physically smaller than those of Europe and North America and rules out the use of such items as doubledeck commuter cars and vista-dome cars.

England, Scotland and Wales are covered by the rail network, which comprises some 11,200 route miles, of which 2,250 miles are electrified. The system is densest in London and the southeast, where an electrified network of 1,000 miles of route carries millions of commuters to and from work in London.

For administrative purposes, British Railways is divided into five regions: Eastern, covering a section of the country east of a line from Berwick to Carlisle, London and along the Thames; Southern, south of a line roughly along the Thames Valley to Westbury and south to Dorchester; Western, including South Wales, Cornwall, Devon, Somerset, Worcestershire and Oxfordshire and tapering to a point at London; London Midland, in the wedge of territory between Eastern and Western Regions and including North Wales, the Midlands, Lancashire and Cumbria to the Scottish border;

and Scottish, covering all of that country. Scottish Region has its headquarters in Glasgow; all other regions are headquartered in London.

Pride of the London Midland Region is the electrified West Coast Main Line, operated jointly with Scottish Region from Euston Station, London, to Central Station, Glasgow, on which route several sections of track are passed for running at 100 m.p.h.

Scottish Region also shares the honors with Eastern Region on the East Coast Main Line from Kings Cross Station, London, to Edinburgh Waverley (with connections to Aberdeen). This line is not electrified, but the trains are powered by "Deltic" class "55" Co-Co diesel-electric locomotives of 3,300 h.p., some named for racehorses and others for regiments in the British army. However, other than these—a handful of less powerful diesel-electric and diesel-hydraulic locomotives, and one electric locomotive—there are no named engines on British Railways, as it is not now the policy of the Railways Board to name locomotives.

On the Western Region, 1976 saw the introduction into scheduled passenger service of the diesel-electric powered High Speed Train, a concept in which a seven- or eight-car train is powered by two 2,250 h.p. diesel-electric "power cars," one at each end, running up to a maximum speed of 125 m.p.h. It is planned to introduce these "Inter-City 125" trains to the Eastern Region's East Coast Main Line in mid-1977, but until then they can only be sampled between Paddington and Swansea and Paddington and Weston-super-Mare.

The railway system is roughly divided into the "Inter-City" network of fast and semi-fast trains between centers of population, cross-country services feeding into the "Inter-City" system from smaller towns, and the commuter services of the main conurbations such as London, Merseyside, the West Midlands and Glasgow. In general, "Inter-City" services are locomotive-hauled, with fully air-conditioned coaches and on-train catering on most (but not all) services; cross-country services by diesel-mechanical multiple-unit railcars, not unlike the North American Rail Diesel Car; and commuter services either by electric multiple-unit trains or the diesels. This is a generalization, since some "Inter-City" diesels and several cross-country services in Scotland are provided by locomotive and coaches formations.

Traditional British "compartment" stock is gradually being phased out and on most "Inter-City" and cross-country services the open saloon type of "day coach" prevails, but with fixed seats of which about half face the direction of travel and half are "back to the engine." On the newest "Inter-City" coaches, second-class seats are usually in groups of four, facing each other across a fixed table, with a central gangway. In first-class coaches, seats are in groups of four on one side of the gangway and two on the other. Toilets are provided in the vestibules of each.

Famous Trains

Sadly, the prestige named train, with a headboard on the locomotive and roofboards on the carriages, is a thing of the past on British Railways.

However, there are still some "ghosts" of these services, even if the names are confined to the timetable, station announcements, and menu cards in the diner.

One of the most famous is the *Flying Scotsman,* whose two services leave London Kings Cross and Edinburgh Waverley at about 10:00 A.M. daily (except Sundays), passing each other near York at about lunchtime. Service from London covers the 393 miles to Edinburgh in 5 hours 43 minutes, with only one intermediate stop at Newcastle-on-Tyne. Service from Edinburgh to London leaves at 9:45 A.M. and reaches Kings Cross at 3:27 P.M. With the introduction of "Inter-City 125" trains on this service, the time is to be cut to 4 hours 30 min.

The equivalent Anglo-Scottish service on the West Coast Main Line is the *Royal Scot* from London Euston to Glasgow Central, entirely over electrified tracks. Here, the train leaves Euston at 10:45 A.M. and, with only one stop at Preston, reaches Glasgow Central, 401¼ miles away, in five hours, at 3:45 P.M. Leaving Glasgow Central at 10:10 A.M., the train makes the same Preston stop, and covers the distance in the same time, reaching Euston at 3:10 P.M.

Show trains on the Western Region are the "Inter-City 125s", from London Paddington to Weston-super-Mare and from Paddington to Swansea. Fastest of these covers the 112 miles from Paddington to Bristol Parkway at an average speed of just under 92 m.p.h., traveling at 125 m.p.h. over some 80 miles of this route. There is no supplement for this high-speed travel.

Scenic routes abound in Britain. The traveler with plenty of time should try the journey from London Euston to Pwllheli, over the Cambrian Coast Line from Machynlleth to Pwllheli. Leaving Euston at 11:40 A.M., he will sample an electrically-hauled air-conditioned 100 m.p.h. train to Wolverhampton, a relatively comfortable d.m.u. from there to Shrewsbury, at an average speed of about 60 m.p.h., a less well-appointed d.m.u. traveling at an average of 39.1 m.p.h. from Shrewsbury to Machynlleth and a rather rough two-car d.m.u. from Machynlleth to Pwllheli, averaging only 27.2 m.p.h. for the 57½ miles, and delivering him to Pwllheli at 6:39 A.M. He cannot return to London the same day, as the last train with a London connection leaves Pwllheli at 5:05 A.M., the connecting service getting to London at 2:28 A.M. the next morning! However, he would be rewarded with fine coastal scenery, a dramatic view of Harlech Castle, and would have traveled over one of the slowest services on British Railways and one of the fastest, all in the same day.

More scenic (and more comfortable) are the Scottish Region services from Glasgow to Fort William and Mallaig and from Inverness to Kyle of Lochalsh. The traveler is urged to make these journeys in daylight in order to appreciate the scenery, even if this means breaking the journey partway, staying overnight, and resuming the journey in the morning.

Classes and All That

There are only two classes of travel on British Railways, first and second. First class is undoubtedly more comfortable on "Inter-City" services, but the degree of greater comfort is not so noticeable on d.m.u. services, and not really worth the extra cost. If you are traveling alone, a first-class sleeper is to be recommended on night services, as this gives you privacy, and you will not have to share space with a restless passenger who spends all night rustling paper bags, or snoring. Second-class travel attracts various concessionary fares (assuming one is not using a Britrail pass), and it is well worth considering whenever these can be used in your itinerary. Britrail passes are not available in Britain, but overseas visitors can obtain them in their own countries through a travel agent.

British Railways publishes a timetable annually in May detailing the services of all regions. This is a massive volume, with more than 1,200 pages, but be warned—amendments are also issued from time to time which can completely change the schedules. For example, in May 1976 the 1,200-page timetable was issued. In October a 160-page book of amendments was issued, these being altered only four days later by an eight-page supplement, with more alterations promised for the next January, so keeping track of all services is a full-time job! However, most BR "Travel Centres" (there is usually one in most large towns and cities, and London has several) are reasonably competent and efficient and can book travel tickets, sleepers and reserved seats, as well as answer queries. You may have to stand in line before being dealt with, though, and if your booking involves the clerk telephoning another center, this can take some time.

Noshing On Board

Most "Inter-City" services have at least a buffet car, though full dining facilities are less widespread. It is as well to check just before traveling, leaving time to buy food for the journey if there is no refreshment vehicle. Food on trains tends to be more expensive than in a "static" restaurant, but the sensation of eating a full meal at 100 m.p.h. is worth the extra. Coffee and tea served from buffet cars is usually "instant" powder. Buffet cars can serve alcoholic drinks at any hour of the day, regardless of the licensing laws of the district through which the train is traveling. Food on trains is cooked on board and served fresh. (Ed. note: many travelers believe the British Rail full breakfast is the best of the daily meals served on board.)

Inter-Station Travel

London is probably one of the most confused capitals in the world for the railway traveler, with some 15 main line stations. However, all of them are on the London Transport Underground system, which is the recommended way of interchanging. This system is a suburban railway in itself, and well worth a day or so if you are interested in urban railways.

Other major British cities with more than one main line station include Glasgow (two), Liverpool (three), and Manchester (two). However, distances between these are not great and local directions should be simple to follow.

Railway museums and preserved railways

Britain's National Railway Museum is at York, within easy walking distance of the station. It is open daily, except for some public holidays, but only in the afternoon on Sundays. The collection is varied and extensive and admission is free.

In London there is a Land Transport Gallery in the Science Museum, South Kensington. This is only a supplement to the National Railway Museum at York and is by no means a substitute for it.

There are some 500 private railway preservation centers and tourist railways running steam trains on summer weekends and daily in the summer season. These range from small centers with only one or two locomotives to major tourist railways, such as the Severn Valley (Bridgnorth, Shropshire) and North Yorkshire Moors (Pickering, Yorkshire) Railways and the "Great Little Trains of Wales," a joint advertising panel of eight narrow-gauge Welsh railways. Information on tourist lines and where one can travel on steam-hauled trains in Britain can be obtained from the General Secretary of the Association of Railway Preservation Societies, Mr. M. D. Crew, BSc, 34 Templegate Road, Whitkirk, Leeds LS15 OHE.

GREECE

By David Tennant

The Greek railway system can be divided more or less into two divisions, with Athens as the meeting point. The main standard-gauge line runs north from here (it in fact starts at Piraeus, the port of Athens and more or less now part of the city) up the eastern side of the country, inland for most of its way but running closer to the Aegean coast for the last part of the route to Thessaloniki (Salonika), the country's second city and also a major port. Here it divides, the busier section running due north to the Yugoslav border. The other section runs first north and then east to the town of Sidirokastron, where it again divides with one line going north across the frontier to Sofia in Bulgaria and the other continuing east to Alexandropolis and thence into Turkey. At Plati, west of Salonika, at the point where the line from Athens turns east, another standard-gauge branch goes west and by a devious route eventually crosses to border into Yugoslavia.

The other main division of Greek railways operates west and south of Athens, crossing the famous Corinth Canal and going right down to Kalamata in the deep south of the Peloponnese peninsula. This is a meter-gauge line, although plans have been approved to standardize it. It is basically one route once it leaves Corinth, running right round the peninsula, with about half being by the sea or very close to it. This line serves Kalamata and Patras (ferries from here to Corfu and Italy), and there are branches to Naflion and Olimpia.

In addition to the foregoing there is also the Athens Electric Railway, which runs from Kifissia (a hill suburb of Athens) through the city center, partially as an underground, down to the port of Piraeus.

Trains in Greece carry both first and second class carriages, even those on branch lines such as those connecting Larissa on the main Athens-Thessaloniki route with the Aegean port of Volos.

Overall speeds in Greece are not as high as in western Europe, largely because of the nature of the country. However, in recent years there has been a marked improvement in speeds, and new track, allowing faster trains, is gradually being extended. Although there is still quite a lot of older rolling stock in operation, new carriages with dining and buffet cars are being brought into service continuously. These are of standard European stock, and on international trains to and from Yugoslavia (and thence into the heart of Europe) coaches may belong to Western European railways or the Yugoslav system. All sleeping cars are part of the Wagons-Lit network, but the *couchette* cars are Greek railway coaches. All restaurant cars are also owned by the railway (which is of course entirely state-owned), and they also operate the refreshment services on other trains through a wholly-owned subsidiary company.

Apart from the Athens Electric Railway already mentioned, trains in Greece are diesel hauled or are diesel rail cars. What little steam is left is mainly freight and confined to the north. Standards of comfort vary from very good to passable, but the railcars on the Peloponnese services are good in both classes. The long distance trains to Salonika get very crowded at certain periods.

Some Leading Trains

Between Athens and Thessaloniki there are three express daytime trains each way and three overnight trains again each way. Of the daylight trains, the most convenient leaves Athens at approximately 9:00 A.M. arriving in Thessaloniki at about 5:00 P.M. It has a light refreshment service (probably to be replaced by a buffet car during 1977) for the entire route. This train then goes on to the eastern Macedonian port of Alexandropolis, reaching there at about 7:00 A.M. the next morning.

The other morning departure (it leaves about 10:45) is the "Akropolis" express, an international train which goes through to Munich via Yugoslavia. It reaches Thessaloniki at about 6:30 P.M. and a dining car goes all the way. The afternoon train (it is not named) leaves the capital at 2 P.M. and reaches Thessaloniki at 10:10 P.M. Again, a dining car goes all the way and it also carries through-carriages as well as second-class *couchettes* for Pithion on the Turkish border. All these trains require a supplement in addition to the normal fare.

Overnight there are three trains. The "Hellas" leaves at 7 P.M., arriving in Salonika at about 4 A.M. The daily through train to Istanbul (not named) leaves at 9 P.M. and has both first and second class sleeping cars and second class *couchettes* to Salonika, which it reaches at 6:15 A.M. (The through coaches then go on to Istanbul, arriving 24 hours later). The third night train is the "Athens" express leaving at 10:10 P.M. and arriving in the northern city at about 7:20 A.M. Both named trains carry sleeping cars (first and second class) and a dining car.

In addition, there are a couple of other daylight trains on the same route (with light refreshment facilities) linking Athens with Larissa.

On the Peloponnese line, there are seven daylight trains linking Athens with Kalamata, some going via Patras, with others traveling the more direct easterly route. The time for the journey varies from seven to nine hours depending on the route and the train. The routes via Patras also call at Olympia. All have light refreshment facilities, as does the one over-night train, and the fastest services require a supplement. There are no sleeping cars.

Suggested Itineraries

Because it is not a very extensive system in relation to the size of the country (and its scenic and historic attractions), the railway does not offer the same opportunity for sightseeing as those in many western European countries. However, the Peloponnese line certainly offers the best itineraries.

For example, one could have a pleasant few hours in Patras by leaving Athens at 8:15 A.M. (approx.) and reaching the port at about 12:30 P.M. The return would be made in the late afternoon, departing at about 5:00 P.M., reaching Athens at about 10:10 P.M. However, one could stay in Patras until 7:24 P.M. and reach Athens by this train at 11:40 P.M. And for a two-day trip, we suggest going to Kalamáta via Patras (leaving Athens about 9:15 A.M., arriving Kalamata at 5:10 P.M.) and returning via the easterly route. You can leave Kalamata at either 8:30 or 11:15 A.M. or 3:30 P.M., arriving in Athens some seven to eight hours later. This is a most attractive trip right through the Peloponnese peninsula.

And if there is only time for a short railway trip from Athens, then take one of the morning trains to Corinth, crossing the canal en route, and spend several hours there. The train journey takes just over an hour and a half.

Tickets, Fares, Costs

There are no "runabout" tickets on Greek railways, although there are reduced rates for children, students and groups. Return and round trip fares are also cheaper than the single equivalents. First class is about 50 per cent more than second class. Tickets can be purchased at stations, some travel agencies and at the state railway office at 31 Venizelou Avenue (for routes north of Athens) and at Agiou Konstantinou 18 for the Peloponnese system. Seat reservations can also be made at these places.

Miscellaneous Information

In Athens there are separate stations for the two systems. The standard-gauge routes to the north depart from the Larissa station, while the southerly system goes from the Peloponnese station. They are very close to each other and both systems go down to the port of Piraeus.

There is no railway museum in Athens and no preserved railways. The Hellenic Railways Organisation Ltd. (initials CH), which is the official name of the railway in Greece, has its headquarters at 1/3 Karolou Street, Athens 107.

HOLLAND

By K. Westcott Jones

The rail system in the Netherlands was built up by two private companies, both under the early influence of British engineers and locomotive designers. Dutch trains, like so many on the European mainland, run on the left even to this day. The merger between the two companies and their absorption by the government took place in 1908, resulting in the N.S. (Nederland Spoorweg) being the only operator.

In the years up to 1939, Holland remained a primarily pastoral land, with a rich overseas empire and a vast shipping fleet. Trade was its lifeblood, particularly with Germany by way of the Rhine and its enormous barge traffic, and with Britain across the North Sea. Manufacturing, land reclamation, big population increase from Indonesian immigration and repatriation, and dense concentrations of industry were to come after the Second World War. It was only then that the railways began to be a vital people and freight mover in this small country.

During the 1930's the main coastal line linking Rotterdam and Amsterdam via The Hague and Leiden was electrified, with an extension to Dordrecht. But the war, and the shattering effects of German occupation, led to widespread destruction of the rail system. Holland's longest bridge, across the Moerdyk, was wrecked, cutting off communication between North and South Holland. It was not until late 1946 that this link was restored, and for some years after, despite the borrowing of equipment from Britain, trains were steam hauled even under the electric wires (Dutch electric engines were found in various parts of Europe, even Romania).

Hard and determined work restored all lines and advanced electric wires during the early 1950's. The last steam engine was retired in 1957.

Rail Services In Holland

With only 12,500 square miles (although this area is being expanded all the time due to reclamation of land from the North Sea), Holland is one-third the size of the State of Pennsylvania. But it has an intense network of railway lines, all carrying passenger traffic (more passengers than freight). No part of the Netherlands is more than 3½ hours by train from any other, and a system of connections makes it possible to catch a train from anywhere in the country to any other part without a wait of more than 30 minutes.

All main lines are electrified on the overhead system, while secondary lines employ diesel traction. The electrics, apart from those making international journeys, are multiple-units, often in bright colors with advertising panels on their sides. Speeds between stations are quite high, even a train stopping at all stations along its route reaching 70 miles an hour. However, no trains in Holland normally exceed 85 miles an hour. Buffet cars are attached to most trains and restaurant cars to those on journeys of two hours and more. They are Wagons-Lits operated.

Obviously, the 52-mile run between the two biggest cities, Amsterdam and Rotterdam, is best served. There is a train every 15 minutes between seven o'clock in the morning and eleven o'clock at night, and even during the night there is at least one train an hour. The best take 58 minutes; the average for semi-fasts (twice hourly) with calls at Leiden and The Hague, is an hour; while trains calling at all stations still manage the trip in 72–74 minutes.

Despite autobahns, no auto could expect to make the trip even at the speed of the slowest train, and there is no direct bus competition, so the trains do good business. There is even an inland line between Rotterdam and Amsterdam, via Gouda, 51 miles. The service is hourly and takes 74 minutes.

International trains run from Amsterdam to Germany very frequently, also to Brussels and Paris, Switzerland and Italy. From the Hook of Holland, where the ferries from Harwich in England arrive, there are widespread services, including Moscow.

From the Hook runs the famous TEE train *Rheingold,* as a section which joins up at Utrecht with the main Amsterdam-Cologne-Basel train.

Electric trains run inland from The Hague and Rotterdam and Gouda to Utrecht, Nijmegen, and Arnhem half-hourly. Even runs to Walcheren Island via the Moerdyk Bridge and Bergen-op-Zoom, through comparatively sparsely populated country, are hourly and electric all the way.

Intense train services, with a ten-minute frequency, operate out of Amsterdam to Utrecht, with expresses going on towards Germany, and down to Eindhoven. Northeast from Amsterdam, around the Ysselmeer (formerly the Zuider Zee), services are less frequent but still half-hourly to Leewarden and hourly to Groningen.

Bargain Tickets In Holland

There is an eight-day unrestricted rail rover ticket covering all trains in Holland available for about $26 in second class and $38 in first class. There is also a "day-rover" (and you can cover all Holland with determination by rail in a 24-hour day) costing about $12 in second class and $18 in first. This "day-rover" can be extended at a daily price of $3 second and $5 first class, up to a maximum of five days.

Preserved Lines And Rail Museums In Holland

The central railway museum for Holland is situated close to Utrecht station. It contains representative types of steam locomotives from the earliest years and those retired in 1957 (large 4.6.0 passenger express engines). One or two locomotives are sometimes steamed.

There are four preserved museum lines on which steam trains operate for rail enthusiasts, called "steam-tramways" to overcome operating legalities. In the North there is *Hoorn to Medemblik;* in the East there is *Appeldoorn to Dieren;* two others less well known run from *Goes to Borsele,* and from *Haaksbergen to Boekelo.*

Pointers For Rail Travel In Holland.

A good all-systems timetable can be bought at main stations, but this is one country where frequencies are so good it is scarcely necessary except to learn the minutes past each hour a service runs.

Care should be taken when boarding multiple-unit electric trains, as they often divide at junctions and it is essential to be in the correct section.

An express supplement is levied from all passengers except holders of Eurail passes or international through tickets for travel on trains classified as "D" expresses.

IRELAND

Because distances in Ireland are not great, there is no elaborate railway system and no need for sleeping cars. Once the network was extensive, but this has been scaled down to mainline operations and some commuter services for the suburbs of Belfast, Cork and Dublin. These are supplemented by a network of bus services in both city and rural areas. Dublin to Cork is a 3-hour journey; Dublin to Belfast 2 hours 10 mins.; Dublin—Killarney, 4 3/4 hours; Dublin—Galway, 3 1/2 hours. Catering services, including bars, are operated on the main line services.

Córas Iompair Eireann (National Transport Company of Ireland) operates train and bus services in the Republic. All CIE trains are hauled by diesel locomotives. There are two classes of rail travel on mainline services, standard and super-standard. Only one class (standard) tickets are issued but for £1 extra per single journey you can enjoy the super-standard luxury. The average rail cost per mile is about 5p for standard class. Seats can be booked three months in advance at a charge of 20p a seat. There is a limit on luggage accompanied by passenger of 60 lb. for standard class. Excess baggage is charged for at 85p per 28 lb. up to 100 miles and at £1.30 for 28 lb. for journeys of over 100 miles.

A 15-day Rail Rambler ticket enables you to travel where and when you like and costs around £18. A Rail/Road Rambler ticket gives the added facility of using buses where trains don't fit your schedule and are about £23. Seats can be reserved on trains at a charge of 20p. Bookings of rail tickets and seats can be made up to three months in advance of traveling.

For young people—the under 23s—Interrail Cards are a good buy if you plan to visit several countries and stay a month in Europe. They can be bought at around £65 in CIE's city office, Middle Abbey St., Dublin, and entitle the holder to half-fare travel on the system which issues it and free travel on 20 other European rail networks. Ireland and Britain are counted as a single network for the purpose of this Card.

Trains in Dublin operate out of two main stations: Connolly (in Amiens Street) for the coast north of Dublin, Belfast and also the south-east, Heuston (Kingsbridge) for the west, south and southwest.

CIE organizes a number of excursion trains, known as "Getaway Trips", at weekends and on special occasions. These are promoted seasonally and to get a list for the time of your trip, contact CIE at 35 Lower Abbey Street, Dublin 1.

ITALY

By P.M. Kalla-Bishop

The long Italian peninsula with a shape on the map that is conventionally likened to a high boot is served by the 9,987-mile Italian State Railways (*Ferrovie dello Stato* or FS), as well as by 31 minor railways amounting to 2,388 miles. Sicily, at the toe of the boot, is included in these mileages, as well as the railways in Sardinia, both these islands being connected to the mainland by train ferries. The elongated nature of the country makes journeys of over 1,000 miles by rail possible, although the longest run by through cars from Milan to Agrigento in Sicily amounts to only 982 miles.

The air traveler is likely to land at Milan, Rome or Naples, while those making a journey overland from the rest of Europe can hardly avoid Milan. The major 527-mile trunk route of the Italian State Railways (FS) runs south from Milan to Bologna, Florence, Rome and Naples. With its extension towards Sicily, this trunk line carries about 30 per cent of the passenger and freight traffic of the FS. The southern half of a new 162-mile *direttissima* between Florence and Rome will open in 1977, designed for trains running at speeds at up to 155 m.p.h.

Italy is ringed by the Alps in the north above the Po River valley, and the Apennine mountains spring from this Alpine mass in the northwest to run the length of the peninsula, with extensions into the heel of the boot and across the Strait of Messina in Sicily. It so happens that the trunk route south from Milan mentioned above runs inland, crossing the Apennines between Bologna and Florence, but most of Italy's main lines follow the coast where the going is easier or lie in the Po valley. Railways run along all the Italian coasts, except for the Po River delta in the north and the heel and spur (the Gargano peninsula) of the boot.

Among the main lines is that from Turin to Rome, which crosses the mountains south of Turin and then runs down to Genoa on the coast with grades as steep as 3.5 per cent on the original line. From Genoa to Rome the line follows the sea, through La Spezia, Viareggio, Pisa, Livorno, and Grosseto. The 134-mile Rome-Naples *direttissima* lies near the coast and it is on this line that the best trains are allowed to travel at up to 112 m.p.h. South of Naples the railway follows the coast below Mount Vesuvius to Salerno and then runs close to the sea all the way to the train ferry docks at Villa San Giovanni, 268 miles from Naples. There is a 6-mile crossing by ship to Messina and after passing through a tunnel near Messina the main line hugs the north coast of Sicily all the 144 miles to Palermo, or runs by the sea south under Mount Etna to Syracuse.

The main line down the opposite coast of the mainland starts at Bologna in the central Po valley and extends the main line from Milan southeast to the sea at Rimini, then running through Ancona, Pescara, Foggia, Bari and Brindisi to Lecce, 497 miles from Bologna and the principal city of the Italian heel. Bologna is one of Italy's great railway junctions and northwards from it a line runs 218 miles to Verona, Bolzano and Brennero on the Austrian frontier, giving access to southern Germany. Other international routes cross Switzerland and run through either the Simplon or St. Gotthard tunnels to converge on Milan, while another from France reaches Turin through the Mont Cenis (Frejus) tunnel.

A west to east main line runs down the northern side of the Po valley and beyond, 377 miles from Turin to Milan, Verona, Venice, Trieste and Villa Opicina on the Yugoslav frontier. From Venice a line runs northeast through Udine for 143 miles to Tarvisio on the Austrian frontier in the direction of Vienna. Other west to east lines include one northeast from Orte, north of Rome, to Ancona, a route of lesser importance from Rome to Pescara, a main line from Naples to Foggia and a secondary route from the train ferry docks of Villa San Giovanni which winds along the east coast of Calabria through Reggio Calabria, Catanzaro Lido and Taranto and so north to Bari. The main line in Sardinia that runs from Cagliari, the capital, northwards to Sassari and Olbia is also very much a secondary line.

All the main lines in Italy are electrified, greatly aiding the speed and efficiency of train service. In all, electric traction is used on 49.5 per cent of the system mileage. Secondary lines are operated by diesel locomotives, the passenger services in particular by diesel railcars, for these latter were used all over Italy as early as the 1930s. Finally, there are about 300 steam locomotives still in service. These have no regular passenger duties and few freight, but stand in reserve or are used for track repair trains—most locomotive depots throughout the country have one or two steam locomotives allocated and they still turn up on almost any route.

The electrification system in use is 3,000 volts, direct current. The latest electric locomotives are in a gray and dark blue livery. The high speed type, rated for a maximum speed of 125 m.p.h., carries a cartoon of a running tortoise on the side and is known as the *tartaruga* or tortoise class. Other high speed stock, both locomotives and electric multiple units, is painted green and gray, but the ordinary run of electric locomotives are in a livery of light khaki and brown. The typical Italian train is hauled by a khaki and brown electric locomotive and if it is a passenger train there will be a string of mid-gray cars behind the locomotive.

Road diesel locomotives are painted green and khaki and diesel switching locomotives are green with yellow flashes. Modern diesel railcars are in various liveries, but the older cars are in khaki and brown. Photographers will find the FS pastel blue shades used on some of the railcars a useful test for color reproduction qualities of the film that they are using. Many varieties of color film reproduce these blues as varying shades of green. Finally, freight rolling stock is the reddish-brown now standard throughout

Europe, except for white refrigerated cars. For 25 years or more standard freight car designs have been built by all European railroad systems.

The Stations

The FS takes pride in the architecture and in convenience of layout of many of its stations, with reason, for the standard is high. The post-war buildings and passenger accommodations of Rome Termini and Naples Central rival any railway station in the world, while the station at Florence, opened during 1935, or the remodelled station at Turin are close behind them in convenience. Milan Central, opened in 1931, is the last in Italy to retain a vast train shed in the old style. The central roof spans 236 feet and on either side are two lesser spans.

Large station buildings of the last century are still to be seen, as at Genoa Porta Principe, Cremona, Bari and Palermo, but the removal of the old train sheds and the substitution of platform canopies rather spoils the effect from the railroad side. Modern and pretty little minor station buildings are to be found all over Italy, for Italian architects have a flair for such designs. Nevertheless, about 100 years ago standard station buildings in various sizes were evolved, together with standard designs for all the other buildings needed by the railway. Many of these older standard buildings are to be seen still, plain and functional in style. The old buildings are not improved nowadays by the dreadful brownish pink or yellow with which they are painted.

Photography of railroads and photography on FS property is freely allowed from all places to which the public normally has access. Except for some urban railroads in Milan, Rome, and Naples, where barriers will be found, the stations and their platforms are free and open to all who wish to use them. Italians make full use of the freedom and family parties see off or welcome any long distance traveler with much display of emotion. Against the freedom of the stations, the train conductor is scrupulous in the examination of tickets and sometimes on trains known to be overcrowded regularly a traveling railway policeman is on hand to enforce the conductor's authority.

Italian trains are of four types, the type being clearly designated in the timetables. *Rapidi* are trains with fast schedules, sometimes first class only for maximum luxury, and fully air conditioned. Many *rapidi* are composed of electric multiple unit saloon train sets, but the latest luxury rolling stock is of the conventional European "compartment" type, each compartment seating six passengers. The next category *espressi* are fast first and second class trains usually composed of standard compartment type rolling stock. Italy uses the standard car types now built for most European railways, some of which are fully air conditioned and may be found on *espressi,* although there is no guarantee.

The semi-fast trains *(diretti)* are the passenger services that tend to be even more overcrowded than the more popular *espressi* trains, for they serve many cities. Train lengths can rise to as many as 22 cars, particularly for those trains running from north to south or on the Turin-Venice main line. Every sort of car can be pressed into service for these trains and the second class passenger may find himself riding on non-upholstered seats, although the timber is suitably shaped to the human anatomy. In this connection it may be noted that nearly 25 per cent of FS passenger cars date from the 1930s and, discounting the lack of cushions for the second class, the first class crimson plush makes a ride an experience from an earlier age.

Local trains as well offer a great variety of rolling stock—it is possible on a Milan commuter train service to travel first class in an electric multiple unit car otherwise used for *rapidi* train services, or again to encounter 50-year old cars with non-upholstered seats on remote branch lines. Most local services are run by electric or diesel railcars and the modern FS diesel railcar is a highly successful unit that Italy has exported to the railroads of several other countries.

Minor railways by their nature run local trains only and a number of them are narrow-gauge (3 ft. 1⅜ in). Among narrow-gauge routes is that from Cagliari to Arbatax in Sardinia, from the railcars of which it is possible to see wild boars at play up in the mountains, or the Circumetnea Railway, beginning which carries the tourist almost all around Mount Etna in Sicily, rising from sea level to over 3,000 feet and down again. Equally narrow-gauge is the Circumvesuviana Railway at Naples which takes the tourist towards Mount Vesuvius, to Pompei or to Sorrento. This line has more sophisticated electronics per mile of its 81-mile system than almost any other railroad in the world. The only reason that its electric cars are not entirely automatic is that it is held necessary that a man should ride them to watch the passengers. As a man rides the train he drives it to keep himself occupied.

Trains and Itineraries

The crack train of the FS is the *rapido, Settebello,* a seven-coach articulated electric train set that makes the 393-mile run from Milan to Rome in 5¾ hours. After leaving Milan something is seen of the Lombardy plain with Lombardy poplar trees in their native setting. The river Po is crossed at Piacenza and the onward section into the province of Romagna runs parallel with the Via Emilia, the old Roman road across the plain. It was hereabouts that Julius Caesar settled his old soldiers in retirement after his campaigns and the field divisions, drainage ditches, rows of vines and lines of fruit trees still meet the railway at a precise right-angle in true Roman fashion. The road cuts across this landscape at an angle for a few miles between Reggio Emilia and Modena, with a dizzying effect on the eye of the passenger.

The first stop is at Bologna, after which the train crosses the Apennine mountains to its only other stop at Florence, passing through the 11-mile, 2,676 feet Apennine tunnel. This tunnel is the third longest railroad tunnel in the world, although still longer tunnels are now under construction in Japan. After Florence the train runs up the valley of the river Arno, with terraced vineyards and cypress trees on either hand, before passing Arezzo and running across the austere uplands of Umbria. After Orvieto the valley of the river Tiber is followed down into Rome. The *Settebello* uses open saloon coaches, but the same run can be made in the latest compartment luxury rolling stock of the *rapido, Vesuvio,* which covers the 527 miles between Milan and Naples in 7 hours 33 minutes.

Milan is a convenient center for visiting some of the northern Italian lakes. Milan Central to Como and its lake is an hour's run on the FS, or the electrified commuter road of the North Milan Railways can be used from their Cadorna terminus in Milan to reach Como. One may there board a lake vessel to Varenna. If the lake vessel is left at Varenna, an alternative rail route will be found for a journey back to Milan Garibaldi station, and travel by the Metro back to Central. Similarly the FS from the Garibaldi station takes 1¾ hours for a journey to Stresa on Lake Maggiore and if the lake vessel is left at Laveno on the opposite shore the North Milan Railways provide a route back to Milan. Lake Garda is about 1½ hours in the train from Milan Central, the destination being Desensano or Peschiera. Should the latter station be used, a magnificent view that encompasses all the southern half of the lake and the mountains at its head is seen from a viaduct as the train crosses.

Tickets and Reservations

Travel by train is cheaper than in most European countries, for the government considers it worthwhile to pay the FS a handsome subsidy to hold down passenger fares. Tickets are available at the railway stations (sign *biglietti* or *biglietteria*) as well as from travel agents. To travel on *rapidi* trains a supplement must be paid which can cost as much as 40 per cent of the ordinary first class fare. Holders of the Eurailpass or the period contract tickets mentioned below are exempt from paying supplementary fares for *rapidi.* Usually the supplementary fare ticket is issued together with the normal ticket by the clerk automatically, but if this is not done and you wish to travel by *rapido* ask for the supplementary ticket, as a small fine is payable if the supplementary fare is paid to the conductor on the train.

Where possible, return *(andata e ritorno)* tickets should be taken, since there is a reduction in the overall fare. At travel agents outside Italy (or at stations on the Italian frontiers) a contract ticket for a period of 15 or 30 days may be purchased. This contract gives the holder unlimited travel over the whole of the FS rail system during the period of its validity. Contracts offer savings should the total mileage traveled in 15 days exceed about 3,000, or 4,500 miles in 30 days. Should you plan to do much travel in *rapidi* trains there will be a saving on lesser mileages, as the supplementary fare is not payable and in any case the contract avoids trouble and wasted time at stations when obtaining tickets.

Agents and stations will sell tickets for journeys ahead of the day of travel and both will deal with seat reservations *(prenotazione)*. In 1969 the FS was the first railroad in Europe with a nationwide seat and sleeper berth computer reservation system. Seat reservation is obligatory on some of the *rapidi* (see notes in timetables) and in any case reservations are advised for heavily-used trains and for sleeping car berths.

Timetables and Information

Timetables of rail schedules are on sale at station newstands throughout Italy and they are the major source of information on rail travel. The *Orario Generale* is the publication with official backing and it costs around $2.00 for the whole country. A cheaper timetable by another publisher is available also, showing the schedules of all trains but omitting many of the auxiliary official notices about terms and conditions, also omitting the page in English explaining how to use the timetable. Both publishers produce smaller timetables giving schedules for north Italy or south Italy only. Sometimes local timetables for particular cities will be found, which include the schedules of local road services as well.

The timetable indicates the *rapidi* trains and shows those trains carrying sleeping cars, restaurant cars and refreshment services. A restaurant car is shown by a crossed knife and fork and a refreshment service by a cup, both at the head of the train schedule. A refreshment service may not amount to more than a man with a box going through the train and selling wine, coffee and sandwiches. A new innovation on some trains is the self-service restaurant car, recognisable because the side of the car is branded with the words "self-service" in English.

Italian stations are well-provided with restaurants and refreshment bars, and again the timetable shows a crossed knife and fork or a cup against the name of the station. In general the larger the station the better the standard of the station restaurant. Restaurant meals are intended to be leisurely affairs, with plenty of time allowed between courses for conversation. A few of the largest stations have quick lunch bars *(tavole calda),* where the meal service is a great deal speedier.

Refreshment bars at Italian stations require prepayment. The system calls for the customer to state what he wants at the cash desk and to pay for it. Near the cash desk a list of what is available is posted with the price. The customer is given a ticket, which he takes to the bar and states again what he wants, then handing over the ticket for it. Normally should a beer be ordered the foreigner will be served with an imported brew. This will be much stronger than *una birra italiana* but at least three times the price. An Italian beer should be specified if the object is mere thirst quenching.

Railway Museum

The state railway museum will be found in Milan in an old convent in Piazza San Vittore off Via San Vittore. The nearest subway station is Cadorna and a new subway extension from Cadorna will put a station even closer at Sant' Agostino. The railway section houses a collection of old steam and electric locomotives which so far total 17, together with old semaphore signals and other railway relics, as well as models of rolling stock.

LUXEMBOURG

This tiny country, barely the size of Rhode Island, has its own rail network, but operates closely with the Belgian National system. The Luxembourg franc is fixed at par with the Belgian franc. This is a rich country, with only 300,000 inhabitants (although many thousands of "guest workers" are employed in iron and steel) and living standards are high from coal, iron, steel, agriculture, cement and ceramics industries.

The Luxembourg National Railways (CFL) comprise two main lines, one running north to south through the country, about 50 miles in length with the capital, dramatically sited Luxembourg City, midway, and another coming from Arlon in Belgium and ending at the capital, about 18 miles distant. On this line, Brussels is 2½ hours away every two hours. A secondary main line runs from the capital into Germany, crossing the Moselle at Wasserbilig (25 miles) on its way to Trier. Another secondary line goes through the beautiful town of Esch-sur-Sure on its way to Rodange (21 miles) and into France at Longuyon. It is very scenic amid the hills and rocks of "Luxembourgois Switzerland".

Heavy freight traffic runs to the big steel works in the south of Luxembourg, such as Dudelange (16 miles), the trains also carrying workers. One or two short branches elsewhere are worked by railcar, but other lines have been closed or lost their passenger services in the past ten years. In all, travelers can ride about 220 miles on the railways of the Grand Duchy, and five-day unlimited tickets are sold for about 250 francs, with another type of ticket giving ten days unlimited use in any 30 days for 500 francs.

Preserved Railway

Close to the steel center of Rodangea, there is a small train works with steam traction called "Train 1900." It consists of two turn-of-the-century wooden cars and an 0.6.0 tank engine, running on five kilometres (3 miles) of line owned by Chemins de Fer at Minieres and built in 1879. It is standard gauge and the ride lasts 12 minutes each way, from Fond-de-Gras to Fuhbosch, costing 100 francs (about U.S. $2.50). The nearest station for connecting is Rodange.

The train makes about five runs daily in the tourist season, and less often at other times of the year. The warning given regarding the two Belgian steam lines applies here—at early or late season there is a risk that the steam locomotive may be off for overhaul, leaving the train to be hauled by a diesel "pug."

No railway museum exists, but a fascinating model collection is open to visitors between 6 P.M. and 10 P.M. on Wednesdays at the Pedagogic Institute at Walferdange (served by CFL trains from the capital), where the

Association des Modelistes Ferroviaires de Luxembourg-Walferdange displays replicas of rail steam history.

PORTUGAL

By K. Westcott Jones

The Portuguese railway system has two gauges, narrow (meter wide) branch lines in the north and 5 feet 6 inches elsewhere. This gauge is the same as that used in Spain and is generally known as "Iberian Gauge."

In their early days, owing largely to British influence and construction (the trains run on the left), Portugal's railways are solid and comfortable, often underrated by travellers and especially tourists.

The CFP (Camino de Ferro Portuguesa) is a State-owned concern based in Lisbon, but with a Northern Division based in Oporto. There is a private railway running from Lisbon along the Tagus Estuary, an all-electric system known as the Estoril Railway. This line, with its frequent services to such important seaside resorts as Estoril and Cascais, is used by visitors to a large extent.

On long distance trains, especially those going into Spain, there is still an air of graciousness about Portuguese train travel. The sleeping and restaurant car services are handled by Wagons-Lits, with blue rolling stock of stately character.

There are pockets of steam working in the north, especially from Trindade Station, Oporto, on the narrow-gauge lines. These are eagerly sought by rail buffs from many parts of Europe and the National Tourist Office is conscious of their value to tourism, a special representative being appointed at Oporto to aid rail groups. A few broad-gauge steam engines still exist at Contumil, near Oporto, and at Regua, 25 miles distant.

A railway museum is planned for Portugal, but equipment and engines are still stored in sheds at the time of writing.

Train Services In Portugal

As befits a main line between two big cities, the link between Lisbon and Oporto, 337 kilometres in length (209 miles), is double track and electrified. It carries a service of eight trains a day each way, the crack ones being the supplementary fare *Foguetas* (meaning comets).

Foguetas make the trip between Lisbon (Santa Apollonia) and Oporto (Porto Campanha) in 3 hours, 40 minutes. Other trains take about 4¼ to five hours, with a night sleeper run slowed down to take nearly seven hours. These crack trains carry a full diner and a buffet; other trains have one or the other. Running is smooth and fairly fast on the wide gauge. This line serves Coimbra the old University City, via a junction called Coimbra B. You change trains here.

Main line trains for Spain, including the famed *Sud Express* to Paris (which has through couchettes changing their trucks at the Spanish-French frontier) and the *Lusitania Express* to Madrid, also start from Lisbon's Santa Apollonia Station. The *Lusitania,* which leaves Lisbon at 9.10 P.M. and gets to Madrid about 12½ hours later, is an elegant train with air-conditioned blue sleeping cars, a buffet car, and Spanish second-class couchettes. It requires a supplement fare for the portion in Spain.

More visitors to Portugal's splendid south-facing coast called the Algarve (where golf is the big thing all year round) are discovering the good train service. This leaves from a station called Barreiro, across the wide Tagus River from Lisbon and reached by ferry boat from the main ferry station (Terreiro do Paco Pier), a 20-minute trip reminiscent of the San Francisco-Oakland trip of days gone by. Train services are all diesel-hauled in southern Portugal.

From Barreiro down to the Algarve, the line passes through delightful countryside, with views to the Arrabida Mountains West of Setubal, and good pastoral vistas all the way down to the south. "Algarve" is an old Moorish word meaning "garden." There are five trains a day each way going to Algarve resorts; most split at Tunes Junction, one section swinging west to Lagos, the other carrying on east to Faro, with two reaching the border at Vila Real, with a ferry into Spain and Seville.

The crack train is the *Sotovento* ("South Wind") running three times a week, first class only, with diner. It takes five hours to Faro (288 kms. or 179 miles), not fast, but scenic and comfortable. There is a night service in seven hours, with sleepers on Friday nights. All daylight through trains have diners.

Trips by the steam meter-gauge lines out of Oporto's Trindade terminus are popular with rail buffs and tourists alike. Big steam tank engines thunder along (they are quite modern), and the best route is to the resort of Povoa, an hour's trip for 24 miles, with about 20 trains each way daily. There are other mountain lines on the narrow gauge, especially at Braga, and from Tua to Braganza. An engine shed with unique steam locomotives, including Mallett tanks, a mile beyond Trindade terminus, served by Boa Vista station welcomes visitors.

Lisbon Suburban

The city of Lisbon has four railroad stations. *Santa Apollonia* serves the main line to Oporto and to Spain. *Rossio* is for electric trains to Sintra Hills suburbs and for secondary diesel trains to mid-Portuguese seaside areas, notably Figuera da Foz. *Cais Sodre* is the riverside terminal of the profitable private Estoril Electric Railway, with intense services along the Tagus Estuary to Estoril and Cascais. *Barreiro,* across the Tagus (by ferry from Terreiro do Paco Pier) is for trains to the south, including Setubal and the Algarve.

Lisbon has a smart modern underground railway system shaped like the letter "Y" starting from downtown. This does not, unfortunately, make direct links with the railroad terminals. Buses are very frequent.

Oporto has three stations. *Sao Bento* is a downtown terminal for trains to Spain, the north, and occasionally the main line southwards. Most express trains under the electric wires use the through station of *Porto Campanha,* a mile or two east of Sao Bento station. Steam meter-gauge services start from *Trindade,* a neat, covered downtown terminal. There are interesting streetcar routes up and down the steep Oporto hills linking all stations. New large Leyland double-decker buses are rapidly replacing the streetcars on city routes.

SCANDINAVIA

By David Tennant

Scandinavia comprises Norway, Sweden and Denmark, with Finland sometimes included, although its ties with the other three are not as close as theirs with each other. However in the area of land (and water) transport, all four countries work very closely, even though Finland has no direct rail link with either of its landward Scandinavian neighbours Sweden and Norway. With the former there is an "end on" rail connection at Haparanda on the Swedish-Finnish border, but as the Swedish railway gauge is "standard" while that of Finland is "broad" (the same as the USSR) there are no through trains.

Transport systems collaborate closely as a look at the timetables shows. For example, there are through expresses linking Copenhagen with both Oslo and Stockholm (and on by ferry from Stockholm to Turku and Helsinki for traffic to Finland). Sleeping cars on overnight international trains within Scandinavia (excluding Finland) are operated by the Swedish Railways.

Frontier formalities are kept to a minimum, as are customs regulations, though this has altered slightly since Denmark became part of the EEC (Common Market), the only Scandinavian country so far to do so.

As far as the rail traveler is concerned, however, the four countries have produced an excellent series of Circular Tour Tickets covering not only their railways but also ferries and where appropriate bus networks. These tickets, which are valid for two months from the date of issue, entitle the traveler to start any tour from any station on that particular tour. On the rail sections you can break your journey at any point, although this facility does not extend to the bus or ferry services. Being "Circular" tickets, once you start going round in one direction you must keep going that way. But you can go either "clockwise or anti-clockwise" on any of the tours. Seat reservations, sleepers, couchettes and cabins on ferries are extra. These tours offer substantial reductions on the normal fares for the distances covered.

Currently there are 13 such tours in existence, ranging from a "shortie" taking in Copenhagen, Malmo, the Swedish university town of Lund, the ferry port of Helsingborg in Sweden, Elsinore (Helsingor) in Denmark famous for being the "home" of Hamlet, Hillerod and back to Copenhagen for a really comprehensive tour to the Land of the Midnight Sun, taking in northern Norway and Sweden as well as Denmark with Finland as a side trip. The former you could do in two or three days, while the latter could be stretched over several weeks (up to eight if convenient). The Circular

Tour Tickets currently cost from about £15 to £80 in second class and from around £20 to £100 in first class. They are, of course, subject to change.

A full-color brochure in English giving details of Circular Tours is available from the four national railway networks, the respective national tourist offices, and many travel agents.

DENMARK

Because of the unusual geographic nature of the country—one comparatively large section of "mainland", namely the Jutland peninsula, and a
series of islands—the construction and pattern of the railway network is
unique. It involves several large and long bridges and a series of train ferry
operations. Although Denmark is the smallest of the Scandinavian countries and one of the smallest in Europe, it has about 2,000 kms (1250 mi.)
of railways plus another 200 kms (125 mi) of ferry routes, the majority of
which link the Danish Railways with those of Sweden, West Germany and
East Germany. Some ferry routes are for freight only.

About 80% of the railway network is owned and operated by the state,
the official name for the system being Danish State Railways (Danske
Statsbaner) or DSB. Diesel haulage is now universal throughout the country, with only the Copenhagen suburban network being electrified.

In recent years the Danish railways have been progressively modernized
and the system is one of the most up to date in Europe. Internal fast trains
are divided into two categories. First is the Intercity expresses known by
the initials "IC" in timetables, giving a regular interval service between the
main cities and towns, with trains composed of the most modern coaches.
The other fast trains are known as Lyntog (lightning trains), shown by the
initial "L" in the timetables. These are express diesel rail car sets with
limited accommodation. Reservation on both "IC" and "L" trains using the
train ferry route across the Great Belt (between the islands of Funen and
Zealand) is obligatory.

As in the rest of Scandinavia, the trains in Denmark are spotlessly clean
and also kept in an excellent state of repair. This goes, too, for the stations
and the train ferries.

Some Leading Trains

Copenhagen is connected with the country's other main cities by the Intercity network. For example, between the capital and Odense on Funen there are Intercity expresses on the hour every hour from 6 A.M. to 11 P.M., taking just under three hours for the 190 kms (118 mi) journey, which includes the ferry crossing of the Great Belt. All of these trains go on to other destinations including Aarhus (the second city), Frederikshaven in northern Jutland (for ferry services to southern Norway), and the port of Esbjerg for ferry services to England. In addition, there are several "Lyntog" trains on this route, including the named *Limfjorden* (to Aarhus, Struer and Frederikshaven), and the *Kongeaen* serving Struer and Sonderborg. All of these trains have refreshment service on board, and full restaurant service is available on the train ferry crossing the Great Belt.

An alternative route from Copenhagen to Aarhus is by train from the capital to Kalundborg on the northwest of Zealand and then the ferry direct to Aarhus harbour (followed by the short train journey into the city center). There are four services each way daily, the 230 km journey taking just over four-and-a-half hours including the three hour ferry crossing. Full meal facilities on the ferry.

The Copenhagen suburban network "S" trains service the seaside suburb of Klampenborg, a popular beach resort in summer.

There are also fast trains from Copenhagen to the islands of Falster and Lolland. Some of these trains are international expresses, using the train ferries from Rodby to Puttgarden in West Germany and from Gedser to Warnemunde in East Germany. Others are local services.

There are no sleeping car services within Denmark, but there is an overnight couchette (second class) service linking Copenhagen with Frederikshaven, Struer (in Jutland), and Esbjerg.

Suggested Itineraries

Perhaps the best "Round Denmark" by train and ferry would be to take the main route from Copenhagen via Odense and Fredericia to Esbjerg. From here go north up the flat, sandy shore of Jutland to the town of Struer, cut across the peninsula to Randers and go north to Frederikshaven. Return via Aalborg to Aarhus and then take the ferry to Kalundborg for the train back to Copenhagen. This can be done very easily in three days allowing for a night each in Odense (Hans Anderson's birthplace) and Aarhus. Of course, the stopovers could be longer and such a trip could ideally take a week with plenty of time for sightseeing.

From Copenhagen, day or half-day trips by train are easily done to the interesting old town of Vordingborg in south Zealand, (about 70 minutes run), Elsinore (for Hamlet's castle—about 40 to 45 minutes with very frequent service), Roskilde with its great cathedral (about 20 minutes) and to Odense on Funen (about 3 hours run). With the last, you could take 8:15 A.M. "L" train and have five to six hours in the city and return to Copenhagen in time for dinner.

Tickets and Fares

In addition to the standard fares on Danish Railways the DSB operates a very good "Rover Ticket" which allows unlimited travel all over the country by train plus appropriate ferries, and connecting bus services. This ticket is valid for either five or ten days. The current cost in first class is $47.60 (£28) for five days and $79.90 (£47) for ten days. In second class the cost is $30.60 (£18) for five days and $59.50 (£35) for ten days. This ticket can be used on the boat train services linking Sebjerg and Copenhagen.

These Rover Tickets must be bought abroad and cannot be purchased in Denmark. They are available through travel agents and overseas offices of Danish Railways.

There are various other concession fares at different times and details of these can be obtained at main stations. The information office in the main station in Copenhagen is open daily throughout the year.

Miscellaneous Information

In Copenhagen there is one main station, the Central, called *Hovedbanegard,* which services all routes into and through the city, including the suburban routes. There is a bus service from the station to the harbor for ferries to Malmo, both the steamer and hydrofoil routes. There are, of course, a number of smaller stations in the city area serving the "S" trains of the suburban network.

The station is one of the finest in Europe architecturally, the main concourse resembling a huge Viking Hall. And it is connected by bus services to all parts of the city.

The national railway museum is in the Dannebrogsgade in the small city of Odense in Funen. It has a collection of rolling stock and locomotives. The country also has an active Railway Enthusiasts club. For full information on its activities write to:

Dansk Jernebane-Klub
Naksovvej 62A
2500 Valby
Denmark.

English is widely spoken in Denmark and at the railway information bureau in Copenhagen there is always at least one person on duty who speaks English. In addition, many of the staff on the Intercity and other fast trains have at least a working knowledge of the language. In country areas, however, a phrase book is helpful.

Seat reservations are obligatory on all trains using the Great Belt ferry route.

FINLAND

Although a comparatively sparsely populated country, Finland's railway network is extensive, running right up to Lapland and from the Russian border to the port of Turku on the west. Built to the Russian gauge of 1,524mm (5 ft. 0 in.) it is mostly diesel although there is an electrification program which is being pushed out both north and west of Helsinki. At the time of writing, about 400 km (248 mi.) of the network was electrified, including the Helsinki suburban network. There is also a substantial amount of steam operation almost exclusively with freight trains, the country keeping a considerable number of steam locomotives in reserve.

The majority of express and diesel and electric trains carry two-class coaches with an increasing number being of ultra-modern design, although there are still a number of older (including wooden-bodied) coaches to be found, particularly in rural areas. There are a number of express trains which carry only second class coaches, although on long distances they also have sleeping cars in both first and second class. Branch lines are often operated by one-class-only diesel units.

The main routes run north from Helsinki through Tampere (the second city) to Oulu on the Gulf of Bothnia, then on to Kemi where one branch goes to the Swedish border (change of gauge there) while the other goes northeast to Rovaniemi (capital of Finnish Lapland) and Kemijarvi. The main east-west route goes from the port of Turku (ferry connections with Sweden) via Helsinki and continuing east through Lahti to Kouvola and the Russian frontier. From Kouvola another main route runs north to Kontiomaki in central Finland and another east-west route runs from the port of Vaasa on the Gulf of Bothnia (again ferry connections from Sweden) right across the country through Seinajoki, Jyvaskyla and Parikkala and Imatra on the Russian border.

There are a number of inter-connecting routes and almost all main cities and towns in Finland have rail connections with passenger services. Because of the many lakes and the vast stretches of forest, the railway travels through some very wild scenery with a number of parts being quite spectacular. The country has no high mountains as in Sweden or Norway, so tunnels are almost unknown, although in some parts considerable obstacles had to be overcome, especially lakes and rivers.

Standards of comfort and cleanliness on Finnish railways are high. Trains are among the cleanest in Europe. Restaurant or buffet cars are carried on main expresses, while on some routes a light refreshment service is provided. These are operated by a subsidiary company of the railway. Sleeping cars (first and second class) are owned by the railway, many now being fully air-conditioned units. On through trains from Russia, the sleeping cars are those of the Soviet Railway system.

Being broad gauge, Finnish trains are remarkably spacious and on the newer rolling stock offer a very high standard of comfort. While there are no high speed expresses as in say Germany or France the main services connecting the principal cities do keep good speeds, especially those linking Helsinki with Tampere and also Turku.

Some Leading Trains

The two main trains from Helsinki north to Oulu via Tampere are called the *Polaria* and *Lapponia,* providing an early morning and mid-afternoon service between the two places. They carry a full restaurant car. To the beautiful country of eastern Finland there is a daily express named for the province which it serves, *Karelia,* running to Joensuu via Lahti, Kouvola and Imatra. And to the northcentral area there is the *Savonia* express to Kontiomaki. Again, these have full restaurant cars.

From Lapland there are daily trains both by day (through trains and also changing at Oulu) and by night. With the latter, there are through first and second class sleeping cars (plus a buffet car) from Kemijarvi and Rovaniemi. The route from Kemijarvi to Helsinki is the longest in Finland, the overnight train taking about eleven hours for the 859 km (533 mi.) trip.

Overnight trains from Helsinki also carry cars right up to Lapland and all call at Tampere both north and southbound.

There is a good service linking the capital with the ferry port of Turku, with seven or so expresses daily of which at least four go right to the harbor at Turku to connect with the ferry route to Sweden.

Public transport in Finland is fairly well integrated with the train and lake steamer services (plus ferries) linking to provide good inter-change routes. During the winter when the country is generally under snow for several months, the rail services are kept going even during the roughest weather, although one must allow for an occasional delay.

Suggested Itineraries

In addition to the through services mentioned above, it would be quite possible and indeed attractive to do a "round Finland" tour by rail. Starting from Helsinki you could go east via Lahti to Kouvoula and into the heart of Karelia, traveling northeast through Lappeenranta, Imatra to Joensuu. From here go west via Jyvaskyla and Haapamaki to Seinajoki. There you are on the main line to Lapland and could proceed north to that fascinating region. The return would be by the main line to Tampere and then via Toijala to Turku, after which you could return to Helsinki by the coastal route.

Depending on how much you wanted to see, this route could be done in anything from one week (rushed, with little time to appreciate the places) to a fortnight (allowing reasonable stop-overs).

A shorter but still interesting round trip would be to follow the above route to Haapamaki and then come south to Tampere and follow the itinerary as above. A week to ten days would be ideal for this—but would depend on stop-overs.

Tickets, Fares and Costs
Finnish Railways issues a leaflet giving full information on fares, including all the various excursion tickets etc. A Finnrail pass is issued for 8, 15, 22 and 30 days, costing respectively in second class $25.50, $34, $42.50 and $52.70 (£15, £20, £25 and £31) and in first class $39.10, $51, $64.60 and $79.90 (£23, £30, £38 and £47). This is issued to foreign visitors only and can be purchased in Finland (passport necessary) at main stations and designated ticket agencies. A Finnrail Pass gives unlimited travel.

On the special express trains (shown as EP on timetables), seat reservation is obligatory and costs 8 Finn Marks. On other expresses it is advisable wherever possible and costs 4 F. Marks.

Timetables are issued free and are obtainable at all main stations and at Finnish National Tourist offices abroad.

Miscellaneous Information
In Helsinki there is one main station in the center of the city. It is an architectural milestone, having been designed by Eero Saarinen, the elder (his son became an equally famous architect in the USA in the post World War II years) in 1912. It is most impressive even if, surprisingly in this land of long winters, much of its platform length is out of doors).

Transport from the ferry docks to the station is by public bus or by taxi, all ferries being met by both.

In Turku ferry services are linked to main trains which come right down to the quayside. Other trains leave from the main station in the city center.

In both cities there are hotels close to the stations and restaurants and buffets in the station buildings.

The National Railway Museum of Finland is an integral part of Helsinki railway station. There is also a Museum Railway at Forssa, about 85 kms north west of Helsinki. Around 8 km of narrow-gauge track is in use at certain times and they have three steam engines, one diesel and several coaches. For further information write to Forssa-Humppila Museum, Box 30, SF 30101 Forssa, Finland.

Note: As Finland is an officially bi-lingual country many names are given in both Finnish and Swedish e.g. Helsinki-Helsingfors, Turku-Abo, Porvoo-Borga etc. Head Office address: Finnish State Railways (VR), Helsinki, Finland.

NORWAY

Norway's railway system has been essentially designed to overcome the formidable natural obstacles of the country, those very aspects, of course, which are so attractive to visitors—high rugged mountains, steep valleys, uneven plateaus, and the fjords. The main lines radiate from Oslo, the capital, north to Trondheim and Bodo (this last was completed as recently as 1962), crossing the Arctic circle en route, west to Bergen, the second city and big tourist center, southwest to Kristiansand and Stavanger, east across the border to Sweden and south again into Sweden and Denmark via the Halsingborg ferry. There are various branches, some more interesting than others, and on the main route north there is a secondary route via Roros which runs east of the other line for about half the distance between Oslo and Trondheim. And from Trondheim there is another route into Sweden. Up in the very far north, the port of Narvik is linked to Sweden by rail, but not to the rest of Norway except by bus and steamship.

The railway is State owned, its official title being Norwegian State Railways—Norges Statsbaner—or NSB. The total route length is about 4,240 kms (2628.8 mi), of which more than half is electrified, including the main lines to Trondheim, Bergen and Stavanger. The rest of the system is diesel worked. It is standard gauge throughout.

Trains carry first and second class coaches with a number being second class only. In common with its neighbors, high standards of cleanliness are very evident on Norwegian railways. New rolling stock is being progressively introduced and on main line trains the comfort afforded in both classes is substantial, with newer stock of the most up-to-date design. In remoter country areas, however, and on certain lesser services, you still come across older coaches which nevertheless are kept in excellent state of repair.

Because of the mountainous nature of the country, average speeds of expresses are not high. But with the introduction of more powerful locomotives (especially on the electrified sections), speeds have been improved noticeably in the last few years. All long distance trains have a dining or buffet car or carry a light refreshment service. Food is good, if somewhat expensive, on these trains, but servings are large. Main overnight trains carry both first and second class sleepers, but no couchette cars.

Norway has a closely integrated transport system with rail, bus and, most vital of all on the long coastlines, ferry services, very closely linked. Timetables show these linked services. It is rare that passengers have to walk more than very short distances when changing from one mode of public transport to another.

Some Leading Trains

The busiest passenger route in Norway is between Oslo and Bergen, a distance of about 470 kms (292 mi), which takes between seven and eight hours. The "prestige" train of the day is the *Bergen Express* which leaves both cities in the afternoon, taking just seven hours for the trip. There is a full dining car and reservation is obligatory. All trains on this route stop at the resort of Voss in western Norway. There is also a fast early morning train from each city.

Between Oslo and Trondheim there are three daytime trains, two taking the main route, the other going on the easterly route via Roros. The fastest service, seven hours for approximately 550 kms (331 mi) is the *Dovre Express* named after the high plateau in central Norway over which it runs. It departs each afternoon with dining car. Again reservation is obligatory. Connecting services on this train from Dombas to the small town and main ferry port of Andalsnes. There is also one through train between Oslo and Andalsnes.

Oslo and Kristiansand have five daytime trains connecting them. The 352 km (218 mi.) journey takes between about four-and-a-half and six-and-a-half hours. The main train is the second class only (new stock) *Sorlands Express* which has a dining car, again reservations being obligatory. Three of the Kristiansand trains go on to Stavanger, of which the *Stavanger Express* is the best. This train takes eight hours for the 585 km (365 mi.) trip. Again a dining car, and reservations obligatory.

From Trondheim, there is one-day train going up to Bodo some 730 kms (455 mi) in distance. It takes around eleven-and-a-half hours for the trip and a dining car goes all the way. En route it goes through Hell (literally, as this is a village about 30 kms (19 mi) from Trondheim) and crosses the Arctic Circle. This train affords an excellent opportunity to see some of the attractively "wild" scenery (but remarkably fertile in places) of the north in comfort.

All the above services have one overnight service throughout the year carrying first and second class sleeping cars and second class day coaches. Each service also has either a buffet or light refreshments available.

Trains in Norway are officially classified as Ekspresstog (express), Hurtigtog (fast), and Persontog (slow).

Some Itineraries

Because of the geography of the country it is not possible to do a complete "round trip" by train. But by using ferries and/or buses it is possible to have several interesting trips leaving from one point and arriving back there.

Starting from Oslo you could take the Bergen Line route to that city. This is without doubt one of the most scenic routes in Scandinavia and indeed in Europe. You could do it in one day without a stop over or alternatively stop at Geilo or Voss, both attractive resorts. From Bergen you could then take the Hydrofoil service to Stavanger, calling en route at Haugesund and

Kopervik, the entire trip taking about four hours. There are four services daily, and it is a most dramatic journey in every way.

From Stavanger you then follow the main line via Kristiansand (stop over there) back to Oslo. As an alternative side trip, you could divert from the main line at Nordagutu and go around the coast to the resort and port of Larvik (an attractive spot), rejoining the main line at Drammen.

With a night each in Bergen, Stavanger, and Kristiansand this route could be a four day "quickie," but it is best to take a full week.

On the Bergen Line at the village of Myrdal in western Norway, there is a branch to the little ferry port (and resort) of Flam on the Sognesfjord. The line is only 20 kms (12 mi) long, but it drops from 2,800 feet to sea level in a most spectacular fashion, passing over many waterfalls (it stops at the biggest for photography), through tunnels and along escarpments, clinging to the edge of the valley. It is unquestionably Norway's most beautiful line, short as it is. You can easily visit the Flam-Myrdal line from Bergen or Voss; get off the main train at Myrdal, take the line to Flam and then return to Myrdal for a later train. Alternatively, you can use this route to get to various resorts on the Sognefjord and other fjords nearby. The ferry links with all trains at Myrdal. If you went by ferry from Flam to Balestrand, one of the delightful tiny resorts, you would change ferries in mid-fjord, an added excitement and perfectly safe.

If going to Trondheim, you could take the main line one way via Lillehammer, Otta, and Dombas, returning by the "secondary" route through Roros, providing a change of scenery for about half the journey.

From Oslo, the train is a very convenient way to visit the interesting towns of Drammen, 40 kms (25 mi.) and Kongsberg, 86 kms (53 mi.). A really interesting day trip by train from the capital is to the town of Tonsberg, which is the port of registry for much of Norway's whaling fleet. It lies at the southern end of the Oslofjord. The 103 km (64 mi.) journey takes about one-and-a-half hours, and there are about eight trains (second class only) each way daily. On the same route but farther on, lies the ferry port and resort of Larvik, about a forty-five-minute ride from Tonsberg. The same trains serve both places and several have light refreshment services. From Larvik also it is possible to return via the inland route, changing trains at Nordagutu on the Stavanger main line.

Tickets and Costs

Rail travel in Norway is comparable in cost with that throughout much of western Europe.

There are no "runabout" tickets for overall rail travel, but reductions are given for groups and certain categories when traveling together. There are also occasional special fares when tickets are issued in connection with special events. Information on these can be obtained at main railway stations. Of course, Norway plays a major part in the Circular Tour tickets for covering the whole of Scandinavia.

Miscellaneous Information

In Oslo there are two main termini—the West Station, which serves the lines to Drammen, Larvik, Kristiansand and Stavanger; and the East Station, serving Bergen, Trondheim and routes to Sweden, both south and east. There is also a small station called National Theatre for the suburban route to Holmenkollen.

Norwegian Railways head office is in Oslo.

Timetables for the main routes are issued free, different ones applying for summer and winter. They can be obtained at main railway stations and also from Norwegian State Railway offices abroad. There is also a National Railway Guide in Norwegian, available only in the country, costing currently 10 N. Kr.

There are at present two preserved passenger railways. The first is the narrow-gauge Holand Railway which runs from Sorumsand to Fossum (3.8km or about 2 miles) about 38 km (24 mi.) east of Oslo. It can be reached by train on the Oslo-Kongsvinger line. It has two steam engines, one diesel and several coaches, operating on Sundays in summer only. Further information from Holand Railways, P. O. Box 31, Winderen, Oslo 3, Norway.

The second line is the Setesdal Railway about 20 kms (12 mi.) north of Kristiansand. It runs for 5 km (3 mi.) along the River Otra and has three steam locomotives, two railbuses and several coaches. It operates on summer Sundays and also on Saturdays in July. The nearest main line station is Grovane on the Oslo-Stavanger line. Further information from Setesdal Railway, Postboks 81 N 4601, Kristiansand S. Norway.

The Norwegian Railway Club was formed in 1969 to promote a general interest in railways in the country and beyond. It works in close collaboration with the State Railways and the railway museum at Hamar (see below). For further information on the Club write to Norwegian Railway Club, Postboks 1492, Vika, Oslo 1, Norway.

The Norwegian Railway Museum is located at Hamar in central Norway some 128 kms (80 mi.) north of Oslo. It has both standard- and narrow-gauge engines and rolling stock as well as old signalling, station buildings and other equipment and is constantly being added to. There is a library and model railway. During the summer, a narrow-gauge locomotive hauls a train of old wooden coaches through the museum grounds. Full information from Jernbanemuseet, N-2300 Hamar, Norway.

SWEDEN

With one of the world's highest standards of living, it is not surprising that Sweden maintains a railway system likewise of first rate quality. Apart from a few branch lines in the central area of the country, the network is owned and operated by the state, the official name being Statens Jarnvagar, with the initials SJ used often. With the exception of short stretches of narrow-gauge track, mainly in the south, the whole system is standard gauge and about 11,200 kms (6944 mi.) in length. About 60% is electrified, the rest being diesel.

Because of the geographical nature of the country, main routes run north and south and east and west, with various links running from these. As the center and south of the country is comparatively flat and more densely populated, the network here is quite extensive. One main line runs to the north, with main branches running from it. This line continues up into the mountains through the iron ore mining area of Kiruna and across the border to Narvik, the far-north Norwegian port. It is completely electrified.

There are other cross-border links with Norway, the most southerly linking Stockholm and Gothenburg with Olso, the Norwegian capital. Another link is in the center of the country and connects Sweden with the Norwegian city of Trondheim. The rail-link with Denmark is by the train ferry route across the narrow straits between Helsingborg (Sweden) and Helsingor (or Elsinore in Denmark). On all these routes there are through train services, with no change necessary at the frontier.

In common with the rest of Scandinavia, the Swedes keep their trains, stations and other railway parts in an excellent state of repair. In recent years there has been an extensive renewing of passenger rolling stock which has resulted in high standards of comfort, particularly in the newest second class express stock. It goes without saying that all cars are very clean.

The system is most extensive in the southern half of the country, with the area west and south of Stockholm being particularly well served. In addition to the main line services, there is a good network of cross country routes, linking the towns and resorts on the Baltic with those on the Kattegat and Skagerrak.

Although Sweden has a substantial amount of industrialization, this is barely evident when traveling by rail, and even where it occurs the general tidiness of the country makes it unobtrusive. The majority of rail routes are in beautiful countryside, varying from the wood and lake scenery of the south central area to the well tended farmlands of the "deep south" to the wide horizon northland with great mountains in the west—plus of course some fine coastal scenery. While it would be an exaggeration to say that you can see the best of Sweden without leaving the railway areas, the trains do serve some of the finest parts of the country.

Some Leading Trains

Top expresses in Sweden are called "Rapid" (Expresstag) and shown by the letter X in the timetables. Other expresses (often those with more intermediate stops) are called "Express" (Snalltag) and the letter "S" is used to mark these in the timetables. Seat reservation in the former is obligatory.

There are several fast expresses ("X" trains) linking Stockholm with the country's two other largest cities—Gothenburg and Malmo. To the former, the best trains take between four and four-and-a-half hours for the 456 km (283 mi) trip. The two main "named" Rapids on this route, the *Stockholmaren* and the *Goteborgaren,* allow both early morning and late afternoon departures from either city and carry either a full dining car or refreshment service. However, as these are mainly trains aimed at business traffic of one kind or another, they do not operate between the June 15 to August 21st vacation period. But there are a number of other trains in operation at that time and throughout the year so this presents no real problem. All trains linking the two cities carry a restaurant car or refreshment service. There is an overnight sleeping car service, with day coaches also offering both first and second class travel between the cities. These are not as fast as the best daytime trains, but speed is of no consequence on this route by night.

Between Malmo and Stockholm there are two routes, a direct one through Norrkoping, Mjolby and Hassleholm and another via Gothenburg. With the former, the 600 km (372 mi.) journey takes around six-and-a-half hours. On the majority of services, a full dining car is carried. Named trains on this route are the *Oresundpilen* (it also serves Gothenburg) and the *Skankingen.* For overnight travel, there is a sleeping car express each night with first and second class sleepers as well as day coaches.

But without doubt Sweden's most fascinating train is the one which runs up the full length of the country, starting in Malmo and ending in Narvik up in the far north across the border in Norway. This train is the *Lappland-spillen* which takes just over 30 hours for the 2123 km (1316 mi) journey. There are through first and second class day coaches the whole way and second class couchettes. This train also carries sleeping cars (first and second class) for the northern townships of Umea and Lulea. The dining car goes all the way.

From Stockholm there are also daily services to the far north with the *Nordpilen* serving Lulea and Kiruna (overnight) and connections to Narvik, again with first and second class sleepers, second class couchettes, and day cars. There is both a dining car and light refreshment service on this route. Another overnight train going to the north from Stockholm is the *Bottenviken,* again with sleepers, day cars, and diners. The time for the run from Stockholm to Lulea (on the coast) is about 12 hours.

In addition, there is a daytime train with first and second class coaches and a dining car. This is the *Adalen* and it takes around 16 hours for the 1130 kms (700 mi. journey).

Suggested Itineraries

If time does not permit a visit to the far north of Sweden, then a good round trip easily manageable within a week starting and ending in Stockholm is as follows. Take the main line route from the capital to Sodertalje, Hallsberg then along the north of Lake Vanern to Karlstad and Kil, then turn south to Mellerud and Trollhatten into Gothenburg. From here go south via Halmstad to Malmo. Turning north again, travel to Hassleholm and then east to Karlskrona, the charming resort area on the Baltic. From here, return inland to join the main Stockholm line at Alvesta and thence north through Mjolby and Norkopjing to the capital.

This is the bare outline of the route, but it can be varied by taking the more direct route to Gothenburg via Falkoping or omitting the visit to Malmo but cutting across the delightful rural country in the south from Gothenburg via Boras and Alvesta to Karlskrona.

A good day trip by rail from Stockholm is south to Sodertalje, then west along the south shore on the salt water lake of Malaren, (Stockholm is at the eastern end of this) to Eskilstuna. From this pleasant town go north to Vasteras. From here the route lies along the north side of Malaren back into Stockholm. The entire distance is about 275 kms (172 mi.). It can be done, of course, in the opposite direction also.

From Stockholm there are good trains to the ancient university city of Uppsala (45 minutes), the ferry ports of Norrtalje and Nynashamn, resort suburb of Saltsjobaden (a half hour run at most).

Mention should also be made of the scenic route into Norway from Stockholm to Trondheim via Ange, Ostersund and Hell (that's in Norway). This attractive but lesser known route takes nearly 13 hours for the 815 km (505 mi.) trip. The train leaves Stockholm at about 10 P.M. and arrives at Trondheim after midday the following day. There are through first and second class day coaches, sleeping and couchette cars for the overnight section, and refreshment services part of the way.

Tickets, Fares and Costs

Rail travel in Sweden is moderately expensive, but if you wish to cut costs use second class travel, as the standards are high.

Within the country, reduced rates apply to family group or Senior Citizens (Old Age Pensioners) only. With the family ticket, three people minimum must travel, e.g. husband, wife and one child—but the child can be any age, from three to twenty inclusive. The reduction is approximately 25% on both single and return tickets. Unmarried children of 21 and over can count as one "parent" in a family.

A group of 10 adults or over get 25% reduction on tickets.

Senior Citizens of 65 and over get 50% reduction on all rail travel. Proof of age must be given. Passport is sufficient for this.

In both Stockholm and Gothenburg, there are 3-day "runabout" tickets which not only allow unlimited travel on local trains, but also on buses, trams and ferries. Current cost is 24 S. kroner ($5.52).

Timetables covering the major routes are issued free at all railway stations and at main information offices as well as at ticket agencies. Tickets may be bought at all stations and also beforehand through accredited travel agencies and at Swedish Railway offices overseas.

A comprehensive travel guide giving details of all public transport services is published in Swedish only. It costs 11 S.kr. ($2.53).

Miscellaneous Information

In Stockholm, the main station is the Central where most trains into and out of the city stop. The public transport services also operate from this point or very close by. The ferry boarding points can be reached by bus or by taxi, and the two main bus stations of Humlegard and Stureplan are also served by city buses from the station. Central is a "through" station. Two small termini serve certain suburban routes. The Ostra East station goes to Rimbo and the Saltsjobanan station is the terminus for the line to Saltsjobaden. They are both within the general central area of the city.

In Gothenburg, there is one main station, the Central, which is a terminus and serves all routes. Bus and taxi services from there to the ferry and ship boarding points.

The dining and buffet cars and the other refreshment services are operated by a subsidiary company of the railway. Full meals on trains tend to be expensive but of high quality. Sleeping car services are also operated by the railway except those on international routes beyond Scandinavia, which are either operated by the country of origin (e.g. USSR or East Germany) or by the West European pool of sleeping cars.

The Swedish Railway Museum is at Gavle about 180 kms (112 mi.) north of Stockholm.

Preserved Railways

Sweden is rich in active, preserved railways. At the time of writing there are seven steam-operated railways in the country. They operate at various times throughout the summer and early autumn. Full information on these can be obtained from the local tourist offices and also from the National Tourist Information Office in Stockholm. These railways are as follows:

Ostarlans Musaijarnvag—Brosarp/St. Olof in Skane. Operates May—mid-September. Standard gauge, about 14kms long.

Ohs Bruks Jarnveg—Ohs Bruks/Bor in Smaland. Near Varnamo. Operates daily in July, Saturdays and Sundays in June and August. Narrow gauge and about 15 kms. in length.

Musaibanan Antan Grafsnas—Antan/Grafsnas in Vastergotland near Alingsas. Operates from mid-May to mid-September on Sundays and national holidays. Narrow gauge, about 11 kms.

Ostra Sodermanslands Jarnveg—Mariefred/Laggasta in Sodermanland. The oldest steam engine in Sweden. It was built in 1888. Daily trips April to October. Narrow gauge, about 4 kms.

Stockholm Roslagans Jarnvegar—Uppsala/Faringe in Uppland. It runs for about 30 kms. on narrow gauge. Open Sundays and national holidays from the end of May to the end of June and again from mid-August to the end of September.

Jadraas Tallas Musaibanan near Gavle where the railway museum is situated. Longest track, around 35 kms. Operates from around the beginning of June through to September.

Gotlands Heffelby Jarnveg on the island of Gotland. This is being restored and put into working order. A number of trips are planned for 1977.

For further information on Swedish Railways write to

> Swedish State Railways (SJ),
> Central Station,
> S—105 50 Stockholm,
> Sweden.

SPAIN

By Murray Hughes

One of Europe's Mediterranean playgrounds, Spain is a tour operator's paradise. Planeloads of sun-seeking holiday makers are whisked from Europe's cities, dumped near a beach with a room in a concrete honeycomb and flown unceremoniously back to their homes. Such holidays afford little opportunity to see what Spain really has to offer and virtually exclude the chance of getting to know any Spaniards. Far more interesting and enjoyable is a trip through the interior, where Spanish life can be seen as it really is and where reminders of Spain's romantic past are in considerable evidence. The best way to do this is by train.

Access

Apart from the Portuguese frontier, all land-based travel to Spain is across the French frontier and through the Pyrenees. There is a good selection of trains to the frontier stations of Cerbere/Port Bou and Hendaye/Irun from many European centers. Examples are the *Hispania-Express* from Hamburg in northern Germany to Port Bou and the group of *rapide* services to Irun from Paris. On most of these however, it is necessary to change trains at the frontier because the gauge of Spanish National Railways' track is 5 ft. 6 in., not 4 ft. 8½ in. like most other European railways.

Nevertheless, starting in Switzerland or France it is possible to reach Spanish soil without changing—a remarkable feat accomplished by only three services, all of which run daily throughout the year. The first of these is *La Puerta del Sol* which leaves Paris (gare d'Austerlitz) in the early evening for Madrid. It conveys first and second class sleeping cars and second class *couchette* cars to the Spanish capital as well as a restaurant car and first-class day coaches to the frontier at Hendaye. A restaurant car and first-class seating accommodations are also provided in Spain, and for some time the Madrid-Irun *Puerta del Sol* featured a cinema car. Special all-inclusive tickets with dinner and breakfast are available for journeys between the two capitals. From Paris to Bordeaux the train runs non-stop, reaching the frontier soon after midnight. Here the sleeping cars and *couchette* cars are lifted up on jacks and the standard-gauge bogies exchanged for broad-gauge ones; the cars are then lowered into position and the train is reassembled before departure for Madrid—its snoring passengers hopefully unaware of the proceedings.

The second through train to Spain from Paris is the *Barcelona-Talgo* introduced in 1974 with first and second class sleeping accommodations only. Departure in mid-evening from Paris gives an early morning arrival at Port Bou. The sleeping cars are not lifted on to jacks, but pass through a special installation where the wheelsets are adjusted from one gauge to another as the train moves over it. Arrival in Barcelona (Termino Station) is just before 9:00 A.M.

The only daytime through service starts in Switzerland. This is the *Catalan-Talgo*—a first class only train forming part of the Trans-Europe-Express network and requiring payment of a supplementary fare. It travels via Lyons, Avignon and Perpignan to Port Bou, where it passes through the wheelset adjusting installation before continuing to Gerona and Barcelona (Termino).

Through the Pyrenees

The Franco-Spanish Pyrenees range, although not as spectacular as the European Alps, offers the traveler some magnificent scenery. Through the heart of these mountains are two relatively unknown railways which cross the frontier. The first passes close to the tiny country of Andorra and is accessible from Toulouse or Perpignan. Originally opened to traffic in 1929, the route is electrified, with gradients as steep as 4 per cent. The French frontier station is located at La Tour de Carol where there are tracks of three gauges: Spanish National Railways' broad gauge, French National Railways' standard and meter gauges. The Spanish frontier station is at Puigcerda, and the route continues to Ribas de Fresser where there is a connection to the meter-gauge electrified rack route serving Nuria, which passes over the highest section of railway in Spain. From Ribas the line descends to Ripoll and eventually to Barcelona (Plaza Cataluna Station).

The second trans-Pyrenean route is from Pau in France to Canfranc, where one changes trains. On this line there are only two or three trains a day and it is well to be sure of their timings before setting out. From Canfranc it is 108 miles to Zaragoza. Both of these routes have numerous tunnels and viaducts and afford excellent views of the Pyrenees.

Structure

The State Railways of Spain (*Red Nacional de los Ferrocarriles Espanoles,* RENFE) was created in 1941 when all 7,980 miles of Spanish 5 ft. 6 in. gauge track were amalgamated. At that time the entire Spanish railway system was suffering severely from the devastation of the 1936–39 Spanish civil war. Subsequently the Second World War further constrained development of the Spanish economy and for many years this and the gauge problem tended to hinder technical and commercial progress.

Today's rail traveler in Spain, although he will experience slower average speeds than in France or other West European countries—something which reflects the more leisurely pace of life—is unlikely to feel that the railways are a relic of the past. RENFE has made in the last few years massive and sustained efforts to modernise and upgrade its network, rolling stock, and operating methods.

The RENFE network is divided into three categories: basic *(red basica)*, complementary *(red complementaria)* and secondary *(red secundaria).* In the first category are about 3,000 miles of line. The most important are the route to the northwest from Madrid serving Palencia, Leon, Oviedo and Vigo; the link between the capital and Barcelona, Spain's second largest city, via Zaragoza; the transverse line in the northeast from Zaragoza to Bilbao and San Sebastian; the route from Madrid to the French frontier at Irun via Venta de Banos and Burgos; the coastal stretch from Port Bou to Barcelona, Tarragona and Valencia; the main route from Madrid to Valencia via Albacete; and the principal artery to the south serving Cordoba, Sevilla and Cadiz, with branches to Malaga and Almeria.

The complementary and secondary categories cover cross-country and branch lines, including several routes into Portugal which handle relatively light traffic.

Services

There is an extraordinarily wide range of passenger services, although not all types of train and service are to be found on all lines. Local and suburban commuter trains are in considerable evidence around the major cities. On the main lines between them, distances are comparatively long and it is this fact more than any other which has tended to shape the service pattern. In no case are main line services frequent by other West European standards and there are only two or three trains a day on many routes. At the bottom of the scale is the *omnibus* or former *correos* (mail train) which stops at all intermediate stations of moderate importance. Next is the *expreso* which caters to traffic between most large towns without intermediate stops. These trains often run overnight and include sleeping facilities and some form of on-train dining. At the top of the list is the *Rapido,* in many cases a luxury service running on the fastest schedule and requiring payment of a supplementary fare.

Further distinctions are made between the types of train used to provide the service, particularly in the case of the *rapido;* different supplements are charged accordingly. Fast daytime services are worked by a variety of diesel railcars. Some of these are know as TAF *(Tren Automotor Fiat)* and consist of three-car sets purchased from the Fiat company of Turin in the early 1950s; late 1976 saw trials with off-the-peg railcars also built by Fiat and similar to the cars leased to the Massachussetts Bay Transportation Authority earlier in the year; these cars may eventually replace the TAF units.

So successful was the introduction of TAF services that RENFE decided to extend the concept and in 1965 a second batch of fast diesel railcars entered service. Known as TER *(Tren Espanol Rapido),* these were of more sophisticated design, again built by Fiat. TER trains can be found on most routes of the *red basica* and consist of two-car sets, with power supplied from a pair of 850 h.p. diesel engines with hydraulic transmission. Whereas TAF trains are second class only, TER services offer both first and second class accommodations, usually with restaurant facilities.

On electrified routes the equivalent of the TER service is the ELT (Electrotren). Outwardly similar, but painted red instead of blue, ELTs offer good schedules and a high standard of comfort.

On nearly all long distance routes there is at least one overnight train with sleeping car and *couchette* facilities. (The Spanish for *couchette* is *litera* and for sleeping-car *coche camas*). RENFE provides second-class *couchette* cars and there is a fixed supplement for use of a berth irrespective of length of journey. Sleeping cars on the other hand are operated by the International Sleeping Car Co and charges for beds vary considerably according to length of journey, class of travel, type of vehicle and accommodation. An extra charge is made where air conditioning is provided.

Talgo

Special mention must be made of the Spanish Talgo services. Anyone who has made use of the *Barcelona-Talgo* or the *Catalan-Talgo* to reach Spain will have noticed the strange appearance of these trains: a low body profile and a series of small units forming a single articulated trainset.

Talgo stands for *Tren Articulado Ligero Goicoechea y Oriol;* the last two names are those of the inventors of the system and the first three words mean "lightweight articulated train".

The idea originated in 1942 when Patentes Talgo SA began experiments to develop an ultra-lightweight train to allow high-speed running over RENFE's at that time dilapidated track. Starting with a set of truck (lorry) axles fitted with railway wheels, an experimental train first ran in 1943. Towards the end of the Second World War the American Car & Foundry company in New York was awarded a contract to build some developmental prototypes, and in 1949 the first Talgo train entered commercial service between Madrid and Irun.

The Talgo principle is as follows: a number of short body units are carried on single axles; each unit is pivoted at the other end on the axle of the unit in front; together the units form an articulated assembly resembling a large caterpillar.

A number of Talgo applications were made in the USA. One of these was the *Jet Rocket,* introduced in 1955 by the Chicago, Rock Island & Pacific Railroad between Chicago and Peoria. A similar train was tried by the New York, New Haven & Hartford Railroad, and the Boston & Maine also ran a Talgo for a short period. Some of the American Talgos have made their way back across the Atlantic to the home of their inventor and can be found on the 4 ft. 8½ in. gauge Langreo Railway near Oviedo in northwest Spain.

Not until 1960 was the Talgo principle extended in Spain. In that year a daily Talgo service was introduced between Madrid and Barcelona via Zaragoza, but these trains were later transferred to the Madrid-Cuenca-Valencia route. In 1964 a further series of Talgo vehicles was purchased by RENFE—100 passenger cars and 10 diesel-hydraulic locomotives of German design. These are the trains which form most of the Talgo services in use today; all offer first and second class accommodations, air conditioning, a restaurant and bar—for which luxuries a hefty supplementary fare is payable.

The unique design of single-axle units prompted Talgo engineers to undertake further developmental work, and experiments were carried out to test the possibility of adjusting the axle width for standard-gauge running. The trials were successful and culminated in 1969 in the introduction of the "Catalan-Talgo" TEE train with adjustable wheelsets between Barcelona and Geneva; the "Barcelona-Talgo" sleeping car service followed in 1974. A triumph of ingenuity, these trains are now a showcase for RENFE outside Spain.

Electrification

Spain's first electrified railway was a 13-mile section of the Almeria line in the southeast, energized in 1911. Three-phase current was used and the locomotives were designed especially to haul the iron ore which had prompted electrification. In 1963 work was completed on the 275-mile Madrid-Cordoba line and 29 locomotives of American design, with bulbous front ends, were employed to haul trains over this route. Other electrification in the 1950s and 1960s was concentrated on the suburban routes around Barcelona, but also spread in pockets along the northern coast where heavy industry flourishes.

By the end of 1973 a total of 2,110 route-miles were electrified. The energy crisis at that time was viewed in Spain more seriously than in some other countries, and as a result a massive 1,710-mile RENFE electrification scheme was approved by the Spanish Council of Ministers early in 1974. The project covers the period until December 1977 and much of the work has already been completed, bringing reduced journey times and more attractive services on several key routes. Most important of these are Miranda de Ebro-Zaragoza-Tarragona/Manresa (-Barcelona), (Madrid-) Guadalajara-Zaragoza, and Alcazar-Albacete-Valencia. Through electric services now operate between Madrid and Barcelona, using both the Lerida and Mora routes east of Zaragoza.

The onset of the energy crisis was not, however, the only reason for RENFE's electrification program. Upward swings in both passenger and freight traffic had been detected and electrification was regarded as necessary to cope with the increasing volume of movements. RENFE's forecast proved to be conservative and passenger traffic continued to increase even during the recession in 1975.

RENFE possesses about 400 electric locomotives. They represent a wide range of the world's manufacturers, but in fact many have been built under licence in Spain. A number of dual-voltage Japanese locomotives provide additional interest, and the keen observer will also spot British, Swiss or American machines. The relatively few small-profile diesels designed especially for haulage of Talgo trains contrast sharply with RENFE's other motive power. Most diesel and some electric locomotives are in a dark green livery picked out with broad yellow stripes.

Steam traction was eliminated from RENFE lines in 1974; steam locomotives can still, however, be found as derelict heaps of decay and rust on isolated sidings. Some of the last of these fiery monsters were oil-fired articulated Garretts and the once ubiquitous 4-8-0 designs.

Passenger Rolling Stock

Most exciting development since the Talgo trains were introduced was the delivery to RENFE in 1976 of a prototype tilting-body four-car 3 kV trainset from the Spanish manufacturer CAF. Known as the *Basculante,* the train derives directly from the Fiat-built *Pendolino* in Italy. Designed to take curves at higher speeds than conventional trains, a proposed series of 10 Basculante trains will allow journey time reductions of about 30 percent on four electrified routes in the not too distant future. The prototype is now undergoing an extensive trial program.

For interurban services such as Sevilla-Cordoba, a large number of three-car series 440 and 441 electric multiple-units is entering service. More of these and an increasing number of ELTs will be introduced as RENFE's electrification program progresses.

Locomotive-hauled rolling stock on main line services is now relatively modern, although vacuum braking is still employed. The Spanish vehicles are interspersed among large numbers of coaches built of German design; nearly all are of side-corridor arrangement, and some of the latest vehicles feature cafeterias and *couchettes.*

Not uncommon until recently were wooden-bodied bogie coaches with wooden seats and open-end balconies; a few are still in use and offer an excellent opportunity to sample railway travel as it was many years ago. A number of sleeping cars also date considerably far back and a glance at the builders' plates will reveal their origins elsewhere in Europe.

Local trains on electrified routes are usually three-car multiple units which are described in the timetables as *tranvias.*

Non-RENFE Railways

The network of Spanish 5 ft. 6 in. gauge lines is closely seconded by 22 railways of varying gauges which are operated by the state organization *Ferrocarriles de Via Estrecha* (FEVE). In addition, there are some 15 independent companies which, together with FEVE, transport about 130 million passengers and about 10 million tons of freight a year.

Most of the FEVE lines are meter gauge and operate in the Basque region and along the northern coast. To travel them all takes considerable time and not a little research. For additional information FEVE headquarters may be contacted at 6 General Rodrigo Street, Parque de las Naciones, Madrid.

Two important independent railways are to be found in Barcelona: the meter-gauge Ferrocarriles Catalanes which runs a line of some 90 miles into the mountains at Guardida, and the 4 ft. 8½ in. gauge Ferrocarriles de Cataluna which operates about 25 miles of electrified route around Barcelona.

Between Leon and Monforte in the northwest is the 50-mile Ponferrada-Villablino Railway where steam locomotives can still be seen.

An extraordinary assortment of rolling stock is operated by these and the several other non-RENFE railways and this will provide endless interest for the rail buff.

Future Outlook

RENFE completed a number of new suburban and local lines in 1975–76. Examples are the line to Prat de Llobregat airport in Barcelona and the Malaga-Fuengirola line on the Costa del Sol, also serving Malaga airport. Other suburban line construction projects are under way in Madrid.

All these schemes are overshadowed by the plan to build a 4 ft. 8½ in. gauge high-speed railway between Madrid, Barcelona and Port Bou. No date has as yet been fixed for start of construction, although RENFE's research effort is now centering on high speed and its associated problems.

Excursions

A journey on a Talgo train is recommended. Talgos are still RENFE's showpiece trains; they remain unique, not least because of the peculiar noise rhythm of single axles on jointed track.

Many Spanish routes offer considerable scenic interest; particularly outstanding are the Malaga-Bobadilla (-Cordoba) line through the El Chorro gorge in the Sierra Nevada and the longer former Central of Aragon Railway route from Zaragoza to Valencia via Teruel. In the north the Palencia to Gijon and Palencia to Santander lines through the Cordillera Cantabrica are both magnificent. Travel through Spain's interior reveals much of the history of the Iberian peninsula, with castles and other ruins dominating many a hilltop. A trip from Madrid to Segovia (about 60 miles) is merited, as this town features a fine example of a Roman aqueduct. Generally the Spaniards are friendly and their guitars often serve as an introduction.

Off the mainland there are two railways in the Balearic Isles: the Mallorca Railway and the Palma-Soller Railway. The extra sea crossing is an optional excursion, however, for Madrid, Barcelona, Bilbao and Valencia are all centers with extensive railway interest.

Timings

Train times are published in the *Guia Renfe,* but the *Horario Guia* offers additional information such as station altitudes and types of traction. Another invaluable guide is the Thomas Cook Continental Timetable, which covers the whole of Europe, Amtrak, Soviet Railways and even China! It also features town maps showing the geographical location of major stations.

For those intending to travel long distances it is worth buying a kilometric ticket—from any RENFE station. These tickets are available for 3,000 km for one person and up to 10,000 km for six. Passengers are not normally allowed to board main line trains unless they have reserved accommodation or their ticket has been endorsed with the train number and date of departure. Incidentally, RENFE was one of the first European railways to adopt a network-wide computerized seat reservation system.

Catering
Full restaurant car service is available in Talgo, TER and some ELT trains, and meals on these trains are reasonable. Cafeteria or snack-bar cars are provided on many other long distance trains. Station catering is generally restricted to provision of rolls and sandwiches; it is better to seek out a nearby bar or restaurant. Spanish food tends to be a little greasy, but seafood specialities are often excellent. Bars frequently provide small tasty dishes known as *tapas* which are particularly enjoyable.

City Transfers
In Madrid the main station serving the north and east at Charmartin is linked by a cross-city underground suburban service to Madrid Atocha for destinations in the south. Madrid Norte (Principe Pio) for Avila and the northwest can be reached by metro.

In Barcelona most trains run to Termino station, sometimes referred to as Barcelona Francia, but through services from Port Bou to Madrid call at Paseo de Gracia, a 10-minute rail journey from Termino. The independent railways have separate stations.

Museums
Spain's national railway museum is located at 44 Calle Santa Isabel in Madrid. Among the exhibits is an 1871 Schneider-Creusot steam locomotive which was once the property of the Andalusian Railway.

SWITZERLAND

By K. Westcott Jones

Switzerland and the State of Colorado have one thing in common, high mountains. In the matter of railways, though, Switzerland—which is only one-sixth the area of Colorado—has eight times the route mileage. No matter how high the mountains, nor how deep the gorges, Swiss railways penetrate and serve the communities. No location in Switzerland is more than ten miles from a working passenger railway.

Highly efficient and regarded with admiration throughout the world, the railways of Switzerland have an enviable reputation for safety and service. The most important inter-city routes are owned by the Government as Swiss Federal Railways, but about half the trackage is in private hands, shared by at least fifty companies, ranging from large and prosperous to tiny and struggling. There is one main route, however, run by Europe's largest railway still not federally owned—the Berne-Lotschberg-Simplon (BLS)—which actually competes as a North-South, under-the-Alps trunk line with Swiss Federal.

When we think of mountain climbing by train, we automatically think of Switzerland. Yet the very first Swiss rack and pinion railway, built to the summit of the Rigi from Vitznau, owes its existence to studies made of the 1860's rack and pinion headed by the locomotive "Old Peppersass" up to the summit of New Hampshire's White Mountains' highest peak, Mount Washington. The engineer of the then Swiss Central Railway, Niklaus Riggenbach, planning a line to climb the Rigi Mountain, heard what Sylvester Marsh was building up Mount Washington and made a visit to U.S.A. to see the workings. From the meeting between these two men, most of the rack and pinion climbs up mountains everywhere came into being.

That great chronicler of Swiss Railways, the late Cecil J. Allen, points out that no other country in the world has so much engineering in relation to trackage. There are 5,900 bridges on all railways, 3,400 of them on Swiss Federal. The grade crossing has long been eliminated on all main and many secondary lines. As for tunnels, the three longest in the world are all in Switzerland (Simplon, Gotthard, Lotschberg are all more than ten miles in length), but when Japan's undersea tunnel to Hokkaido is ready, that will take pride of place.

The Swiss look upon their railways with pride, although there is now widespread car ownership and consequently a slight but definite falling off of rail usage. But for every Swiss riding a Swiss train, there are two foreigners. These include tourists, business travelers, and "guest workers" (of whom some two million are in Switzerland during certain seasons aiding the hotel industry).

Normal fares are high, and the more difficult the line, the higher the charge, culminating in the upper section of the Jungfrau Railway (Europe's highest) where the rate escalates to 12 Francs ($5 U.S.) per mile. But so many concession tickets exist that all visitors are cushioned against high fares, and only the chance emergency traveler would pay full rate.

Because of labor shortages and higher costs, Swiss trains do not all present that spotless gleaming look so long associated with them. Internally, they are clean; externally, only the "SBB-CFF" designation on the sides of Swiss Federal cars are wiped clean, unless crack express trains are involved.

Electric traction from abundant water power was harnessed to work the railways at a very early stage, and by 1955 the entire system was under the wires, except for one mountain-climbing line. Only one small passenger line is worked by diesels. However, nostalgia and the tourist business have resulted in a widespread re-steaming of lines for pleasure purposes (see later).

The Swiss have struck nearly the correct revenue and profit balance between freight and passenger workings, *one* for *one*. This is a lesson for the world, particularly USA (where freight is 22 to passenger's one) and Britain (where freight is only 0.6 to passenger's one).

Train Services In Switzerland

The timetable is enormous; it embraces the Alpine postal motor coaches. Yet Switzerland is no bigger than the states of Massachusetts and Connecticut put together—and with about the same population. The rail section alone has 392 small-print pages of time tables. No traveler in Switzerland should make rail or bus (or lake steamer) journeys without it. The cost is Sw. Frs. 5.50 (just under U.S. $2.50) and it is called "Amtliches Kursbuch," "Indicateur Officiel," or "Orario ufficiale," according to which of the three major Swiss languages (Swiss-Deutsch, French, or Italian) you wish to use. A very high proportion of people in travel and tourism speak fluent English, as it happens.

Switzerland originates trains, and it passes international expresses. In fact, the business of passing international trains is and always has been good business for Switzerland. It is a founder-member of the TEE (Trans Europe Express) high speed, all first class, deluxe system, and ten out of the 34 TEE's are handled at some point in Switzerland. Swiss Federal Railways' electric multiple-units are used for the TEE *Gottardo* and the TEE *Cisalpin,* both Swiss-originating, and also the TEE *Iris* (Zurich-Strasbourg-Brussels in seven hours).

Swiss Federal Railways operate a fast, highly efficient, inter-city network between Geneva, Lausanne, Berne, Olten, and Zurich, and from Basle to Lucerne, Basle to Zurich, and Zurich to Lucerne. Distances are not, of course, great, the overall run from Geneva to Zurich being 287 kms. (178 miles), but frequency is hourly with a timing of 3¼. All trains carry first and second class cars, and the Swiss Dining Car Company provides one of its red vehicles on all trains running during normal mealtimes. In general, fast trains run hourly, and stopping trains also hourly, on main lines. Time keeping is not so precise as it used to be due to an ever-increasing volume of freight and passenger traffic, but almost all arrivals (excepting international trains) are within five minutes of scheduled time.

The great operation is the Gottard route, Zurich and Lucerne to Lugano and on into Italy. More of this anon. Swiss Federal trains run eastwards from Zurich to Winterthur and the Lake Constance area, also to Sargans (for Austria) and Chur. On this latter line, express trains run every two hours. From Lausanne, Swiss Federal trains run up the Valley of the Rhone to the Simplon Tunnel, their national limit being Brigue Station at the western entrance. There is one interesting meter-gauge route owned by Swiss Federal which also makes a rack and pinion climb with electric traction. This is the Lucerne-Interlaken line over the Brunig Pass. More Swiss Federal routes ply westwards from Olten and Berne to Neuchatel and the French frontier.

Private Railways In Switzerland

All other railway lines, and they run into thousands of kilometers, are private. The most important (and the most profitable, for unlike many railroads today it pays a steady 4% dividend) is the Berne-Lotschberg-Simplon (BLS), operating as a standard-gauge electric main line from Berne to Brigue, with extensions over acquired lines to Biel, Zweisimmen, and Interlaken. It has the *most powerful locomotives in the world,* giant electrics working in tandem on heavy expresses—and freights—pounding up the heavy grades to the eleven-mile-long Lotschberg Tunnel and putting out 8,800 horse power.

The BLS line is a competitive alternative to the North-South Swiss Federal traffic via the Gotthard Tunnel. Its Lotschberg Tunnel is being double-tracked, having been built electric, but single, in 1913. Traffic has grown to fantastic proportions, and it is fortunate in having a monopoly with no roads through this part of the Alps. It works a profitable shuttle service of trains through the tunnel hauling autos and their passengers. This has grown from 20,000 cars a year in 1950 to over a quarter of a million today. BLS expresses carry international stock as well as their own, and the best trains have BLS restaurant cars attached. Despite tremendous gradients and heavy trains to be hauled, the 95 miles from Bern to Brig are covered by expresses in 100 minutes. This is currently the world's most efficient passenger traction. . . .

Most of the Grisons in the eastern part of Switzerland, where the Alps are most concentrated and the valleys among the highest in Europe, are served by the Rhaetian Railways (Rhaettische Bahn). This progressive rail system, based on Landquart, is owned by the Cantons of the East. It is all electric with smart modern trains running on meter gauge, the latest electric engines carrying names, and the best trains equipped with neat restaurant cars. It does, however, run steam specials for enthusiasts (see later).

The Rhaetian Railways serve Davos, St. Moritz, the Engadine Valley, the Bernina Pass with a line going across the Italian border to Tirano, and Arosa. Connections are made with Swiss Federal at Landquart and at Chur. Its major engineering work is the seven-mile-long Albula Tunnel. Crossing the Bernina Pass, the railway is over 7,500 feet above sea level, and for line clearance, giant rotary snowploughs are used which in very severe conditions are pushed by extremely powerful steam locomotives.

Because of the number of important and fashionable ski resorts served by the Rhaetian Railways, peak traffic is in winter, when as many as 18 trains a day are run to St. Moritz over two routes. The best expresses take 2 hours, 5 minutes for the 77 miles from Chur to St. Moritz, which is excellent work for meter gauge and tremendous gradients. The average is only 2¼ hours.

Among the very many private lines are some with significant route mileage and good equipment. All except one are electrified, though a few maintain steam for pleasure runs. The Brienzer-Rothorn Bahn climbs to its 8,600-foot summit by steam power alone, a 55-minute ride from Lake Brienz to a mountain top, not unlike Mount Washington's cogwheel, but with rather more modern steam power.

In some cases, private railways link up for a through working arrangement. From Lucerne all the way to St. Gallen in Northeast Switzerland there is such a co-operative, the Sudost Bahn (Swiss Southeastern Rly Company) handing over its train at Rapperswill to the Bodensee-Toggenberg. Very handsome restaurant cars are provided on this 2¼-hour trip; evening journeys with music while you dine! The *Glacier Express* is a world-famous train running in summer only *over* (rather than through) the Alps from Zermatt through Brigue and the Upper Rhone Valley to St. Moritz. This traverses the Brig-Visp-Zermatt Railway (partly rack-and-pinion), the Furka-Oberalp Railway (part of which has to be dismantled every winter), and the Rhaetian Railways. It crosses the highest bridges in Europe. There is a restaurant car on its scenic four-hour journey.

Based at Interlaken, and handling immense tourist traffic passed to it by the BLS and from the meter-gauge Swiss Federal's Brunig Pass Railway, is the Bernese-Oberland Railway. This plunges into the high valleys and reaches Lauterbrunnen and Grindelwald. Here it hands over to colleagues, the Murren Railway, and the Wengernalp Railway. Finally, at Scheidegg, the Jungfrau Railway takes over and ends up 12,000 feet above sea level just below the summit of the mighty Jungfrau. The 5½-mile trip by Jungfrau Railway is the most expensive train ride in the world (about U.S. $5 a mile). The B.O.B. (Bernese-Oberland Bahn) works with the other lines of the Oberland for marketing and promotion. These lines are highly successful, for most of the resorts they serve are popular in summer and winter and cannot be reached by any other means of transport. There are no roads to more than 50 places in Switzerland reached by rail. This is how the Swiss want it, for it maintains peace and quiet and safety in the mountains. Zermatt is the largest roadless town.

Magnificently scenic is the Montreux Oberland Bernoise (M.O.B.), with an electric line climbing steeply above Lake Lucerne's eastern end and threading the mountains to Zweisimmen and Spiez. It serves Gstaad, one of the top ski resorts of Europe, and comes to an end at Zweisimmen, where the BLS subsidiary takes over (change of gauge).

Another private railway makes an international connection into Italy, like the Rhaetian. It is the Centovalli Railway, running from Locarno through Camedo to Domodossola, 35 miles.

Newest of the private railways is an extension of the Lucerne-Stans Railway to Engelberg, finished in the early 1960's. It gives good access on a line 23 miles long to popular, medium-cost ski resorts. The meter-gauge electric trains run 24 times a day each way, taking about 53 minutes, and some have buffet facilities.

Numerous other private lines are short spurs or mountain climbing ventures, most of them successful. In the Lake Constance area, mention should be made of the Mittel-Thurgau Bahn (Weinfelden-Kreuzlingen-Constance, 16 miles) because it actually enters German Federal Territory. In the Southwest of Switzerland there is a private line running into France —the Martigny-Chatelard, which works with French Railways to link Chamonix with Martigny in the shadow of Mont Blanc.

Preserved Steam Railways And Museums

"Steam Over Switzerland" is the title of a recent book by George Behrend. The fact that it can run to book size indicates how many tourist steam rides exist in modern Switzerland. The Swiss National Tourist Office produces an official booklet called "Steam in Switzerland" and it lists twenty lines which run steam excursions regularly or occasionally.

Swissair actually sells on the American market special tours for railfans, flying them to Zurich, then having them escorted on trips on preserved steam lines and some of the more interesting electric routes.

The Swiss Federal Railways have about five engines capable of being steamed for special excursions. There are also antiques brought out from time to time to celebrate special occasions. The private railways have held on to one or two examples of the last steam power they bought, while others have actually purchased steam engines from Austria and Germany to operate specials.

The first country in the world to go (with one minor exception) all-electric is sensible and efficient and commercial enough to recognise the value of steam trips. Being one of the world's few non-bureaucratic democracies, Switzerland gives its people and its visitors, what they require without upsetting the main transport structure.

Here is the 1976 list of steam operations in Switzerland, showing the name of the company and where it is based. It does not include Swiss Federal specials.

APPENZELLER BAHN Herizau, North East Switzerland. (Bought steam from Austria.)

Blonay-Chamby (Enthusiasts' private system) reached by rail from Montreux.

BERNER OBERLAND BAHN Interlaken.

BRIENZ ROTHORN BAHN (All steam, mountain railway) Lake of Brienz.

BODENSEE TOGGENBURG BAHN St. Gallen, N.E. Switzerland.

BRIG-VISP-ZERMATT BAHN Brig, Zermatt.

BRUENIGBAHN (Steam enthusiasts' line) Kaegiswil on Brunig Line.

MITTEL THURGAU BAHN Weinfelden, N.E. Switzerland.

RHAETIAN RAILWAYS Chur and Grisons.

SURSEE-TRIANGEN-BAHN Sursee, between Olten & Lucerne

SENSETALBAHN Laupen, 12 miles West of Berne.

SOLOTHURN-ZOLLIKOFEN-BERN-BAHN Worblaufen, just outside Berne.

SIHITAL-ZURICH-UETLIBERG-BAHN Zurich area.

VEREINIGTE-BERN-WORB-BAHNEN Worb-Dorf, close to Berne.

VITZNAU-RIGI BAHN Lake Lucerne—classic Rigi climb.

WALDENBURGERBAHN Zurich.

FURKA-OBERALP BAHN (works steam in conjunction with Rhaetian Rlys). Dissentis, Grisons.

The above are railways, but steam listings also include particularly fine paddle steamers operated on the lakes. The BLS owns a beauty on Lake of Thun. The Zurich Lake has several, Lake Lucerne has four, and Lac Leman (Lake Geneva) five, owned by private companies. There is also one on Lake Constance.

The *Swiss Transport Museum* is at Lucerne, just outside the city on the lakeshore. Its rail exhibits are numerous and splendid, including a full working model of the Gotthard Railway. There is a full-size paddle steamer, the "Rigi", in the grounds.

Preserved steam engines can be found at a few points. One is a Brunig Line rack and pinion tank engine (circa 1926) preserved at Meiringen on the Brunig Line. The earliest Vitznau-Rigi steam engine, based on Mt. Washington's "Old Peppersass," is at Vitznau, Lake Lucerne.

Riding The Gotthard Line

Switzerland is synonymous with mountain scenery and railway engineering. Both are exhibited in strength to the thousands of passengers who travel every day by heavy express passenger trains over the famous Gotthard Line.

Until the St. Gotthard Tunnel was built and opened to traffic in 1881, there was no straightforward rail route through the Alps. Trains had to go around them, either down through France and along the Italian Riviera, or east through Austria. The ten-mile bore of the St. Gotthard started in 1871 under the direction of engineer Louis Favre, who did not live to see final completion, dying in the Tunnel in 1879. He is buried close to the tracks in the churchyard at Goschenen, at the northern entrance.

The Gotthard Line starts at Arth Goldau, lines from Zurich and Lucerne having come together there. The climb is breathtaking, the train swinging around curves and climbing gradients of nearly 3%, yet at 45 to 50 miles an hour. Rushing torrents and high mountains with snowcapped peaks always in view enthrall passengers. There is the drama of the spiral tunnels, three of which lift the train 1700 feet. Opposite Wassen Church, the line is lifted 400 feet, and passengers pass the church three times, each time at a higher level.

When the train rushes into the great tunnel at Goschenen, the language is Swiss-Deutsch, the architecture Germanic, the weather probably cool and definitely North European. Eleven minutes later, after hurtling through the tunnel at an altitude of 3,750 feet, the train emerges at Airolo. All at once this is the Mediterranean climate, soft, warm, with palm trees. The language is Italian and the architecture South European. The descent down through the long Valley of the Ticino is superb and scenic in a different way to the northern ascent. The 171 kms. (113 miles) from Arth Goldau to Lugano take only 150 minutes by heavy expresses, while lighter TEE trains, not stopping at Arth Goldau, do the 142 miles from Zurich to Lugano in 169 minutes.

The Lotschberg Line

Northbound trains emerging from what is still the world's longest main line rail tunnel—the 12 mile Simplon from Italy to Switzerland under the Alps—stop at Brigue station. Those taking the BLS route to the north leave the Swiss Federal, which carries on down the middle of the Rhone Valley, and swings off to the right.

The immensely powerful electric locomotives get an immediate grip on the heaviest trains and the climb on the BLS, despite gradients of 2% and more, is made at 55 miles an hour. The fall away of the Rhone Valley to the left has no parallel in railroading; it is just like climbing by aircraft in propeller days, only much smoother. On the right is a precipice, a sheer mountain wall. Soon, on the left, it becomes a precipice dropping 3000 feet down to the Valley of the Rhone.

The BLS on its ledge is magnificently engineered. The track is in superb condition. The train thunders across the great Bietschtal Bridge, a huge steel arch straddling a narrow ravine whose bottom is 255 feet below the wheels.

After twelve miles of fast climbing, the express enters the tight Lonza Valley, where the gradient steepens to nearly 3%, yet the speed does not fall below 50 miles an hour. Very heavy avalanche protection is noted high above the cuttings. Then comes Goppenstein Station, with an approach road and dozens of open flat cars for hauling autos through country where there are no highways. The 10-mile-long Lotschberg Tunnel is entered and speed rises to 60 miles an hour. Ten minutes later, the express bursts out at Kandersteg, having shifted from the watershed of the Rhone to the watershed of the Rhine. After that it is steeply descending track, turning and twisting yet at speed, all the way to the lakes of Central Switzerland and the Oberland. The federal capital, Berne, 95 miles from Brigue, is reached barely 100 minutes from the start, every one of the 6,000 seconds of the trip being packed with scenery or tunnel darkness, admirable coach comfort, and food and drink if desired.

Swiss Bargain Tickets

Although individual journeys by Swiss Railways can be quite costly, numerous reduced rate tickets can be obtained, especially by visitors. Best of all are the SWISS HOLIDAY PASSES, valid for 8, 15, 21, or 30 days. These permit use of all trains in the country, Swiss Federal or private, without extra charge or without obtaining ticket. The exceptions are special mountain lines, for which a reduction of 50% or 25% in the case of a very few of the most scenic is allowed.

A Swiss Holiday Pass costs 100 Francs (US $4) second class and 140 (US $5.60) first class for 8 days; 140 ($5.60) and 200 ($8) respectively, for 15 days. They must be bought through travel agencies or through the Swiss National Tourist Offices abroad—not in Switzerland.

Eurailpass is honoured throughout Switzerland.

The Swiss Holiday Ticket is a useful thing. If an ordinary ticket is bought involving travel by rail into Switzerland covering not less than 150 kms. in the country, then extension journeys are half-price, while five excursion tickets are attached allowing trips on steamers or funiculars at half-price.

There are day excursion fares on some lines, special weekend tickets, and tickets valid on Alpine Post Buses at half rate. The BLS Company runs "Blue Arrow" rail excursions several days a week, including trips to Stresa in Italy.

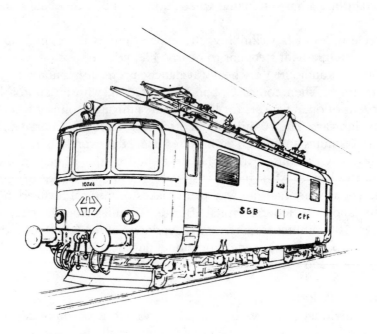

EASTERN EUROPE

By
K. Westcott Jones

ALBANIA

All of Albania's tiny railway system is new, built in the past ten or fifteen years with Chinese help. Tirana is the capital, an inland city, and Durres (known in King Zog's day, pre-War, as Durrazzo) the port on the Adriatic Sea. One line links the port with the capital 24 miles away, and another line runs 45 miles inland to the town of Elbasan. There is an even newer link from Tirana to Lac which may soon be extended to the Yugoslavian frontier at Lake Ohrid to join that country's system.

The Ministry of Communications of the People's Republic of Albania no longer permits foreigners to ride its trains, but some tourists did during a brief period when visitors were allowed in fairly freely. Most trains are reported to be modern but spartan, all one class, very crowded, some hauled by diesels and some by modern tank engines probably obtained from Eastern Europe before Albania became isolationist and China's friend in Europe. There are eight trains each way between Durres and Tirana, running at about 28 to 30 miles an hour average.

BULGARIA

The State Railways tend to fan out eastwards from the hilly capital, Sofia, towards the Black Sea Coast. There is one important main line running to the West, where the frontier station, Dimitovgrad, is on the approaches to the Dragoman Pass leading down into Yugoslavia. This route is traveled by international trains such as the *Orient Express* (Direct Division) and the *Marmara Express*. Although carrying through cars and at least one couchette and one sleeper from Western Europe, these international trains attach a good many Bulgarian cars at Sofia, or even at the frontier, and run as locals while in the country, without restaurant facilities.

There are some lines, especially from Sofia to Plovdiv and Varna, with electric traction. Diesels are widely used, but some steam haulage remains, including some of the very last "twelve-coupled" tank engines in the world, only otherwise seen in Java (Indonesia). Cars are steel and modern, with comfort standards high in first class, improving (plastic with a hint of softness) in most seconds. On the 292-mile journey from Sofia to Burgas and the 353-mile trip to Varna, Bulgarian State sleeping cars, couchette cars, and diners are used. A good frequency gives three night trains and seven day expresses. Average express train speeds in Bulgaria are in the 50–55 m.p.h. range.

The fastest trains are not the internationals. which the State Railways seem to delight in turning into locals, but some internal expresses of their own, headed by the early morning trains (one about 6 A.M.) from Sofia to Varna, the country's leading port and holiday area. Many popular beach resorts lie to the north of Varna, but Balkantourist, the official tourist organization of Bulgaria, seems to be unaware of the existence of the State Railways and has never made mention of trains. This rift between State organizations in a Communist country has not been explained to the West. Ask for travel information at any Bulgarian State tourist department office in Europe or America, and they'll talk about planes, buses, and driving, but trains—which are really quite good by international standards—are dismissed with a shrug.

Nevertheless, Sofia's main station has complete information (but only in the local tongue or German). It also has many cafes and restaurants, where a bad rate of exchange for hungry transit passengers is notorious. Several hotels are clustered within a short walk of the terminus, but local bureaucracy does not encourage the traveler seeking a night's sleep.

CZECHOSLOVAKIA

This is without doubt the most extensive rail network in Eastern Europe, as befits the most developed industrial nation (with the possible exception of East Germany) in the Soviet Bloc. The Czechoslovak State Railways radiate from Prague (Praha), the capital. The main line is that to Brno and Bratislava, now completely electrified. The 249 miles to Bratislava are covered by the fastest trains in the country, with a good deal of international traffic coming from East Germany and continuing on to Hungary. The best trains take five hours, with an average timing of five-and-a-half hours. The *Balt-Orient* Express takes this route.

On the longer and hillier line from Prague to Kosice via Poprad-Tatra (center for the holiday areas of the Tatra Mountains) there are overnight sleeper trains, also electric hauled. The best express, the *Tatran,* takes 6¼ daylight hours for the 281 miles. Another is the morning express *Dargov,* taking seven hours.

Some lines are not electrified and on these a mixture of steam and diesel traction will be found. Czechoslovakia has a comparatively modern fleet of steam engines, all equipped with the Austrian-invented Giesl injector which improves efficiency, and the giant (4.8.2) engines are a great sight for rail buffs. We have ridden on the footplate of one of these, double-heading the *Balt-Orient* on its steam section through Moravia between Cseska-Trebova and Brno.

Steam is widely used on Prague suburban services and eastwards from Prague towards West Germany. It is also found in the northern and northeastern parts of the country.

Most main line trains have either restaurant cars or buffets (though this may consist of only 12 seats in a car at the rear of a train).

Supplements are payable for travel by express trains except for persons buying tickets outside the country.

The most scenic line in Czechoslovakia is the narrow gauge electric mountain railway climbing into the High Tatras from Poprad-Tatry to Stary Smokovec (an eight mile ride taking some 40 minutes). There is an electric rack and pinion line from Strba to Strbske Pleso in the Tatra Mountains, with best frequencies during the winter sports season.

There are one or two preserved steam lines in the hill country of Slovakia, and the Czechs pay tribute to steam rail buffs by allowing a pre-war Pacific engine to operate excursions from time to time. The Transport Museum in Prague has some locomotives, including the model (2.6.4) most loved by Dvorak, the great composer who was a railway enthusiast.

Prague has three stations, the *Stredni* (Central), a terminus, *Hiavni* (Main Station), and *Smichov* (for suburban services). Most expresses leave from Main Station, including all international trains.

GETTING THERE. Rail links with Western Europe are most frequent to Austria, with three trains a day from Prague (Main) to Vienna via the Ceske Velenice border point, and three trains a day to Vienna from Bratislava via the Devinska border point. There is a through service between Paris and Prague via the Cheb border point, and one to Stuttgart the same way, both from Prague Main. Another train from this Prague station goes to Nuremberg via the Ceska Kubice border point. There is also one through train a day from Prague Main to Linz in Austria, crossing the border at Ceske Budejovice.

The *Paris-Prague Express* has through cars and couchettes, plus Wagons-Lits from Paris to Frankfurt and a restaurant car from Frankfurt to Prague. The overall journey takes 19½ hours. Several hotels are within easy walking distance of Prague Main Station, also the offices of CEDOK, the State Tourist Organization which handles travel and accommodation bookings.

EAST GERMANY

There are through coaches to East Berlin from Paris, Ostend, Hook of Holland, Basel, and, from several large West German cities. Western rail frontiers: Herrnburg, Schwanheide, Oebisfelde, Marienborn, Gerstungen, Probstzella, Bad-Schandau, Gutenfurst and Frankfurt/Oder, at all of which entry and transit visas can be obtained. Alternatively, you may be given a pass and instructed to collect your visa at your first destination point. The Reiseburo will fix this for you. There are about three trains a day between Berlin (East) and Hamburg, twelve to Hannover, three to Munich and Frankfurt.

Berlin is the hub of the Deutsch Reichsbahn (East German State Railway System), where the main stations are Friederichstrasse and Ost. Services through the West Berlin enclave are operated by the D.R., also to points in West Germany such as Hamburg (Altona) and Hannover. The partition of Germany after the war leaves the East German network somewhat short in track mileage, with attenuated natural routes. Berlin to Leipzig (113 miles), Berlin to Dresden (119 miles), and Leipzig-Dresden (75 miles) are the only frequent and fairly fast main lines with some trains averaging 60 miles an hour. Berlin to Warnemunde and Sassnitz, both on the Baltic, are important seaport and holiday routes, which also serve Rostock (three hours from Berlin).

While the Leipzig and Dresden lines are electrified now, a good deal of interesting steam traction remains on the D.R. Some engines (Pacific models of the 01.5 class) are semi-streamlined and are much admired by international rail buffs. Diesels are used on some international trains, to Hannover for the Hook of Holland service, and eastward to the Polish border.

Most trains are well equipped with new cars, and Mitropa red-painted restaurant cars grace most main line runs. There are also modern Mitropa sleepers on night services, especially to other parts of Eastern Europe. Track up-grading has been going on, but a lot of lines are still fairly slow running.

Fares and on-train costs are very low by West German standards, but supplements are charged aboard express and semi-fast trains. Only the "personnenzug" (all-stations locals) charge the basic fare.

Long-distance trains in and out of East Berlin, particularly those traveling toward Poland, can be terribly overcrowded. Reservations are vital.

The main railway stations *(hauptbahnhof)* in all towns and cities are substantial places in central sections, with ample meal and snack facilities.

HUNGARY

The Hungarian State Railways (MAV) is an efficient and well run organization providing almost all parts of this comparatively small, land-locked country with frequent service. International connections to the West, especially to Vienna, are the best of the Eastern European countries except for East Germany. MAV stands for Magyarorszac Vasuti Terkepe.

Electrification is well advanced from the Austrian frontier to Budapest and from Budapest eastward and northeastward. Diesels of both Russian and Hungarian design haul most express trains on non-electrified routes, while steam still reigns on routes to Lake Balaton and to parts of the Great Hungarian Plain. A large fleet of comparatively modern (4.8.0) locomotives, regarded as the best and most functional all-purposes steam engines in Central Europe, are widely employed.

In general, all main line trains are comfortably equipped, always with a smart restaurant car, and sometimes with a bar-buffet as well, fitted at one end of a passenger car. First class compartments are in red plush and quite luxurious, while the age of wooden seats in second class has disappeared in favor of green leather or plastic. Speeds are in the 50 to 55 miles an hour range for express trains, the best being on the 119 miles from Budapest to Szeged (just under 2½ hours). On the Miskolc Line, 112 miles, the best train (Lillafured Express) takes only two hours.

An excellent timetable is published which may be available for purchase at main stations. Ask for "Hivatalos Menetrend." It contains a very detailed map and also lists bus services in relation to trains.

Station buffets and restaurants in the larger Hungarian stations are modestly priced and surprisingly good. Once, when changing trains with quite a wait involved out on the Great Hungarian Plain, we lunched in the buffet at Puspokladany, and were offered—at a splendidly laid table—eight choices of main hot dish, from which we selected a very good double Wiener Schnitzel.

Budapest maintains a superb railway and transport museum, with the larger exhibits, including a streamlined tank engine which in 1934 held the European speed record for steam traction and an original restaurant car of the *Orient Express,* being shown in the State Park. There are one or two preserved lines of narrow gauge, both steam and electric, one of them climbing into the Buda Hills from Obuda across from the City of Pest.

Getting There

London to Budapest is 1,108 miles. Two suggested routes—London-Ostend-Brussels-Cologne, Frankfurt am Main, Nuremberg and Vienna, or

London-Paris-Strasbourg-Munich-Vienna. Sleepers or couchettes are available from Ostend or Paris.

The frontier crossing stations by train from the surrounding countries are:

From Austria: Bruckneudorf-Hegyeshalom; Wulkaprodersdorf-Sopron; Mogersdorf-Szentgotthard. *From Czechoslovakia:* Komarno-Komarom; Sturovo-Szob; Cana-Hidasnemeti; Slovenske Nove Mesto-Satoraljaujhely; Fil'akovo-Somoskoujfalu; Rusovce-Rajka; Lenartovce-Banreve. *From the Soviet Union:* Chop-Zahony. *From Romania:* Episcopia Bihor-Biharkeresztes; Curtici-Lokoshaza; Salonta-Kotegyan. *From Yugoslavia:* Subotica-Kelebia; Koprivnica-Gyekenyes; Beli Manastir-Magyarboly; Kotoriba-Murakeresztur.

Apart from the direct route of the *Ostend-Vienna Express* and the *Orient Express* from Paris in summer, Budapest can also be reached from Basel and Vienna on the *Wiener Walzer* express. Two other expresses, the *Wien-Budapest Express* and the *Arrabona Express,* run from Vienna in summer only.

By Train. If you travel via Basel-Zurich-Innsbruck-Salzburg-Vienna (*Wiener Walzer Express*), from Ostend, Cologne and Vienna (*Ostend-Wien Express*), or from Paris via Munich and Vienna (*Orient Express*), you will arrive at the *Keleti Palyaudvar* (Eastern Railway Station). The *Pannonia Express* from Berlin, via Dresden and Prague, also arrives here. The station is over 90 years old, but has been extensively rebuilt and enlarged. There is a statue of George Stephenson, "Father of Railways," on top of its elegant facade. Connected by a moving staircase is a station of the "Metro" (subway), with frequent trains running to the city center and on under the Danube to the Southern Railway Station.

If you travel by the *Baltic-Orient Express* via Stockholm-Berlin-Dresden and Prague, you will arrive at the Nyugati Palyaudvar (Western Railway Station) which stands on the Korut (Grand Boulevard) just before it reaches Marx Square. This was the place from which the first Hungarian train started in July, 1846. The entrance hall is decorated with the statue of Kato Haman, a "Communist martyr of the Hungarian workers' movement".

Finally, if you arrive from Rijeka and Zagreb, you will find yourself at the *Deli Palyaudvar* (Southern Railway Station), at the Western end of *Vermezo* (Field of Blood), the largest park of the Inner Town of Buda. Trains to Lake Balaton start from here.

Lake Balaton's Southern Shore

To Balatonboglar: Apart from the Nagykanizsa-Budapest *railroad* line and Motorway No. 7, Boglar is connected with Kaposvar by an ancillary road. *Bus* connection with the neighbouring villages and the resorts on the southern shore. *Balatonfoldvar* lies along the Budapest-Nagykanizsa main *rail* line. *Buses* to the neighbouring villages and to the other resorts on the southern shore.

Balatonszarszo is linked to Budapest by the same *railway* line as the others along the southern shore.

To Balatonszemes: Rail connections with Budapest are the same as the other southern shore resorts. *Buses* to neighbouring villages, other resorts.

To Fonyod: The *railroad* stations are on the Budapest-Szekesfehervar-Nagykanizsa line; the Kaposvar line branches off here.

Siofok has three *railroad* stations (Siofok, Balatonszeplak, Upper and Lower stops), which are all on the Budapest-Szekesfehervar-Nagykanizsa main line. There are regular *steamer* connections.

Transdanubia

The *railroad* line to *Dunaujvaros* branches off from the Budapest-Pecs main line at Pusztaszabolcs and leads through Dunaujvaros to Paks. There are through trains from Budapest.

Gyor is an important *railroad* junction, a stop on the Budapest-Hegye-shalom-line. The international main line to Vienna passes through here and the main line Budapest-Gyor-Sopron and Gyor-Szombathely branch off here. (The latter goes on to Graz.)

A rail junction, *Kaposvar* has direct *rail* connection through Dombovar with Budapest, along the Budapest-Pecs line through Gyekenyes with Za-greb-Rijeka-Venice—direct international trains from Budapest to Yugoslavia pass through Kaposvar. The Fonyod and Siofok branch lines link it with the Budapest-Nagykanizsa-Murakeresztur main line. The Szentbalazs-Szigetvar and the Hencse-Hedrehely-Barcs branch lines start from here. From the *bus* terminal near the railroad station and from Szecheny Ter 13, long-distance buses start towards the county's villages and tourist centres, and there are eleven local bus lines.

Komlo can be reached by *rail* on the Dombovar-Godisa-Komlo line which branches off from the Budapest-Pecs main line at Dombovar.

Koszeg can be reached by *rail* on the Szombathely-Koszeg branch line.

Mohacs is the terminus of the Budapest-Pusztaszabolcs-Pecs-Mohacs *railroad* line.

Nagykanizsa is a *railroad* junction, its station (a good mile from the centre) is on the Budapest-Szekesfehervar-Nagykanizsa main line. It is also the terminus of the Nagykanizsa-Murakeresztur and the Nagykanizsa-Szombathely-Sopron lines.

Papa is an important *rail* junction, the Budapest-Gyor-Szombathely-Szentgotthard main line passes through it and it is the starting point of the Papa-Tatabanya and Papa-Csorna branch lines.

Pecs is the most important *railroad,* highway and bus junction of Southeastern Transdanubia. Three express and four slow trains connect it both ways daily with Budapest; the fastest express covers the journey non-stop in 3 hours; in the summer direct trains via Dombovar and Kaposvar to Fonyod, Keszthely. Rail connections to Villany-Mohacs, Szigetvar-Barcs-Gyekenyes-Nagykanizsa-Szombathely.

Sopron is served by the main *rail* line Budapest-Gyor-Sopron and Szombathely-Sopron; the lines to Austria stop here, a frontier-station.

After Budapest, *Szekesfehervar* is the most important communication center in Hungary. Here the main *railroad* lines of Budapest-Szekesfehervar-Nagykanizsa-Murakereszter and of Budapest-Szekesfehervar-Celldomolk-Szombathely diverge; the city is the terminal station of the branch lines to Bicske, Komarom, Pusztaszabolcs and Sarbogard.

Szekszard is connected by the Sarbogard-Bataszek branch line with the Budapest-Pecs and Dombovar-Baja main *railroad* lines.

Szigetvar is a railroad junction; the Pecs-Nagykanizsa line passes through it, and it is the terminus of the Kaposvar-Szigetvar branch line.

Szombathely is the most important railroad junction of Western Transdanubia; it can be reached from Budapest in 3½ to 4 hours. Both the Budapest-Gyor-Szentgotthard and the Sopron-Szombathely-Nagykanizsa main lines pass through it; it is the terminus of the Budapest-Szekesfehervar-Szombathely line and branch lines start from here to Hegyeshalom, Koszeg, and Rum. Tramways and local buses.

Tata's railroad station is Tata-Tovaroskert, on the Budapest-Gyor-Hegyeshalom main line.

Tatabanya's four railroad stations are all on the Budapest-Gyor-Hegyeshalom main line and on the Papa and Oroszlany branch lines. Local buses.

Veszprem is a railway junction on the main Budapest-Szekesfehervar-Szombathely line. A branch line to Zirc, Pannonhalma and Gyor starts here. The station lies about 2 miles north of the town center, with which it is connected by a bus service.

Zalaegerszeg's railway station is on branch lines which join the main lines to Szombathely, Nagykanizsa and Budapest via Zalalovo, Zalaszentivan and Ukk. Local buses.

Zirc lies long the Cuha Valley section of the Gyor-Veszprem railroad line. From here a branch line starts to Dudar.

The Great Plains

Baja can be approached from the west and the east by two main *railroad* lines: one connects Dombovar and Bataszek with the town, the other, Kiskunhalas. The branch line to Gara and Hercegszanto starts from Baja.

To Bekescsaba: Here two main *railroad* lines meet: the Budapest-Szolnok, Bekescsaba-Lokoshaza and the Szeged-Bekescsaba lines. The narrow-gauge line of Bekescsaba-Bekessamson starts here.

To Cegled. The Budapest-Cegled-Szolnok-Debrecen-Zahony and the Budapest-Cegled-Kecskemet-Szeged main *rail* lines pass through Cegled, which is also the starting point of the Hanthaza branch line and the narrow-gauge railway to Vezseny.

To Hajduszoboszlo: By the Budapest-Debrecen main *railroad* line (about 120 miles from Budapest, 11 miles from Debrecen). Frequent express and regular trains in both directions are met by local buses at the railway station for the short trip to the spa.

To Kalocsa: By *rail* from Budapest on the Budapest-Kelebia line, taking the branch line at Kiskoros.

To Kecskemet: The town is a *railroad* junction; the Budapest-Cegled-Kecskemet-Szeged main line passes through it; it is the terminus of the Budapest-Lajosmizse-Kecskemet line; it is the starting point of the Kunszentmarton and Fulopszallas branch line and the Kiskunmajsa and Kiskoros narrow-gauge lines.

Nyiregyhaza is on the Budapest-Debrecen-Nyiregyhaza-Zahony main rail line; it is also the terminus of the main line runing through Miskolc and Tokaj. It is the starting point of many branch lines to neighboring districts.

To Szolnok: The Budapest-Szolnok-Debrecen-Zahony rail line and the line connecting the southern half of the Trans-Tisza District with Budapest via Szolnok-Bekescsaba-Lokoshaza both branch off close to the town. It is the terminal station of the Budapest-Ujszasz-Szolnok main line. From here, branch lines start to Hatvan, Kiskunfelegyhaza and Hodmezovasarhely.

POLAND

Although Poland borders Russia and was once a part of that country, Polish trains run on standard gauge and are much more Western European in character and appearance than Russian lines. In the main, the system radiates from Warsaw, the capital, out to the Baltic Coast at Gdansk and Gdynia, northwest to Sczeczin, the big port on the Baltic, south to Cracow and the Polish Highlands, east to Russia and northeast to the Mazurian Lakes, west to East Germany via Poznan, and southwest to the great Silesian industrial basin. Lines also go southeast to Ukrainian Russia and the big city of Lvov (once Polish).

The big British tour firm "Magic of Poland" runs a series of rail tours worth taking if you are a buff—they call them "Magic of Steam in Poland" and there is plenty. With large deposits of brown coal available, many Polish steam engines are in service. But don't expect high speeds and clean white smoke from them, for Polish coal is far removed from Welsh and Pennsylvanian anthracite.

From Warsaw to Cracow the service is frequent and fairly fast, with diesel traction on the best trains and electrification on the way. The 198 miles take 4½ hours by the best trains, and there are restaurant or buffet cars on them, but also people—often en masse. Onwards through the Highlands up to Zakapane, the ski resort, is wonderfully scenic but slow going—nearly five hours for the 90 miles. There is talk of getting this line under the wires in the near future and running speeds will then be doubled.

Faster runs are met with on the main line to Silesia, with 3½ hours for the 197 miles to Katowice by the evening express *Gornik* from Warsaw Central. Summer trains to the Baltic Coast (where Sopot is a particular favorite for its beaches) take about six hours for 215 miles, and even the best train, locally called a "Torpedo" (Kaszub in Polish) needs slightly under five hours. Reservations are advisable for the expresses, especially for group travel.

Several trains to and from Berlin run right through Poland from East to West and vice-versa on the Berlin-Brest Litovsk line, on the way to Russia. Some of them, unaffected by the change in the width of the tracks at the Russian border, carry on to Leningrad or Moscow. Warsaw has through trains to the Hook of Holland and Ostend and a car-carrying (Auto) train for the British market.

Both restaurant and sleeping cars run inside Poland, under the overall control of Polish State Railways but wearing on their sides the mouthful "Przedsiebiorstwa Wagonow Sypialnych i Restauracyjnych", happily being shortened to "WARS" on new equipment. The restaurants are good, with willing if overworked service, and prices are moderate. We were squeezed unwittingly into one on a very crowded train from Gdynia to Warsaw one September day, having already lunched. But they let us eat light snacks most of the way to Moscow; otherwise, there was no place on the train, 1st or 2nd class, to stand, let alone sit.

Warsaw now has a Central Station, and nearly all long-distance trains go through it or originate there. The old Main Station has been turned into the Railway Museum.

ROMANIA

Radiating from Bucharest, the large capital famed for its boulevards, is an excellent network of railways serving all parts of this Latin land set in Eastern Europe. Although the first railway, dating from the late 1860's, was British-built and linked the capital with the Danube 37 miles away, the French influenced further railway construction, and indeed influenced Romania in many ways.

There is a superb line from Bucharest to the Black Sea at Constanza, crossing the Danube by the magnificent Saligny Bridge and causeway system, built in 1890–1895. This line, 140 miles long, is much used by tourists, for Constanza lies within a few miles of the Black Sea resorts, Mamaia to the north of it, Eforie and ultra-modern seaside spots with the names of planets, to the south. It carries six good trains each way daily, some of them very long and most conveniently equipped with two diners.

The State Railways restaurant cars have a rather sound rule which allows passengers only 45 minutes seated at table. This cuts down the lines of hungry and thirsty hopefuls making the four hour trip.

Another line used by tourists goes from Bucharest for 143 miles northeastwards to Galati near the Danube Delta, where there are boats downstream. This region is famed for its birdlife, the finest in Europe.

The next most important tourist line is the one from Bucharest into the Transylvanian Mountains, electrified to Brasov, 166 Kms. (about 105 miles). Sinaia, a mountain health resort, is on this line. Express trains run to Cluj, to Arad, and Oradea, beyond Brasov, so all important expresses such as the Balt-Orient and the Orient pass through. Romania's fastest trains, the *Decebal* and the *Transylvania,* take this route.

One more important line runs west of Bucharest, via Craiova to Timisoara, close to the Hungarian border. It runs beside the Danube near Turnu Severin, site of the vast Danube barrage (shared with Yugoslavia). Part of the 533 km. (330 miles) route is electrified, and it carries rapid trains, one named *Traian* (after the Roman Emperor).

While most main lines in Romania are electric or diesel, there are some well kept steam engines in various parts of the country on secondary routes. An unusual rack and pinion standard gauge mountain railway is to be found at Subcetate, with steam haulage by elderly Austrian tank engines. This has become a tourist attraction, much to the amazement of the locals who fail to understand why foreigners want to go uphill in a steam train doing 5 miles an hour when a bus on the nearby road runs at 30 miles an hour.

To enjoy Romania by rail, and the trains are good, with clean equipment and comfortable first class accommodations (leather or plastic in 2nd. class), it is wise to buy a timetable ("Mersul Trenurillor") for the C.F.R. (State

Railways). The price is low, but the information comprehensive and readable. Even if one cannot understand the language, there is a keyed map.

Dining and sleeping cars are attached to long distance trains throughout the country. There are no restrictions on foreigners traveling, but most trains become crowded despite a fairly good frequency. Reservations can be made for rapid trains (which require supplementary fares).

Many towns and resorts have two stations, one called 'Nord', which is both French and Romanian for north. Bucharest (Buccaresti) Nord is the main terminal in the capital. Buses and street cars serve it, but officially marked taxis are in short supply, giving rise to unofficial ones which can be more expensive and sometimes undesirable for foreigners. While there are cafes and one excellent hotel in the immediate vicinity of this terminal, it is at least a mile to the heart of the city, where most of the better hotel and restaurant facilities exist.

SOVIET UNION

All Soviet trains start exactly on time (if they are not mysteriously cancelled altogether); there is a broadcast warning five minutes before departure but no whistle or "all aboard!" call, so you must be careful not to be left behind. There are four classes, of which the *deluxe* offers soft seats and private washrooms; the other classes have washrooms at the end of the cars. The *first-class* service is called "soft seat", with spring-cushioned berths; there are two or four berths in each compartment. There is no segregation of the sexes and you might find yourself sharing a two-berth compartment with someone of the opposite sex. The *second* or "hard-seat" class has a cushion on wooden berths, available in two-, three- and four-berth compartments. The *third class*—wooden berths without compartments—is used mostly in local service and rarely sold to foreigners. Each two-berth compartment has a small, table reading lamp, a wardrobe closet and a radio speaker—which, fortunately, can be shut off except when the conductor uses his master switch to wake everybody as the train nears its destination.

The best train service in the U.S.S.R. is the *Red Arrow Express* (Moscow-Leningrad); the longest route is that of the Trans-Siberian Railway, with a mystique all of its own. During the time it takes to get from Moscow to Irkutsk, for example, you'll find yourself plunged into a different world. People wear pyjamas or dressing-gowns, there is much tea-drinking and talk—and you are likely to find someone speaking some Western language with whom to strike up a friendship. The dining cars are well equipped, the meals have generous portions and tea and snacks are available almost constantly. In every car, the conductor keeps a samovar on the go night and day and serves you refreshing hot lemon tea in tall glasses.

Railway tickets are called coupons and are sold in a stapled cover without which they are not valid—so you must make sure that the conductor only removes the appropriate section. The baggage allowance is 77 lbs. in the compartment; any excess must be placed in the baggage car. The Soviet trains use broad-gauge tracks and their running is smooth and there is more space than in the European trains. The passenger trains are divided into three types: fast, express and long-distance trains of sleeping coaches alone. There are, of course, local commuter trains into all major cities.

Foreigners may not purchase rail tickets at will, but only to destinations covered by their visas. It is normally necessary for Intourist to obtain tickets for visitors to the country. But for travel to the outer suburbs of such cities as Moscow and Leningrad, where tickets are dispensed by machines, rides costing up to half a Rouble may be made (and this may cover journeys of 30 miles). Some routes are not open to tourists at all. Timetables are almost impossible to buy but details (in Russian) are posted at stations.

Many main lines in Russia (and almost all the way across Siberia) are electrified. The fastest train in the country is the July- and August-only *Aurora* from Moscow to Leningrad, covering the 403 miles in 4 hours, 59 minutes at an average speed of 81 miles an hour. In the reverse direction, however, it takes 5 hours, 53 minutes. The all year round day train, one class and quite comfortable with reclining seats and a restaurant car, takes 7½ hours. The overnight *Red Arrow* (11.55 P.M. from both ends of the line) takes a comfortable 8½ hours and is all-sleeper. This busiest main line in the Soviet Union is mainly flat except for an easy crossing of low hills near Bologoye, and is virtually dead straight, for that is how a despot tsar ordered it to be built back in 1850. Although fully electrified, steam engines will be seen at various points along the route, particularly Bologoye and Kalinin, coming in from branch lines and on freight workings.

Getting There

From Britain: Direct services carrying a Soviet sleeper-coach are available throughout the year from London in conjunction with Harwich-Hook of Holland or Dover-Ostend boats. They offer a comfortable two-day journey through Central and Eastern Europe with no need to change compartments or trains. Soviet sleeper-coaches are designed for long-distance travel—as we shall see when discussing travel within the U.S.S.R.—and the compartments normally have two berths (first class) or four berths (second class). There are washstands in first class compartments. In winter, a minimum inside temperature of 64 F. (18 C.) is maintained. Each coach has its own conductor. On most sections of the route, a restaurant car is attached. Tea, coffee and biscuits are served by the conductor, but many travelers on long hauls buy food in stations.

During the summer, the through train departs daily from London's Liverpool Street Station, at 9.40 A.M. and goes via the Hook of Holland. In winter it runs on Mondays, Wednesdays, Fridays and Sundays. It arrives at the Byelorussky Station in Moscow at 4 P.M. two days later. Trains via Ostend run from London's Victoria Station, leaving at 10 A.M., daily in summer and on Tuesdays and Fridays in winter. The summer schedule includes stops at Berlin and Warsaw.

Moscow and many other Soviet cities have direct rail connections with Helsinki, Berlin, Hook of Holland, Paris, Rome, Prague, Vienna, Budapest, Belgrade, Bucharest and Sofia. You can even enter by train from Tehran to Moscow (92 hours, about $70 (£39), once-weekly in each direction).

The Russian gauge is 5 feet, just 3½ inches wider than the standard gauge in the U. S. and Western and Central Europe. By means of a Soviet-developed technique, through cars (mainly sleepers) are hoisted up at frontier stations (Brest-Lisovsk for Poland and Western Europe) and the trucks unscrewed, then changed for those of the gauge required. Only when crossing into Finland is this process omitted, for Finland also has 5 feet gauge, arising from the days when it was a Russian-dominated country.

From Finland: A pleasant way to visit the U.S.S.R. is to enter from Helsinki by train. Trains leave Helsinki about noon, arriving in Leningrad late in the evening (and go on to Moscow the next morning). The through train from Helsinki to Moscow leaves in mid-afternoon and arrives in Moscow the next morning.

Moscow

Moscow has nine railway stations, which handle 400 million passengers annually. The lavish Moscow Metro (subway) links most of the railway terminals (*Vokzal* in Russian), either directly or involving only a short walk.

The Byelorussian Railway Station (Byelorussky Vokzal Square): Trains to and from Berlin, Warsaw, London, Paris, Smolensk, Minsk, Brest and Vilnius.

The Kazan Railway Station (2 Komsomolskaya Square): Trains to and from Rostov-on-Don, Kazan, Volgograd, the Central Asian Republics and Siberia.

The Kiev Railway Station (Kievsky Vokzal Square): Trains to and from Chop, Belgrade, Bucharest, Budapest, Karlovy Vary, Prague, Sofia, Cierna, Jassy, Kiev, Kishinev, Lvov, Odessa, Uzhgorod and Chernovtsy.

The Kursk Railway Station (29 Chkalov Street): Trains to and from the Crimea and the Caucasus, Armenia, Azerbaijan, Georgia, the Mineralniye Vody spas, Kursk, Tula, Orel and Kharkov.

The Leningrad Railway Station (1 Komsomolskaya Square): trains to and from Helsinki, Leningrad, Kalinin, Novgorod, Murmansk, Petrozavodsk, Pskov and Tallinn.

The Paveletsky Railway Station (Leninskaya Square): Trains to and from the Donets Basin and Volgograd.

The Riga Railway Station (Rizhskaya Square): Trains to and from Riga and Baltic health resorts.

The Savelovsky Railway Station (Butyrskaya Zastava Square): Trains to and from Uglich, and secondary routes to Leningrad.

The Yaroslavl Railway Station (5 Komsomolskaya Square): Trains to and from Siberia and the Far East, Moscow-Peking Express.

The Central Railway Enquiry Office (tel. 266–90–00) will provide information about departures and arrivals.

Leningrad

The second city of the Soviet Union is a huge railway center, with five terminal stations (called *Vokzal* from the London Vauxhall Gardens, where a tsar first saw a railway station in the 1830's!).

The *Finland Station,* famed for Lenin's engine preserved under glass and commemmorating his entry into the city in 1917, serves North Russia, Karelia, and Finish cities, plus northern suburbs.

The *Moscow Station* (Moskovski Vokzal) serves the main line to the capital.

The *Vitebsk Station* (to Vitebsk and Kiev).

The *Varshavski Station* serves southern Leningrad suburbs, the important main line to Pskov, Vilnius, and Warsaw, also to Riga.

The *Baltiski Station* has trains to Riga and Tallinn, and southwestern suburbs.

A metro (subway) almost as lavish as the system in Moscow is being expanded. At present it links the Finland Station with the Moscow and Vitebsk terminals.

The Baltic Republics

You can reach Tallinn in about 7 hours by train from Leningrad and 19 hours from Moscow. There are connections to all major Soviet cities. Finnish and Soviet steamers sail regularly on the Tallinn-Helsinki Line. Tartu is 3–4 hours by train from Tallinn.

Riga is 16 hrs. 45 mins. from Moscow by train on the *Chaika* ("gull"), taking seven hours, a soft and hard class express with restaurant car, diesel hauled.

Vilnius is 14 hrs. 10 mins. by train from Moscow. From Poland, it can be reached via Grodno and Minsk. It is linked to most Soviet cities, but foreign tourists are not allowed to use the routes from Kaunas, Minsk, or Kaliningrad.

The Ukraine

Next to the Leningrad-Moscow line, the route from Moscow (Kiev Station) to Kiev and Odessa handles most main line passenger traffic. Many tourists use it, especially if taking a cruise out of the port of Odessa. It is 542 miles to Kiev, almost all flat and agricultural steppe-country. The fastest trains run only during the summer season, when the 8:39 A.M. from Moscow reaches Kiev in just over 13 hours. The *Odessa Express,* nightly all year round at 10:15 P.M., gets to Kiev at 10:26 next morning, and to Odessa (949 miles from Moscow) by 8:43 P.M. It is not yet electrified and average speeds on the route, considering the fairly level track, are not remarkable. The best trains have soft and hard class seating and sleeping cars, and restaurants. Curiously, since Odessa is the "Home City" of Pushkin the Poet, the express train of that name runs from Moscow to Kiev and then to Lvov and Budapest without serving Odessa.

Moscow to Rostov is a well-traveled route, via Kharkov. It is 485 miles to Kharkov, and 836 to Rostov, the 9:45 A.M. from Moscow taking 9½ hours to Kharkov. On this route the overnight *Ritsa* and *Kavkaz* expresses are the most comfortable.

Many people want to visit Volgograd (famed in the war as Stalingrad. It is 668 miles from Moscow's Kazan Station, and one fast train, the *Volgograd,* leaves at 2:35 P.M. to reach the city on the Volga at 8:50 A.M., equipped with soft and hard class, a deluxe sleeper, and restaurant car.

Travel by rail in the Caucasus and Central Asia is a slow but interesting business, with mountains to enjoy if few on-board amenities.

Samarkand

It is 2,213 miles from Moscow (Kayan Station) to the Golden City of Samarkand. The journey by a daily train called *Uzbekistan* takes 54 hours to Tashkent (2,094 miles), while an unnamed daily with soft and hard class cars takes 69 hours to Samarkand. It is only fair to point out that passengers using the faster and more comfortable *Uzbekistan* to Tashkent can fly by *Aeroflot* in about 45 minutes to Samarkand. However, some may consider the extra 15 hours by train, winding through hot, dry, scenic mountains, worthwhile as an experience—may we suggest one way?

The Trans-Siberian Railway

The 5,778 miles of railway stretching from the Pacific Coast of Siberia to Moscow is by far the longest continuous track in the world on which through trains are operated. The title "Trans Siberian" came from the English language; Russians call it the "Great Siberian Railway," but under the Czars—who built it between 1890 and 1900—it was the "International Railway."

In its early years it was a vital and rapid link for Westerners, especially diplomats, who used it to reach the capitals of China and Japan. Today it constitutes the greatest single travel experience a tourist can have, and offers Americans a through route from the Orient to Europe, while Europeans get a fairly cheap and interesting transit to Japan and Hong Kong. Yet its biggest foreign users are Australians, traveling with it to or from Europe as an adventure.

A second rail link with the Far East—a new Trans-Siberian line, more than 2,000 miles long—is nearing completion. Apparently it will run much farther away from the sensitive Chinese border area than the old line—625 miles from the frontier at its nearest point.

For foreigners, it doesn't start at Vladivostok, for that is a military port with limited access. The regular ships of the *Soviet Far East Line* come into the port of Nakhodka, about 50 miles to the north, having sailed from

Yokohama and Hong Kong. A smart-looking boat train meets the ship (at
least twice weekly in summer) and runs for 564 miles to the Soviet Far East
city of Khabarovsk. Here passengers must change trains, but it is an Intourist requirement that passengers spend a day in the city, sightseeing (at
least when eastbound), when they either go on by the Trans-Siberian or
take a plane across the Soviet Union. (*Alaska Airlines* have some charter
flights direct from Anchorage into Khabarovsk, *Japan Air Lines* weekly
flights from Niigata.)

That first sight of a Russian train at Nakhodka is an encouraging one, for
its new green-and-cream cars are airconditioned, offering two-berth sleepers with a shower between two compartments, an excellent diner, and a
powerful electric engine. But the latter only hauls the train for about 50
miles to Nadezhdinskaya near Ussurisk Junction, where the electric wires
cease. A large Soviet diesel takes over here for the remainder of the run
to Khabarovsk. That first night is an easy one on the train, leaving the port
at 8 P.M. with dinner and then a good sleep as the express rolls along
through the darkness at about 45 to 50 miles an hour. The next morning,
lady attendants call passengers with tea from the samovar, typical Russian
tea in a glass, and while breakfast is taken in the diner, the Ussuri River
may be seen on the left of the train, with wild forest and hill country
stretching away on the other. In the forests are the last surviving Siberian
tigers, plus a good deal of wild life which no one is likely to see.

The boat train is due at Khabarovsk at 11 A.M., and although until
recently a 26-hour stopover was called for, even westbound, it now appears
that due to the increase in passengers one can go through the city changing
trains on the same day. So on Day Two there is a two-hour sightseeing of
this big and rather strange Far East city, founded by Erofey Khabarovsk on
his trek to the Siberian Pacific in 1858. Today it has a population of half
a million and boasts a splendid waterfront along the wide Amur River with
a view to the distant hills of China.

At 1 P.M. the Trans Siberian Express itself comes into the station from
Vladivostok. Steam is the predominant traction from Ussurisk Junction for
over 1,500 miles to Chita, but the electric wires are going up fast, and by
1977 the whole line is expected to be electrified. As it is, the 4,000 miles
from Chita to Moscow represent the longest electric railway in the world.
You always know where you are during daylight—the kilometre posts
show the distance to Moscow.

The train itself is a disappointment compared to the boat express. There
are "soft"- and "hard"-class cars, a diner, a baggage car, and three seating
coaches for short-haul passengers. Both "softs" and "hards" have four
berths, the only difference being that the "softs" are made up and have full
carpeting, while "hard" class passengers must hire their own bedding.
There are no showers, only washrooms at both ends of each car. Wide
corridors in "soft" are carpeted, with fold-down seats, and shaving plugs
are placed on the outer walls so men with electric razors shave in public!

It is probable that one or two of the new "SZ" type, two-berth sleepers are being attached to this train now, a type similar to those on the boat express.

The Trans-Siberian trains, called *Rossia* and numbered One and Two (No. 1 is westbound), run daily from May to September, four times a week in winter. The basic train sets, in red and cream (marked with brass Cyrillic characters on the side denoting "Moscow-Vladisvostok") were built in 1949 and are *not* air-conditioned. The train is sealed in winter, with heat furnished by the train attendants stoking stoves; in summer the dry, burning heat of Siberia, with plenty of dust about, makes travel conditions unpleasant at times. Normal garb for Russian passengers is very informal: trousers and shirt, often pajamas. The four-berth compartments are not divided as to sex and it may happen that three men share with a woman, although for tourists boarding with Intourist at Khabarovsk, using airline-type boarding cards, there is an official attempt to avoid this.

Day Two

The afternoon of Day Two sees the Trans Siberian train rolling across the mighty Amur Bridge and through dry country with the high hills of China never far away. To get the best out of this journey, travelers MUST have a knowledge of the Cyrillic alphabet (it only takes 48 hours to master), for without it they cannot read the timetable displayed in each car and will not know where they are when the train stops. Even more important, they will not know *how long* the stop is going to be. The train adheres very strictly to schedule—it has to, because the Siberian Railway is extremely busy throughout its length. It is double track and boasts CTC (centralized train control) but passes a fast freight every 30 minutes and a number of passenger trains not going the full length of the line. There are 91 stops from Vladivostock to Moscow, 79 of them affecting those passengers who join at Khabarovsk, and the time at stations ranges from two minutes to a maximum of 17 (at Irkutsk). It is normal to get out and walk up and down the platforms, perhaps to buy things from the station "bazaars," but only one warning blast is given before the train starts away. The "soft" car attendants try to keep an eye on their passengers to prevent their being left behind. Moscow Time is kept throughout the train's run, which can vary up to seven hours from local time.

As darkness falls the train is rolling smoothly through the dry, hilly country of the Soviet Far East (they do not regard this region as Siberia proper). The dining car is open all day from nine in the morning until ten at night, and its menus are in six languages. Only those items on the huge and optimistic menus which have pencilled prices against them are available. Being a better "shop" than most in the towns and villages through which it passes, the train's diner is often visited by locals who buy beer and ice cream to take away. This can lead to shortages for passengers, and no replacements are made until Irkutsk is reached. Meals are fairly cheap, foreigners paying by means of Intourist coupons purchased in advance (but taking change in roubles and kopeks). The food is fairly good at times, rump steak fried in breadcrumbs apparently being a stable and consistent favorite. Breakfasts are massive affairs, at least for Russians, who seem to visit the diner for four meals a day.

Passengers tend to retire early, soon after ten at night, but the car attendents serve tea at that hour, or cocoa on request. The heavy cars, 56 tons on average, rolling on their wide five-foot gauge, ride easily on excellent track (except that after the spring thaw there may be bad stretches) and sleeping is comfortable. But a lot depends on your traveling companions!

Days Three and Four

As Day Three brightens and the attendants begin their rounds with the inevitable tea at eight o'clock, one has settled into the routine of the Trans-Siberian. It is like traveling in a coastal freighter, with tiny cabins, making a lot of stops in small ports. The wide corridors are the promenade decks and the diner is the saloon. There are drinks parties in the "cabins" and you learn a certain amount of Russian!

The scenery is mainly upland forests with rivers and lakes often in sight. The ubiquitous silver birch trees (*beryozka,* a symbol of Russia) are now more in evidence. There is a good exercise stop during the morning at Skovorodino, where 15 minutes are spent changing engines. The train is now 756 miles from Khabarovsk, with 4,500 still to do!

Before noon, the splendid Shilka River comes in sight, and the train runs on its right bank all day. If one is interested in trees and glimpses of wild life, it is worth sitting on a corridor seat and just watching this little known part of Siberia unfold. Later in the day, the country becomes very dry again as the train enters the fringe areas of the Gobi Desert.

Day Four dawns with a semi-desert aspect, with Manchuria and Mongolia well away to the south. The highlight of the morning is the 15-minute stop at the city of Chita, junction for the former Chinese Eastern line to Harbin and Korea. In the early afternoon a transformation takes place as the train begins to climb away from the Gobi region into the Trans-Baikal area, the true Siberia. The range then crossed is the Yablonoi, little known to Western travelers, where summits touch 9,000 feet. The train goes through at altitudes above 4,000 feet and the temperature in winter plummets like a stone, while in summer it is noticeably cooler. The helper engine comes off at Mogzon, then another stop is made at a station called Petrovsky Zavod. All around are the dense forests, the Siberia of fact and fiction. We stay on the high plateau the rest of the day. Late at night a stop is made at Ulan Ude, junction for Peking.

Days Five and Six

Day Five dawns alongside the fierce Angara River, amid tremendous mountain scenery on the southern side of Lake Baikal. This is the only river to escape from mighty Lake Baikal, into which flow more than 300 rivers.

Irkutsk at breakfast time is the longest stop, 17 minutes, where you get a change of linen and towels, and the diner is restocked. Its crew, though, goes right through to Moscow, and so does the electric engine up front. The big city glimpsed from the modern station has been called "the Paris of Siberia!"

Thus ends the more romantic section of the great journey; for the rest, there are some highlights, but mostly a great deal of forest. It is ideal for catching up on sleep and reading. There are mountains and lakes on the way from Irkutsk, with the train still above 3,000 feet.

Very early on Day Six the train stops at Krasnoyarsk, which means both "red" and "beautiful." There are enormous hydro-electric schemes on the River Yenisei hereabouts. All day the Siberian plain unfolds, with its millions of trees, lakes and streams. Speed averages 43 m.p.h. Late at night we enter highly industrialized Novosibirsk, crossing into the station by the Ob Bridge, longest and most important on the line. Only 30 miles north is Akademgorodok, a Soviet science and space city.

Days Seven and Eight

Going west you don't see anything of famous Omsk, on the Irtysh River for the stop is early morning on Day Seven. This is the junction for the South Siberian Railway. Contrary to popular belief, the Trans-Siberian doesn't pass through Tomsk, but misses it by 100 miles (you change at Taiga Junction).

There is a run of ten hours across the plain to Sverdlovsk, an important Urals industrial city which occupies a favored place in Soviet history. Soon after leaving it, winding through the comparatively low but rocky Urals, we pass a sign showing Asia to the east and Europe to the west. It is downhill, gently, most of the way through coniferous forests and wide fields, until the stop at Kirov late in the evening. This is the last important place short of Moscow, now only 595 miles away.

Day Eight, last on the train, dawns with the train amid grain fields and forests as it whirls across North Russia, bearing west southwest towards the capital. This is the morning you get your bills for services rendered by the attendants (all those glasses of tea and cups of cocoa). The price is very modest but they shy at tips although happy to accept a present. At 11.55 A.M., if the train is on time, and it usually is, Moscow's Yaroslavl Station, a beautiful copy of a Russian fairy castle, comes in sight and the journey ends amid the bustle of the great Square of the Three Terminals (Komsomol Square).

YUGOSLAVIA

The large rail system of Yugoslavia is a mixture of West and East, with emphasis on linkage with Western Europe. Hard terrain and huge coastal ranges have prevented easy rail building, and early lines ran through the softer country of the Danube and Sava valleys across Serbia. Only in 1976 was a vital standard-gauge link opened between Belgrade, the capital, and Bar on the Adriatic Coast.

The Belgrade-Bar Railway is one of the outstanding engineering achievements of Europe in recent times. It is 288 miles (464 kms) long, electrified throughout and built under the wires, passes through 46 major tunnels and over earthworks and viaducts reminiscent of the Mexican Chihuahua-Pacific (itself not opened until 1961). This is now the main route to the coast from the capital, surpassing planes and even cars (much loved and owned by the relatively affluent Yugoslavs of today). It carries a service of five through trains a day in each direction, all calling on the way at Titograd. Best time is nine hours, by an early afternoon departure, a train called *Lovcen*. There are sleepers on overnights and through cars to Hamburg and other West German and Channel points. Restaurant or buffet cars are attached to day trains on what is Europe's newest railway, but speeds, by the very nature of the terrain and the recently laid track, must be kept down to around 32 m.p.h. average.

Most main line trains from the West enter Yugoslav at Jesenice on the Austrian border, but there are two other crossings, one on the Italian border at Sezana near Trieste and the other at Maribor, where the line comes from Spielfeld in Austria. In summer a host of international trains cross these borders, for the Dalmatian Coast is a highly popular tourist area. Trains to and in Yugoslavia are heavily patronized. There are through cars to Split, and Rijeka, also by spur lines, and Sibenik and Zadar can be reached as well. All are leading coastal resorts.

The fastest and most frequent trains on the JZ (Yugoslavian State Railways) are to be found on the double track Balkan main line, Ljubljana to Zagreb, Belgrade, and Nish. This is electrified to Belgrade, while on the line to Nish and Skopje, American General Motors diesels haul the expresses.

This is the famed route of the former Simplon Orient Express (a train founded in luxury in 1921 as an offshoot of the *Orient Express,* dating from 1883, and abandoned in squalor early in 1977). Today it is traversed by such trains as the *Akropolis Express* (fastest train to Greece), the *Hellas Express,* the *Athens Express,* the *Tauern, Dalmacia* and *Skopje* expresses. There is, in fact, a constant procession of international and domestic express trains along the 575 kilometres (355 miles) of line from Ljubljana through Zagreb to Belgrade.

One outstanding business train, the unattractively early 5:40 A.M. from Zagreb, runs the 416 kms (258 miles) to Belgrade in 4 hours 34 minutes, the country's fastest train. It, and its return service at 3 P.M. from the capital, is called the *Emona Express.*

Yugoslavian State Railways grade their trains as Poslovni (rapide—the fastest), Expresni (express, the next fastest), Brzi (meaning fast, and not very), and Putnicki (omnibus, or all stations, slow). Unless you have tickets bought outside Yugoslavia, a supplement has to be paid to ride the first two categories. Some international trains carry blue and gold Wagons-Lits; internal long distance and a few international trains have red Yugoslav sleeping cars. There are a fair number of buffet and restaurant cars belonging to the Sleeping and Restaurant Car Enterprise of the JZ.

The majority of tourists going to Yugoslavia head for the magnificent coast, hundreds and hundreds of miles of rock and mountain, beaches (mainly shingle) and islands. Trains can take them to points along the coast, even by means of diesel hauled narrow gauge—to Dubrovnik via the main line from Belgrade to Sarajevo and Mostar. But there are no links *along* the coast, where a fine highway has now been built with an express bus service running virtually every half hour. Until 1966, Coastal steamers provided the only communication.

Some secondary lines out of Belgrade and Zagreb still employ steam traction, especially on shorter suburban runs. A few engine sheds maintain interesting studs of steam locomotives, built in Hungary, Austria and Germany. Yugoslavia builds its own diesels now, as well as electrics, but also imports some from America. However, new passenger cars are especially good, long and somewhat similar to the best German cars. These are exported to Israel (for the Tel Aviv-Haifa expresses) and to other countries.

Fares have risen markedly over the past few years, but going second class by train is still the cheapest means of transport in the country. It is not comfortable, except for some expresses which admit seconds (the best are first class only) and always very crowded.

Links with Hungary are good, with three border crossings and a main line from Belgrade to Budapest via Novi Sad on the Danube and Subotica carrying such trains as *Istanbul Express, Pannonia Express* and *Marmara Express* in six to seven hours for the 354 kms (220 miles) including frontier formalities. Four express trains daily connect Zagreb with Vienna via Maribor.

There are two lines across neighboring Roumania's western borders, but the Danube is not bridged all the way downstream from Belgrade and the Yugsoslav and Roumanian rail systems, visible and parallel to each other for many miles, make no physical contact.

The new Bar Railway has the finest scenery to be observed from in Yugoslavia, but mention must be made of the route into Bulgaria from

Crvni Krst near Nish, where international trains climb to the Dragoman Pass. This is wild and dramatic country, much appreciated by riders of the *Simplon Orient* in its great days. Fjord-style scenery is superb on the meter-gauge line from Mostar to Dubrovnik.

Belgrade (Beograd) main station is an unroofed terminal into which all express trains back up. Another station used by local services, Dunav (the Danube Station) is a through station. Zagreb Station is noted for its very long platforms; it is a through station, but all trains stop there. Zagreb is the leading rail center of the country; it was formerly the Austrian-Empire city of Agram.

THE MIDDLE EAST

JORDAN

Like most Arab countries, Jordan has shown little interest in railroads, passing from the camel era into fast cars and buses with scarcely a gap. But railways are now being built on a large scale, intended to move heavy bulk freight, including phosphates, from the Red Sea port of Aqaba to the capital, Amman, with spurs to mining areas.

A railway once traversed Jordan (or Turkish Trans-Jordan as it was known before 1914) on its way to Medina for Mecca. This was the famous Hedjaz Railway, opened in 1904 to take pilgrims from Turkey and other Middle East countries to Mecca. It was largely destroyed in 1917 during guerrilla attacks by Arab and British forces under Lawrence of Arabia.

Expensive attempts to revive the Hedjaz line in recent years have so far succeeded only in upgrading the length from the Syrian border through Amman to Ma'an, about 290 miles. It still has its original awkward gauge 3 feet 5¼ inches, but a modern standard gauge link is under construction from Damascus (Syria, which see) to Amman.

At present, trains in Jordan run on an occasional basis except for a regular twice weekly Damascus-Amman train (with cafe-restaurant), which takes six hours for the 142 miles. Only regular departures southwards over the 233 miles to Aqaba are freights, but tourist trains can be hired if there is a large enough party. A variety of steam locomotives, dating from the 1904–14 era and built in several different countries, can be seen at work around Amman and in the depot.

SAUDI ARABIA

The giant oil-rich Arabian Peninsula, which won independence from the Turkish Ottoman Empire in 1918, lost its only railway in the course of many hard-fought battles. The *Hedjaz Railway,* Turkish-built with German aid, opened in 1904 and ran as far as Medina (for Mecca) for Moslem pilgrims. Nearly 500 miles of line from Trans-Jordan to Medina was so badly damaged by guerrilla attacks in 1916–17 (notably those led by Colonel Lawrence—"Lawrence of Arabia") that no trains could run. The Hedjaz then lay completely derelict for 45 years.

An international consortium worked at restoring the Hedjaz Railway with funds supplied by Syria, Jordan, and Saudi Arabia. From 1964 to 1969 engineers worked at it, but succeeded only in upgrading the Jordan section and building some new culverts in Saudi Arabia before both funds and government interest died away. All along the way engineers found scores of fascinating old locomotives wrecked but well preserved in sand.

King Ibn Saud was a railway enthusiast, and he dreamed of a modern Trans-Arabian rail system linking his capital, Riyadh, with the Iranian Gulf and the Red Sea, plus a revived Hedjaz Railway. Before he died he saw the first part of that dream come true.

Aramco (Arabian American Oil Company) built a fast, modern standard-gauge line for the king, financed by oil royalties. Starting on the Gulf at Dammam, it runs through Dhahran, with spurs to oil wharves and residential zones, for 354 miles via Hofuf to Riyadh. When opened in 1952 it was the most up-to-date railroad in Asia, with some of the fastest trains East of Suez.

The king lived long enough to see streamlined trains with meal service cars and air conditioning running from the Gulf to his hot, dry, inland capital in nine hours. Saudi Arabians took to railroad work and soon became good engineers under Aramco training. But the succeeding king and those ruling subsequently have shown greater interest in Cadillacs on highways and private luxury jets overhead. The extension of rails to Mecca and Medina was surveyed, but never built.

The *Dammam-Riyadh Railroad* never became the *Trans Arabian,* but still runs quite well. A daily schedule taking nine daylight hours, with Budd railcars coupled together, has first and second class accommodations and buffet service.

One tiny, narrow-gauge railway built at Aden by the British during their colonial days and now long perished, was the only other trackage on the vast Arabian Peninsula.

ISRAEL

Train travel is the cheapest means of transportation in Israel. Its nationalized railways (only one class, but with one car bookable in advance) can take you to Haifa, Tel Aviv, Jerusalem, Beersheba, Nahariya, and way points. Engines are diesel, rolling stock is modern, although some coaches are not heated in winter. The fastest trip is the one between Tel Aviv and Haifa; the most scenic is from Tel Aviv to Jerusalem. Plan carefully to avoid the Friday afternoon rush and holiday crowds. Examples of regular fares: Haifa-Jerusalem, IL 13.30; Tel Aviv-Beersheba, IL 8.70; Tel Aviv-Haifa, IL 9.

Developed from the former Palestine Railways, the Israeli system is expanding and now offers services to Dodoma. Extension for freight and passengers to Eilat, on the Red Sea, is planned.

A fine new railway station has been opened in Haifa, and also serves as a bus terminal. Express trains depart for Tel Aviv virtually every hour (no trains from sundown Friday until sundown Saturday) taking 65 minutes for the 52 miles. New Yugoslavian diesel-hauled rolling stock is used on some, while others consist of German-built multiple units.

The twisting, hilly line from Tel Aviv and Lod Junction up to Jerusalem shows the finest views of the Judean wilderness. In winter, snow can occur at higher levels on this route, especially in the mountaintop city of Jerusalem. More than once in recent years, *Israeli Railways* have demonstrated their efficiency by using snow ploughs and keeping services running when roads were paralyzed.

TURKEY

The youth of many nations feel drawn to this large, rather poor, semi-occidental country, and young foreigners ride Turkish trains in great numbers. They ride minibuses, jeeps, ordinary buses—but most of all, the trains. Any departure of the famed *Taurus Express* from the Asian shore of the Bosphorous opposite Istanbul will have a fair number of tourists, but unlike pre-war days, they will probably be found in 2nd class, sharing meal packets with locals.

Yet Turkey has some trains with equipment for gracious and luxurious style, sleeping cars being found on many long-haul services. The *Anatolia Express* 8 P.M. nightly from Istanbul (Hayda Pasha) to Ankara, is Turkey's *Blue Train,* with luxurious sleepers and restaurants and a few sitting cars in the rear. The train takes 11-¾ hours for the 359 rugged miles up to the high, inland capital. Faster and smarter, but less gracious, is the 9:15 A.M. *Bogazici,* 1st class only plus restaurant car, a diesel multiple unit which roars uphill in 9-½ hours. Three times a week, the famed *Taurus Express* makes a 10:35 A.M. start, with sleepers for almost everywhere in the Middle East, a restaurant, and some 1st and 2nd class sitting cars. It takes 11¼ hours to make the trip. Other trains use this busy line, including the *Dogu (Eastern) Express* for Kars on the Soviet border, and the *Vangolu Express,* a night run which extends to Lake Van and—once weekly—to Teheran.

Watch out for the description "fast mail" in timetables relating to Turkey and the Middle East in general. This means quite the opposite of what it meant in the US when mails were the fastest timings. In Turkey and further East, "fast mail" is a mixed way-freight.

European Turkey has shrunk to a small country at the end of the Balkans. One rail route runs through it to the Bulgarian frontier, carrying a few well-known trains including the fabled *Direct Orient Express* and the

Stamboul (Istanbul) *Express,* nowadays busier than ever but no longer as romantic or luxurious as once they were.

Asian Turkey has a wider network of railways, some built (and at one time operated) by the French, others by the Germans of long ago. There are many very interesting steam locomotives to be seen, including heavy Turkish-built 2-10-0's dating from 1960. Outside Izmir (formerly Smyrna), we have seen steam engines from seven countries in the space of one hour. Diesels have made their appearance on major trains, with multiple units for the Limiteds, while electric wires are in evidence both in Istanbul and Ankara. However, in the mountains of the southeast, the heavy trains thunder upgrade with two big steam engines up front, and sometimes one helping in the rear. There is plenty of sound and smoke and smell (from doubtful coal) for the keener rail buffs.

Many hundreds of rail buffs make organized tours to Turkey every year to watch steam in action over the high, dry Anatolian Plateau and up the mountain grades. There are many centers, large and small, at which rail sights and sounds can be rewarding. On the Black Sea coast at Samsun, there is steam narrow gauge.

Passengers crossing the Bosporus by ferry to Hayda Pasha or Istanbul should note that while the trip is only 15 minutes, traffic problems on the European side and gaps in the ferry service mean that a good two hours should be allowed for connections (in addition to which the trains are often very late at either end).

IRAQ

For all practical purposes, railways began in the land once called Mesopotamia during its Turkish Empire days, just as the Ottoman rule was coming to an end. But the British army, taking Mesopotamia early on in the 1914-18 war, laid most of the rail system which operates to this day.

Oil rich Iraq is embarking, together with Syria, on an expansion program of its railways. There will be a new, fast route linking Damascus with Baghdad, Iraq's capital. Meanwhile, the existing rail line comes in from Turkey, crosses a strip of Syria, then runs through Mosul and Samara to Baghdad. This was the historic railway built by the Kaiser's Germany for the Ottoman Turks in the 1909-13 period. The line, standard gauge, runs on across the desert to Basra on the Gulf and Umqasr, another Gulf port.

There is a narrow (meter) gauge line running northeast from Baghdad to Kirkuk (noted for its oil fields). For freight and military purposes only, it extends to Erbil and from a junction at Juloula to Khanikin.

Train services are sparse, but express trains, with compartments making up into sleepers (bedding charges payable) and air conditioned cars, run on the main line each day. Speeds average just under 30 miles an hour for "fast mails." The 337 miles from Baghdad to Basra are run overnight in

11½ hours by the best train, 1st and 2nd class only. On the narrow gauge, the 198 miles to Kirkuk takes 10 hours, daylight travel only. There are no restaurant cars.

SYRIA AND LEBANON

Taurus Express, an evocative title, was once part of the international pre-jet set's way of travel. The train still runs, taking through sleeping cars from Istanbul (Hayda Pasha) to Syria twice a week on a 38-hour schedule.

But it barely reaches into Syria, serving only Aleppo. Construction is under way to link Damascus, oldest city in the world still inhabited and Syria's capital, with Aleppo by a fast, standard-gauge line.

The present standard gauge in Syria, operated by *Syria and Lebanon Railways,* runs south from Aleppo through Hama and Homs to Akkari (on the Lebanese border) then down through Tripoli to Beirut, a total distance of 246 miles. There is a daily train between Aleppo and Homs, taking six hours for the 96 miles, and a thrice weekly "express" doing the run in three, normally extending through to Beirut, which is reached in 7¾ hours. With the present troubles in Lebanon, this is liable to suspension beyond Akkari.

Damascus sends its *Hedjaz Railway* down to Jordan on 3 feet 5¼ inch gauge, but only twice weekly. It does, however, run two trains a day to the Syrian-Jordan border at Deraa, taking about 3¼ hours in a diesel railcar for 80 miles. Big things planned for the *Hedjaz Railway* (see Jordan) have not reached fruition.

A narrow-gauge railway with rack and pinion sections runs from Beirut to Damascus. It is often out of action these days, but when running it was a popular Sundays only excursion trip behind sturdy little steam engines.

IRAN

Until the end of the 1930's, Iran (or Persia, as it was better known) had no railroad system of any kind. War brought rapid completion to a major project when British and American railroad builders laid a line from the Persian Gulf through Teheran, the capital, to the Russian frontier and Bandarsham on the Caspian Sea. This line soon carried enormous freight loads and played a big part in supplying the Soviet Union with arms in the war against Hitler.

In post-war years, rail construction has gone ahead rapidly, and it is the Shah's intention to have a fast, modern railway network as good as any in the developing world. Contracts have been let for high-speed electrification on specific routes.

Teheran now stands at the hub of five rail routes, one going to Tabriz and Lake Van in Turkey, allowing through couchette service all the way to Istanbul (Hayda Pasha). Another goes north to the Caspian, while one strikes east to Meshed. Two run southward, one to Bandar Shapur on the Gulf, the other to Zarand, with an extension soon to be opened to Kerman.

When the 260 miles of projected route from Kerman goes through to the existing railhead of the Pakistan system at Zahedan (well inside Iran), *rails will extend all the way from Europe to Karachi and India!* An overland route in seven or eight days by train from western Europe will have a tremendous impact on cheap travel. Laborious and insecure bus routes will disappear overnight, and even the 25-day, semi-luxury tour buses may find it hard to compete.

For a rugged, mountainous Middle East country that had few roads and no railways 40 years ago, it is amazing to note the fine, high-speed services already running on the Meshed line. A French-style "Turbo" speed train covers the 576 miles from the capital in 8 daylight hours (over 70 miles an hour average, with stops). An overnight sleeper train takes 14 hours. The speed train requires a hefty supplementary fare.

From Teheran to Tabriz is 457 miles of mountainous terrain. The best train takes 14½ hours. This line carries the through train to Turkey and also a through sleeper to Moscow via Djulfa and Leninakan. Both these international services are run weekly at present.

To Zarand on the way to India there are 648 miles of line carrying trains three times a week, with an overnight sleeper express to Isfahan, a popular tourist center. Trains run daily from Teheran to the Caspian shore at Bandarshah (308 miles) either by day or overnight, and two trains a day go down to the Gulf, both involving overnight journeys for the 582 miles.

Zahadan is linked to the Pakistan railroad system. Regular service is interrupted in case of cholera epidemics in Pakistan. Inquire in Zahedan about eventual resumption of services. The station is located 3 km. (2 miles) east of the city. The opening of the rail section between Isfahan and Kerman is planned.

Being modern and ambitious, the *Royal Iranian State Railways* provide what are described as irreproachable conditions in first class sitting and sleeping cars. First class fares are three times the cost of third and about twice second class fare.

AFGHANISTAN

There are no railways in Afghanistan, and it is unlikely that any will be built from internal resources. However, external pressures (including the World Bank) may eventually lead to Afghan spurs from the future Europe-India line.

Since 1973, rails have linked Istanbul (Hayda Pasha) with Teheran and eastern Iran, while westward extensions from India and Pakistan are already on the borders of Afghanistan. The missing link, currently covered by buses on a poor but improving road, is less than 500 miles.

PAKISTAN

Pakistan's railways are run by a nationalized company, known as PWR *(Pakistan Western Railway),* and the network covers practically the entire country. Although there are still steam locomotives in a few remote parts, most have been replaced by diesels. Almost all lines are Asian broad-gauge (5 feet 6 inches), but there are some lengths of meter gauge. Electrification work is in progress on main lines. There are four classes: 1st, 2nd, intermediate, and 3rd.

There are numerous facilities at the disposal of the tourist—sleeping cars, transport of cars, and compartments which include kitchenette, toilet, and shower. Although it is possible to arrange for these facilities from intermediate stations, it is better to do so from the main cities.

Baggage allowances are 115 lbs. for 1st class passengers, 80 lbs. for 2nd, 60 lbs. for intermediate, and 50 lbs. for 3rd, excluding bedding. Children traveling half-fare are entitled to half of the above weights. The following examples are fares from Karachi to Lahore: 1st class, Rs 158, 2nd Rs 76, intermediat Rs 39.60 on mail runs and Rs 29.40 on regular, and 3rd Rs 25.80 and Rs 20.40. Only 1st and 2nd class are recommended to westerners.

There is also a "travel as you like" scheme, which allows unlimited rail travel for a month from the date of issue of the ticket. It costs Rs 413 for 1st class and Rs 206 for 2nd, and children travel half-fare. There are modest supplements for extras such as air conditioning, bedding, towels, and reservations. All expresses, chief of which are *Karachi-Lahore-Peshawar, Karachi-Quetta,* and *Lahore-Quetta,* have dining cars.

If you miss a train on which you have a reserved seat, you must get your ticket refund from the stationmaster within three hours of the train's departure. Failing this, you can write a letter of explanation to the Vice-Chairman of the PWR in Lahore or to the Divisional Superintendent of PWR in Karachi. A refund will be given for the fare less 10%.

Finally, there is the ultimate luxury of renting an entire car. This can be of Category "A" with air conditioning, private bedrooms, drawing rooms, dining room, kitchen, and servants' quarters. It can be uncoupled at any station and left as long as desired. Bookings must be made well in advance.

Several times a year, *Galaxy Travels Pakistan Ltd.,* of McLeod Road, Karachi, organizes rail tours of Pakistan in style, with a side visit to Kabul in Afghanistan (not by train, as there are no rails in that country). The all-inclusive price for 17 days is about Rs. 1100.

Although the newly developed city of Islamabad, near Rawalpindi in northeast Pakistan, is now the capital, Karachi remains the commercial center of the nation. The railway system, largely built by the British when

Pakistan was part of India, tends to radiate from this big port on the Arabian Sea.

Express and long distance trains leave from the Cantonment Station at the southern end of Karachi's Frere Street. They go daily to Hyderabad (Sind), Multan, Lahore, Rawalpindi (still the station for Islamabad, to which a connecting line is under construction), Sahival, and Peshawar on the northwest frontier (station for the legendary Khyber Pass).

Mightiest river of Pakistan, and one of the great rivers of Asia, is the Indus, almost bisecting the country to flow via a delta into the Arabian Sea. Railway lines run up the Indus on either bank, serving Moenjo Daro, Jacobabad, and Shikapur. Train travel to Baluchistan and Quetta (which is rebuilt from the ravages of earthquakes), and also to Zahedan in Iran, is by way of Jacobabad, and the PWR system even across the border.

Summer temperatures in the Sind and lower Baluchistan can exceed 125 F degrees in the shade between April and June. Air conditioned cars are highly desirable and worth the extra money. By mid-June, the southwest monsoon has set in to relieve the heat. By contrast, Quetta and its surroundings are bitterly cold in the November-February period.

The most intensive network of railways in Pakistan is based on Lahore, main city of the Pakistan Punjab, as befits its dense population.

The high, cold valleys of the north cannot be reached directly by rail. In fact, Gilgit and Hunza are still only accessible by mule track or aircraft. The railhead for Kaghan, Nathiagali, and Abbottabad is Havelian.

There is a fascinating and scenic mountain railway with steam traction running three times a week from Peshawar to and through the Khyber Pass, ending at Landi Kotal. This line, climbing to over 3,500 feet on wide gauge without rack and pinion assistance, is popular with dedicated rail buffs.

SOUTH AND SOUTHEAST ASIA

BURMA

by Hugh Ballantyne

When Burma became independent from the British Empire in 1948, it adopted an isolationist policy with a one party, socialist type government and promptly closed its doors to visitors. Only in recent years have tourists been allowed visas for entry and these are severely restricted to a maximum stay of seven days, so for these reasons little has been seen of the country or Burma Railways in modern times.

Burma has a tropical climate and in the south three large rivers originating in the mountain ranges of China and Tibet flow across wide plains down through the heart of the country on their way into the Indian Ocean. The plains are flanked on all sides except the south by hills or ghats which are generally wild and sparsely populated areas, remote and quite inaccessable to a short-stay visitor.

The railway system, state owned, comprises 1,910 route miles of meter-gauge track. The principal artery is the 385 miles long main line running due north from the capital city, Rangoon, to Mandalay, Burma's second city. It is interesting to note that this line from Rangoon as far as Pyinmana, a distance of 220 miles is double track (with British style left hand running) and this is one of the longest stretches of meter-gauge double track in the world. From this main line, six branch lines run off east and west, two principal ones being from Pegu to Martaban in the southeast and, nearer Mandalay, a mountainous line east from Thazi Junction to Shewenyaung. This latter branch reaches a maximum altitude of 4,608 feet, which is the highest point on the system. Along the main line there are five places between the two cities with steam locomotive depots which are, in order going north, situated at Pegu, Pyuntaza, Toungoo, Pyinmana and Thazi Junction. At the first two places, American wartime-built 2–8–2's known as "MacArthurs" (officially class D) are allocated and work pickup and freight trains plus the daily mixed train from Pegu to Martaban. Thazi Junction retains four Garratts for main line freight workings.

The shed for Rangoon, the largest on the system, is a roundhouse situated at Malagon Junction three miles east of Rangoon Central station and contains mainly diesel locomotives. At Mandalay there is a diesel depot visible at the south end of the station platform and the steam depot is located three miles south at Myohaung Junction.

In the Mandalay area, four branch lines radiate off the main line. The longest of these goes north to Myitkyina, another west to Alon, a short line just out of the city north to Madaya and a branch eastwards into the Northern Shan States, which is noted for its fine scenery, gradients and zig-zag, to Lashio. Unfortunately, this line is in an area prohibited to visitors, beyond a town called Maymyo.

Another line of importance from Rangoon goes northwest to Prome, and in the area of Rangoon itself there is a circular suburban track around the north of the city serving Insein, Kambe and Malagon Junction, plus many local stations in the built up area of the city.

Finally, there are two completely isolated sections of railway, both steam operated. The longer is in the southwest of the country running from Henzada Shore on the banks of the River Irrawaddy, to Bassein and Kyangin and the other, which is the most southerly railway, running from a town called Moulmein to Ye, a distance of 89¾ miles. The Ye line is notable for the fact that at a place called Thanbyuzayat a connection was once made with the infamous Burma-Siam Railway, constructed by the Japanese using forced British and Allied P.O.W. labour in 1941/43 under such savage conditions that it became known as the "Death Railway." Ten old 4–6–0 and two 0–6–0's operate on the Moulmein-Ye section.

The Burma Railway system was entirely British built and the British influence is still strong both in operating methods and facilities provided. Unfortunately, the railway has declined from being an efficient and well operated line to one that is run down. For all this, it is still of considerable interest and operates about 200 steam locomotives of fourteen different classes and 120 diesels in five classes. The steam types range from 0–6–0ST to Garratts built across the world in America, England, Japan and Switzerland. However, prospective visitors should note that steam locomotives are thinly spread out over the entire country and, with time limits and prohibited areas, you could not hope to see all the locomotives in service.

Steam operates some mixed and freight trains and most switching outside the Rangoon area, but nearly all trains on the main line to Mandalay, principal trains on the secondary routes to Prome and Martaban, and the Rangoon suburban services are diesel operated, with B-B type locomotives built in Japan in 1971 or older 1200 hp B-B and Bo-Bo-Bo's of French design. Rangoon has little steam activity, although a limited amount of pilot work is done by ST class 2–6–4T's. The main locomotive works and repair shops are situated at Insein, nine miles northwest of Rangoon. Heavy steam repairs are still carried out here and the works switcher is a delightful little 0–6–0ST, number SL3, with an open-backed cab built by Avonside in 1928.

Practical Information

Travelers to Burma can only arrive by air at Rangoon and with your seven days' visa careful planning of your visit is necessary. The first problems to overcome are that no timetables are published and that all signs and notices on the railway are in Burmese script which is quite unintelligible, particularly as numbers are not of Roman type. Fortunately, many Burmese, particularly older people, speak some English, so assistance is usually available and at Rangoon and Mandalay stations no language difficulty should be encountered.

The main line train service is:

	No. 3 up	No. 1 up	No. 11 up
Rangoon dep.	7 A.M.	11:30 A.M.	3:35 P.M.
Thazi Jct. arr.	4:24 P.M.	12:32 A.M.	4:30 A.M.
Mandalay arr.	7 P.M.	4 A.M.	8:35 A.M.
	No. 4 down	No. 12 down	No. 2 down
Mandalay dep.	7 A.M.	3:55 P.M.	9 P.M.
Thazi Jct. arr.	9:21 A.M.	7:03 P.M.	11:42 P.M.
Rangoon arr.	7 P.M.	8:10 A.M.	12:40 P.M.

All these trains run daily and two classes are provided, upper class and lower class. To travel anywhere on the day express, advance booking is essential with at least two days' notice if you want the luxury of a cushioned seat, which is only available in upper class cars. Lower class have upright wooden seats. Also note that a seat ticket must be obtained before a travel ticket will be issued. The fare for the 385 miles journey is about $12 upper class, $3 lower class and, by comparison, the Union of Burma Airways (UBA) fare is $18. Stations in Burma are dirty, with only the most basic toilet facilities and the trains are little better, although for the upper class car on the Mandalay train, which is kept fairly clean. Travel by lower class is only for the hardiest. In particular, one should avoid the so-called restaurant car on the Mandalay train, as it is absolutely filthy and Burmese standards of food hygiene are virtually non-existent. However, the day express maintains a reasonable average speed of about 40 m.p.h., so if you take your own food and drink and like train travel, a reasonable trip can be made at low cost. Main line trains keep fairly well to schedule.

On other lines, there are generally one or two trains a day, one usually departing early morning and, sometimes, an afternoon service, but careful inquiries must always be made locally before buying a ticket.

There are only three official tourist hotels in Rangoon. The most expensive and least convenient for the city center is the Inya Lake Hotel. Down in the commercial center nearer the docks and about 1½ miles from the Central Station is the Strand Hotel. The third and most convenient hotel for the railway traveler is the Thamada Hotel which is only a few minutes easy walk from the Central Station. A good room with air conditioning and bathroom will cost about $6 per night plus meals. Tolerable English-style meals are served at reasonable prices and there is a good bar service. Drinks are expensive and a bottle of beer costs about 75 cents. Airport buses pick up and set down passengers at all three of the tourist hotels and ramshackled taxis are readily available to and from the airport at any time.

The following is suggested for a seven-day visit endeavouring to see as much of the railway system and country as possible in the time.

Day 1.—Sightseeing in Rangoon. Make reservation on the train to Mandalay.

Day 2.—Fly out by UBA to Henzada to see railway system radiating from here. Interesting steam locomotives. Return in the afternoon by air.

Day 3.—Fly out by UBA to Moulmein to see the second isolated system. Return by air at 3:30 P.M. or take 12.30 P.M. ferry across estuary to Martaban and have train ride back to Rangoon. Train departs 1:30 P.M. arrives Rangoon 7 P.M. The ferry boat makes a connection with the train.

Day 4.—Take train No. 3 to Mandalay.

Day 5.—At Mandalay.

Day 6.—Take morning train to Maymyo 40 miles along the Lashio branch and return in afternoon by road in shared taxi-jeep service. Ample vehicles for hire during daylight hours at reasonable cost.

Day 7.—Fly by UBA morning flight back to Rangoon.

After Mandalay there are no towns of any real size and accommodations and food in each—unless one is extremely adventurous and has a strong stomach—cannot be recommended.

The only good hotel in Mandalay is the government run Mandalay Hotel—cost of room with bathroom about $8 per night—meals extra. This hotel is just over a mile from the station and a taxi ride from the station is advisable.

Letters to railway headquarters in Rangoon for information and permission to visit locomotive depots and Insein Workshops remain unanswered, but railway staff do not mind photographs being taken, nor will permission to visit depots be refused provided the shed master is asked first and he will almost certainly want his photograph taken in return.

The Burmese are quiet, reserved people, but polite and friendly, and, in particular, those who worked on the railway in British days are very helpful to visitors. The present government regime has imposed a most austere way of life upon the people and visitors must accept lower standards than prevail in the western world, but for all that the country is a most interesting one to visit.

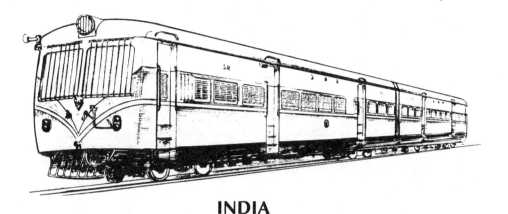

INDIA

By Lt. Col. A. A. Mains

India's first passenger train ran in 1853, from Bombay to Thana—a distance of 21 miles; in the following year the line from Calcutta (Howrah station) to Raniganj was opened; and by 1880, all the major cities of India had been connected by rail. The present railway system is the fourth largest in the world, having a route total of 37,700 miles. It is the second largest system in the world under one management, the U.S.S.R. claiming first place.

The original trunk lines were built to the gauge of 5 ft. 6 in., the widest in the world at the present time. Subsequently, a substantial network of meter-gauge lines were added and these still account for about 40% of the total capacity. There are also a few narrow-gauge lines of 2 ft. 6 in. and 2 ft., but except for the scenic mountain railways, these would not come within the range of the usual tourist.

All the major cities are linked by the broad gauge, so change of trains due to break of gauge is rare. On the other hand, there are some areas which are served entirely or mainly by meter gauge. These areas lie in the northern parts of the states of Uttar Pradesh, Bihar and Bengal, and Assam in the north and east, the states of Tamil Nad, Mysore and Kerala in the south and Rajastan and Gujerat in the west. The latter area is one of interest to tourists as it includes the towns of Jaipur, Jodhpur and Udaipur. In the south, the tourist center of Mysore is also on this gauge.

Speeds are low compared with Western countries, although many improvements have been made in the last few years, such as air-conditioned cars; this is also true of the standards of accommodations and catering. The climate and distances are not conducive to rail travel for the tourist or business man. It is almost impossible to keep non-air-conditioned cars free from the all pervading dust, and the speed of air travel is emphasized by the distances between main cities. It takes a little over 2 hours from Bombay to Delhi by air, but 19 to 24 hours by rail. But, for seeing the countryside and the peoples of India, rail travel is the answer. The relatively long station halts—most of the fast trains stop about once per hour for about ten minutes—give the traveler an opportunity to stretch his legs and to observe the fascinating variations of dress, especially female, as his journey progresses.

India is a paradise for the railway enthusiast. There are still 8,000 steam locomotives to 1,700 diesel and 800 electric, and while most of the fast trains are now electric or diesel hauled on the broad gauge, steam is still king on the meter. The mountain railways, the Simla and Darjeeling lines in the Himalayas, the Matheran Hill Railway near Bombay—all narrow gauge—and the Nilgiri Railway meter-gauge rack railway in the south are well worth a visit.

Classes of Accommodation

Basically, these are first and second class, as these cars are found on all trains except on a few unimportant branch lines where the trains are second class only. Above the first class is luxury accommodation—Air conditioned (AC) class—but this is only found on about 30 broad gauge and 10 meter gauge trains. These trains generally cover travel between all the major cities and tourist centres. In addition, there are certain air-conditioned second-class services, usually shown in the timetables as "II AC"; these comprise air-conditioned second-class sleepers, for which a first-class fare is charged, and second-class chair cars, the fares for these being higher than the normal second class. These facilities are only found on certain "special type" expresses. Air-conditioned cars consist of two- and four-berth compartments, with transverse upper and lower berths opening off a corridor which has toilets, Western style and Eastern at the ends. These coaches are usually vestibuled. They are well equipped and bedding, including towels, and toilet paper is provided without extra charge. An attendant is on duty in each car. The compartments are larger than those in Western countries and the standard of comfort compares favourably. First-class cars are similar in layout and have an attendant, but the standard of accommodation is comparable to the European *couchette*. Some first class cars, but by no means all, are vestibuled. Second-class air-conditioned sleepers provide *couchette* type berths in open saloons and second-class air-conditioned chair cars have reclining seats. In both first class and second-class air conditioned sleepers, the lower berth must be utilized to full seating capacity between 6 A.M. and 9 P.M.; thus a 4-berth compartment will seat six by day. Bedding may be hired either on the train, in the case of certain important trains, or at the starting station, on payment of a small fee. Western travelers should provide their own toilet paper except in AC class. Ordinary second class has hard seats and is usually very crowded. It is not recommended for western travelers.

Train Services

All the major cities are linked by "mail" trains which, except for the special expresses, are normally the fastest trains. Most have AC class accommodation and many, but not all, have Dining Cars. The most famous is *The Frontier Mail*—Bombay (Central) to Amritsar; before 1947 it continued to Peshawar on the northwest frontier, now in Pakistan. *The Deccan Queen* is a luxury day train, but it is not air-conditioned—Bombay (Victoria Terminus) to Poona (Pune). This is a scenic route, as the line rises about one thousand feet in sixteen miles, winding up the hillside, through twenty-five tunnels and over eight high viaducts. This line is electrified. In recent years a tourist train, *The Taj Express,* with AC class accommodations and a dining car has been put on between New Delhi and Agra, leaving at 7:15 A.M. and returning at 7 P.M. It takes three hours to cover the 124 miles.

There are also the special expresses, of which the best are *The Rajdhanis,* which carry only AC class and II AC class passengers. These trains have cut the overall time from Bombay to Delhi by 5 hours and from Calcutta to Bombay by 7 hours. They only run on two days in each week. The *Air-Conditioned Expresses* carrying AC class, II AC class and ordinary first and second class also run on a limited number of days in each week from Bombay and Calcutta to Amritsar vai Delhi and New Delhi to Madras, but are no faster than the ordinary daily *Mails.*

Comparative Distances and Times

Broad Gauge Bombay—Delhi 860 mi. (1,384 km) *Rajdhani Express*	
	19 hrs
Frontier Mail	24 hrs
Bombay—Calcutta 1,223 mi. (1,968 km)	36 hrs
Delhi—Calcutta 892 mi. (1,437 km) *Rajdhani Express*	16 hrs
Mail	23 hrs
Delhi—Madras 1,294 mi. (2.185 km)	40 hrs
Meter Gauge Delhi—Bikanir 289 mi. (463 km)	12 hrs
Delhi—Jodhpur 388 mi. (625 km)	15½ hrs
Delhi—Udaipur 466 mi. (750 km)	20 hrs

There is also an express crossing the border from Amritsar to Lahore in Pakistan, but as yet through services from Calcutta to Bangladesh have not been restarted.

Itineraries

Indian Tourist Offices abroad or the Tourist Guides at the offices of the Western and Central Railways at Bombay, the Eastern Railway at Calcutta and the Northern at Delhi will assist in planning itineraries.

There are few day trips which can be taken because of the distances involved, but a visit to Agra from Delhi can be made in a day by using "The Taj Express," which allows nine hours for sight seeing. The scenic route to Poona (Pune) can also be enjoyed in a day by leaving Bombay at 7 A.M., arriving in Poona at 11:35 A.M. and returning at 3:25 P.M., reaching Bombay at 7:40 P.M. The extremely picturesque narrow-gauge Matheran Hill Railway is on this route and can be visited during the day.

Timetables, Fares and Reservations

A "Tourist Timetable" can be obtained free of charge at Indian Government Tourist Offices abroad which gives much useful information. For the railway enthusiast there is the "All India Railway Timetable" published by the Railway Board, price Rs.3 (about 40 cents), but this is difficult to obtain outside of India.

Fares are low by Western standards, only AC class approximating to those charged in the West. They are calculated throughout India on a kilometer basis, becoming cheaper for greater distances. The mileage rate is:

For short journeys of 200 km (124 miles)
AC class $0.08, I class $0.03, II AC (chair class) $0.25, II class $0.009.
For longer journeys of 2,000 km (1,242 miles)
AC class $0.05, I class $0.025, II AC (chair class) $0.016, II class $0.006.

These fares apply over the whole system except for the Rajdhani Expresses, for which special fares inclusive of reservation fees and meals apply and a few fast trains for which a surcharge of Rs.10 ($1.25) AC class, Rs.5 ($0.62) I class, RS.3 ($0.37) II AC (chair class) and RS.1.50 ($0.18) II class, is charged irrespective of distance traveled.

Specimen fares are: Delhi—Agra, 200 km—AC class $11, I class $5, II AC class $4, II class $1.25. Delhi—Madras, 2,200 km—AC class $52, I class $35, II AC class $22, II class $8.

Prior reservation is essential for all mail and express trains; the fee is Rs.0.50 ($0.06).

There are various concessions and reductions. "Travel as you like" tickets give unlimited travel for 21 days and can be purchased by foreign nationals at AC class $200, I class/II AC class $80, II class $25. These tickets are on sale only at the Central Reservation Offices at Bombay, Delhi, Calcutta and Madras. Circular Tour tickets for travel over 2,400 km with break of journey, without any restrictions, are sold at a reduction of 15% on tariff rates. Return tickets in AC and II AC class, valid for one month, are issued at a 15% discount. There are also student concessions for I and II class tickets only.

Information can be obtained from Indian Tourist Offices abroad but reservations cannot be made nor tickets issued outside of India.

Catering

No one need starve on a journey in India. All large stations have refreshment rooms at which Indian food can be bought and many have a restaurant serving Western food. Dining cars are provided on the principal trains, but the number of these is relatively small, since only some 35 broad-gauge trains and 8 meter-gauge trains have them. There are buffet cars on a further 4 broad gauge and 12 meter-gauge trains. On trains without a dining car, the conductor or car attendant will telegraph ahead to the nearest restaurant or refreshment room, free of charge, and the meal will be served to the passenger in his compartment. The cost of meals is very reasonable, although the choice may be limited. Full breakfast $0.56, lunch or dinner $1.00. Refreshment rooms and tea stalls at stations where Western food cannot be obtained can usually provide omelettes, toast or bread and butter, tea or coffee, and iced minerals are obtainable on all major trains. Drinking water provided from official sources, i.e. dining cars and refreshment rooms, is said to be safe to drink. Alcohol is not sold on any trains or at stations.

Hotels and Accommodations at Stations

There are only two railway hotels in India at Ranchi and Puri on the main line from Calcutta to Madras, but major stations have "retiring rooms." They cannot be reserved in advance and are for short term occupation only. Charges are well below hotel prices. All I class waiting rooms have couches on which passengers may sleep at night, using their own bedding.

Railway Museums and Preserved Railways

The All India Railway Museum in Delhi opened in January 1977. There are no preserved railways in India, although it is unlikely that the Darjeeling Himalayan would have survived had it not been for tourist interest.

The Hill Railways are, however, of special interest. The Kalka-Simla Railway starts from Kalka and climbs to Simla in just under 60 miles. Kalka is at 2,400 feet above sea level and 5,200 feet is reached in 23 miles. The line then drops down to 4,600 feet only to climb again to reach Simla at an altitude of 6,700 feet. The scenery is superb and the ruling gradient is 1 in 33. The gauge is 2 ft. 6 in. and trains are now diesel hauled.

The Darjeeling Himalayan Railway is a steam operated 2 ft. gauge line, with features of great interest, notably the reversing stations and the double loop by which the railway gains height. It climbs to 7,400 feet at Ghoom, the highest altitude attained by any railway in the Indian subcontinent, before dropping down to 6,800 feet at Darjeeling. The ruling gradient is 1 in 25 with some lengths of 1 in 22 and a short length of 1 in 20.

The Matheran Hill Railway near Bombay is a 2 ft. gauge line of only 12 miles, with gradients of 1 in 20. It is now diesel operated. Regrettably, only the Matheran Hill Railway can be visited as a day excursion. Fares on the hill railways are high to compensate for high capital and operating costs. The normal kilometer rate applies, but the chargeable distance is higher

than the actual. For example, Kalka-Simla is charged at 287 km as against
an actual distance of 96 km.

Photography
The photographing of railways and railway subjects without prior per-
mission is strictly forbidden. Permits are issued by the Railway Board in
Delhi, but patience is needed, for it can be a long and tedious business.

SOUTHEAST ASIA

Some countries have excellent rail systems, while others are not as well equipped. International rail travel is presently limited to the Singapore-Bangkok express, and you have to change trains near Penang. This two-day trip is quite romantic, especially if you like to speculate about your fellow passengers' possible missions and intrigues—and there is always at least one air conditioned coach. There is sleeper service between Bangkok and Butterworth three times a week, and daily sleeper service to Singapore. Ferries run between Penang and Butterworth. Sleepers are air conditioned. The famous rail line between Saigon and Rangoon, which the Japanese tried to finish with their bridge over the River Kwai, is still not complete, and other international travel is not possible even where the rails exist, as in Vietnam and Burma.

SRI LANKA (CEYLON)

The British came to Ceylon after the Dutch administration ceased and built a railway system as good as the one they bequeathed to India. It was a broad gauge project, 5 feet 6 inches, with sturdy tracks.

Today, the railways are intact, with main lines radiating from Colombo Fort *north* to Anuradhapura and on to Talaimannur (for the ferry to Ramasswaram in South India), also to Jaffna via the extraordinary Elephant's Pass, *northeast* to Trincoma Lee (once a major British naval base and now a developing seaside resort); *east* to Batticaloa, and in an *easterly* direction with a touch of *south* in it, to Kandy (the ancient capital) and Bandarawela through high mountain country.

There are also less important lines running due north from Colombo to Negombo (passing Bandaranaike International Airport) and Chilaw, also directly south to Bentota and Galle. A narrow (meter gauge) line runs from Colombo Fort through the Keleni Valley, very scenic, very slow, and popular with rail buffs because some trains are still hauled by interesting steam tank engines.

Almost all traction in Sri Lanka these days is diesel, but four heavy Beyer-Garrett steam locomotives are retained as helpers in the really high country from Kandy to Nanu Oya, over 6,000 feet elevation. These make a fine sight at night pounding up the steep mountain grades.

Tourist Trains

Unique among railway systems, the *Sri Lanka Government Railways* operate 32 packages for tourists, using special Japanese-built air conditioned trains from Colombo Fort. Passengers are collected by bus at their hotels and taken to the station for early morning starts. There are observation salons and restaurants aboard these trains, which go to especially interesting and scenic parts of the country and are accompanied by professional guides. Kandy is a frequent destination, while others run to Galle, Sigiriya (for the monumental rock), Anuradhapura, Nanu Oya (for the Nuwara Eliya hill station), and Polonnaruwa.

The Mountain Journey

Neatly proportioned trains with observation cars at the rear pull away from Colombo Fort bound for the mountains. Their passage is through some of the most gorgeous scenery in Southern Asia.

From Colombo, it is a fast journey on easy grades for 40 miles to the important junction of Polgahawels, then the train twists and climbs through low mountains with dramatic panoramas of the plains and the sea. The main line just misses Kandy, passing through Kandy Peradenya (site of one of the world's finest botanical gardens) at about 2,200 feet.

The line swings away southeastwards, climbing all the while, with magnificent views of deep green tea estates and ravines and soaring mountain tops. From the right hand windows you can see Adam's Peak, nearly 8,000 feet, a superbly shaped mountain revered by pilgrims. It is set in a wilderness sanctuary of forest and mountain where much wildlife survives.

The train climbs on to the Horton Plains, passing through tunnels and over high bridges as it tackles the longest and steepest broad gauge climb in Asia. At Nanu Oya, it has reached over 6,000 feet above sea level and runs through cool, green countryside. Here a narrow-gauge spur line used to go off for six miles northwards to Nuwara Eliya, but today buses and taxies have taken over. Nuwara Eliya is a very English-style hill station, nearly 6,700 feet high, with golf course, race course, English Club, and mock-tudor village with big, traditional hotels.

The train on the high, main line loses altitude slightly as it swings around to Bandarawela in the heart of Ceylon's tea country and finally comes to its terminus at Badulla, some 5,000 feet above sea level. Deep down to the south lies the Ruhunu National Park, home of elephant, tiger, warthog, and many other wild animals.

SINGAPORE

You can reach Singapore by train either from Bangkok in Thailand, which is a two-and-half-day journey, or from Kuala Lumpur in Malaysia. First class, reserved, air conditioned compartments are available.

The railway line running into Singapore Island is the property of the *Malayan Railway,* which provides through services to cities in West Malaysia. The terminal station on Keppel Road is also owned by Malayan Railways (Station Hotel, close by the terminus, has 34 air conditioned rooms, several bars, dining room, and coffee shop).

No local train services are provided on the line within Singapore and all trains go through to Malaysia. There are three daily expresses to Kuala Lumpur, one day train, which has a buffet car (taking only 5 hours), and one night train (with air conditioned sleepers) taking 7½ hours. There are through cars to northeast Malaysia via Gemas.

An aerial tram system with enclosed gondola-style cars carries passengers from Mount Faber south to Sentosa Island.

MALAYSIA

The *Malayan Railway* (or the Royal Malayan State Railway, to give the system its full title) operates 1,666 kilometers (1,033 miles) of rail, including some 35 kms. in another country (Singapore). The main line, in fact, starts in Singapore, runs across that highly-developed island as a single track without offering local service, and crosses into Malaysia by the famous road and rail, water pipe and oil, causeway over the Straits of Johore to Johore Bahru. It then runs up the tropical heart of Malaysia, past rubber plantations and rich forests, to Gemas.

Here, the line divides, the western route becoming the more important. It runs to Kuala Lumpor ("KL" to all in Southeast Asia), entering one of the most picturesque railway stations in the world, built at the turn of the century, as were many surrounding major structures. The Station Hotel (23 air conditioned and 17 non-air-conditioned rooms) occupies the first floor, below the railway headquarters. Passengers may take day rooms here at modest cost. The Majestic Hotel, in similar architectural style (31 rooms), is directly opposite the KL station.

The northwestern line continues through Selangor State and tin mining scenery to Ipoh, known as the "Tin Capital of the World," and Butterworth, where a frequent ferry service links the station with Georgetown (Penang) on Penang Island. Then the line runs due north through Alor Star to the Thailand border, where the Thailand government railway continues to Bangkok.

The northeastern route swings away from the KL line at Gemas and passes through hundreds of miles of sparsely populated jungle country via Jerantut and Kuala Lipis to enter wildly tropical Kelantan State, eventually reaching Kota Bharu almost on the South China Sea. Here it links with the Thailand railway system at Tumpat. There are no through trains on this route.

Apart from one important branch from KL westward to Port Klang, that is the extent of the rail system in West Malaysia. A new line has been projected and building may soon begin between Butterworth and Kota Bharu, effectively linking the northwest and northeast routes just below the Thailand border.

Most important and most popular of all trains from a visitor's point of view is the *International Express,* operated three times weekly from Butterworth to Bangkok. On Sundays only, a deluxe sleeping car starts in KL, operated under the ASA (Association of Southeast Asia) scheme. This runs in the *North Star* express to Butterworth and is switched to the *International Express,* giving a once-weekly through service from capital to capital. There is a dining car throughout the run.

There are three trains daily between KL and Singapore, the fastest (with a buffet parlor car) taking 5 hours, the most comfortable (an overnight sleeper with some air conditioned cars) taking 7½ hours. These timings over a distance of some 250 miles are not bad for the 3 feet 6 inches gauge. Air conditioned sleepers are charged at $M 10 per night. The KL-Singapore first class single fare is $M 36.40, and from KL to Butterworth, $M 72. In second class, approximately half these rates are charged, with $M 3 for non-air-conditioned sleeper berths (usually four to a cabin).

Automobiles are conveyed by train over hundreds of roadless miles on the northeastern line. Along this route are stops where jungle safaris begin, passengers alighting from trains to be met by canoes or even, in come cases, pagoda-equipped elephants.

The *Sumpitan Emas* (which means "Golden Blowpipe") runs daily from Gemas to Tumpat. Sleeping cars, two of them air conditioned, are attached at Gemas, one having come down from KL, the other up from Singapore. The express has a buffet diner.

Sabah (East Malaysia)

The *Sabah State Railway,* based on the East Malaysian capital of Kota Kinabalu, has about 235 kms. (just over 150 miles) of line. From Tanjong Aru near the capital to Tenom is 75 miles, and rail service by diesel railcars is daily. There is service also to Sandakan.

This is one of the scenic wilderness adventures much beloved by tourists, so facilities for the charter of railcars seating from 15 to 138 passengers are very fluid. Local and overseas travel agencies arrange these charters frequently. The trip on the 3 feet 6 inch gauge takes about 3¼ hours and passengers see mighty mountain ranges, dense jungle, and wildlife, particularly monkeys. There is a charge of $M 432 to hire a 15-seat railcar for the round trip.

There are reports of steam engines still working trains in Sabam (including Sarawak, where an isolated line works inland from Kuching). It is said that steam can be used on passenger trains to Tenom for $M 8.20 per person.

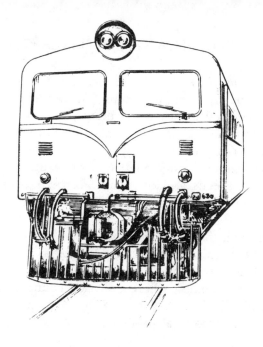

THAILAND

The *State Railway of Thailand* operates a modern system over 2,480 miles of track. There are four main trunk lines, to the north, northeast, east and south. Sleeping cars and/or air conditioned carriages are available on all long-distance trains: dining cars offer adequate, but not very interesting, food. Trains are clean and comfortable, and timetables reasonably accurate. Second class sleepers of latest Japanese type should not be eschewed at B 75.

Daily services cover all main destinations within the country from Bangkok. There are two main stations in Bankok—Hualampong and Bangkok Noi (which is in Thonburi on the further side of the river from the main city). Be sure to check which one your train leaves from.

Fares are reasonable and tickets can be reserved in advance. First class fare to Chiangmai, one way, is B390 and the overnight sleeper express leaves Bangkok at 5:00 P.M. daily for the 17-hour journey, which is very pleasant and relaxing. You can make an international rail journey northeast to Laos if you have the right documents.

The greatest travel opportunity offered by the railroad system out of Bangkok is to Kuala Lumpur in Malaysia three times weekly and, by an easy connection in KL, right through to Singapore in about 52 hours.

Dining cars in Thailand offer local foods, and foreign visitors may feel they leave something to be desired. But the staff are usually friendly and willing—if the car is not too busy they will often make you an omelette. On night trains, especially the *Northern Express* to Chiangmai, breakfast will be brought through to sleeping berths, including ham and eggs! Wines may not be available in the diner, but there is plenty of cold beer, and we have seen Mekong whisky being served as a wine substitute.

The *Royal Thai State Railways* are well maintained and spotlessly clean. This applies equally to the remaining "MacArthur" 2–8–2 steam locomotives seen from windows when on freight or secondary passenger trains and to floors and furnishings of sleepers and coaches. A little man with a brush, pan, and duster is constantly busy.

Track throughout is laid to 3 feet 6 inches gauge and is generally in good order, though speeds are low. The *Northern Express,* 5:00 P.M. from Bangkok, is the best train in Thailand, taking 19 hours for the 465 miles, with about 15 stops. First stop is at Don Muang, Bangkok Airport, which is rail connected, though sparsely served.

The northeastern line runs for 387 miles to Nong Knai (on the Laos border) and also to Ubon, 356 miles. There is an eastern route running to Aranyprathet (158 miles) where a physical connection exists with the railways of Cambodia. This was the time-honored way of getting to Angkor Wat, but war and political problems have prevented through service in recent years.

BANGLADESH

There was never any rail connection between the west and east wings of Pakistan during the twenty-five years they were under the same government. Most of Bangladesh's rail system is meter gauge, closely linked to India or dependent upon river connections. It suffered much damage during the rebellion and subsequent war involving India and Pakistan.

LAOS

There were no effective passenger railways built in Laos when it was under French administration. Plans may develop under the Communist Pathet Lao Government for some rail construction to match what is happening in neighboring Vietnam.

Rail access to the capital, Vientiane, is by *Royal Thai State Railways* to Nong Khai on the Mekong River, with a ferry crossing and short bus or taxi ride on the Laos side.

In general, the Mekong River is the Laotian highway, but a few good roads with bus services also provide surface transport.

KHMER REPUBLIC (CAMBODIA)

The recent Communist takeover and closer linkage with Vietnam is expected to add to the threadbare rail system of the Khmer Republic.

Until recent years there was good train service from Bangkok to Phnom Penh, the capital, calling at the Cambodian towns of Sisophon, Battambang, and Pursal. It went on to Kampot and Ream on the Gulf of Thailand.

A line branched off at Sisophon to Siam Reap close to Angkor Wat, and was heavily used by international tourists in the 1920–39 period.

VIETNAM

The long war wrecked all lines, but latest information is that the coastal route built by the French from Saigon north to Hanoi is being restored and upgraded. From Hanoi to the Chinese border the tracks are in good condition and carry through sleepers to Peking and even Moscow. It is understood that the former meter gauge on the coast is being widened.

EAST ASIA

CHINA

Railroad construction came late to Imperial China, forbidden—it is alleged—by successive emperors. By the 1880's, when the United States already possessed some 90,000 miles of track, China had a mere 11. This was a short line built by the British outside Shanghai, but it served more as a novelty and joy ride than a transport link. It lasted 20 years.

Not until 1911 were Hong Kong and Canton, only 112 miles apart, joined by rail. In the China of the early 1920's, under international influence and a Republic (threatened by warlords), railways took shape rapidly. American, British, and French builders helped join Peking and Shanghai, Nanking (Chiang's republican capital) and Shanghai, Hangkow, and Canton. First class travelers were aided by the Wagons-Lit Company, with its international sleeping cars, and although comfort rode the trains, security and speed were lacking.

Wars with Japan chopped China into sections. Then came World War II, when Chungking became capital and the Japanese occupied all China's seacoast and principal cities. This, at least, resulted in improved railroads, for the Japanese flair for rail construction was already well advanced. Peking and Canton, 1,500 miles apart, were finally rail linked, although a line of sorts, broken only by river crossings, had been put through in 1937–38. But China has broad gauge, and Japan uses mostly 3 feet 6 inches, so rolling stock for passengers did not arrive during the war years.

After the Communists took over under Mao Tse-tung in 1949, it was Russian influence that transformed the rails of China. Today it is Russian rolling stock, and Russian motive power built in China under Soviet technicians, that dominate the trains. During the ten years of close working relationship between Russia and China (which ended in 1960), new lines were built, including a direct route from Peking to Ulan Bator in Mongolia, shortening the journey to Moscow by 1,500 miles. The typical Chinese "express" train of the period was composed of symmetrical cars with distinctive ventilators on their roofs, hauled by a P.36 or "Stalin" type steam engine, either from Lurgansk or built under license.

The picture is virtually unchanged in 1977, although the Chinese are taking steps to stamp their own identity on rail travel. For foreigners, travel is heavily restricted and only very limited, special-purpose tourism is allowed. Rail travel for foreigners is largely confined to Hong Kong-Lowu-Canton, Canton-Hangkow-Peking, and very occasionally Canton-Shanghai, Shanghai-Peking.

Train Services in China

We have experienced only the main service on China's "open window," the 89 miles of track linking the Hong Kong border with Canton's Kwang-chow station. This route is traveled frequently by foreigners entering China, especially in late February for the Canton Spring Industrial Fair.

Certain large cruise ships, such as the *Queen Elizabeth II* and *Rotterdam,* are allowed to send up to 600 passengers on excursions from Hong Kong to Canton, when two special trains are operated. But in all instances, even with foreign Prime Ministers, passengers must alight at Lo Wu and walk across the covered bridge into China, joining the Canton train at Shamchun beyond the "Bamboo Curtain."

Comfort and a very high degree of cleanliness are immediately apparent. The Russian system of soft and hard classes applies; with sleeping car trains, this means soft (made up beds in compartments) and hard (berths without bedding and uncarpeted floors). Speeds have improved, the best train over the 89 miles taking 105 minutes, but in the main, they are still on the slow side. Tea and light refreshments are served at seats on short-distance express trains, and long-haul trains have restaurant cars, reputedly very clean and modest in price.

There are three trains a day from Shamchun (Lo Wu) to Canton, each with connections to and from Hong Kong. Freight trains are backed across the bridge in both directions, the engines never going beyond the border. Traffic is quite intense and is increasing. All trains on both sides are now diesel hauled, the present generation of the *National Railways of the People's Republic of China* still showing marked Soviet railways design and influence as regards diesel power and major steam power (which will be seen along the route and at Canton).

From Canton, a good day express runs to Shanghai in 8 hours, with soft and hard seating accommodations and meal service. There is also a daily train heading due north and right across China to Peking. It takes exactly 36 hours to cover the 1,444 miles, involving two nights and one day. The 40-miles-an-hour average (there are major stops at Changsha, Hangkow and Chengchow) exceeds that of Russia's Trans-Siberian over most sectors.

The legendary *Shanghai Express* still runs, taking 22½ hours for the 900 miles from Shanghai to Peking. This is about 4 hours quicker than during its prime in the late 1920's, when Chinese passengers were rare and top international service fed and pampered foreigners. Today, a foreigner is so rare he or she will be a source of wonder and amazement, even to soft class sleeping car users.

Train travel in China for foreigners today depends first upon the vital visa being issued, then upon the China Travel Service, whose only office outside the Republic is in Hong Kong, and thirdly upon Luxingshe, the official state tourist organization looking after foreigners. Apart from the busy Hong Kong-Canton route, which is always by train, choices seem to be ignored. It is reported that Luxingshe will say "today there are no trains—you must fly," and later on during an itinerary, "there are no more planes—you will travel by train."

HONG KONG

This British Crown Colony retains the 22-mile-long section of the former *Kowloon-Canton Railway,* which runs through the New Territories (leased from China until 1993) to the frontier at Lo Wu. The standard-gauge railway is intensively used, with passenger trains at least hourly, reached by ferry from central Hong Kong. Three each day connect at Lo Wu with trains for Canton, and passengers with the appropriate visas and other documents walk across the bridge over the Shamchun River between British and Chinese customs posts, where a Chinese train waits.

Passengers not going through to China are not permitted to travel to the frontier station, but must leave the train at Sheung Shui, about 2 miles on the Hong Kong side.

The railway goes through a long tunnel after leaving Kowloon, taking it under Lion's Rock and providing the shortest route to Sha Tin Bay, the Chinese University campus, the popular shopping area of Tai Po, and the Fan Ling Golf Club. Trains are always crowded and carry three classes of passengers. The 55-minute journey is cheap and quite scenic, giving a glimpse of South China in minuscule, with plenty of rice paddies and water buffalo to be seen.

The peak tram is Hong Kong Island's best known "railway," a funicular climbing 1,400 feet from Queen's Road East low level station.

JAPAN

Commodore Perry's fleet anchored in Tokyo Bay in 1853 and brought a steam train and some track when it forced the Shogun to open up trade with the Occident. This tiny example of what railroads could do was left behind by the Black Ships, and from it sprang one of the great rail networks of the world.

Under Emperor Meiji (1868–1912) Japan's railways grew into a fine, well-run system on 3 feet 6 inches gauge. Travelers during this period compared the Japanese trains most favorably for their comfort, cleanliness, and service with European and American ones. But not for speed; that was to come later.

In the latter part of the 19th century and the early part of the 20th, Japan eagerly copied everything mechanical from Europe and America. The early railways showed this trend, while Tokyo Central Station, planned in 1909 when the Japan National Railways Board was set up and completed in 1914, is an almost exact copy of Amsterdam Central.

But later, Japan built up its own rail image, and after 1964, when the high speed New Tokaido Line started running from Tokyo to Osaka, the world tried hard to copy Japan. Japanese engineers were called in to help at Trenton, New Jersey, when development work was going on with the Department of Transportation's *Metroliners* on the New York-Washington run. They have been consulted by the French, Germans, and Italians on high-speed projects now taking shape.

By building the standard gauge New Tokaido Line, financed by a huge World Bank Loan (now repaid), Japan became the first country to operate passenger trains at a scheduled speed in excess of 100 mph. To their credit, they had built up the Old Tokaido Line on its 3 ft. 6 inch gauge to high standards or frequency under electric wires. They also held the world record for speed on this gauge, recording 104 miles an hour, while some sectors were traveled at 73 m.p.h. average in the early 1960's.

Today, the Old Tokaido Line is mainly carrying freight, while passengers use the new line *(Shinkansen)*. The frequent expresses and semi-fasts often carry *half a million people per day*. During the 1970 World's Fair in Osaka, one busy day saw 685,000 passengers carried on New Tokaido Line trains, yet no one had to stand. Airline routes have long crumbled before such remarkable demonstrations of surface travel efficiency and speed, but at first they flew "competing" routes.

We tried an experiment in 1965, and again in 1969 (about the last year jets tried to fly the Tokaido route). Starting from the International Hotel in Kyoto, one of us took the airline limousine to Osaka Airport and flew to Tokyo's Haneda Airport, the other taxied to Kyoto New Tokaido Station, rode the famous *Bullet Train* to Tokyo, then took a surburban train to Hammamatsucho, where he took the Monorail to Haneda Airport. The rail user arrived at the meeting point at Haneda just as the jet from Kyoto/Osaka was discharging baggage.

Repeated in 1969, with the *Hikari* trains speeded up, the comparison was made from Osaka city center to Tokyo city center. It resulted in the rail user having to wait one hour and twenty minutes in Tokyo for his airborn companion (whose flight was not delayed)! Today, 94% of all traffic on the route is by train, the remainder mostly by road.

The New Tokaido Line, built from scratch with no grade crossings and only twelve stations, is 515 Kilometers long compared with the Tokyo-Osaka distance of 560 kms. by the Old Tokaido Line. There are 65 kms. of tunnel, 100 kms. of elevated track, and 44 kms. of bridges. Curves are especially gentle and gradients very slight. Normally, express trains run at 200 kms (125 m.p.h.) but get up to about 220 kms. (137 m.p.h.) on certain stretches. There are speedometers in the buffet and dining cars for passengers to observe progress. The extensions to Kyushu and northward from Tokyo are faster, allowing speeds of 250 kms. (156 m.p.h.) on a regular basis.

Although some 6000 kms. of route will be operated on the Shinkansen system by 1985, the majority of Japan's routes will still be on 3 feet 6 inch gauge. Although very creditable speeds are maintained on these tracks, the keynotes of the smaller trains will be as today, frequency, efficiency, good service, cleanliness, and opportunity to view grand scenery. Only five countries in the world operate vista-dome cars for scenery (invented at Burlington in 1945): USA, Canada, France (Maritime Alps only), Germany (Rhine areas only) and Japan (Kinki Nippon Railway, a private line).

Japanese National Railways

Apart from the growing number of Shinkansen, the 3 feet 6 inch gauge lines of J.N.R. carry a daily quota of 496 limited express trains and 1175 semi-fast trains. In addition to these, of course, are many thousands of commuter electric services in and around the major cities.

Services are often deluxe aboard limited expresses, and every semi-fast is equipped with a "green car" (first class) on long distance routes. There are sleeping cars, too, the best in Asia, an "A Class" roomette (not quite so large but as well equipped as an American one) costing Y6400, and a lower berth (as in Canada) Y4900. "B" grade sleepers, more like couchettes in Europe but with refinements and only requiring second class fares, cost Y1400 for a lower, Y1300 for a middle or upper. All sleepers are air-conditioned.

Every limited express carries a diner, and some semi-fasts have refreshment cars. Both Western and Japanese meals are served in diners, and a full service of alcoholic drinks is available in the diners. There are rolling trolleys, often with waitresses handling them, on most trains. There is also a definite "non-tip" system aboard J.N.R. trains.

A few of the most traveled tourist routes use English for announcements (all Shinkansen trains are operated in Japanese and English). Other less internationally traveled lines are in Japanese only, so a good map is highly desirable, although some station names even in remote areas will have an English translation of the name set up somewhere.

Private Railway Companies of Japan

There are about 150 private railway companies sharing some 30% of Japan's total rail mileage. As in Switzerland, where a similar system applies, some of them are quite large and prosperous, others are small and in financial straits.

One of the best known and most used by foreigners is the successful *Kinki Nippon Railway* (called "Kintetsu" by the locals). It owns the only vista-dome equipment in Asia, and runs standard gauge limited expresses throughout the Kinki and Tokai districts. The main line links Osaka with Nagoya, others serve Nara and Kyoto, with a scenic route to Ise-Shima National Park. The Kyoto-Nara trains take 36 minutes and carry much tourist traffic.

The *Hankyu Corporation* provides express train services between Kyoto, Osaka, Kobe, and Takarazuka. The trains are mainly electric with special expresses called "tokkyu".

The *Fuji Express Company* has a rail line from Otsuki to the five lakes and Mt. Fuji district, taking about an hour. The *Odakyu Railway* has a line to Gotemba from Shinjuku, taking about 100 minutes, and serves Lake Hakone from Shinjuku (Tokyo) to Yumoto. It also serves Enoshima, a popular resort. There is a four-day Hakone Area pass valid on the Odakyu Line and its buses, for Y2600.

Other companies include the *Tobu Electric Railway,* the *Nishi Nippon,* the *Hanshin Company,* the *Tokyo Electric,* and the *Nankai Railway* (trains from Osaka to Wakayama and boats on to Shirahama).

Fares and Other Practical Notes

Japan's *Shinkansen* "bullet trains" have the reputation of being the fastest, most punctual and most comfortable trains in the world. Special features of the *Hikari* super-expresses include compartments for wheelchair passengers, and diners as well as buffet cars. The trains do not have baggage cars, and only limited overhead rack space, so travel light.

The *Hikari* covers the 556 kilometers between Tokyo and Osaka in 3 hrs. 10 min., stopping only twice in between. From Tokyo it reaches Okayama, 733 kilometers away, in 5 hrs. 30 min. The *Kodama* (slower express) has more stops in between, and takes an hour longer. Neither stops for more than two minutes at any station, so hurry to get on or off.

In 1975 the extension of Shinkansen service beyond Okayama to Hakata, 1,078 kilometers, began functioning. Forty-five Hikari super-express trains operate daily between Tokyo and Hakata. The shortest traveling time between the two cities is now 6 hrs. 56 min.; slower Kodama trains take 7 hrs. 48 min. By 1979, five new Shinkansen routes should be in operation: the Tohoku, between Morioka and Aomori; the Hokkaido, between Aomori and Sapporo via the world's longest undersea tunnel; the Hokuriku, between Tokyo and Osaka via Toyama on the Japan Sea; the Kyushu, between Hakata and Kagoshima; and the Nagasaki, between Hakata and Nagasaki.

Other projected lines are planned for completion by 1985, when the Shinkansen network will cover 6,000 kilometers, connecting remote places in Kyushu to others in Hokkaido.

The Hikari leaves Tokyo every 15 or 20 minutes, with the Kodama operating in the intervals between the Hikari's departure times. Should your Shinkansen express ever be more than two hours late, you are entitled to a refund of the express charge. An announcement in English informing foreign passengers of the refund is made on the train. If a delay of more than two hours is anticipated, super-express fares are reduced 50 per cent.

Hikari fares are: Tokyo-Kyoto, Y2,610 + Y2,700: total Y5,310; Tokyo-Okayama, Y3,410 + Y3,300: total Y6,710; Tokyo-Hakata, Y4,510 + Y4,500: total Y9,010. Green Car—first-class—charges are computed on the basis of distance. Twenty-six cities are connected by telephone to Shinkansen trains. Three-minute calls cost Y300 for short distances, and Y600 for long distances. Japan National Railways sells hotel reservation tickets combined with Shinkansen tickets, at the "green windows" of its major stations. Japan Travel Bureau provides a similar service for both luxury hotels and business hotels combined with Shinkansen tickets.

More leisurely rail trips can be made on the older lines, which provide a creditable cover of the Japanese islands. So long as you get a seat, which at least on the long-distance trains is only a question of selecting and reserving in advance, railroad travel competes favorably with other methods.

Several private railroad lines in the Tokyo and Kyoto-Osaka areas offer excellent service, mostly to resort areas but occasionally also to distant cities. Around Tokyo are two popular private lines, the *Tobu* line to Nik-ko, and the *Odakyu* route to Hakone, both using air-conditioned "ro-mance" cars. These, like the other private lines, are on an all-reserved, one-class basis and have refreshment stands on each train.

In the Kansai area, the *Kinki Nippon Railway* provides double-deck vista dome cars between Osaka and Nagoya through the scenic Kii Penin-sula region and operates a fine air-conditioned train from Osaka to Nara.

Economy travel. It is possible to buy reduced-rate excursion coupons when visiting a number of places designated by Japan National Railways. These tickets are available at the principal JNR stations, and at any office of the Japan Travel Bureau and Kinki Nippon Tourist.

Special discounts are available to foreign tourists in parties of 15 plus.

"Japan Tour Tickets" are available for overseas visitors, together with hotel and sightseeing coupons, to those who travel on special routes pre-pared by the JNR. Applications are accepted at the JTB offices in Tokyo, Kyoto and Kobe, 4 to 21 days prior to the date of departure.

Fuji-Hakone-Izu

Five Lakes and Mt. Fuji district. Japanese National Railway trains Leav-ing Shinjuku Station in Tokyo, an 85-minute semi-express ride on the Chuo Line takes the traveler to Otsuki Station, where it is necessary to change to the privately-owned *Fuji Express Company's* rail line. This takes you to the lake via Fuji-Yoshida in another hour. Six trains daily from Shinjuku go directly to Kawaguchi without the necessity of changing. Best train leaves at 8.46 A.M., arrives 9.29. The *Odakyu Private Railway* line to Gotemba from Shinjuku Station connects with a bus at the former city, the motorized portion of the journey being a one-hour trip from Gotemba to Lake Yamanaka. (The Odakyu rail sector takes 1 hour 40 minutes.)

To *Lake Hakone* and its area, a comfortable way is by the *Odakyu Rail-way's* route from Shinjuku Station in Tokyo to Yumoto, taking 80 minutes by the line's modern romance cars, all-reserved limited expresses. More complicated, but going via Yokohama and Odawara, giving you a glimpse of the sea, is the *Japanese National Railway's* route from Tokyo Station to Odawara. At Odawara, you change to the *Hakone-Tozan Railway* line which goes up the Hayakawa River valley through Yumoto, Miyanoshita, and Kowakidani, to Gora (45 minutes). From Gora, you can go even further by cable car (9 minutes) to Sounzan. A ropeway connects with the high-altitude lake directly. From Yumoto and/or Gora-Sounzan, you can take a taxi or bus to the lake. From Yumoto to Hakone town itself is about 45 minutes, and from Miyanoshita, about 30 minutes. From Hakone to Sengokuhara is another 40 minutes, and from the latter through the high-lands to Miyanoshita, 20 minutes by car. A direct highway from Hakone to Atami via Ten Countries Pass (Jikkoku-toge) is a 75-minute drive, and a different route, the Taikanyama road, leading to Yugawara, takes 90 minutes.

Regular *Japanese National Railway* Tokaido line expresses (which go all the way to Kyoto and Osaka) reach Atami in about 90 minutes, and on the new line in one hour. It can be reached in 2 hrs. by express. The comfortable *Izu Express* takes about one hour from Ito to Shimoda. Through service from Tokyo to Shimoda is also provided by JNR daily in cooperation with the Izu Electric Railway Co. Automobile travel to Atami takes up to four hours if traffic is bad.

Driving beyond Atami will take you over one hour to Kawana, at least one hour from there to Imaihama and at least another hour to Shimoda. From Imaihama up the central mountain range in the middle of the peninsula will take you 40 minutes to Yugashima, and another 35 minutes to Shuzenjo. But the quiet, lovely mountain town of Shuzenji itself can be reached directly from Tokyo by JNR express in 2 hrs. 20 min.! Trains depart Tokyo every day at 12:45 and 1:18 P.M., with extra trains provided on weekends and holidays.

To *Shizuoka*. There are nearly 30 express trains from Tokyo to Shizuoka daily, taking about ninety minutes to make the trip on *JNR's* New Tokaido line. From the Fuji-Hakone area the traveler should catch the *Kodama Express* of the New Tokaido Line at Odawara or at Atami.

Nikko

The best way is by the expresses of the *Tobu Electric Railway,* which are quite plush. They leave Tobu Asakusa Station about every half hour, take about 1½ hours to Nikko, from early morning. The JNR trains, from Ueno Station, are less frequent, on about the same schedule. All express seats on both lines are reserved; ask your hotel or travel agent. Both lines also run frequent ordinary trains; these are cheaper, non-reserved, take about 2½ hours.

Shonan

If you arrive in Japan by ship you will already be in the heart of the Shonan area. If you are going from Tokyo you should catch the *Japanese National Railways* Shonan expresses leaving Tokyo station every half hour and taking 30 minutes to reach Yokohama, or the Yokosuka expresses leaving every 15 minutes. You may continue on the latter line to Kamakura, Zushi, Yokosuka, and Kurihama, and on the former to Atami. The main Tokaido line from Tokyo to Kyoto is the route on which the Shonan trains operate to Atami via Oiso and Odawara. To reach Enoshima, the "Miami of Japan", one can go to Kamakura on the JNR train and then take a taxi for a 15-minute trip. A new monorail line links Ofuna Stn., JNR, with Enoshima Stn. in 13 minutes. But a direct route passing through interesting countryside and on a far superior train is the Odakyu express from Shinjuku station, with all reserved seats on some trains. You can also reach Odawara by another track of the same all-reserved Odakyu. Expresses continue on to Fuji-Hakone.

Chiba-Kanto

Very good express trains leave on the hour from Ueno station. and reach Mito station, 75 miles away, about minutes later, for a one-way fare of Y1,250. Public transportation east of Tokyo to Chiba and west to the Chichibu-Tama National Park region is highly developed. The *Red Arrow* express from Ikebukuro on the Seibu line takes 83 mins. to reach Chichibu. Five semi-expresses of the *Japanese National Railways* depart daily from Shinjuku and Ryogoku stations (successively) for Chiba and thence down the west coast of the Boso Peninsula to Tateyama, two going on to Awa-Kamogawa. Time: 3 hours. Six similar trains go to the east coast passing through Oami and Ohara for Awa-Kamogawa. Time: 2 hrs. 45 min. There are also four semi-express trains daily for Choshi. The *Skyliner* is a super-express destined to connect Tokyo and the Tokyo International Airport at Narita.

Kyoto

From Tokyo there are about 90 super-express trains daily, taking from 3 to 4 hours to reach Kyoto. Ordinary expresses take 6–8 hours. All these trains have buffet cars, reclining seats, telephones, etc., and are very comfortable. Rapid interurban service from Kobe takes about an hour, from Osaka about 30 minutes. There is frequent plane service Tokyo-Osaka, and bus service from Osaka International Airport to Kyoto; actual flight time is about 1 hour; but the extra commuting and waiting time required make the super express trains really more convenient.

From Kyoto Station by the National Railway to Osaka, Kobe, and beyond, take the rapid *(kaisoku densha)* on Track 4. From Sanjo Station to Osaka (Yodoyabashi) by the Keihan Electric Railway, about an hour by limited express *(kyuko)*. From Kawaramachi to Osaka (Umeda) by the Hankyu Electric Railway express *(kyuko)* or special express *(tokkyu)*. Change at Umeda for Kobe (Sannomiya). These lines all have departures every 20–30 minutes during most of the day, JTB runs a fancy transfer bus Kyoto-Kobe. One trip each way per day, fare four times that of the railways.

Kyushu

The *Japanese National Railways* is continuing to expand its electric line services throughout the island. Otherwise, diesel and steam are still used. The special *Yunoka* semi-expresses (one each day) run a direct Hakata (Fukuoka) to Beppu schedule in three hours. This train continues on to Tosu and returns on the same line. Hakata to Nagasaki by limited express is just under three hours.

In 1975, the Sanyo and Kyushu extensions to Hakata of Japan's famed Shinkansen super-express network were completed. The shortest traveling time between Tokyo and Hakata is now 6 hours 56 minutes, by the Hikari super express. The Kodama takes 7 hours 48 minutes. Next in speed to the bullet trains are the limited and regular expresses. Direct limiteds from

Tokyo reach Hakata in 17 hours, Nagasaki in 20 hours, Kagoshima in 22 hours.

The Japan Alps

This is a large area and there are three separate routes from Tokyo to and through the mountains, plus an important seacoast route running from east to west along the northern shores of the country. First is the *Joetsu* line of the *Japanese National Railways,* running north from Tokyo's Ueno Station through Takasaki, up to Iwappara and on to Niigata. There are special expresses; the *Toki,* from Ueno to Nagaoka and Niigata, that leave frequently and take less than four hours to cross the country. Ordinary expresses take about five hours to travel the same distance. Typical time lapses are Ueno-Iwappara, four hours; Ueno-Kusatsu, three-and-a-half hours on the train plus a one-hour drive.

The second line, the *Shinetsu,* also runs from Ueno Station to Takasaki, but here it branches off to the west through Karuizawa, and turns north to Lake Nojiri and the famed Akakura skiing grounds. A limited express, the *Asama No. 1,* leaves Ueno Station every morning for Karuizawa and Nagano. The new train proceeds to Toyama, Kanazawa.

The third and most southern of the three lines from Tokyo, is the *Chuo,* which leaves from Tokyo at Shinjuku Station and passes through Kofu, Lake Suwa, and on to Matsumoto, the gateway to the Alps.

Tohoku

Sendai, the capital of the region, can be reached in 4½ hours by limited express train from Tokyo. The comfortable *Japanese National Railways* streamliners use the coastal route, affording some scenic views of the Pacific. The JNR trains on the main line to Hokkaido are reasonably good, but there are only two or three first class streamliners, and none match the famed Tokyo-Osaka expresses for luxury and comfort. The main line trains pass through Mito, Sendai, Morioka, and Aomori. Another route with expresses is Tokyo-Utsunomiya-Fukushima-Yamagata-Akita-Aomori. There are two daily limited expresses running along the coast of the Japan Sea from Aomori to Osaka, via Hirosaki and Niigata, and vice-versa. A southbound train leaves Aomori at 4:40 A.M., reaches Akita at 7:28, and Niigata at 11:03 A.M. Osaka arrival is 8:03 P.M. Two daily expresses also operate between Sendai and Niigata across the country, the morning train leaving Sendai at 7 A.M., arriving at the western terminus at 1:09 P.M. A lesser line runs from Tokyo to Niigata, and thence, with changes, up to Akita.

Hokkaido

It is a 14 hr.–15 min. trip from Tokyo to Hakodate, via Aomori, by limited express train and ferry boat. Construction of a new super express railway line, already projected, will reduce rail travel time. After 25 years of study, the Seikan Undersea Tunnel is to be built, connecting Honshu with Hokkaido by passing under the Tsugaru Straits. It will be the longest tunnel in the world. By 1978, rail travel from Tokyo to Sapporo is expected to occupy a mere 5 hours 50 minutes.

Steam in Japan

Despite ultra-modern high-speed trains, some pockets of steam traction continue to survive, especially in Kyushu and Hokkaido. A few very interesting locomotives will fascinate rail buffs in Hokkaido, including one or two remaining Baldwins.

A magnificent steam shed-museum is maintained outside Kyoto, with examples of about 25 classes (and more being added). Every day, different engines are steamed up for visitors, and there are opportunities for short rides, as well as climbing onto footplates.

Finest steam power in Japan is the C62 class, 4.6.4 locos rebuilt from 2.8.2's in 1949. A few may still be at work in Hokkaido; two examples will be seen in the Kyoto shed-museum.

Tokyo Stations

Tokyo Central is a through station with a great number of tracks, those furthest to the East being the standard gauge ones added when the New Tokaido Line was built.

In its central building is the Tokyo Station Hotel, 62 rooms (but 36 without bath). It is completely air-conditioned and has a swimming pool. Full meal arrangements, Japanese, Chinese, and Continental.

Shinjuku is the second most important station. That, too, is a through station. Indeed, there are no rail terminals in Tokyo. Some trains may start from Ikebukuro, or from Shibuya, or even from Shimbashi. All these are linked by the Yamanote suburban line.

The Shinkansen line stations are as near as possible to those of the older lines they have largely superseded. At Yokohama, though, the old and new stations are over a mile apart, and in Osaka there are 1¾ miles separating the new from the old (with a rail connection).

Ohme Railway Park

A fine collection of historic steam locomotives is preserved in the open at Ohme Railway Park, in the Tokyo Area. Engines from both state and private lines are on show, with examples of rolling stock.

KOREA

To most of the younger generation, Korea means south of the 38th parallel. This is where most travel occurs these days and where transportation facilities are developed to Western patterns. But to older people, Korea once meant the magnificent *South Manchurian Railway,* built and maintained to superb standards in the era of international travel during the period 1900–1914. The Japanese created it as a link with the Chinese Eastern and the Trans-Siberian lines. It ran to Seoul from the north and to places which meant a lot in the history of the period, such as Port Arthur. Most of the trackage of the S.M.R. is now in North Korea or China, very infrequently traveled by Westerners. There is a through sleeping car from Moscow to Pyongyang, North Korea's capital. However, no rail routes cross the 38th parallel today.

South Korea

The *Korean National Railroads* have their headquarters in Seoul and radiate southward. Seoul to Pusan is the crack line, and over its 350 miles high-speed trains, almost comparable to those of Japan's new Tokaido line, operate fast, efficient services. Standard gauge is used, which allows speeds up to 100 miles an hour, and the track bed to Pusan follows the original South Manchurian route to the city-port, where ferries cross to Japan. "Special Expresses" have air conditioning, dining cars, Pullmans, and obligatory reservation of seats.

Other main lines in South Korea include the *Honam* line from Seoul to Mokpo in the southwest, and the *Chungang* line, Chongyangri to Pusan. Secondary lines offer quite satisfactory standards of travel and a chance for rail buffs to see occasional steam engines.

THE PHILIPPINES

Rail rates on Luzon are reasonable. The *Philippines National Railways* (PNR), with the main terminal (called Tufuban) at Recto Avenue, Manila, dispatches six passenger trains daily to the Northern Lines, passing through the provinces of Rizal, Bulacon, Pampanga, Tarlac, Pangasinan and La Union. First class passengers bound for the summer capital of Baguio are taken up by cars from the debarkation station at Damortis, La Union, and the third class passengers make the trip by buses. Actual terminus of the Northern Line is Dagupan on the Ungayen Gulf. First class fare in deluxe air conditioned coaches is approximately US $4 one way from Manila to Baguio. To the Southern Lines are dispatched daily the *Bicol Day* and *Night Express* trains, the *Mayon Ltd. Express Train* and two motor car trains, passing through the provinces of Rizal, Laguna, Quezon, Caramarines Sur and Albay. The Manila-Legazpi (Bicol Express) fare one-way is approximately US $7; and the Manila-Legazpi tourist class fare one way on the Mayon Ltd. is approximately US $5.75.

Virtually all Philippine passenger rail services are concentrated on the important and relatively well populated island of Luzon. Apart from a few sugar estate and industrial narrow-gauge lines, the only other railway is on Panay, where a line of about 70 miles in length runs from Roxas in the north to Iloilo City, a port-resort.

The Luzon lines are dramatically scenic in parts, southern expresses from Manila to Legazpi City having the perfect cone of Mayon Volcano in sight on any fine day all the way from Naga to the terminus (about 90 minutes). Southern-route trains also pass close to the Pagsanjan Falls and Rapids.

But the Philippines have never been railway islands, even in Spanish and early American (from 1900) days when rail building was at its height in the world. Nor are they road islands. They are, however, the last great stronghold of the inter-island passenger ship, with three companies offering services, often of high standard. There is, of course, a wide air network.

TAIWAN

Transportation here is a problem. Trains, buses, and planes are punctual and well run, but there are not enough of them to handle the great number of people who want to travel. The facilities are therefore crowded, and purchasing bus or train tickets is often impossible. The way to get around this is to buy your tickets through a travel agency. Although they will be a little more expensive, this will save you much frustration and valuable time.

There are a number of trains that operate daily to and from Taipei. The ride to Taichung is about 3 hours—to Kaohsiung about 6. The main trunk line stops at almost every big city on the west coast. Remember, you can't buy roundtrip tickets! Your return ticket must be purchased either by you or your hotel, and it is advisable to do this the day before you intend to leave.

The facilities on tourist express trains of the *Taiwan Railway Administration* are of high standard, with air conditioning, hostess service, towels, free tea, and reading material. There are always restaurant cars on these trains. They are called *Kuan Kuang* and *Chu Kuang,* making four south-bound and five north-bound runs a day between Taipei (the great, over-populated, sprawling capital) and Kaohsiung, some 240 miles along the west (China Sea) coast. They take six hours, running on well maintained 3 feet 6 inch gauge track, a legacy of railway building when the Japanese held the island of Taiwan (then Formosa). The trains are diesel hauled and charge slightly higher fares than first class on normal passenger services.

In good weather—and here one must mention the long rainy seasons in Taiwan—this can be a most scenic and interesting journey. At the city of Taichung, about midway on the route of the tourist trains, buses connect and make a trip eastward to Taiwan's greatest tourist attraction, Sun Moon Lake.

A branch line goes off from Chiayi, about two-thirds of the way to Kaohsiung, up to Alishan, a region under the control of the forestry bureau. Reservations well in advance are essential on this limited service. It reaches a particularly splendid mountain area and Alishan, at 7461 feet, has the distinction of being the highest railway station in East Asia. As a matter of fact, they are shifting it downhill to a new location at 7251 feet and building a big 1000-bed hotel on top of it, but Alishan will still retain its 'highest' rating.

Taiwan's east coast has railways which are not physically connected to the main system. A long line runs north-south from Hualien to Haituan and Taitung, highly scenic when it is not raining and humidly overcast. There is steam traction to delight all rail buffs, and narrower gauge.

Plenty of big Japanese-built steam engines can be seen at work on the busy port route from Taipei to Keelung. This line passes near the National Palace Museum, containing most of Imperial China's treasures brought out by Chiang Kai Shek's forces in 1949. There is more steam on the short Tamsui line.

In general, rail travel in Taiwan is fairly cheap, but the *Kuan Kuang* express charges NT$ 331 (about US $10) and the *Chu Kuang* NT$414 (about U.S. $12.50). Most ordinary trains charge a fare of about 3 U.S. cents a mile in 1st. class.

THE PACIFIC

INDONESIA

For some 300 years, the Dutch occupied the large Southeast Asian islands of Sumatra, Java, the Celebes, and part of Borneo—then called the Netherlands East Indies. Whatever the shortcomings of the long occupation, modern Indonesians agree that its legacy of an extensive rail system on Java and a lesser one on Sumatra was beneficial.

Unfortunately, no improvements to the railways were undertaken after 1941 following invasion by the Japanese, and by the end of the war in Asia, the entire system was in ruins. Much of the good track had been dismantled and carted away by the Japanese for use in other military spheres. There followed an anti-colonial war, and it was not until 1949 that the Indonesian Republic was formed with secure control of the islands. By then, it was not possible to travel by train between any major cities.

Repair work was slow and the track was bad. A private Dutch railway company line linking Bandung with Surabaya via the south coast had been laid to 4 feet 8½ inches standard gauge. Most of this had been wrecked or taken away during the war, so it was eliminated completely, leaving the Java system all 3 feet 6 inches gauge. The socialist leanings of the Sukarno government of Indonesia (1949–1966) severely discouraged any frills when main lines were restored to working order. Trains were crude, with no restaurant cars and no sleepers.

This was in utter contrast to the excellent services of 1940, when the fastest narrow gauge trains in the world were thundering from Batavia (now Djakarta) to Surabaya, equipped with luxurious first-class, sleeping, and restaurant cars. Even an order for an air-conditioned train with sleepers from East Germany was opposed by the Communists as being a train for elite travelers.

All this, however, changed with the overthrow of the Sukarno government and a return to moderate pro-Western policies. A new railways division was formed, called P.J.K.A. (Perusahaan Jawatan Kereta Api), which announced a couple of Five Year Plans and has made good on the first one, with the second one not far behind schedule. New and heavier tracks, faster trains, better rolling stock, and more restaurant cars have all resulted, though the only sleeping car train is the one from Surabaya to Djakarta. Today, sections of the Java system are back to 60 miles per hour, running on the narrow gauge.

Meanwhile, the elderly—and often ancient—rubs shoulders with the new, making Java and Sumatra paradises for rail buffs, especially those with keen steam interests. No less than 79 classes of steam locomotives have been retained, mostly in East Java and Central Sumatra. Some are lightweight engines built more than 90 years ago, while others are oddities surviving from orders placed by the Dutch with Bavarian builders in the early 1900's. There is also a large number of quite modern Krupp all-purpose steam engines delivered in the mid-1950's for the Sukarno regime. Many modern German and American diesels are in use. There are now 7,246 kms. of 3 feet 6 inch gauge and 645 kms. of very narrow gauge line worked in Indonesia.

Java

There are two trunk routes, both over 500 miles long, from Djakarta, the capital, to Surabaya—one via the north coast through Cirebon and Semarang, the other via the center of the island at Bandung and along the south coast via Jogjakarta and Madiun. Important lines go from Surabaya to Malang and eastwards to Bangywangi for the ferry to Bali, while others run from Djakarta up to Bogur and westwards to Merak for the ferry to Pandjang in Sumatra.

The overnight *Bima* between Djakarta and Surabaya is the crack express of Indonesia, an air-conditioned sleeper train with restaurant car which provides dinner, bed and breakfast with the fare, whether you ride first class or economy. This is one of two East German built trains whose acceptance was delayed by politics. An American or German diesel unit heads it, and where the track is restored the speed is quite high. Although *Bima* means night bird, part of its 15½ hour journey is made in daylight.

Fastest train of Indonesia, and the fastest in Southeast Asia, is the *Gunung Jati,* running from Djakarta to Cirebon (219 kms.) in 150 minutes. Its speed reaches 65 miles per hour. The *Parahyangan* is fastest of the several daily trains running from Djakarta to Bandung (2,000 feet above sea level). A restaurant car express, often with meals served at your seat by waitresses, it makes the 174 uphill kms. in 148 minutes. A useful train for tourists wishing to ride the rails is the *Mutiara Timur* (Eastern Pearl), a daylight express from Surabaya to Bangywangi for the ferry to Gilimenuk on Bali (20 minutes sea trip and seven hours on the train).

A number of steam-hauled trains run from Surabaya to Malang, hauled by unique 12-coupled tank engines. Steam is otherwise confined to freight work or to light spur lines and suburban services, but there is a fantastic working museum piece in Surabaya—none other than an urban steam tram service.

Madiun is the main center for repairing steam locomotives. It is a major town in East Java, with frequent train service. The sheds and repair workshops can be visited, and groups of rail buff tourists arrive frequently from Australia, USA, Britain, and other parts of the world. Here one may see veterans of steam long disappeared from the rest of the world.

At Ambarawa in the hilly heart of Java, a steam museum has been developed in which it is intended to keep one engine representative of each class. There is also a cog-wheel railway from here up to Bedono which is operated as a steam rail mountain tour offered to 20 or more persons booking the train. A Swiss-built rack engine hauls the train.

Giant Mallett engines built in Germany may be seen on steep freight lines (Hannomag DD52 class 2.8.8.2 engines, the largest working Malletts in existence). These haul mixed trains in the Nagrak area of West Java, and colored postcards of them are on sale. Javanese railmen regard them much as the Union Pacific did their "Big Boy" Malletts of the 1940's and 1950's.

Sumatra

This huge island, much larger but less heavily populated than Java, has three separate railway systems. There are plans to link the ferry landing port of Belawau (Medan), where the vessel from Penang in Malaysia berths, with Pandjang in the south where the ferry runs across to Java. But there are several hundred miles of tropical jungle, mountains, and forest to overcome between the gaps, and the Central Sumatra system is no help. being mostly narrow gauge and based in Padang on the west coast. This system has a series of short lines to the rubber estates and forests, steam worked, in some cases by interesting rack-equipped engines. These survive mainly because of coal haulage from Ombilin to the coast.

North Sumatra has a long line from Banda Atjeh on the extreme tip down to Rantauprapat, which is being extended to Wing Toot. It serves Medan and the Malaysian ferry and has a new diesel hauled express called *Putri Hijau* between Medan and Tanjunbalai. The north system has about half a dozen new diesel locomotives, but the predominant traction is steam of various interesting types, all teak burning.

The South Sumatra railway routes have been upgraded so far as track and equipment are concerned. There are now eight new diesels and a pair of night express trains *(Sindang Marga)* run between Kertapati and Lubuklinggau. Day expresses (this word is rather loosely used) are diesel hauled now between Kertapati and the Java ferry at Pandjang. They are called *Raja Basah 1* and *2,* while night trains (with somewhat crude couchette-sleepers) run also from Kertapati to Pandjang as *Sriwijaya 1* and *2.*

Madura

Only one other island in the thousand-strong Indonesian Archipelago has railways, and that is Madura, offshore from Surabaya. It is famous all over the world for its bull races, but is always overshadowed by Bali (where railway buses run on good roads to the Java ferry).

Madura is reached by a short ferry trip from Surabaya to Kamal, where steam-hauled trains run northwards a short distance to Bangkalan and eastwards nearly the length of the island to Pamekasan.

Other Information

Djakarta has two stations, but all main line trains work into Kota (the main station). Surabaya has three stations, Gubeng (for the main line to Djakarta), Kota (for Bandung), and Pasar Turi. Taxis and pedal cabs connect them.

The P.J.K.A. timetables are on mimeographed sheets available free of charge in English, but they only list the main line trains and carry no information about suburban or mixed services. They do show the fares, which are modest by Western standards.

Scenery on Java consists of teak, water buffalo, and people, for the island is overpopulated. There are plenty of glimpses of mountains and distant extinct volcanoes. In Sumatra, tropical forest is the primary view from any window.

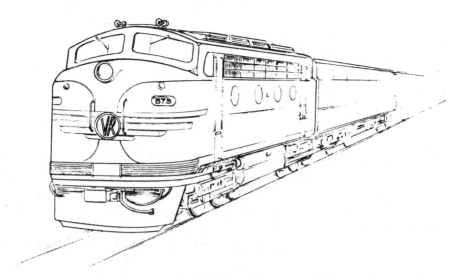

AUSTRALIA

Nearly 30,000 route miles of rail track cover the more densely inhabited parts of the Australian continent and some of the sparsely populated areas as well. This compares favorably with the United States, nearly twice the area of Australia with ten times the population, where trackage is about 200,000.

But until fairly recently, the Australian tracks were of many different gauges, and rail travel for passengers as well as for shipment of freight, looked to be on the way out, challenged by air and road transport. However, a mammoth investment program in new gauge track, relaying, modern equipment, and iron ore discovery has resulted in a complete change of situation. Today, Australia is in the forefront of railway development and some of her trains are among the best in the world, while her iron ore and coal freights rival and even exceed those of the biggest tonnages in the United States.

Australia developed out of British-settled colonies, some of them started as convict stations at the end of the 18th century following the loss of the American colonies. When railway construction began in the mid-1850's it was colony by colony, each regarding the neighbor as a different country. The gauges were chosen without regard to through running, so New South Wales, the oldest colony, chose standard gauge (4 feet 8½ inches) while Queensland opted for 3 feet 6 inches and Victoria built to 5 feet 3 inches. Later, Tasmania (entirely separated from the mainland) constructed at 3 feet 6 inches, as did Western Australia, while South Australia, showing good sense, linked up with Victoria with 5 feet 3 inches. However, South Australia also built a good deal of 3 feet 6 inch gauge railway. In 1900, the only through running possible was between Melbourne and Adelaide.

Not unlike the situation in Canada years earlier when West Coast settlements demanded a rail link to the East as the price for joining a federation, Western Australia agreed to join the Commonwealth of Australia in 1901 only if a railway was built across the continent.

This formidable task, across desert and waterless plain, took until 1917, with construction by the Commonwealth Government to a gauge of 4 feet 8½ inches between Port Augusta 200 miles North of Adelaide to Kalgoorlie, the gold mining town in Western Australia, a distance of some 1,200 miles. So a passenger taking a train from Sydney in New South Wales to Perth in Western Australia faced six changes of train and gauge. His journey took him from Sydney southwards on 4 feet 8½ inches to Albany on the Victoria border. Here he joined a train of 5 feet 3 inch gauge to Melbourne. From Melbourne he took the then solitary inter-city express, called *Overland,* to Adelaide on 5 feet 3 inches. Headed northwards for 100 miles to Port Pirie Junction, he was on 5 feet 3 inches but changed at the Junction for 3 feet 6 inches for a short ride to where the 4 feet 8½ inches Commonwealth line began near Port Augusta. He stayed with this train a day and a night to Kalgoorlie, where he changed for the last time, to 3 feet 6 inches and the *Westland Express* for a 360 mile run to Perth. The whole trip took five days and nights!

Slight easings at Port Pirie improved matters in 1937 but it was not until 1962, when standard gauge went right through from Sydney to Melbourne, that changes were reduced to four in all. Journey time came down to four days and nights.

Then came the dramatic and costly scheme, finished in 1970, which converted Western Australia's main line to standard and put a new line through South Australia to join with existing upgraded gauge at Broken Hill. The first train, the superb *Indian Pacific,* rolled across Australia from sea to sea in three days, 101 years after Union Pacific achieved unified gauge in America.

Great Trains Of Australia

Several of Australia's latest trains rank among the best in the world. They run under the banner of "Railways of Australia" rather than the various States, as was once the case, and the ownership of several is by the Australian National Railway Commission (which took over the former Commonwealth Railways). The A.N.R.C. operates all the former Commonwealth lines plus the Tasmanian Railways and the non-urban railways of South Australia.

Top train is the magnificent *Indian Pacific,* a streamliner running four times a week in each direction between Perth and Sydney, 2,460 miles in 65 hours. It carries first and economy class passengers, all in sleepers, the firsts with showers and private toilets. The train is air conditioned throughout, with double windows and venetian blinds between the windows controlled from inside the compartments. It has a diner serving excellent meals included in the fare, while a cafetaria lounge serves the economy passengers, and an observation lounge, a bar, and a music room (with full-sized piano) the first class. On its long straight run across the Nullarbor Plain it speeds at a 60 miles an hour average, held for a thousand miles. It is always full up and berths should be applied for three months in advance.

Next in line is the *Trans Australia Express,* called the "Trans" by Australians. This, too, is now a streamliner. It runs three times a week from Perth to Port Pirie, with onward connection to Adelaide by a 5 feet 3 inch gauge train. It, too, has a music room and piano. Journey time from Perth to Port Pirie is 40 hours, with four hours on to Adelaide.

The *Southern Aurora* is an excellent inter-city streamliner, all sleeper and first class, between Melbourne and Sydney, running nightly and taking 12¾ hours for the 600 miles. An unusual innovation for business and other travelers is its restaurant, which opens for service at 7 P.M. while standing in Melbourne's Spencer Street Station, an hour before departure.

The "Rora", as Australians call it, was introduced in 1962 after introduction of the standard gauge between the nation's two largest cities. Prior to that, the best train was the famous *Spirit of Progress,* introduced in 1937 as a steam streamliner between Melbourne and the border station of Albany, where the most hated words in Australia ("All change, Albany") were heard, calling passengers out onto the very long platform for the trudge to the New South Wales train for Sydney standing on its different gauge.

The "Spirit" still runs, but as a through train, with cars for Canberra as well as Sydney. It carries first and second class passengers and has a diner. A third express runs through from Melbourne to Sydney and vice versa every day. This is the *Intercapital Daylight,* with first and second class seating cars and a continuous service diner with stools up to a waitress-served counter. It takes from 8 A.M. to 9 P.M.

From Melbourne's Spencer Street Station, an overland express has run to Adelaide without a change of gauge for more than ninety years, thanks to both Victoria and South Australia (in part) having the 5 feet 3 inches gauge. The present "Overland" has been a streamlined air-conditioned train, diesel hauled, with first and second class sleepers and a club lounge, for more than ten years. Rolling stock is continuously being improved, but it has never had a diner on its 7:30 P.M. to 9 A.M. schedule. Breakfasts are served in bed and coffees and sandwiches at night in the club car, but full dinners are arranged in dining rooms at the main stations at both ends of the line.

The legendary *Ghan* is a remarkable combination train that runs to the "Dead Heart" of Australia, terminating at Alice Springs. There is no effective road up from South Australia to "The Alice", so large numbers of autos and "piggy back" trucks are hauled on the end of the *Ghan's* rake of passenger cars. These can then set off along the great tarmac road that stretches from Alice Springs to Darwin. The *Ghan* actually starts at Maree, South Australia, where a number of coal mines work. Passengers and freight go up to this point from Port Augusta over standard gauge, and change to the 3 foot 6 inch *Ghan,* a long streamliner with diner and good sleeper equipment. It then takes 24 hours heading northwards across desert country through occasional tiny townships such as Oodnadatta, following the line of the overland telegraph built in 1879 by camel caravans. Because Afghan drivers were imported with their camels to thread this line through waterless country, the train that followed became known as the *Afghan Express,* but, typically Australian, became shortened (this time officially) to *Ghan.*

Those camels, their work done, were released and founded the wild herds of camels met with occasionally in the Outback.

An entirely new standard-gauge railway is now under construction from Tarcoola, on the Trans Australia Railway, northeastwards to Alice Springs. When it is completed, the old 3 feet 6 inch gauge line will be abandoned from Marree onwards. It is relatively slow and subject to washouts on the rare occasions when rain falls. The new route, due to be ready in 1979, will be longer but faster and of stronger construction.

New South Wales has some good country trains, most of them with air-conditioned equipment and diners, serving the major towns inland. The best named expresses are the *Brisbane Limited* and the *Gold Coast Motorail.* The former runs nightly from Sydney to Brisbane, where the gauge has been standardized into South Brisbane station and will soon be extended across the river into the city proper. It takes about 15½ hours for the 600 miles. There used to be an ordinary *Brisbane Express,* now merged with the Limited, so that the latter carries deluxe sleepers, ordinary first class and second class coaches, plus a continuous service dinette handled by squads of waitresses.

The *Gold Coast Motorail* is an all-sleeper, car-carrying train, with autos hauled on the rear. It runs from Sydney to Murwillumbah on the New South Wales-Queensland border, to serve the famous "Gold Coast", a Florida-Type development based on Surfer's Paradise. The train is the Australian equivalent of America's "auto trains" from Virginia to Florida, and carries a good diner.

The *State of Queensland* is all 3 feet 6 inches and plenty of it, with a long coastal main line and several very long inland thrusts. On these tracks run a fleet of streamliners, none of them daily but most two, three or four times a week. The *Sunlander* runs from Brisbane to Cairns, nearly 1,200 miles, in 38 hours; the *Capricornian* runs the shorter length, Brisbane to Rockhampton; the *Westlander,* as its name implies, heads inland from Brisbane to Toowoomba and the Darling Downs, terminating at Quilpie; the *Midlander* runs inland from Rockhampton, to Longreach and Winton (Outback towns where the famous Australian airline QANTAS—meaning Queensland and Northern Territories Aerial Service—was founded back in 1920); the *Inlander* takes a long, lonely route from Townsville to Mount Isa.

All these trains are air conditioned, have first and second class sleepers, coaches, and carry a grill car or food-bar car. Their speed is not high due to the gauge, but most run at 40 miles an hour or more where circumstances permit. They all require one night on their journeys, except *Sunlander* which takes two, twice a week.

Incredibly, the fastest trains in Australia are found in Western Australia. They are diesel multiple units running on the new standard gauge between Perth and Kalgoorlie. Called *Prospector,* these trains have become very popular, with daylight runs, hostesses serving meals at seats, and a seven-hour time card for the 336 miles. The units often run at more than 70 miles an hour.

Western Australia has one other "name train," this one on the 3 feet 6 inches. It is the *Australind,* a refreshment car, coach and first class day train from Perth to Bunbury, taking about 3½ hours for the 120 miles.

Urban And Country Trains Of Australia

Soon after the end of World War II, most Australian trains had reached a very dilapidated condition, with old rolling stock mostly of wooden construction showing signs of "bow shaped" bending. The locomotives, with few exceptions, were elderly steam-driven ones dating from the early years of the century.

Both Sydney and Melbourne already had intense electric suburban services, but again the equipment was old, forty years and more, with wood the main feature, broken doors and shabby seats. Many Australians believed the days of trains were over, the blossoming airlines (Trans Australian Airlines, the government's "baby," and ANA-Ansett, a private enterprise line) taking over the longer trips, while cars and buses did the urban and outer-urban journeys.

But a transformation took place, due to hard work and heavy investment. Even now it is by no means complete, but the railway, for both long and short haul, is again in vogue and a pleasure to ride. For one thing, there are showers in the sleeping cars of all long-distance trains, and most double bedrooms have private showers.

Wide extensions to the electric lines have been built, with underground sections in Sydney. Brisbane's network of commuter lines is in process of electrification. Adelaide has a suburban service with multiple-unit diesels.

Sydney has a great many double-decker electric commuter units, quiet and fast. Those taking the outer-suburban runs to Gosford and inland to the Blue Mountains at Katoomba are well upholstered and carpeted throughout. Formerly the New South Wales Government Railways and now the Public Service Commission of New South Wales, the railway in that state is the largest single employer of labor in the Southern Hemisphere. Electrification began in Sydney in 1926.

In Melbourne, bright new electric trains have appeared, and the underground loop is rapidly taking shape, which will extend the suburban electric area. Already, Flinders Street Station, with its 18 platforms and 20 tracks, has the largest number of passenger train movements in the world except for London's Clapham Junction (which passes 2,400 trains a day).

Victorian country services have a long way to go yet so far as equipment and facilities are concerned, but an overnight train to Mildura has good sleepers. Out of Sydney Central Station, 37 country trains a day are upgraded, with good rolling stock and at least cafeteria cars if not full scale diners.

Several of the long distance country trains penetrating Western New South Wales, notably the *Silver City Comet* which runs from Sydney to Broken Hill, show their passengers vast mobs of kangaroos, some of them trying to pace the train. These animals never go near roads for fear of hunting, but seem to realize that near rail lines they are safe.

A number of services link Sydney and Melbourne with Australia's Federal Capital, Canberra. It is just over three hours from Sydney by the fastest diesel multiple-unit express, up to the capital in the morning and down to Sydney in the evening.

Determined passengers may travel in the caboose (equipped with three seating compartments) of freight trains in many parts of Australia, particularly Queensland and Tasmania, and in Western Australia.

Scenic Highlights On Australia's Railways

There is a short and very hilly 25-mile run from Cairns in Northern Queensland up into the Great Dividing Range at Kuranda. It is really part of a system going inland to Forsaythe and Ravenshoe, served by mixed traffic trains on a thrice-weekly basis.

But so scenic is the initial tropical run to Kuranda that special tourist trains, often with up to 12 cars, are put on each day at 9 A.M. The trip takes about 90 minutes, including stops to view waterfalls and to alight for photography. From Kuranda, passengers may either return in the train or make a bus tour over two or three itineraries, returning to Cairns that afternoon.

Electric outer suburban trains run from Sydney to Gosford across the Hawkesbury River on a long, low bridge, showing some of the finest river and forest scenery in Australia.

The rail route over the Blue Mountains from Sydney to Katoomba and on to Lithgow is dramatic. This is an outer suburban electric service operated quite frequently. Two business trains leaving Sydney Central between 5 P.M. and 6 P.M. for the Blue Mountains have been known for many years as the "Fish" and "Chips."

Made by only one train a day now that an integrated rail-coach service runs, the journey from Brisbane up to Toowoomba (105 miles) twists and turns amid the Great Dividing Range in one of the finest and steepest rail climbs in Australia. The fast bus up from the plains to Toowoomba misses the scenic highlights slow moving train passengers enjoy for nearly two hours.

The Ride Across The Continent

Let no one say the Nullarbor Plain is boring. We have ridden this trip three times and it is always fascinating. Aboard *Indian Pacific* or the

"Trans" the passenger rides in a luxury hotel with all conveniences, yet the scenery is always changing. Sometimes the great plain is alive with color where desert plants have grown after a rare shower. Sometimes there are mobs of kanagoos and emus if water is present. The cloud formations can be beautiful.

Tiny railway communities, named after former Prime Ministers of Australia, are stopped at or passed at speed. They live for, on, and by the railway, all their supplies, even their school and cinema and library, coming by train. There are usually neat houses plus a paddock and a station building, with passing loop and siding trackage. Sometimes a small flying doctor airstrip and a windsock shows up across the way from a community. But to stray out of sight beyond the line of rail is perhaps to be lost forever.

The train runs on the world's longest straight stretch, 297 miles from Nurina to Ooldea. Both *Indian Pacific* and "Trans" average 65 to 70 m.p.h. along here with smooth running, and many passengers choose this time to take a shower.

Only as darkness falls the first day from Kalgoorlie (second night out from Perth) can people get out at a 30-minute station stop, at Cook, South Australia, where the diesels are refuelled. Next morning, they see the Woomera Rocket Base in the desert, then hills and the start of big bushes, even trees. Wildlife becomes more prolific, with emu, kangaroos, and birds, before Port Augusta is reached.

Australian Rail Bargains

On short trips, especially on suburban electric trains, rail fares seem high, but the longer distance you go, the cheaper it becomes. On the trips across the Nullarbor Plain to and from Western Australia, meals and sleepers are included in the fare for both first and economy class.

An "Austrailpass" was introduced shortly before the United States started its "USArailpass" in early 1975. This allows unlimited *first class* travel over 27,000 miles of passenger track for 14 days at a cost of Aus. $70 (US $78), which can be extended to 21 days for Aus. $110 (US $123), and Aus. $140 (US $157) for one month. These rates do not include meals or sleepers, but such charges can be paid as extras, and in fact a sleeper berth costs Aus. $4 (US $5) for the night aboard Queensland streamliners and Aus. $5 (US $6) aboard trains such as the *Southern Aurora*.

The full first class return fare from Sydney to Perth including meals and sleepers (roomette) is Aus. $264 (US $296). With an Austrailpass, the extras to pay are $160 (US $179), so with a 14-day pass used only on this one trip, it is cheaper than buying normal fare.

The Austrailpass is marketed in North America, Europe and Japan, especially by the Thomas Cook organization. It cannot be purchased on the spot in Australia.

Steam In Australia

From a fleet of over 6,000 steam engines in 1952, Australia now has only 31 left on the books in active service, all of these switching in Victorian country districts. The Trans Australia line was first to go diesel, entirely for water-shortage reasons. The new "Trans" with diesel traction started in 1951.

American built and British built diesels came in, but the Clyde works in Victoria supplies most of the diesels today. As for electrification, it is so far confined to the extensive Melbourne suburban system and that of Sydney, plus two stretches of main line in New South Wales—84 miles west to Lithgow and 36 miles northwards to Gosford.

Many preserved steam engines get a chance to go out on the tracks with enthusiasts' specials. Magnificent semi-streamlined green Pacific engines of the "38" class of the New South Wales railway (which were built at the same time as and on main frames supplied by Canadian Pacific Angus shops when CPR's Royal Hudson Class was being developed) survive to the tune of three at Eversleigh Works near Sydney. Older engines exist there, sometimes working trains for the Australian Railway Enthusiasts Society or the various chapters of the Railway Historical Society.

There are working steam engines in Brisbane and most weekends see them out on the tracks with specials to Toowoomba or Gympie. South Australia has several in good shape, including some giants built by American designers based on the Pennsylvannia's immediate post-war steam streamliners. Steam workings from Adelaide are almost daily from April to October, the details given with care on the morning radio news. West Australia, too, has its engines, the best known being at Bunbury where a special steam run called *Leschenault Lady* takes place frequently into the Jarrahwood Forests. Victoria also holds a few engines in reserve for ceremonial specials.

Rail Museums

The largest and most interesting museum is at Redbank in Queensland, between Brisbane and Ipswich. Displayed in the open, and run by the Queensland Division of the Australian Railway Historical Society, Redbank shows 12 steam engines illustrating the steam history of the State. Admission is free.

In Victoria, amid the Dandenong Ranges some 35 miles east of Melbourne, the "Puffing Billy" steam train climbs the hills on a daily schedule. It is not only a prime tourist attraction but one of the finest narrow-gauge passenger railways in the world.

Adelaide's Mile End, just a mile from the terminal station, has a massive museum with over 20 engines, some being restored, others in working order (and sometimes brought out onto the tracks). Admission is free.

There is as yet no National Museum for steam locomotives, since the history of railways has developed through the different States.

In Victoria, Swan Hill is a vast open-air museum depicting life in a country district on the Murray river at about the turn of the century. In addition to farm machinery, there are classes of Victorian Railway steam engines working at that time. Admission to Swan Hill is Aus. $1.

Steam locomotives preserved as monuments may be seen in various communities throughout Australia. Both rail fan groups (the Australian Railway Historical Society and the Association of Australian Railway Enthusiasts) are very strong and active, and more preserved lines may soon be in action.

Tasmania has a pleasant little named train, the *Tasman Limited,* running every weekday from the North Coast at Wynyard through Devonport (where the car ferry from Melbourne berths) and Western Junction (Launceston) to Hobart. It crosses the central mountains in daylight and gives a very scenic ride to about 80 passengers, all of whom enjoy reclining seats and meals and drinks served by hostesses.

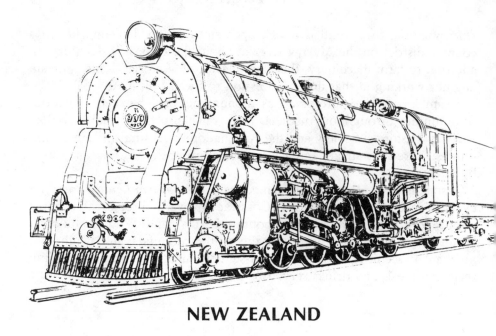

NEW ZEALAND

Although explorers and whalers made spasmodic attempts to establish settlements on New Zealand's North Island in the very early days of the 19th century, it was not until 1840–2 that planned colonization took place. Advance parties laid out the towns of Dunedin and Christchurch ready for fleet arrivals in 1850. Wellington had been settled to some extent in 1841 and declared the capital in 1852, but it was in Christchurch that the first railway was projected—a short line to connect the town with the port of Lyttleton.

December 1, 1863 is the agreed date of the opening of the first steam-hauled public railway in New Zealand, from Christchurch to a wharf on the Heathcote River, a mere 4½ miles laid to a wide gauge of 5 feet 3 inches. Slow progress with railway construction, due to the mountainous nature of both islands of New Zealand and the small population, led to a decision to abandon wide gauge in favor of 3 feet 6 inches.

By the mid-1870's, the lines were taking shape and eventually they played an enormous role in the development of New Zealand. The government took over most of the struggling lines, but a very famous private company, the Manawatu, remained independent until 1908. Its line ran from Wellington to what is now Palmerston North, about 84 miles, and showed a distinct American influence, using Baldwin locomotives, American-style cars, and the first dining cars to be seen in New Zealand. After the government took over the Manawatu Railway, the diners went to an important tourist train running to Rotorua (whose hot springs and geysers were challenging Yellowstone Park in Wyoming for the valuable "Jet Set" tourism of those days). Taken off in 1915, on-train refreshment facilities were not seen again in New Zealand until 1971. The Manawatu Railway had one other claim to fame: in 1892, with a Baldwin 2.6.2 engine, a world speed record for the 3 feet 6 inches gauge was established, 15 miles in 15 minutes, with a maximum of 64½ miles per hour.

It was not until 1909 that the two largest cities of New Zealand, Auckland and Wellington, were finally linked by rail. For many years, passengers had traveled by rail between Wellington and New Plymouth and then taken an overnight steamer to or from Auckland. Completion of an overland route had been prevented by very rugged terrain known as the King Country, where Maori wars had continued until quite late in the 19th century, and volcanoes in what is now National Park.

It seemed to be the policy of the New Zealand Government Railways from just after the start of World War I (which for New Zealand was August 1914) until a new outlook in the 1960's to run a basic service without frills. No attempts were made to offer luxury trains, and services onboard and at stations were minimal. Even the best express in the country, the Night Limited on the trunk route from Auckland to Wellington, stopped twice for refreshments. There were mad scrambles for hot meat pies and tea, and it was alleged that this was how so many young men in New Zealand developed the shoulders for playing rugby—only 10 to 15 minutes were allowed for 500 people to be fed!

The locomotives and rolling stock were, however, kept in good order, always quite clean, while fares were modest and speeds remarkably good considering the narrow gauge and mountainous country. Some electrification was effected in the Wellington suburbs and in 1921 through the 5½ miles of Otira Tunnel near Arthur's Pass on South Island under the Southern Alps.

With air and road travel building up in the 1950's and 1960's, no New Zealanders had a good word to say for their railways. Some routes were cut out or retained for limited freight only. North Island was most affected, with no trains to Rotorua and none north of Auckland except for specials. Railways were losing money while rail subsidiaries such as the touring buses and ferries were making it.

A sudden rail revival took place under what is believed to be Australian and Japanese influence. Australia had been modernizing her system and unifying her many gauges, while the Japanese had achieved world fame with the new Tokaido Line. At the same time, seeing her prime market, Britain, starting to enter the European Common Market, New Zealand needed to export meat and dairy produce to Japan. Reciprocal imports were called for, and railway material was chosen, as well as other engineering items.

The turning point came in 1970–71 with the introduction of fine new trains. One of them, the overnight "Silver Star" between Aukland and Wellington, was equipped more luxuriously than anyone in New Zealand had ever seen before. Today it is ranked among the ten best trains of the world. Up-to-date and reliable diesels were obtained, replacing older diesels which had not been better than the well-built steam locomotives they worked alongside. Steam was retained for main line running in the South Island until the winter of 1970, but even that succumbed to diesel traction on a refurbished daylight express called "The Southerner."

North Island

Apart from an intensive suburban electric network radiating from Wellington up the Hutt Valley and into the nearby steep hills, and for some local diesel suburban units out of Auckland, trains carrying passengers are few in number. But those few can be considered good.

Wellington's large and impressive railway terminal, built in the center of the city in the 1930's, is headquarters for the system. Passenger trains go to Auckland by the main trunk route, to New Plymouth via Wanganui, and to Napier by way of Masterton.

The trunk line is served by a daylight railcar called *Silver Fern.* Fast and comfortable, this makes the trip between 8 A.M. and 7 P.M. in both directions, giving wonderful views of the Raurimu Spiral up to National Park and the three dramatic volcanoes, Ngaurahoe, Ruapehu, and Tongariro (7,515, 9,175, and 6,517 feet respectively), the first two quite active and smoking through their snow-capped summits. *Silver Ferns* have hostess service, with meals and drinks served at seats. Seven stops are made en route and there is a commentary given during the trip.

Overnight on the trunk line is the famous *Silver Star,* New Zealand-designed with Australian overtones, and Japanese-built. It takes 12½ hours (from 8 P.M. to 8:30 A.M.) for the 426 miles, two hours quicker than the former *Night Limiteds,* which made two meal stops. Passengers aboard *Silver Star* have two-berth bedrooms equipped with private toilets and showers; and there are single rooms as well; there is also a neat buffet car staying open until midnight, while breakfast is served in bed!

A slower train, consisting of older *Night Limited* steel stock with sitting cars and couchettes, makes its way nightly between the two big North Island cities between 4:30 P.M. and 6:50 A.M. It calls at twelve stations en route, two of them for quick meals.

An appalling disaster occurred on Christmas Eve, 1953, due to volcanic activity in National Park. A sudden eruption blew out an entire lake which in turn swept away a trestle bridge just as the faster of the two *Night Limiteds* was entering it. Some 150 persons were swept away to their deaths in the silt as the first six cars and the locomotive fell crashing to the river bed.

New Zealand is called the "shaky Isles" because of minor and major earth tremors, eruptions, and geysers, but nowadays extra watches are kept on the transport system, especially along the stretches above 2,000 feet in the National Park area.

Blue Streak is the name of a fast railcar running Monday to Saturday from Wellington to New Plymouth. It takes about 6½ daylight hours, and is supplemented on Sundays and Fridays by an ordinary train in the afternoon, taking seven hours. *Blue Streak* offers the same on-train facilities as

Silver Fern railcars. The perfect cone of 8,210 foot Mount Egmont is the scenic highlight.

The Endeavour, named after Captain Cook's ship, runs between Wellington and Napier, Mondays through Saturdays, in 5½ daylight hours. It has refreshment services. Connection is made at Napier with an ordinary train which runs for four hours to Gisborne. This passes along the shores of Hawkes Bay.

That is the sum total of the main line passenger trains of North Island, but if the quantity seems thin, the quality has been revitalized; and after all, the population is barely one and a half million. Foreign tourists, perhaps to the tune of 100,000 a year, are big users of the daylight trains, while *Silver Star* is prime transport for the nation, sought even by business travelers. Its cost is equal to flying, at 20 New Zealand Dollars (about $25 U.S.) inclusive of berth. Other trains are much cheaper, with about $5 N.Z. charged to New Plymouth.

North Island To South Island

The New Zealand Government Railways own three train ferries which take trains and autos from Wellington to Picton across the Cook Straits. Two of them, *Aramoana* (4,160 tons) and *Aranui* 4,524 tons) carry a large number of foot passengers as well. The trip, across what must be viewed as some of the windiest waters in the world, takes 3½ hours, but there is shelter from islands and fjords after two hours of open sea. There are up to four departures daily in each direction, the 10 A.M. and 6:40 P.M. from Wellington, and the 2:20 P.M. and 10:40 P.M. from Picton operating all year.

Both passenger ships have cafeterias and bars and a few cabins, but the open seating is quite adequate. A bus or taxi links the ferry terminal in Wellington with the railway station; no passenger train equipment is rolled aboard, only freight cars. At Picton there is a wharf shared with buses and the railway to Christchurch but only one railcar and one mixed train daily use it, a good train-ferry connection being offered only in the northbound direction.

As with trains, tickets should be bought as far as possible in advance from the New Zealand Government Travel Bureau Offices, but they may also be purchased at main railway stations and at the ferry terminals.

There is a longer ferry journey direct from Wellington to Christchurch by the 9,000 ton *Rangatira* of the Union Line. This takes ten hours, mostly overnight but with some daylight sailings, with departures five days a week. The ship has berths for all passengers, a restaurant, and a movie!

South Island

Larger than North Island, the South Island has a vast mountain range, the Alps, and is sparsely populated with a climate akin to Southern England in the North and to Scotland in the South. Its trunk rail route is from Christchurch (population 240,000) to Dunedin and Invercargill, along the South Pacific coast and across the Canterbury Plains.

Crack train is the six days a week *Southerner,* air conditioned, and equipped with a constant service buffet car. There is bar service at seats in the smoking section of the train, and seating comfort is exceptional. The *Southerner* leaves both Christchurch and Invercargill at 8:40 A.M., the southbound train calling at Dunedin at 3:05 P.M. and reaching Invercargill at 6:45 P.M., the northbound making the Dunedin stop at 12:21 P.M. and getting to Christchurch at 6:35 P.M. When there are night sailings by the Union Line's *Rangatira* to Wellington, *Southerner* runs through the tunnel over the route of New Zealand's first railway to the ship's side at Lyttleton. The train makes six intermediate stops on its 374 mile journey. From Dunedin to Invercargill it is the most southerly train in the world, in latitude 46 degrees South.

There is dramatic coastal scenery with some robust headlands to watch for, and from the Canterbury Plains looking westwards on a clear day the whole line of the Alps can be seen. Including lunch, the great ride aboard *Southerner* costs just $10 N.Z.

New Zealand's most scenic train ride is on the twice daily railcar from Christchurch to Greymouth and Hokitika, clear across South Island, climbing to Arthur's Pass at 2,500 feet and then through the 5½ miles of Otira Tunnel, where elderly electric engines dating from 1921 still cope competently with freight traffic. Dropping down to Greymouth there are fine views of the Tasman Coast, as the railcar runs on to the former goldmining area of Hokitika.

The railcars take just over 5½ hours for the 130 miles, but this includes some climbing on grades as steep as 1 in 25 (4%). There is only one departure on Sundays.

A long journey up the Pacific Coast to Picton, some 230 miles, takes 6 ¼ hours by a daily (except Sundays) railcar. Scenery is pastoral rather than impressive, but there are some fine views of the Kaikoura Range also of surf beaches and Norfolk Island pines lashed by seaspray on a windy day. There is a mixed train at night (8 hours).

South Island boasts a grand steam train trip called *Kingston Flyer.* This is isolated from the main rail system but can be reached by NZGR bus. It links Lumsden and Kingston in the Southern Lakes area, runs for 40 miles (two hours) and consists of vintage 1920's cars in spotless condition hauled by a preserved Ab class Pacific of a once numerous class introduced in 1915. It is an extremely popular and usually overbooked tourist attraction from early December to Easter. Reservations must be made well in advance.

AFRICA

By
K. Westcott Jones

NORTH AFRICA

ALGERIA

French from 1840 to 1960, Algeria was treated as a Department of France and given railways accordingly. Built to standard gauge, the trains ran with a pre-war speed and efficiency admired in many countries.

The system is basically coastal, to provide a link between Casablanca in Morocco and Tunis, at one time all French. The main lines are between Algiers and Oran, the two biggest cities, and eastwards between Algiers and Constantine (the dramatically- sited hill city founded by the Romans).

There are two penetrations southwards over the Atlas Mountains to the Sahara. One goes to Saida and Colomb Bechar (built originally for Foreign Legion purposes), the other to Biskra and Touggourt (built for tourism in the earlier part of this century when these places were winter sunspots much favoured by the "International Set").

The lines running eastwards from Algiers were much used by Americans of the First Army during the North African campaign, and spurs were constructed. Traffic has never risen again to such intense proportions as when troop trains and hospital trains were running between Algiera and Bone (now Skikda). General Eisenhower had his headquarters in Algiers and used special military trains on several occasions. Track and signalling improvements carried out by American engineers at this time are still in use.

The 422 Kms. (262 miles) of route between Algiers and Oran is the busiest passenger line in Algeria today. There are five trains each way daily, three with buffet service, one with couchettes for overnight travel. The best trains take 5¼ hours; a daytime slow takes 7½ and the night train 8¼ hours.

One train from Oran, the 12:40 P.M., runs through to Casablanca in Morocco. It is an overnight journey, but there is a sleeping car from Oujda, at the Moroccan border, to Casablanca and others going westward from Oran terminate at Tlemcen.

Because of oil and gas riches in the desert, there is important traffic on the inland route to Colomb Bechar. A night train with first class sleepers branches off the Algiers-Oran line at Mohammadia and runs the 430 miles to Bechar in 14½ hours overnight. It has a fully equipped diner. Other Saharan lines just get Micheline railcars from Constantine (to Biskra) and Annaba to Tebessa.

There is a daily through train from Algiers to Tunis. This is a long trip by way of Annaba and Constantine, 984 km (600 m.), and the train, the only named express in former French North Africa, is the *Transmaghreb,*

EGYPT

In the last century, Egypt's importance as a major land mass on the route to India and the Far East led to early railway construction. The Suez Canal, linking the Mediterranean to the Red Sea, was not opened until 1869, but 30 years before that, an overland route existed between Alexandria and Suez, first by camel caravan and later by train. The British Peninsula and Oriental Navigation Company (P. & O.) created the route, using a fast ship in the Mediterranean and another one on the Red Sea. A Lieutenant Wagram built up and became responsible for the overland connection, involving camels to Cairo and onwards to Suez, a journey of 175 miles taking four days.

British interests built a railway ostensibly for the Khedive of Egypt in 1854, linking the Khedive's summer palace at Alexandria with his winter palace at Cairo and his yacht at Suez. But in reality, the railway's prime business was to link the two P. & O. mail ships, transhipping freight, mail and passengers in one day instead of four.

Once ships could transit the Suez Canal 15 years later, the railway lost its prime importance and never really regained it. But having said that, it is necessary to make clear that the rather skeleton railway network in Egypt today is well used and fairly important to the nation's economy. In the immediate pre-war period, it played a big part in tourism, and before politics stopped the link, there were through sleepers from Istanbul via Palestine and a bridge over the Suez Canal at El Firdan to Cairo. This link, due to the creation of the State of Israel and the destruction of the bridge as well as the railway line along the Canal from Ismailia to Port Said, no longer works and is little remembered.

Water is the lifeblood of Egypt and the main railways follow the Nile or its Delta or the Suez Canal or the sea coast, since that is where the people are.

Trains In Egypt

The busiest rail line in Egypt is between the two chief cities of Alexandria and Cairo. It is 129 miles long, by way of Tanta on the Delta and Benha Junction (where the line to the Canal goes off), laid through well-watered, highly agricultural, flat country. There are 23 passenger trains each way daily, four of them quite fast, taking only 2½ hours with two or three stops. Trains making all the stops take between 3½ and four hours.

Ordinary services are second and third class, with white painted cars, wooden seats in third-class and plush in second. They are always crowded and many people ride dangerously on the roofs or on the rear ends. The express, or "rapide" trains are Hungarian-built, streamlined diesel units,

HEALTH ON THE MOVE

While we don't suggest that you turn into a traveling hypochondriac, here are a few points to consider for making sure your holiday isn't spoiled by avoidable health upsets.

Flight Planning

Sleep well before you leave

Plan to arrive at your normal bedtime

Go easy on the food and alcohol on board

Wear loose comfortable clothes

Wrap yourself in a blanket to sleep—the body temperature drops

Take it easy for 24 hours after arrival (especially after a big time change): no important meetings immediately

Montezuma's Revenge and Allied Ills

Be wary of shellfish, icecream, salads and unwashed fruit

Drinking-water can be deadly—avoid village pumps

Make sure food is well-cooked—avoid any that has been left on display

Shun restaurants with flies

Bottled mineral water is usually safe—as is Coke and Pepsi

A good treatment for diarrhea is *Kaomycin* (an antibiotic with kaopectate) every four hours—or take *Lomotil* plus *Neomycin; Entero-Vioform* is no longer recommended

Mosquitos can be more serious than vampire bats; malaria can be prevented by regular dosage with *Proguanil* or *Paludrine—Chloroquine* is best for treatment

Hot Tips

Never wear nylon in the heat—cotton is best

Keep your intake of fluids going with plenty of salt

Go easy on sunbathing for the first few days

Always use a good quality cream or lotion

If you have heat prostration—*don't drive*

air conditioned, and carrying only first and second class. These do not permit roof riders. There has been no steam traction in Egypt since 1956, which is not surprising in a land without coal or wood, but with reasonable quantities of its own oil and access to abundant, cheap Middle East supplies (cheap for Arab countries, that is).

Supplementary fares are levied for travel in air-conditioned trains. Buffet, dining, and sleeping car services are run by Egyptian State Railways. Air-conditioned, first class sleepers are single berth, and air-conditioned seconds are two berth, each carrying an air-conditioned supplement as well as the sleeper charge. These are found on all trains going up the Nile to Upper Egypt, serving the popular tourist destinations of Luxor and Aswan.

Another busy line is that from Cairo to Ismailia on the Suez Canal, but at the time of writing, tracks are not yet restored from war damage on the extensions to Port Said and Suez. A coastal route, built by the British after the Eighth Army's wartime advance following the Battle of El Alamein, runs from Alexandria to Mersa Matruh (calling at El Alamein on the way three hours after leaving Alexandria). Once a week, a train nudges up towards the Libyan frontier at Sollum, to El Alamein (much used by British & German visitors) three times a day.

Cairo has two stations, one the big, pretentious Main Terminal, the other a smaller affair for Helwan and Heliopolis electric suburban services and the 85-mile desert run direct to Suez. This one is called Cairo Pont Limoun.

From Main Station each evening there are four "rapides" and two expresses going up the Nile. The best runs only between October 1st. and June 30th., mainly for tourists, and it leaves at 7:35 P.M. with first and second class sleepers and diner, to reach Luxor (419 miles) at 7:30 the next morning. Two trains, the 4:25 P.M. (sleepers only from July through September) and the 8 P.M., go all the way to El-Sadd-El-Ali, the Aswan High Dam, 556 miles from Cairo. There is also a 7 P.M. "rapide" with first and second class sleepers and diner, calling at Luxor and ending at Aswan at 10 A.M. Aswan itself is seven miles north of the High Dam. The object of going to El-Sadd-El-Ali is to make connection with steamers and hydrofoils on the Nile (Lake Nasser) to reach the Upper Egypt monuments and to attain the Sudan at Wadi Halfa, where a Sudan Government Railways train waits to cross the desert to Khartoum.

Upper Nile scenery which sleeping car passengers observe on awakening is quite dramatic, but in the main, Egypt out of the window is sepia-colored, with scattered palm trees. Running is fairly smooth on well maintained standard-gauge track, and single-berth sleepers are definitely good; but one should not expect gourmet meals in the diners (nor anywhere in Egypt). At Luxor is the fabulous Valley of the Kings, deep clefts amid high, sun-burned rock. The daylight train ride from Luxor to Aswan is fascinating, with a mixture of desert, river, rock, and mountain, with cultivation spreading out from the river, mainly on the western bank.

Anything less than 2,000 years old is new in Egypt, so there are no railway museums as yet and no preserved railways. In fact, we do not know of a single preserved steam locomotive in the country, which is unfortunate, for some excellent Atlantic engines ran for many years (until 1955) on shorter routes.

LIBYA

Apart from a meter-gauge line out of Tripoli built fifty years ago by the Italians, there are no railways in the enormous, mainly desert, country of Libya.

Colonel Gaddaffi's oil-rich Libya seems to have spent money on roads, but there is no indication of any railway development as yet. It is certain that the unfinished Italian line is not in use.

During the last war, when British Eighth Army and German Afrika Corps actions surged backwards and forwards, there were one or two short military lines, and the British Army had one near Benghazi. These are now completely out of action.

MOROCCO

It was not until 1912 that the first mile of rail track was laid in Morocco. Formerly, this strange North African land had been undeveloped, living from the sea, and transporting by ship or camel caravan or horse. It was the takeover by the French that led to railway building, but primarily for the purpose of exploiting mineral wealth and moving troops. Later, some lines were used for tourism. As in all former French North Africa, gauge is standard (4ft.8½in.).

But even now, after twenty years of independence from the French (and from the successive international rulers of the Tangier Free Zone), the Kingdom of Morocco has not added a single mile of line to the network left by the French. One must conclude that the French-built system did, in fact, do the job.

During 1975, by means of a massive "Green March," a non-violent invasion of the former Spanish colony of Sahara to the south, the territory has "agreed" to become part of Morocco. This has sparked off the first railway thinking in two decades, largely because the Sahara territory is rich in phosphate and other minerals, and Moroccan wishes are to haul the products by rail, rather than see them continue to be shipped from the port of El Ayoum (the capital of the former Spanish Sahara). A line for minerals and passengers has been projected from Marrakech southwards to Agadir, Sidi Ifni, and to El Ayoum. If completed it will be longer than all the railways in Morocco put together.

Rabat is Morocco's Royal Capital, an expanding city with suburbs growing up, already choked with road traffic. For the first time, there is talk of a "shuttle" type of commuter railway.

Trains In Morocco

It is probably true that there are still five times as many camel trains as railroad trains in the large Kingdom of Morocco. Rail service is sparse, confined to a few lines of mainly single track.

The trunk route is from Casablanca to the Algerian frontier at Ouijda, 678 kilometres in length (about 420 miles). The line serves Rabat, the capital, Meknes, and the Imperial City of Fez. There are three through trains each way daily, all equipped with buffet cars, one of them with air-conditioned first class cars, and another with first class sleeping cars. Sleepers and diners in the country are owned by Moroccan Railways but staffed by the Wagons-Lits Company. One train & runs beyond the frontier to Oran in Algeria.

The best train, a day "rapide," takes 11 hours for the 420 miles. The two night trains take 11¼ and 12 hours. Third class cars are only attached to one train, the slower night express. The line is electrified.

Tourists use quite different trains to these trunk-route services. The one most consistently used is the daytime Tangier-Rabat-Casablanca air-conditioned, diesel, multiple unit, a train introduced in the early 1960's and distinguished by the fact that it has for years appeared in airline timetables. British European Airways, now the European Division of British Airways, shows it in connection with its flights to Tangier as a way of getting to Rabat (no airport and in the 1960's no landing rights at Casablanca).

Tangier is on a single track branch going off the main electrified line at Sidi Kacem. It runs northwards for 201 Kms. (126 miles) through pleasant, hilly country and along the coast to Tangier Port, linking with ferries to Gibraltar and Algeciras (South Spain). The diesel train (see above) leaves Casablanca at 7:35 A.M., first and second class only, with diner, and air conditioning throughout. It arrives at 1:50 P.M., having averaged 45 m.p.h. for the 277 miles. Going south, it leaves Tangier Port at 3:10 P.M. (after the arrival of the two ferries) and makes it to Casablanca by 9:44 P.M.

There are two other trains on the Tangier-Casablanca line, both slow with first, second, and third class cars but negligible refreshment facilities. Both take about eight hours, one by day and one at night; the day train has a buffet car between Sidi Kacem and Ouijda.

Until airline service came direct to Marrakech, the electric train service between Casablanca and the popular desert oasis resort was heavily used by tourists. The French electrified it on construction back in 1924. Today, the original box-fronted wooden electrics are still at work. They haul trains of three classes (always with a stand-up buffet in one of them) over the 150 miles of semi-desert in about 3½ hours. There are normally three passenger trains a day each way, increased in the peak winter months when

Marrakech is not only a winter sunspot but a ski resort for the close-by 8,000 foot Atlas Mountains.

There are two stations in Casablanca, Port and Town, well separated. Only one Marrakech Line train runs into Port, which is the departure station for Tangier.

Train travel in Morocco is basically cheap, but for air-conditioned trains there is a stiff supplement, and first class, which is plush and comfortable, is also fairly costly.

A mineral line concerned with phosphates branches off the Marrakech-Casablanca route and runs to Safi on the coast.

TUNISIA

France took over the administration of Tunisia in 1912, at the same time she added Morocco to her North African Empire. But the Bey of Tunis, unlike the Sultan of Morocco, had realized the value of railway communication, and—with French engineering help—he had already built some lines. His capital, Tunis, was linked with the port and naval base of Bizerta 58 miles away, and also with the Algerian Railways starting 120 miles to the west at Guardimoau on the frontier. There were also some meter-gauge tracks.

The French later put a few extensions in, but basically the system remains today as it was then. Some of it, in the western part of the country, is standard gauge, while the East and South are meter gauge. A mineral line, also carrying passengers, has reached to the desert at Tozeur.

Most interesting and most used of Tunisian railways by visitors is the white painted electric suburban system out of Tunis. Early electric units dating from the 1920's go to the popular seaside resort of Sidi-bou-Said and—important from a tourist point of view—to Carthage and its ruins. The line also goes alongside the canal down to La Goulette, the port for Tunis recently developed (which has taken over much of Bizerta's traffic).

Tunis has three rail stations, none of them inspiring. The standard-gauge terminal sends off four railcars a day over the 58 miles to Bizerta (taking 1¾ hours) and four rail cars a day to the Algerian border (taking about 3½ hours for the 120 miles). Its big event of the day happens at 12:51 P.M. when it dispatches the westbound *Trans Maghreb* to Algiers, an express with first, second and third class cars, first and second class couchette cars and a diner. Half an hour later, the incoming *Trans Maghreb* completes the big action and the crowds die away.

Tunis' electric station is just a hut off the main street but Tunis East is a covered terminal sending meter-gauge railcars to the major resorts in the east and south. Some tourists use these; more should, for Tunisan roads are dangerous and the death rate is high. These railcars, with first and second class accommodation, go to Hammamet, Sousse, Sfax, and Gabes. They run six or seven times a day each way. The 90 miles to Sousse takes two hours. Only one a day makes the whole trip to Gabes (busses for Djerba Island and the Saharan South), 260 miles to the South, in just over seven hours.

Alone among North African countries, Tunisia has a preserved train which is used for enthusiast groups and tourists in general. It is the original special train built for the Bey of Tunis, and has been restored with exotic oriental lounges added. It runs on the meter gauge and has to be diesel hauled at present, since Tunisia has no steam locomotives. The train can be chartered, and is called *The Red Lizard,* or *Le Lezard Rouge.*

STEAM IN EAST AFRICA

For several years, East Africa has been a favorite with railbuffs for its magnificent array of steam locomotives. A great many big Garratt engines are in service in Kenya, Uganda, and Tanzania. The biggest in the world on narrow gauge are the giant "59" class Garratts (named after mountain ranges) used on the Mombasa-Nairobi freights. These, in straight competition with diesels, won hands down in all aspects of operation, but diesels haul the passenger trains over the line and have done so since 1964.

A large variety of steam engines may be seen and photographed at Nairobi Shed. In other parts of East Africa, a security blanket has now descended on railways, and no one is allowed to photograph officially. Passenger trains on lesser routes and spur lines in all three countries are steam-hauled by 2.8.2 "Tribal" class engines built in the early 1950's. All East African engines are painted red and in Kenya most are well maintained.

BURUNDI

Burundi is a part of the former Belgian Mandate of Ruanda-Urundi, taken over from German East Africa in 1917. It became independent, with Rwanda, in 1963. The capital is Usumbura. At one time a railway was planned to run up from the capital to Lake Kivu at Bukavu, but nothing came of it once a good road and local air service were provided. A line was built just on the Zaire (Congo) side of the border, from Kalandu half way to Bukavu.

ERITREA

A former Italian colony now joined uneasily to Ethiopia, this hot land on the Red Sea was fortunate in having high mountains and cool plateaus close to its main seaport of Massawa (a place with the unhappy distinction of having the highest annual mean temperature in the world coupled with the highest humidity).

The Italians built a railway very early on, completing a 75 cm. narrow gauge line in 1887 up to Ghinda. Then they widened the gauge to 95 cm. but did not reach Asmara, 7,143 feet above sea level and blessedly cool, until 1911, although it was only 73 miles from the coast.

The line was pushed westwards into a fertile valley and ended at Biscia in 1925. It never reached the Sudan border, where a line from Khartoum had already crossed the Eritrean border from Kassala to Tessenai.

A rather tattered railcar, called a "litorina" by Fiat who built it and its sister in 1935, still makes the trip up from Massawa to Asmara. It takes about four hours and reveals one of the most spectacular railway climbs in the world, reminiscent of Peru. But now there is a highway and the railway route has fallen into some decay. Rail grade is 2½% and freight moves very slowly (a mixed train with stream traction at last report took ten hours). There is no indication of service of any kind on the railway, or what is left of it, westward from Asmara.

ETHIOPIA

A single delicate thread of meter-gauge railway links the 8000 foot high capital of Ethiopia with its main outlet to the Red Sea, a town in French territory. It took a long time to build—over twenty years in fact—from 1897, when it was projected from the French port of Djibouti, to 1917, when the first train entered Addis Ababa. During that time, the railway changed ownership several times, ending up as a Franco-Ethiopian Company which enjoyed remarkable prosperity until Mussolini's forces invaded Ethiopia (which they called Abbyssinia) in 1936.

It is 488 miles from Djibouti to Addis, and the three times weekly passenger service takes just under 24 hours. This is done in two stages—overnight from Djibouti by a locomotive-hauled train as far as Dire Dawa, 3,900 feet, then a diesel-electric unit by day from Dire to Addis. There are no restaurant cars, but sleepers are provided from the coast to Dire Dawa. Breakfast is taken at Dire, in a run-down station hotel, and lunch at a fly-blown buffet at Awash.

This is one railway which has been hard hit price-wise by aircraft, for it is cheaper to fly, quite apart from speed and comfort. This applies to both 1st and 2nd class, but not to 3rd, which is very cheap, but slow. Those riding 3rd class don't travel on the diesel unit but on one of several freight trains with mixed accommodations.

The journey between Dire and Addis is breathtaking from a scenic point of view. One American oilman who likes to ride the railway describes it as "grassy valleys and gorges reminiscent of the best in Colorado." It is, of course, cool and fairly dry on the highlands, but the section from Dire Dawa to the coast is a Red Sea Hell type of humid heat, much like a furnace.

Diesel traction has been used for many years between Djibouti and Dire, and is now taking over for the rest of the line. But a few strange varieties of meter-gauge steam power can be seen on the Awash-Addis Ababa sector.

Air conditioning has been reported fitted to sleepers on the Djibouti-Dire Dawa overnight run, but this adds to the cost. The aging Fiat railcars on the highlands are considered very comfortable for 1st class and quite good in 2nd, but there are few, if any, amenities.

Recent disturbances in Ethiopia resulted in destroyed bridges and serious interruption to both freight and passenger workings. The only surface alternative is a dirt road most of the way which heavy trucks negotiate. The main export from the highlands and bulk traffic of the railway is, of course, coffee. It was here the coffee bean was discovered and later sent all over the world to suitable climates.

Eritrea is now a part of Ethiopia in a political sense, although this is disputed by rebels. Rail services are reported seriously damaged in mountain areas. (See Eritrea.)

KENYA & UGANDA

They called it the "Lunatic Line" when construction started back in 1898 at Mombasa on the Indian Ocean. It was going from "nowhere through nowhere to nowhere." But the builders and the promoters had a lot of faith. Besides, in building a railway through unknown East Africa to the remote inland country of Uganda, they hoped to put down the Arab slave trade.

The line took shape, snaked its way through the uplands, met lions and suffered nearly 200 men eaten alive in the Tsavo area, including Superintendent Ryall who was taken from his parked sleeping car by a maneater. But it got to the highlands and set up a base at a well called Nai-robi in then deserted Kikuyu country. In 1900 this became a small town of construction workers' tents and huts.

The route took them over the Rift Valley escarpment down which trains were lowered on an inclined plane assisted by ropes. It went on across the Highlands and over the fierce Mau Summit, encountered savage tribesmen, but made it to Kisumu on the shores of Lake Victoria by 1901. Here a prefabricated ship was launched, and Kampala, capital of Uganda, became accessible to the outside world in under four days.

Nowhere else in the world, and at no time in history, has a journey been so dramatically shortened, from a six months walk full of danger to a four day ride in comparative comfort and safety. Freight gained spectacularly— no longer restricted to what a human head could carry.

The railway achieved its purpose, putting down the slave trade and opening up Uganda, but it also created the country of Kenya in passing and developed what has become East Africa's major metropolis, Nairobi. As the years went by the line was improved by elimination of the inclined plane and a new route up over Timbaroa into the Highlands, making through train service to Kampala which climbed to 9048 feet, highest point achieved by rail in the Commonwealth.

Service has been extended in Uganda to Kasese in the foothills of the Mountains of the Moon, and northwestward to Gulu and the edge of the West Nile. It is still a vital lifeline, although the highway from Mombasa to Nairobi was paved in 1963 and road traffic competition now exists. The rail gauge is meter, which has limited speed.

The journey is full of interest, but political problems on the Kenya-Uganda border mean that luxurious 38-hour through train service three times a week by the "Uganda Mail" is a thing of the past. The "Night Mail" over the 308 miles between Nairobi and Mombasa now leaves at 6:30 P.M. and arrives at 8 A.M. All 1st and 2nd class compartments make up into sleepers, and the restaurant on board serves the cheapest, and best consistent with price, food in Kenya. The train is not, however, air conditioned, mainly because the mile-high altitude of Nairobi is chilly and heat suffering would only take place down at the coast, when the train is rolling through cool darkness or dawn. Passengers in the up direction *always* see wild animals from the windows as the train crosses the Athi Plains—usually zebra and giraffe.

MALAGASY REPUBLIC

This large island-nation in the Indian Ocean, formerly the French colony of Madagascar, has been an independent state within the French Community since June 1960, and has a big population of some six millions, many of whom are more allied to Malaysians than Africans. It possesses some 535 route miles of railway.

There are four railway routes, the most important being the line which links the high inland capital of Tananarive with Tamative, the chief port, 229 miles distant, on the east coast. The trains are French in origin with perhaps Asian overtones, well run but not used much by tourists due to an intense and relatively cheap air network. One good Micheline auto-rail service does carry tourists, in modest numbers. Mixed trains (diesel-hauled) and four wheeler autorails don't.

One very scenic route runs southward from Tananarive and climbs to the hill station of Antsirabe, a spa set at 5,000 feet surrounded by mountains up to 8,800 feet. It is 99 miles from the capital, a 5-hour trip. On the way up from the port to Tananarive a branch line goes northward to Lake Alaotra, 105 miles from the junction at Moramanga.

Down in the south of what is the fourth largest island in the world, a detached line runs from Fiannarantsoa to the east coast, covering a distance of just over 100 miles, ending at the open roadstead port of Manakara.

Best train in Malagasy is the day "express" from Tamatave to Tananarive, taking just under ten daylight hours. The gauge is meter everywhere in the island except on Nossi-Bey Island (ex-naval base) where sugar lines operate on 60 cms. Steam has died out except on the sugar plantations, but decaying locos may yet be seen in yards.

MAURITIUS

This large Indian Ocean island, member of the British Commonwealth, and French-speaking to a large extent had a major rail network on standard gauge until 1960, based on Port Louis, the capital, and Curepipe, with lines running north and south. Few traces remain, but in the Historical Museum at Mahebourg a passenger car, some signals, and a few locomotive models bear witness to what was frequent service attractively run over some 200 miles of track.

MOZAMBIQUE

Until 1975 and the changed political status of Mozambique, railbuffs from Britain, USA and Australia went to the remote parts of this big southern African country to hunt down the rarest steam engines in the world—the Nampula Atlantics. It was like a chase after a scarce animal species, and these were the last locos of that famous and once popular 4.4.2 wheel arrangement invented on the Philadelphia-Atlantic City lines about 1896.

Railbuffs found them and photographed them and rode them. At last count (mid-1975) there were four existing in the Nampula region. Now no one knows for sure and the present government of Mozambique says nothing. Tourist and visitor trade has been all but stopped.

The capital, Maputo, had, or perhaps still has, a good deal of American steam power, including the last big tank engines built by Baldwin, and some Canadian and American 4.8.2's of the type built just after the end of World War II.

Main line passenger workings to South Africa, up the famous line along which Winston Churchill escaped from the Boers in 1900, are diesel hauled. The trains still run and have air-conditioned rolling stock. The 1976 timetable showed three trains a day over the 88 kms (55 miles) from Maputo to Rossano Garcia on the South African border, plus one through train to Komatipoort (93 kms) which carries on to Pretoria. But the line from Beira to Salisbury, once Rhodesia's lifeline to a port, has no service beyond the border, nor is there any train on the line to Bulawayo from the coast.

The new left-wing government of an independent Mozambique has closed the border to Rhodesia at Malvernia, and at Vila de Manica on the line to Salisbury from Beira.

Mozambique became a rail-oriented country in the late 1880's, under the Portuguese. Its rail system flourished in a land where few good roads existed, and its best trains fired the admiration of visiting Rhodesians, whose own equipment is neither very comfortable nor very fast. There was never a direct link with Natal to the south; all passenger and freight traffic to South Africa moves, and has always moved, uphill to the High Veld, westward. But there were plans to extend the existing South African Railways line from Durab to Golela in North Natal (388 kms. from Durban) for a few miles to cross the Mozambique border and join up with the rail system there. This may not now take place, but will probably swing north-westward into Swaziland.

Not unlike Angola, Mozambique had three distinct rail systems—in the south based on the capital, in the center based on Beira, and in the north (tropical) around Nampula. Life-blood of the Mozambique system was its freight and passenger workings to South Africa, Rhodesia and Malawi.

SWAZILAND

No scheduled passenger service as yet, but see Golela, South Africa.

REUNION

A mountainous island in the Indian Ocean close to Mauritius, Reunion is a French Overseas Department with 300,000 inhabitants, a considerable percentage of them French.

There is a meter-gauge railway carrying passengers for 38 miles along the rugged west coast. It runs from Pointe des Galets to St. Benoit, by way of the capital, St. Denis. It is a very scenic and picturesque line, but uses bone-breaking and aging Micheline railcars, on four wheels.

SUDAN

The Sudan Government Railways can claim a remarkable distinction in that they operate more than 700 miles away from any rail tracks. The secret lies in their owning the stern-wheeler steamers on the Nile, which reach upstream as far as Juba, some 700 miles from railhead at Kosti.

Sudan has a fairly effective, if sparse, rail system built by the British soon after the turn of the century. The most important line runs from Wadi Halfa just below the Egyptian border (and not very far by river from Abu Simbel) right across the utter wastes of the Nubian Desert to Khartoum. This is a journey of 557 miles, and the twice weekly deluxe train (it has air-conditioned sleepers and a diner) takes exactly 24 hours.

The gauge is African Standard, 3 feet 6 inches, and the traction is mainly diesel,—in a country where water is desperately short one would expect this. In Khartoum and close to the Nile there are some steam engines still in use.

Other Sudan railway services are the Khartoum to Port Sudan (on the Red Sea) link, three times a week, taking 21 hours via Atbara, and Khartoum to Port Sudan via Kassala, also three times a week but taking 45 hours. There is also a long, lonely line from Khartoum to Nyala and Wau, taking 48 hours, on a thrice-weekly basis.

The White Nile Service, which used to be an important overland link to Central Africa, leaves Khartoum every Tuesday for Kosti, 238 miles, a journey of 13½ hours. Here the passengers for South Sudan transfer to a stern-wheeler proudly displaying "Sudan Government Railways" on its sides. The boat takes 11 days (if the water levels are satisfactory and weeds do not clog the paddles) to reach Juba. There used to be a bus connection for Uganda (58 miles away) to meet the boat at the railway-owned Juba Hotel. Up to 1939, this was an essential link in the legendary Cape to Cairo overland journey, but 1st class traffic has fallen away to negligible proportions, the trains and boats being mainly 2nd and 3rd class today.

TANZANIA

This used to be German East Africa, and a railway was started from the port of Tanga even before the British built their "Lunatic Line." It took from 1891 to 1911 to reach Moshi near Mount Kilimanjaro.

Another railway, the Central Line, began at Dar-es-Salaam in 1905 and reached the inland town of Kigoma on Lake Tanganykia (close to Ujiji where Stanley found Livingstone) in 1914. This line, just over 760 miles long and of meter gauge, was the last built by the Germans before the 1914–18 war ended their sovereignty over Tanganyika. The British took on a Mandate and built more railways, an important one running northward from Tabora on the Central Line to Mwanza at the southern end of Lake Victoria, while a 131-mile branch went to Mpanda.

After the war the railways of Kenya, Tanganyika and Uganda were merged into the East African Railways and Harbours and links were built between them. The Tanga line is connected to the Kenya system at Voi. The combined system worked well under a commission based at Arusha in Tanganyika, even after all three nations had become independent.

Tanzania was formed by a merger with the offshore spice island of Zanzibar. Political troubles in the early 1970's have led to a breakup of railway workings and today they are starved of funds and traffic; only the lines in Kenya work well. Foreigners are not encouraged to ride the Central

Line and so far few have traveled on the Chinese-built "Tanzam." Steam traction predominates, but light-weight rails make speeds slow on the narrow gauge. Until 1969, 1st class accommodation was maintained in good condition and buffet or dining cars were attached to Dar-Mwanza and Kigoma trains.

THE TANZAM RAILWAY

The world's latest long-distance railway was officially handed over to its owners, the Governments of Tanzania and Zambia, by the Chinese Vice-Premier on July 14, 1976. It was built in record time by some 15,000 Chinese skilled and semi-skilled workers and is intended to get Zambia's copper out to Dar-es-Salaam. From Lusaka to Dar is about 1800 miles, but the new railway, cutting through virtually unknown and largely virgin country, is just over 1200 miles in length, from Kapriri to the Tanzanian capital. The trip takes 36 hours and there are first, second and second-class coaches, as well as a dining car, which serves only curry and local maize dishes.

It is called "The Great Uhuru Railway" by its new owners, for it was built to free Zambia from reliance upon Rhodesia and Angola in exporting her copper. However, since the change of status of Angola, the railway has already lost its essential political purpose and copper is going over the Zaire-Benguela line again, shortening the journey to European and U.S. markets.

The "Tanzam" is a remarkable feat of engineering, built to African Standard 3 feet 6 inches gage, which joins with Zambia but requires transhipment to Tanzania's meter system. It climbs to a maximum of 6000 feet en route. Trains have been running over its length since early in 1976, but few people have seen it, let alone used it, apart from locals and the Chinese. During the latter stages of construction, it is reported that a Tanzanian Minister who tried to inspect it was kept at bay by rifles.

An interesting sidelight is the fact that Tanzania has ordered **five new steam locomotives** from India, allegedly as standby power on the long, lonely route, while it already has some Chinese steam and Zambian diesels supplied.

ZAMBIA

Zambia achieved independence in 1964, taking over from what was Northern Rhodesia, the 'Country of the Line of Rail.' There is still a single line of rail running from the Victoria Falls Bridge (frontier with Rhodesia) right across the country in a northeasterly direction to the Zaire frontier. It serves the copper belt and the capital, Lusaka.

The line is of 3 feet 6 inches gauge and is 497 miles long. From the town of Ndola within the copper belt, branch lines serve Luanshiya (24 miles), Kitwe (41 miles) Mufulira (82 miles) and Chingola (82 miles). There is now the new "Tanzam Railway" going off to the northeast from a place near Kabwe and opening up virtually unknown territory, running for several hundred miles through hot, rugged country to the border with Tanzania.

Passenger trains no longer cross the Victoria Falls Bridge from Rhodesia. Air and road transport have largely taken over from the once trunk route of the "Line of Rail" and passenger services are on the basis of a mail train once a day averaging under 20 miles an hour. This carries 1st, 2nd, and 3rd class passengers and a buffet; 1st and 2nd class compartments make up into sleepers at night with bedding supplied at nominal cost.

Canadian technical assistance has been supplied to the Zambian Railways, which use mainly Canadian-built diesels, although there are some heavy steam engines, mostly Garratts, remaining from the former Central African Railways. Freight trains are frequent in the busier parts of the copper belt.

SOUTHERN AFRICA

ANGOLA

Threading right across the huge country of Angola, which was a Portuguese colony for 500 years until 1975, is a railway which has fascinated railbuffs all over the world. It is known as the Benguela Railway, built in relatively recent years in order to move Katanga (in the former Congo) copper to the Atlantic port. Begun in 1913, it did not reach the high country of Angola until 1929 and was completed to the border with the then Belgian Congo late in 1931.

The Beguela Railway, of 3 feet 6 inches gauge, was built steam and remained steam all the time it was part of the Anglo-Portuguese partnership in a company called Tanganyika Concessions. It was immensely profitable and possessed unique features, not the least of which were forests of fast-growing eucalyptus trees used for fueling the engines and the supreme luxury of its 1st class sleeping cars and diners.

It is 838 miles from Lobito Bay on the west coast to the frontier with Zaire (Congo). There are no spur lines, but the first 40 miles to Benguela are through fairly well populated country and carry an urban-type service. The line climbs inland up the escarpment from Benguela, attaining a maximum altitude of 6038 feet in the first 250 miles. It then runs across the high country, descending gradually to about the 4000-foot mark. Inland, along the right of way the eucalyptus forests grow, and engines stop for refueling at giant piles of eucalypt logs. A very high degree of thermal efficiency has been obtained from this fuel, so that a big Garratt engine could haul 250 tons up a grade of 3%. In fact, enthusiasts might like to note that the overall efficiency has been brought to a point where one tonne-kilometer was achieved by burning only 0.58 grams of eucalypt wood, and that at a time when the logs cost a mere $2.60 per tonne (1000 kilos). The average profit for the railway between 1965 and 1973 was $4 million a year.

No one knows what the future holds for the Benguela Railway since Angola became independent and was involved in a fierce civil war. It is uncertain how many of its Portuguese employees remain. In the years leading up to independence the track was often sabotaged at the Zaire end of the line and the border was closed to passenger trains. Until 1973, groups of railbuffs on tour traveled the line as far as Silva Porto, about 406 miles from Lobito Bay. Now even the Portuguese names of the towns along the route are being changed. Of late years, diesel locomotives have been arriving from the United States.

The steam engine stock of the Benguela Railway stood at 109 at the time of independence, many of them giant wood-burning Garratts. In the high country, passenger trains were hauled by five very powerful wood-burning 4.8.2's built by North British Locomotive Works in Scotland in 1955. Down on the coastal stretch, local trains and freights used coal, for it was easy to import from South Africa, with whom the then sovereign power had good relations. Most American visitors delighted in the three or four Baldwin locomotives dating from 1921. Four passenger trains a week went as far as Luso, 644 miles from Lobito Bay, taking about 37 hours, but in very great comfort and, indeed, elegance for 1st class.

Some majestic scenery is traversed in the first 40 miles uphill from Beguela. but most of the rest of the journey is noted for its typical African bush and the unusual forests built up from seedlings imported from Australia.

Other Railways

Apart from the famous Benguela Railway, one of the most successful, profitable, and admired railways in the world in recent years, two other systems serve Angola.

One is based on the capital, Luanda. It runs inland for about 300 miles to Malange, and has two short branches to Dondo and to Golungo Alta (a hill station). It also has an urban line running northeastward to Panguila. Some diesels were delivered by 1968, but the prime mover was steam traction, using a variety of engines, but mostly big German Krupps-built 2.10.0's. The system belongs to the State but is not profitable.

The Luanda system is isolated from the Benguela Railway and both are isolated from the third system, deep in the south of Angola, based on the port of Mocamedes, a name likely to have been changed as we go to press. This has a deep penetration line inland to Vila Serpa Pinto (named after a famous Portuguese explorer), some 500 miles from the coast. At the astonishing city of Sao de Bandeira, situated on a high plateau like a lost world, to which the 3 feet 6 inch gauge line spirals up madly to reach 5000 feet, a branch goes off southwestward to Vila de Almoster.

Diesels had made considerable headway on this system, where little water is available. The main line, thrice-weekly passenger trains were diesel hauled by 1967 and even freights had diesel traction. However, as late as 1974 some reserve steam was reported at Sao de Bandeira.

Plans were afoot to extend the Luanda and Mocamedes lines, but were interrupted by the civil war.

MALAWI

The famous missionary Dr. Livingstone began the recorded history of Malawi (then Nyasaland) in 1859. The name was changed to Malawi when independence was gained in 1964 after the break-up of the Central African Federation. The country is centered on its great lake, 355 miles long, 10 to 50 miles wide, and over 2000 feet deep.

A short railway line comes up from Blantyre, the main city, to Chipoka and Salima for lake service steamers (which are run by the Malawi Railways). Only 43 miles from Blantyre the capital, Zomba, set on a plateau, is reached; the line carries on for about 200 miles to Salima. Diesel railcars are used, stopping for refreshments, and the journey takes some 12 hours on the 3 feet 6 inch gauge.

Malawi's lifeline railway comes in from Mozambique and the port of Beira to cross the border at Nsanje, 242 miles from the Indian Ocean port. It runs on for another 107 miles to Blantyre, which has two railway stations (one each for up-country and the lake).

Headquarters of the railway system is at Limbe, on the line to the south just beyond Blantyre. Most traction is by diesel railcar or diesel locomotives hauling freight, but there is some reserve steam on the not-very-heavily-used railway system. Special tourist tickets are issued to visitors in 1st class only, covering meals en route, but these are only for the route to the lake. The week-long steamer trips around Lake Malawi by rail and railway-owned vessel, are the key tourist and travel features of the country.

ZAIRE

When Belgium abruptly gave up sovereignty over the Congo in 1960 (the name was not changed to Zaire for several years afterwards), there existed 2,800 route miles of railway, widely scattered and not interlinked. The lines fed into river routes or roads, and the whole country represented an amazing exercise in transhipment of people and goods. It all worked well, and the railways were efficient for their part, but nothing was fast— speed was left to SABENA the Belgian airline, and, now, internally, to AIR ZAIRE.

Civil wars and strife, including the temporary secession of Katanga Province, damaged some lines and prevented planned extensions of the system as well as the fulfillment of some electrification projects. It is not certain if the proposed extensions have gone ahead, but Zaire has been a unified nation for several years now and railway expansion is expected to be a transport priority.

Prior to the state system, there were three main railways, OTRACO, BCK (which became KDL after 1955) and CFL. It was all African Standard gauge of 3 feet 6 inches except for 78 miles of meter and some miles of narrow (60 cm.) line. More than half the total mileage was run by BCK-KDL, from the border of Northern Rhodesia (now Zambia) up to Port Franqui on the Zaire River. This served Lubumbasha (formerly Elizabethville) and linked with the Benguela Railway of Angola at Dilolo. It also provided through train service to Bulawayo in Rhodesia with onward connection to Cape Town. These international links are now casualties of politics or war.

The Lubumbashi-Kolwezi section of this Katanga Line is electrified, and the trains are the smartest in Zaire, with good sleepers and diners, but speeds are rather low, averaging about 24 miles an hour. The 1st class traffic of Congo days has fallen off, but from all reports, 2nd and 3rd class remain busy. The former BCK was opened in 1909 and progressively extended.

When numerous passenger liners called at Matadi at the entrance to the Zaire River, the 248 miles of line completed in 1898 running beside the impassable lower river to Leopoldville (now Kinshasa, Zaire's capital) was the most used railway in the country, especially among foreigners. This was the OTRACO system, and a daily 1st and 2nd class express used to do the run in ten daylight hours. It is understood that an all-classes train with restaurant car covers the distance in 10½ hours at the present time.

Back in 1906 the CFL built meter-gauge tracks on the upper river and linked it to Lake Tanganyika. It operated from the Stanleyville region, now called Kisangani. Then there was the Kivu line, only half of it ever finished, which would have stood a better chance starting from Usumbura and is now a "streak of rust" replaced by a metalled road.

Railbuffs try to make the long journey by Benguela Railway from Lobito through Angola to Lubumbashi, a four day trip when trains are running. With political and civil war troubles, it hasn't operated for several years, but freight trains run and it is hoped that a political alliance may soon enable through passenger trains again. They are steam on the Beguela to Dilolo then diesel or electric in Zaire. There are no reports of active steam in Zaire.

BOTSWANA

The long single line through Botswana, on which diesels supplied from Britain for the Botswana Government are used in waterless country, may

not be the only railway in the nation (formerly Bechuanaland Protectorate), by 1981.

There are reports that a railway might be built by the Chinese from
Francistown making a wide detour around Rhodesia to join the Zambian
Railway more than 600 miles to the north. From here, freight could be
worked to the point 125 miles north of Lusaka where the new Tanzam
Railway begins its long haul to the east coast. Sir Seretse Khama has been
to Peking to discuss positive aid for this ambitious project.

RHODESIA

Since Rhodesia declared UDI (Unilateral Declaration of Independence)
in 1965, the railway system has become truncated and has lost, progressively, three routes to other countries. The first to go was that across the
Victoria Falls Bridge into what was Northern Rhodesia and became
Zambia (although it is Zambia, with her copper exports, which at first
suffered the major loss). Then came two routes to Mozambique, one to
Beira and the other to Lorenzo Marques (now called Maputo).

Rhodesia depends upon two routes to the South, one via Botswana and
the other (only recently completed) via Beit Bridge across the Limpopo
River directly into the Republic of South Africa. Both are increasingly
threatened by guerilla activity and in June 1976 three diesel engines were
blown up, two trains being derailed.

It was Cecil Rhodes and his "Cape to Cairo" railway dream who opened
up the country which still bears his name. As the line of rail pushed on
through Matabeleland and Mashonaland, settlers followed in its wake. By
1903 the Zambesi River had been reached, a year after Cecil Rhodes' death
(he left the bulk of his vast fortune to Oxford, creating the Rhodes Scholar-
ship). Soon afterwards the great bridge was spanning the gorge beside the
Falls. Sadly, virtually nothing crosses it these days, but in recent years one
track had been removed to allow a motor road to parallel the single line
of rail.

The International Set (fairly described as the "Jet Set" of the 1900–14
period) soon descended on Victoria Falls, and comfortable if very slow
trains carried many hundreds of first-class passengers on Rhodesia Railways' 3 feet 6 inches gauge to the very brink of the "Smoke that Thunders." There the train rolled across what was the greatest and loftiest bridge
in the world at the time—426 feet above low water in the gorge.

Bulawayo is the link-pin of the Rhodesian railway system, reached in
1897. It is 4,400 feet above sea level and surrounded by the Matopo Hills,
which hold the grave of Cecil Rhodes. From Bulawayo, the main line goes
southward, into and through desert country which is Botswana and then
into the South African Republic at Mafeking. Northwestward lie the Falls,
the line first traversing Wankie with its coal mines and game areas. To the

northeast is Salisbury, capital of Rhodesia, 298 miles and 10½ hours away by Rhodesia's best and fastest train, the nightly first and second class mail with buffet car.

Despite a shortage of oil, the mail is almost certain to have one of Rhodesia's surviving diesel locomotives at its head in both directions.

But a heavy Garratt of the "19" class, built in the early 1950's, will more than likely take the Victoria Falls train, which carries all classes of passengers (even fourth) and leaves nightly at 7 P.M., to reach the Falls, 291 miles away, at 7:45 the next morning.

There are three branch lines in Rhodesia carrying passenger traffic, mostly hauled by steam. One is the Bulawayo-West Nicholson line, 124 miles long. Another is from Gwelo (about two-fifths of the way from Bulawayo to Salisbury) to Shabani, 82 miles, and the third also runs from Gwelo, for 123 miles to Fort Victoria.

The passenger-mail train from Bulawayo to Cape Town comes and goes three times a week. It is diesel-hauled to the Botswana border by a Rhodesian engine, and another diesel takes over for the run through Francistown and Mahalapye to the Republic of South Africa's border, some 420 miles. This long single line is the only railway in *Botswana,* a sparsely inhabited independent nation headed by Sir Seretse Khama, which has most of the Kalahari Desert in its territory. From Mafeking southward, the Bulawayo-Cape mail usually reverts to steam traction for some distance.

Due to troubled borders and occasional attacks by guerillas, one cannot be sure that Rhodesian trains will run according to the long-standing time-tables. New security measures are making things rather difficult for rail buffs, who until recently went in large numbers from America and Britain and were given many facilities at locomotive sheds and even on footplates.

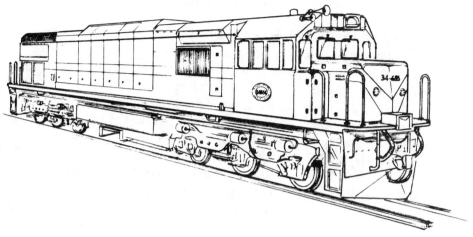

SOUTH AFRICA

There is no doubt that the Republic of South Africa is one of the few really great railway countries of the world. Its vast area is spanned by 12,250 miles of African standard gauge (3 feet 6 inches) route miles, some 2,400 miles of which are electrified. In addition there are 1,390 route miles to SW Africa. On these tracks run the most luxurious train in the world, plus some very fine expresses of international standard, and a great many steam engines maintained in excellent condition, including some fairly new ones of mammoth size.

It is a country visited by as many as 23,000 rail buffs on organized rail tours in the course of a year, coming mainly from Britain, the United States, Australia, West Germany, Japan, Canada, and New Zealand. Their aim is to see and ride behind as many as possible of the 2,300 steam engines in active service. But tourists as well as rail buffs especially appreciate the fabulous *Blue Train* which runs weekly from Pretoria to Cape Town via Johannesburg and Kimberley.

The *Blue Train* concept dates from 1938, but entirely new ones, built on the Rand of Transvaal, were put into service in 1972. Air conditioned, fully carpeted, noise-proof, dust-proof, the staterooms equipped with showers and, in a few cases, with sitting rooms and marble bath tubs, the train carries 103 passengers looked after by a crew of nearly 30. It runs the 999 miles from Pretoria to Cape Town in 26 hours, which is excellent for the relatively narrow gauge, and is electric hauled from Pretoria to Kimberley, diesel hauled (by three blue-painted diesels) from Kimberley to Beaufort West, then electric hauled to the Cape. Even the *Blue Train,* however, is switched at Pretoria by a steam engine, specially kept and blue-painted for the task. It is the only major express on the main line that has diesels; others, such as the *Orange Express, Drakensberg Express,* and *Trans Karoo Ex-*

press, are steam hauled from Kimberley through De Aar Junction to Beaufort West. As on all main line "name trains" in South Africa, the *Blue Train* has an elegant diner and cocktail lounge.

Formation Of South African Railways

In the beginning there were four territories, Cape Colony (British), Natal (British), Transvaal (independent republic), and Orange Free State (also an independent republic but closely linked to the Transvaal). The first actual railway began in 1860, from the Point at Durban to the city, only four miles. But an engine had been delivered to Cape Town a year before this to work on construction of a line from the Cape to Wellington, originally 4 feet 8½ inches gauge over the 56 miles. The building of this line took from 1857 to 1864. The original engine that worked this line is preserved in a place of honor at Cape Town's superb new terminal on Adderley Street.

Other lines were started in Natal, such as Durban to the Bluff in 1865, while the Cape Province line pushed forward very slowly, climbing on to the high, dry Karoos (semi-deserts rising in steps to the High Veld). The Boer Republics of Transvaal and O.F.S. were farming regions using the outspanning ox wagon system and no railways were planned.

Discovery of diamonds at Kimberley, war between the British colonies and the Boer states in 1888 (the First Boer War) and, later, discovery of gold on the Witwatersrand in the Transvaal gave the impetus to faster rail construction. In Natal, the discovery of vast deposits of good coal on the Transvaal border resulted in rapid rail construction.

The Cape line reached Kimberley in 1889, 647¼ miles inland. Because of its diamonds, this soon became a big city with tens of thousands of prospectors and workers digging the "Big Hole" (largest man-made excavation on the surface of the Earth). It was Cecil Rhodes, Prime Minister of Cape Colony, who forced the railway onwards, to try to achieve his dream of a "Cape to Cairo" railway. The line went northward to Vryburg, Mafeking, through the then Bechuanaland Protectorate across the Kalahari Desert to Matabeleland (later Rhodesia). Mafeking was rail-linked by 1894, Bulawayo by 1897.

Meanwhile, a line was built inland from Delagoa Bay (Mozambique) to Pretoria, the Boer Capital, which was reached in 1896. Other lines appeared in the Transvaal and Orange Free State, but what was to become South Africa's largest city, Johannesburg, did not get a railway link until just before the outbreak of the Second (and more serious) Boer War in 1899. During this war, which lasted over two years, the famous war correspondent, Winston Churchill, was taken prisoner off a train on the Natal line running up from Durban to Ladysmith, and made his escape from a Boer camp in Pretoria by hiding in a freight car on the Pretoria-Delagoa Bay railway.

With the final defeat of the Boer Republics, in which railways played a big part (bigger even than in the American Civil War), there came rapid development of Johannesburg and the Witwatersrand as a gold mining area. Many railways were built and Cape Town was soon linked via Kimberley. This became the trunk route of South Africa rather than the line to Rhodesia (which never did reach Cairo, but managed to attain Bukama on the then Congo River, more than 2,000 miles from Cape Town, and opened up enormous copper deposits on the way).

In 1910 South Africa was unified as a Dominion under the British Crown, which was to last until 1961, when it became an independent republic outside the Commonwealth. All railway organizations merged, except for some private and industrial lines. The new title was South African Railways and Harbours Board. This had expanded profitably through four decades, officially taking over the German lines of South West Africa in 1923 and thus acquiring another 1,390 route miles. Crack train of the new Union of South Africa was the *Union Express* from Cape Town to Johannesburg and Pretoria, the forerunner of the 1938 series of *Blue Trains.* Passengers by mailships of the Union Castle Line plying between Cape Town and Southampton had priority on this train along with members of Parliament (the Union had, and still has, two seats of Parliament, at Pretoria in the winter and Cape Town in the summer). From an original schedule in 1911 of 36 hours for 999 miles, timings were reduced to 28 hours and, with the new *Blue Train,* to 26 hours.

All the South African Railways are, with the exception of one long freight line, of narrow gauge.

Great Trains Of South Africa

The leading express trains in the Republic of South Africa tend to be known by colors. The *White Train,* for example, is very V.I.P., used by the President and by visiting dignitaries, but it has also been chartered to an American tour group of rail buffs. The *Blue Train,* built as two complete units in 1972, is the world's most luxurious train, a weekly service between Pretoria, Johannesburg, and Cape Town. It is rightly regarded as a five star hotel on wheels, and its fortunate 100 passengers are shielded from the outside world in cossetted elegance. It has the fastest timing in Southern Africa, 145¼ miles from Kimberley to De Aar in three hours.

The *Orange Express* is not really orange in color, but passes through a large portion of the Orange Free State on its twice-weekly run from Durban through Bloemfontein and Kimberley to Cape Town. It runs the 2,091 kilometers (1,296 miles) in 40½ hours, being steam hauled for nearly 450 miles of the route (Bloemfontein to Beaufort West). There is also the "Drakensberg Express," which does a twice weekly shuttle between Durban and Johannesburg, electric haulage all the way, and covers the *Orange Express* route once week. It is the old Blue Train, now painted green, and is air conditioned and luxurious, the second finest train in the Republic and the grandest train in the world to enjoy steam traction. Both "Orange" and "Green" run the 69¼ miles from Orange River to De Aar in 106 minutes, at an average of 39¾ M.P.H., the fastest steam haulage in Africa.

Despite its recent name change to *Trans Karoo Express,* the five-days-a-week fast train between Cape Town and Johannesburg, running on days that the *Blue Train* does not, is still called *The Brown Train.* It has steam traction from Kimberley to Beaufort West (across the non-electrified gap) over 350 miles. This train has good twin diners and a pleasant cocktail lounge.

Other crack trains are not linked to colors. The *Trans Natal Express* runs nightly between Durban, Johannesburg and Pretoria in 15 hours, as well equipped as the *Trans Karoo.* The *Rhodesia Mail* runs twice weekly betweek Cape Town and Bulawayo (in Rhodesia) via Mafeking; the *South Wester* is weekly, between Cape Town and Windhoek.

The Steam Sheds—Visitors Welcome

There are about 1,700 active steam locomotives working in South Africa, plus another 400 stored or staged as strategic reserves. Some of the largest steam locomotive depots ("sheds") are to be found in the Republic, and permission to visit is easily obtained. In some hotels, notably at Kimberley, Bloemfontein, and De Aar, there is information in rooms about this, with a number to call for a permit.

The best known steam sheds, meccas for rail fans from all over the world, include Beaconsfield (Kimberley); De Aar (where the famous Mr. Gordon Watson, known as "King in his steam castle" in many countries, is Loco Foreman, or shed master); Bloemfontein (where Mr. Phillip Williams is in charge of what was until 1972 the world's largest shed, it still has many engines); Capital Park (Pretoria); Germiston (near Johannesburg); Paarden Eiland (Cape Town, where Mr. Visagi holds the key office, once occupied by a brother of the famous transplant surgeon Chris Barnard); and Sydenham (Port Elizabeth, with Mr. Eddie Jacobs in charge).

The largest concentration of steam trains may be seen on what is now known as the W.G.S.R. ("World's Greatest Steam Route") over the 237 Kms. (138 miles) of double track between Kimberley and De Aar across the Karroo. Some 68 steam-hauled trains (and about five diesel hauled, including the *Blue Train* twice or four times weekly) pass each day. There are good lineside vantage points, even picnic spots with seats provided, and small hotels overlooking the tracks exist at Modder River, Witput, and Krankuill. To quote from the North West Cape and Kimberley area tourist brochure "these names ring clanging bells with rail buffs all over the world." A daily passenger train running in daylight (with dining car) serves all stations between De Aar and Kimberley.

The Garden Route and Other Scenic Lines

From Cape Town to Port Elizabeth along the "Garden Route" is 1,085 kilometers (674 miles). It takes 41 hours by a well-equipped passenger train (first and second class sleepers and diner) running daily in both directions.

This train is electric hauled from Cape Town to Worcester, a four hour, 140 mile journey, then steam hauled most of the rest of the way. Four different Beyer Garratt locomotives are used, plus a 4.8.2 of the 19D class which works for over nine hours between Outshoorn and Klipplaat. Among the highlights are the entry to Mossel Bay, a pleasant seaside resort, the coastal run to George, the storming of the Montague Pass over some of South Africa's most magnificent scenery, the ostrich country near Outshoorn (where thousands of ostriches will be seen, many pacing the train), and the great climb to the Tourwaterpoort Pass. Mountains and gorges, seashore and rolling hills are in sight most of the time.

Avis rent-a-car at George are enterprising, and on notice from the train conductor at Mossel Bay, will have a five-seater car or a nine seater "combie" waiting with driver for the arrival of the train. This paces the train up over the Montague Pass on a dirt road, giving photographers the incredible spectacle of the Garratt blasting its way up the steep grades with a heavy train. The car ride ends at Camfer, down the other side from Topping (Summit) and currently costs 19 Rand (about 21 US Dollars) for a five-seater or 25 Rand (about 27.50 U.S. Dollars) for a "combie." Many rail enthusiasts use this service and rejoin the train at Camfer.

Port Elizabeth is a growing, prosperous port and resort on the Indian Ocean. It is the end of the rail "Garden Route." Onward travel to Durban is by road or air, as there is no direct rail link.

Rail Museums

Steam locomotives are spotted at stations all over the Republic as monuments. There is a forty-strong museum of veteran locomotives at De Aar Shed in the care of Mr. Gordon Watson, the famous Locomotive Foreman. A big South African Railways museum of engines of all classes is being prepared at Kraaifontein, about 20 miles North of Cape Town. The Wemmer Pan (J.T. Hall) Museum is within three miles of Johannesburg, where several small steam engines plus street cars and veteran road vehicles are on display. In the massive Johannesburg railway station a large museum displays models of all types of steam locomotives that have run, or are running, in South Africa. All main stations have their monument engine, some outside in a place of honour, as at Bleomfontein and Johannesburg.

South Africa pays due tribute to its steam railway history, as well as its very active steam locomotive present. As for the future, it is reckoned that steam traction—in this country of abundant coal and labor but no native oil—will survive at least ten more years from 1976.

An even narrower gauge (2 feet instead of 3 feet 6 inches) exists in several parts of the country for freight purposes. Best known is the Port Elizabeth (Humewood) to Loerie and Aventuur line, no less that 170 miles long. On this most Saturdays is run the *Apple Express.* Two types of narrow-gauge steam engines are used, one a Garratt, but diesels are also found on this route. In Natal, 2 foot-gauge systems work over very mountainous country from Umzinto near the Indian Ocean inland to Ixopo and Donnybrook, and from Port Shepstone to Harding. Passengers are only carried by special arrangement in cabooses. The engines are quite new, splendid little Garratts (2.6.2 + 2.6.2) built as recently as 1968. There are no diesels on the busy Natal narrow gauge lines.

The high Drakensburg Mountains, rearing to over 11,000 feet, are reached spectacularly by a rail line from Bloemfontein to Aliwal North (about the coldest place in Southern Africa) and then by a branch which climbs by reverse switch-backs (like those in the Peruvian Andes and up the Himalayas to Darjeeling) to attain Barkly East. Mixed trains run daily.

This is near the Lesoto Border, a sparsely populated country surrounded by the Republic of South Africa and formerly known as Basutoland. The only railway to enter Lesoto is a branch from the Bloemfontein-Aliwal North line which junctions at Sannaspos and goes to Marseilles and then across the border to a terminal at Maseru, 5,000 feet above sea level.

The main line from Durban through Natal to Johannesburg threads the Drakensburgs, but it is electrified and has been since 1925. There are long tunnels, the only significant ones in South Africa, and the expresses cover the highest section in darkness.

There is another spectacular route, this time steam hauled, which climbs over the Lutzberg Pass. It runs from Rosmead on the Karroo down to Klipplaat and Port Elizabeth. Some American rail fan groups, especially the larger ones, charter special trains to make this run in daylight, but the normal passenger service climbs in darkness. A through train running three times a week from Mossel Bay on the coast of Cape Province goes to Johannesburg, and in summer has through cars for Victoria Falls, making the longest steam-hauled journey in the world today: Mossel Bay to Rosmead with steam, then Bloemfontein to Kimberley, and Kimberley or Warrenton to Mafeking, and (in Rhodesia) Bulawayo to Victoria Falls. It climbs three passes on its route, the Montague, the Swartzberg, and the Lutzberg.

Some Facts About South African Rail Travel

A large timetable should be carried on journeys covering all main and secondary lines. It is cheap to buy (the equivalent of 35 cents) and contains all distances and altitudes along with a host of other information. For suburban services around Johannesburg, Cape Town, and Durban, smaller, separate timetables are needed, costing the equivalent of 8 cents.

Trains in South Africa are divided into "whites" and "non-whites." It is an offense for either racial group to enter the cars of another. The "non-white" cars are usually in the front of the train, a position railfans like to occupy. Unfortunately, they cannot, and there is no physical connection between the two sections of the train.

Most trains carry first, second, and third class cars, but for "whites" only first and second class may be used. There are first and second class as well as third in the "non-white" section.

The vast majority of railway personnel are Afrikaans-speaking whites, but they have a good command of English and are generally helpful. Locomotive engineers and firemen are always "whites" as are dining car staff. By tradition, "Cape Coloureds" handle the bedding and on-train cleaning.

Fares are modest in relation to most parts of the world but have risen sharply in recent years. Meals are the cheapest anywhere in Southern Africa, a four-course meal with coffee in a diner being R.1.50 (about $1.75).

SOUTH WEST AFRICA (NAMIBIA)

The driest and emptiest land on Earth, South West Africa is a mandated territory of the Republic of South Africa, although the mandate is contested by other African countries, who call it Namibia. The railway system is run entirely by South African Railways, using the standard gauge of Africa (3 feet 6 inches), and diesel traction has been employed throughout since 1965, almost wholly on account of the shortage of water.

But it was the Germans who built the first railways in this parched hunk of Africa. The unwanted territory was taken in the name of the Kaiser in 1885 after it had been declined by Britain following a report which declared it to be "only sand and rock and wild animals." The Germans began by laying—with great difficulty—a narrow gauge (2 feet 6 inches) line from the relatively cool but eternally dry coastline at Walvis (Walfisch) Bay for 255 miles inland up to the high plateau where they made their capital at Windhoek, 5,500 feet.

It was this little railway that did more to open up South West Africa than any other thing or person, and as a result, the tiny "back-to-back" 0.6.0 + 0.6.0 locomotive that hauled the first train in 1902 has been preserved as a national monument outside Windhoek Station. It is called "The Little Locomotive," much respected by the whites of the country, a large percentage of whom are Germans. Another locomotive is also declared a national monument in Windhoek, up by the Horseman Memorial outside the Government Buildings. This is the last narrow gauge engine and carriages in service (replaced in 1962), a 2.6.0 tender engine of 2 foot 6 inches gauge and the cars it hauled on its last run in the Tsumeb region in the northern part of South West Africa.

German South West fell to South African troops late in 1914 and the country has been run by Pretoria (with local overtones) ever since. Work on changing the gauge took, in all, some 40 years, but the main line to connect at De Aar Junction on South Africa's trunk route was done early and through trains have operated from Cape Town to Windhoek for well over 50 years.

Alluvial diamonds were discovered in 1907 when a German Railway foreman named August Stauch found a number of them at a place called Kolmanskop, 10 miles in from Luderitz Bay, the territory's second port. Since then, vast areas of the empty land have been declared "forbidden zones" and a total clampdown on entry by any unauthorized persons (and it is incredibly difficult to become authorized) coninues to exist. For long stretches, passengers are forbidden to alight from the Keetmanshoop-Luderitz Bay train as it runs slowly·along its permitted corridor to the sea.

South West Africa is described in the official guidebook as "not a pretty country nor a gentle one." But it is awe-inspiring and grand and we who visit its crisp hot emptiness look forward to a return trip. It is perhaps a mixture of Arizona, Death Valley, and Nevada, but in the north there is swamp and some 38,000 square miles around Etosha are kept as a game reserve—the biggest in the world. Passenger trains no longer run all the way to Tsumeb, but from Otijiwarongo (260 miles from Windhoek) travelers are conveyed by bus to either Tsumeb or the Etosha Pan (for game viewing). There is another freight-only line on which passengers are conveyed by bus; this is the 140 mile section to Gobabis from Windhoek.

The rail link from Windhoek to the coast carries a good overnight train, first and second class and all compartments making up into sleepers. It also has a buffet diner on Fridays and Sundays. The trip takes 11 hours, and those going westward will see the utter desert of the Namib, where no rainfall has ever been recorded. Yet it is still the habitat of graceful antelope (oryx) and Bushmen can find water deep down below the surface. There are hard, bare mountains and curious shifting sand dunes, and a cool-current coastline with dangerous surf from Swakopmund to Walvis Bay.

From Windhoek to the border of South Africa at Upington on the Orange River is a long, lonely haul of 623 miles. The scenery is mostly semi-desert. Only two small towns exist along the way, Keetmanshoop (junction for the Luderitz Bay Line, 226 miles long), and Karasburg. Nowhere else in the world is so empty except the crossing of the Nullabor Plain in Australia, where the Trans Australian expresses are air conditioned and fully equipped with the latest facilities. The *South Wester* is not a bad train, each compartment making up into a bedroom at night, and with a dining car and good service, but it is rather slow and not luxurious. The train takes 25 hours to Upington, and another 12½ hours to De Aar Junction, where it takes the S.A.R. main line for Cape Town, still another 515 miles away.

Traveling about this remote, 317,000 square mile country can be hot, dry and dusty, but winter nights are cold. A South African Railways timetable is essential, not only for train services but also for details of the road coaches operated from railheads and over stretches where passenger trains no longer operate. Since there are only half a million people of all races scattered about the territory, public transport services are remarkably good, but there is only one jet airport, some 40 miles from Windhoek, with links to Johannesburg and the Cape. Small propeller aircraft operate internal flights, mostly on charter but there is a scheduled service to Walvis Bay.

SOUTH AMERICA

SOUTH AMERICA

Only in the southern part of South America is there any co-ordination of rail services allowing through trains to run long distances. It is possible, in theory, to travel from Rio de Janeiro to the extreme south of Chile by way of Uruguay and Argentina. In practice, this journey would involve eight changes of train, some of them onto narrow gauge railways. In the northern part of the South American continent, railways tend to be links from ports to high inland cities, isolated from each other. North of the Tropic of Capricorn it is not possible to travel by rail from one capital to another.

The densest and most effective railway network belongs to Argentina, eighth largest country in the world, which has 27,000 miles of railway. The British built most of it, starting in 1857, and because of the flat "Pampas" (like the Mid-American Prairie), the lines were cheap and easy to lay. Nevertheless the standards were high and several great private companies continued a policy of expansion and development up to the end of 1946, when the system passed into the hands of President Peron's government. The old company names disappeared, being replaced by those of founding army generals. In the main, though, the network is in good shape and some very satisfactory passenger trains operate on long hauls.

Chile, too, has a sound railway system, running north and south (generally called the "Longitudinal Railway"). This is natural in a land which is over 2,600 miles long but less than 100 miles wide.

There are only 5,200 miles of railway, two-thirds of it State-owned. One major railway, the *Antofagasta,* is still a British private company, serving the copper mines of C'hquicamata and bringing it down to the Pacific port of Antofogasta.

Brazil has many different railways, most of them now in state hands, but little money has been spent in recent years and some are in poor repair. Strides are being made with the trunk routes from Rio to Sao Paulo, to Santos, and southwards to Montevideo. There are 23,000 miles of railway made up of five different gauges, and divided into "economic islands." The failure to link up so many lines led first to a superb system of coastal passenger ships, and later a well developed internal airline network.

The richest country in South America, Venezuela, spread over 360,000 square miles, has almost no railways at all. It used to have a narrow gauge rack and pinion line from the La Guiara to Caracas and Maracay, but nothing exists now in working order. The Government is at present conducting a survey with the aim of laying modern high speed railways.

As a tourist promotion for the major nations of South America there is an "AMERAILPASS", which may be bought from the *Association of Latin*

American Railways, Florida 783, Buenos Aires. It allows unlimited travel for a month (or two months) over some 30,000 miles of line in Argentina, Paraguay, Chile, Uruguay, Peru, and Brazil, and it costs approximately $75 (£42) in first class (the only acceptable method of travel for tourists on most trains) for 30 days. For overnight travel, holders can upgrade, for $3 (£ 1.70) to sleeping space.

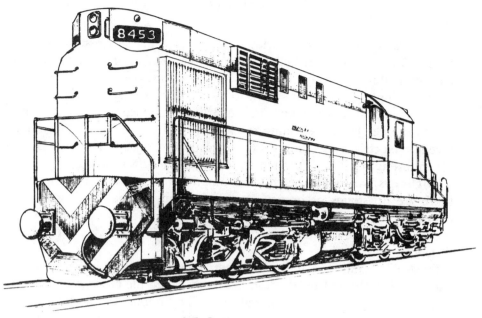

ARGENTINA

The State Railways in Argentina have a network of 25,000 miles, one of the largest in the world. All name trains, such as *El Libertador* to Mendoza, *Los Arrayanes* to Bariloche, *Rayol del Sol* to Cordoba and the crack *Expreso Buenos Aires,* are diesel-drawn, with new deluxe dining cars and sleepers built by Fiat in Cordoba. Many carry uniformed hostesses and have wall-to-wall carpeting. Sleepers are nicely decorated and most are air-conditioned. You can travel to Asuncion by the Urquiza line; to La Paz by the Belgrano line, or to Chile via Mendoza or Salta. Belgrano is metre gauge, but the rest are 5 ft. 6 in. broad gauge, which makes for smooth travel.

The railways have been in the hands of the government since 1947, when the major British companies were sold. Great and famous names, such as *BAGS* (Buenos Aires Great Southern Railway), *The Central,* and *Pacifico,* ceased to exist almost overnight and were replaced by the names of army generals who have contributed to Argentina's history.

The first railway in the country was built from Buenos Aires in 1857. Lines were easy and cheap to build across the enormous flatlands, no less than 250,000 square miles of Argentina being "pampas," or temperate grassland. Today, everyone thinks of the country in terms of the four great railways radiating fanwise from the capital.

Argentina became Britain's eighth "dominion" through the railways. It is almost impossible to illustrate now the importance of the railway companies operating in Argentina to the British people, but they contributed nearly a quarter of the national wealth, their profits buying very cheaply the "roast beef of old Argentine;" their fuel requirements keeping British coal flowing out of U.K. ports at the rate of 40 million tons a year; and wheat and linseed oil also coming very cheaply through railway profits.

Hundreds of thousands of Britons held shares in the great companies. When Britain, impoverished by World War II, was forced to sell the Argentine Railways to the Peron government for barely a year's supply of beef, a crippling blow was struck to the U.K. economy.

The great railways remain, but the British influence is now very slight. Dutch diesels, Japanese rolling stock, Italian (Fiat) pullmans and diners, Swedish electrical signaling, have replaced the once exclusively-British (even to engineers and firemen from England) railway scene.

Highways will never be much competition to railways in Argentina; there are no stones or gravel to surface them and paving is a terribly expensive business, suitable only between densely populated areas (which means around the capital). Air travel is popular, if expensive, over longer distances.

Since 1947, the *B. A. Great Southern,* operating from its vast and elegant terminal, Plaza Constitucion, has been called the *General Roca Railway* (*ferrocarril* is Spanish for railway). The *Central Argentine Railway,* radiating from the largest and most dramatic of the terminals in Retiro Square, became the *Bartolome Mitre Railway.* Next door to the "Central's" Retiro is a less pretentious structure, home at one time of the *Central Cordoba State Railway* (one of the few non-British systems of pre-war days). This railway has been renamed the *General Belgrano Railway.* A battered train shed, also in Retiro Square, was base of the not very prosperous, but highly active Buenos Aires *Pacifico,* now called the *General San Martin,* which still runs out of the rundown terminal. From Plaza Once, the one-time *B. A. Western's* base, runs the *Sarmiento Railway.* The ex-*Central Buenos & Entre Rios Railway* (from Lacroz terminus) became the *General Urquiza.* The old *Midland,* operating from Puente Alsina, is now called the *Ferrocarril Nacional Provincia de Buenos Aires.*

A superb underground railway system, with five lines, links Plaza Constitucion with Retiro via the "C" line, while Plaza Once is connected with the "B" route. Plaza de Mayo is an interchange station.

Main line trains for Mendoza, some 600 miles to the west of Buenos Aires and the starting point of a narrow gauge rack railway over the Andes to Chile, include the deluxe *Libertador,* highly recommended for its air-conditioned sleepers, pullmans, and diners. It runs twice weekly, with Santiago connections. Buenos Aires-Mendoza time is 14 hours.

Longest ride in the country is to San Carlos de Bariloche in the southern Lake District, 45 hours by the *General Roca Railway* via Bahia Blanca. The fastest rides are to Mar Del Plata, 248 miles in about 5½ hours, and to La Plata, 35 miles in 54 minutes. Junin, on the Pampas, 159 miles on both the *Mitre* and *San Martin* railways, is reached in under 4 hours. While speeds are nowhere very high, running is smooth. Scenery is, for the most part, flat except in the northwest, the extreme west, and the far south.

BOLIVIA

The fifth largest country in South America, with the world's highest capital, Bolivia has a mere 1,400 miles of railway, some 800 now government owned. It is all narrow (one metre) gauge. Most was built by Bolivia's victorious enemies in the past to compensate for massive land grabs.

The quick way to La Paz, 12,500-foot-high capital lying in a bowl of the Altiplano, is from Arica in Chile. This international line is 278 miles long and its thrice-weekly diesel rail cars take 10 hours. There are more than 30 miles of rack and pinion track, and the greatest altitude is reached at General Lagos, 13,930 feet, just short of the Bolivian frontier. Although high, the scenery is not as tremendous as on other routes, perhaps the best part being the descent into the amphitheater of the capital.

Bolivia has taken over her portion of the British-owned Antofagasta Railway and the section—in doubtful repair—from La Paz to Ollague is at an almost uniform altitude of 12,000 feet.

There is train service from La Paz to Buenos Aires three times a week, taking four days for the 1,500 miles. Trains leave La Paz in a southeasterly direction and pass through Oruro (junction for Cochabamba, second city of Bolivia), then Rio Mulato (junction for Sucre), and finally Unyuni, where the line to Antofagasta goes off to the right. The line to Argentina crosses the border at Villazon.

The six-mile section down from the Altiplano into La Paz is electrified; trains are taken down gently in loops, the slow progress compensated for by views of three mighty Andean peaks all above 20,000 feet: Illampu (21,490 ft.), Illiman (21,315 ft.) and Huayna-Potosi (20,407 ft.).

Colossal, overpowering views and clear atmosphere make rail travel—however slow and uncomfortable—the only way to go in Bolivia. (Reports have been received that the condition of coaches on the Bolivian part of the La Paz-Buenos Aires run is often unspeakable.)

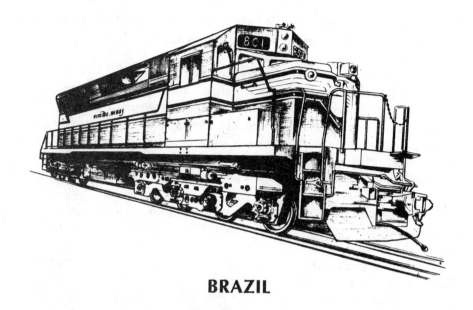

BRAZIL

The largest country in South America, Brazil borders all other South American countries except Ecuador and Chile. This means it has nine different frontiers, yet only one of them (to Uruguay) is crossed cleanly by international rail tracks. True, there are routes by railway into Bolivia and Argentina, but they involve changes and ferries across rivers. Six frontiers are not even approached by rail (nor even by reliable roads).

Statistics tell us that in this enormous country 91 per cent of the railways are located in the coastal belt less than 300 miles wide. There are 23,125 miles of railway, of five different gauges (90% are of metre gauge).

The British built most of the railways, including the shortest, yet most successful and profitable the world has ever known, the *Sao Paulo Railway,* 50 miles of 5 ft. 3 in. gauge linking Santos with the highland city. All of them have now either been sold to the Brazilian government or their leases have expired (the Sao Paulo Railway duly ran its 90-year course).

Name changes of rail systems occurred with the new ownership. Most curious of all was the old British line from Pernambuco running inland, *The Great Western of Brazil,* changed now to *Northeastern of Brazil.* Pernambuco, itself, is now known as Recife. The Sao Paulo Railway became *Estrada do Ferro Santos y Jundiai.*

Brazil's spectacular new capital, Brasilia, 3,000 feet up in Goias State, 600 miles inland, has been poorly connected by rail. Declared the capital in 1960, it was at first reached only by air or unpaved road. Now a line has reached it from Sao Paulo via Anapolis and another is under construction from Rio de Janeiro and Belo Horizonte.

A grand old railway is the *Leopoldina,* British-owned until 1950, which runs from Rio de Janeiro to Vitoria, 410 miles to the north. It also has a line with rack and pinion gradient climbing up to Teresopolis, 3,000 feet and 56 miles from Rio. It used to have a rack and pinion line to the nearer hill station of Petropolis, but this has been closed since 1964, and one of its elegant little steam engines is preserved in the town's main park. The Leopoldina has its base at the Barao de Maua station in Rio.

The crack line in Brazil is between Rio and Sao Paulo, 253 miles by the *Central of Brazil Railway* via the Paraiba Valley. Because of severe air competition (a half-hourly shuttle), there are only two express trains a day, the night train being the deluxe *Cruzeiro do Sul,* taking seven hours, but with sleeping cars. It starts from Rio's Central station. It is truly amazing (but in keeping with North American thinking) that two cities, one of 4 ½ million and the other 3½ million population, should have such limited train service!

The *Sorocabana Railway* runs southwards from Sao Paulo to the south of Brazil and on into Uruguay. It takes over five days on an international train riding on metre gauge!

Second most spectacular of Brazilian railway journeys is one of barely 100 miles, up from the port of Paranagua to Curitiba, 3,000 feet high. The run is accomplished by a fast diesel unit called the Littorina in just under three hours, and it affords some magnificent views of sub-tropical jungle, mountains, and waterfalls. An early morning mixed steam train, which we used one way, runs up the line in 4½ hours.

No visitor to Brazil should miss taking a trip by train from Santos to Sao Paulo, a 50-mile journey during which the whole train is hoisted up the forbidding 2,300 foot escarpment of the Serra do Mar. One of the wonders of the world when it was built by a British company in the late 1850s, the *Sao Paulo Railway* was an instant success. It gave the highlands of Brazil easy access to a port; it developed the then-small town of Sao Paulo (1860 population was a mere 25,000) and turned it into the world capital of coffee; and it gave the coastal people—then fever stricken—a means of escape to the healthy high interior. The S.P.R. made enormous profits and paid big dividends, but it also ploughed back development money.

For nearly 90 years the railway had a monopoly, but after World War II, Canadian technical assistance led to the building of the Anchieta Highway up the Serra. Freight traffic still keeps the railway profitable, but passenger trains are fewer and less well patronized than they used to be. Standards under the E.F.S.y J. remain high.

The 10:00 A.M. *Cometa* from Santos is a streamlined diesel train with comfortable first and second class accommodations and a buffet. It runs past the foot of the incline 9 miles from Santos, then it is hooked on to endless wire ropes which drag it up five separate steep inclines, with counterbalance weights coming down. The views are dramatic, the speed—considering the climb—remarkable. Freight trains and long passenger trains are split into sections, but the Cometa stays together. From the summit (Alto da Serra) the train travels fast on its wide gauge past 20 miles of factories to the elegant terminal in the heart of Sao Paulo. It is amazing to discover that your arrival time is only 11:40 A.M.

CHILE

Stretching from the Antartic to the tropics, Chile is 2,600 miles long, but no wider at any point than 110 miles. Naturally, the main railways run north and south, while international lines run east or northeast (into Argentina and Bolivia). There is a rail link into Peru, her northern neighbor, but only by a short, isolated railway running from Arica to Tacna, a mere 40 miles. This was, in fact, the second railway to be built in South America, dating from 1851.

The Chilean State Railways are a very important force in Chile, owning some 4,000 miles of line out of 5,185 miles of railway in the country. They own coastal ships, several ports, and a chain of good resort hotels, including some beyond the limits of rails (like the Cabo de Hornes at Magellanes). Chilean State Railways also handle internal tourist matters, the only body doing this efficiently.

Tickets for first class rail travel in Chile are hard to come by in summer, and on the *Trans-Andine Railway* demand always exceeds supply. Travelers are advised to use the services of a *competent* travel agency in Santiago, preferably Wagon-Lit/Cook, who have ticket allocations. Weaker agents only understand air bookings.

Flechia del Sur (Southern Arrow) is the name of the best train, traveling quite fast down the 661 miles of broad gauge (5 ft. 6 in.) track on the *Longitudinal Railway* from Santiago to Puerto Montt. It takes 17 daylight hours in summer. But there are daily trains all year round on this trunk line, including the *Nocturno,* leaving Santiago's Alamosa Station at 8:45 P.M. nightly.

While conditions have deteriorated in recent years due to political and financial troubles, the equipment on these trains ranks with the best in Latin America. Restaurant cars are excellent and there are comfortable saloons with deeply reclining seats, called "pullmans." There are also sleeping cars on night services. Time keeping, however, can be haphazard.

Electrification has made great strides in Chile, as befits a country using many water-powered turbines and the joint constructor of the first electric main line in the Americas (Santiago to Valparaiso). Personal experiences on the Longitudinal Railway in the late 1960s showed us electrification reaching farther and farther south, but lack of funds and materials have prevented its completion all the way to Puerto Montt. Diesels take over from electrics on the main trains, but steam engines are still in use on spur lines. Attractive steam engines built in Britain and America are seen on branch lines, particularly from Loncoche Junction to Villarica (station for the glorious resort of Pucon).

All along the Longitudinal Railway, the monarchs of the Andes are in sight, often as snow-capped, near perfect, volcanic cones. The scenery in the Chilean heartland is pastoral; farther south there are views of forest and lakes.

North from Santiago, the Longitudinal is a very different proposition. The broad gauge route goes to Valparaiso, but the northbound Longitudinal starts at a station called La Calera on the Valparaiso line. It is only metre gauge and much slower, with a frequency of only two through trains a week. Iquique is the effective northern terminus, although a short line on a different gauge runs north to Pisagua, a nitrate port about 100 miles away.

Antofagasta is the main railway center of North Chile. It is headquarters of the British-owned *Antofagasta Railway,* which has metre gauge services to the high copper mines and also runs a weekly through train to La Paz in Bolivia, with sleeping and restaurant cars as well as diesel units, to the frontier. A new railway, opened in 1948, runs east from Antofagasta across the Andes to Salta in Argentina; it reaches an altitude of 14,680 feet over the Chorillos Pass. Through trains to Buenos Aires, with sleeping and dining cars, run twice weekly (once in winter) and take four days.

Exciting indeed is the shortest and most abrupt crossing of the Andes from Chile. This is the *Trans-Andine Railway,* a narrow gauge rack and pinion system shared by Argentina and Chile. This way, the altitude is kept to just under 11,000 feet, an important factor for tourists with heart conditions or unable to breathe thin air.

The *Trans-Andino Combinacion* starts from Santiago's Mapocho Station at 7:45 A.M. on Mondays, Wednesdays, and Fridays. At Llay-Llay station the through cars are switched to a Valparaiso-Los Andes train and this carries on eastwards to Los Andes up the Aconcagua Valley.

Chilean customs are cleared at Los Andes, and a change of train from Chilean broad gauge electric to Trans-Andine metre gauge is made at the same time. At noon, the Trans-Andine train, electric hauled by a fairly new Swiss engine and modern cars obtained for the World Ski Championships at Portillo in 1966, sets off for the high pass.

Rack and pinion are soon engaged and the train climbs steeply. Refreshments are sold at seats, but the angle of climb can spill coffee. Decades of writers have tried and failed to do justice to the magnificence of the scenery. All agree it is the finest rock and canyon panorama in the world, dominated as the train grinds higher by the giants of the Andes, Aconcagua (22,834 feet) on one side and Tupungato (22,310 feet) on the other. The trains goes under La Cumbre Pass by a tunnel, reaching a maximum altitude of 10,900 feet, then enters Las Cuevas station about 3 P.M. Here a change is made to an Argentine diesel unit, which descends through wonderful desert scenery to Mendoza, reached at 7:45 P.M. (12 hours from Santiago). Argentine customs are cleared on the train.

COLOMBIA

Colombia is the fourth largest country in South America and, with a population of nearly 16 millions, it is the third largest in population. However, set among the cordilleras of the Andes, the country has presented enormous difficulties to builders of railway and road. Despite completion of the *Atlantic Railway*, linking the 8,800-feet-high capital, Bogota, with the Caribbean at Santa Marta, and a new line up the western shore of the Magdalena River, there are still only 2,300 miles of narrow gauge railway.

As recently as 1921, the only way to reach the capital was up the Magdalena River aboard stern-wheelers, which often stuck on sand spits. The average journey time from the coast, 800 miles away, was 12 days, but three weeks was no exception. Then, having arrived at Girardot, there was still 8,000 feet to climb by a railway 88 miles long, built before the turn of the century, by a British company.

Air travel came early to Colombia and grew rapidly. *Avianca,* the main Colombian airline, is the oldest in the Americas, having been founded in 1920. But internal air travel is fairly expensive and, due to weather conditions and tremendous mountains, not as safe as in most countries. A demand for rail and road travel has led to building programs for both in recent years.

In 1961 the Atlantic Railway was completed, linking Bogota with Santa Marta, and when the President opened it he declared that "Colombia was now a Nation unified". The line is 550 miles long and was financed by a World Bank loan in 1955. Modern equipment was supplied by Sweden, France, Germany, and the United States. Assistance was given by *Avianca,* which provided five planes to fly surveyors and work parties, while Avianca's helicopter division at Girardot was employed to swing vital parts into position in difficult terrain. This is one of the few examples of air-rail constructional co-operation.

The inaugural passenger train ran on August 1, 1961, carrying the President of Colombia for the whole journey. We first rode the line, by courtesy of Colombian Railways, in the cab of the Swedish diesel unit with the engineer, the following February. There are two passenger trains daily, a slow, locomotive-hauled train taking 22 hours, and a fast Swedish diesel set taking 17 hours (at the time of our trip 18½ hours, for the track was not yet bedded down). The diesel does the run in daylight hours, after an early morning—and usually fog-bound—start from the high capital. Meal stops are made briefly, but a small, adequate buffet on the train serves hot dishes and beer.

The descent to the Magdalena River at Puerto Salgar is steep and scenic, but most of the journey is through dense jungle and tropical plantations, with some fine river views and glimpses of distant mountains. There are some fine bridges along the line.

Medellin, a city 5,000 feet high with a population of three quarters of a million, is reached by rail from Puerto Berria on the Atlantic Railway. The line climbs easily from the river for nearly 100 miles, passing through industrial developments for the last 20 or so to the city. Passenger trains take 13 hours from the capital.

A railway runs southwards to Cali from here, second city of Colombia with 835,000 population. It is the industrial and cultural center of the Cauca Valley, set at an altitude of 3,290 feet, with a sub-tropical climate. The main railway from Cali runs down to the Pacific at Buenaventura, 105 miles away to the West. This was constructed prior to the turn of the century and made Cali more accessible—and at first more important—than the capital.

The Buenaventura-Cali railway is busy, but single track. It is a smaller version of Ecuador's spectacular Guayaquil-Quito line. The climb is not so high nor so steep, but it does pull up out of very luxuriant jungle to the higher slopes of the Cauca Valley at 5,000 feet with tremendous views before dropping down some 1700 feet into the city. Passenger trains take six hours to make the 105 mile trip. Via Medellin, and Puerto Berrea, Bogota can be reached by rail from the Pacific.

While modern diesels and diesel units are found in increasing numbers of Colombia's main railway routes, steam buffs will be pleased to see and hear some Baldwin locomotives built at Philadelphia (usually 4.6.0's) more than half a century ago. Their chime whistle is a delight. A small stud of them lives at Girardot, and at branch line terminals.

ECUADOR

Five railway lines add up to a total of 698 route miles, but two routes are totally isolated, and only 288 miles (from the main port of Guayaquil up to Quito, the 9,300 feet high capital) are in good condition and well used by tourists as well as locals.

Headquarters of the railway system is Riobamba, a town of 40,000 people nestling close to the mighty volcano of Chimborazo.

Apart from a diesel railcar service on the main line from Guayaquil to Quito, described in some detail later, all trains are either freight or "mixed", and the latter can mean just one wooden coach attached at the end of the train. It may, on the newly extended Quito-Ibarra-San Lorenzo line, mean a fairly good first-class car and a creaking second-class behind it. The gauge is 3 feet 6 inches, which results in some tight turns and jolting travel. Apart from the main line, train timings are described as "somewhat unreliable."

The two isolated lines curling inland from ports (Machala to Pasaje and Arenillas; Bahia de Caraquez to Chone) are mainly for banana and agricultural produce. Rail buffs would get pleasure more from watching and photographing than from riding.

Train Ride to the Sky

The world's mightiest roller coaster stretches in a crazy, rollicking 288-mile ride from Guayaquil to Quito and back, via the *autoferro,* a one-car "train" which looks like (and may be) a school bus on a railway chassis, with 30 tiny, and hard, non-reclining seats. Service is daily, including Sunday, and the magnificent tour is a guaranteed highlight on any South American trip. Despite the noise, which is at times almost unbearable, and the lack of heat or food (pack a lunch), the 12- to 14-hour ride (from

Guayaquil to Quito, but only 11 hours in the reverse direction) is a real travel adventure. If you are in a hurry to get between the cities, however, you can hire a taxi from your hotel and make the trip for about $85 (for two) along the Pan American Highway (good condition) in about 7 or 8 hours.

The rail gauge is 3 ft. 6 in., and it carries, in addition to the autoferro, a daily mixed train, usually steam-hauled. This leaves Duran at 5 A.M., but only manages to make 150 miles to Riobamba by nightfall. It stays the night here, leaving at dawn to reach Quito by mid-afternoon, switching operations permitting.

The trip is very bumpy, and not for the faint of heart, for the switchbacks and turns are enough to take the breath away from a mountain climber. Probably the best way to give an idea of the trip is to reproduce the stations listed on the ticket, with their altitudes:

Altitude in Feet	Station	Miles from Guayaquil	Altitude in Feet	Station	Miles from Guayaquil
15	Duran (Guayaquil)	0	10,379	Luisa	142
20	Yaguachi	14	9,020	Riobamba	150
42	Milagro	21	11,841	Urbina	170
100	Naranjito	31	10,346	Mocha	178
300	Barraganeta	43	9,100	Cevallos	186
975	Bucay	54	8,435	Ambato	196
4,000	Huigra	72	8,645	San Miguel	219
4,875	Chunchi	76	9,055	Latacunga	227
5,925	Sibambe	81	10,375	Lasso	239
8,553	Alausi	89	11,653	Cotopaxi	250
9,200	Tixan	95	10,118	Machachi	263
10,626	Palmira	103	9,090	Aloag	266
10,000	Guamote	112	9,891	Tambillo	273
10,388	Cajabamba	132	9,375	Quito	288

After scanning the elevations and then examining the geography between Guayaquil and Quito one begins to appreciate the magnitude of the challenge construction engineers accepted when this road was planned. The obstacles before the builders were formidable. From the sea-level left bank of the Guayas River the track extends out 54 miles over flat savanna lands. At the 54th mile the road begins a dizzy climb to 10,600 feet within the next 50 miles. To accomplish this, the track climbs at a 5½ percent gradient along such engineering triumphs as "Devil's Nose"—a double switchback zig-zag cut out of solid rock.

After a brief stop for both man and machine to catch their breath the *autoferro* starts out again climbing even higher to Urbina at 11,841 feet above sea level. Urbina lies at the foot of snow-capped Mt. Chimborazo, which towers another 10,000 feet above the tracks and presents probably the most spectacular view seen from any train window anywhere in the world. As the journey continues, 309 bridges, tunnels, and bends are passed, and Mt. Cotopaxi dominates the bright, clear blue mountain sky. After crossing, climbing and descending these Andean ranges a final descent is made to Quito, where a tired but satisfied group of rail veterans disembark. The *autoferro* leaves Guayaquil at 6 A.M. on Mondays, Wednesdays and Fridays; it leaves Quito at 6 A.M. on Tuesdays, Thursdays and Saturdays.

Listed below is a brief summary of the trip from Guayaquil to Quito with the most important stops identified. Best bet, however, is to take the trip in the opposite direction to get the most spectacular scenery in daylight. The Quito-Guayaquil trip, being mostly downwards, takes only 11 hours, and leaves Quito at 6 A.M. An advance reservation is always needed because the trip is extremely popular and space is very limited. One-way fare is about 80 sucres, a little over $3.

Passengers are ferried across the river from Guayaquil to the station in Duran at 6 A.M.

First stop is Yaguachi, a small village 14 miles from Guayaquil. First important stop is Milagro, where scores of Indian women greet the train with native fruits and *allullas* (a small, tasty, cookie-like bread). At the 54th mile of the journey, the train arrives in Bucay, where a larger engine is often connected for the steeper grades ahead.

From Bucay the trip becomes spectacular as the lush tropical fields pass by and the Andean ascent begins. The train climbs through the Chanchan River gorge to the small village of Huigra.

The most breathtaking segment of the journey starts an hour from Huigra. After inching along a steep canyon ledge high above the Chanchan River, the engine begins the slow pull up the Nariz del Diablo (Devil's Nose), which consists of a series of zig-zags that climb 1,000 feet in the gorge above the river. Tunnels, bridges, and steep cliffs highlight the arduous climb up the perpendicular ridge. The air cools and the tropics fade to a green haze far below.

Next a series of small Indian mountain villages pass by. Chanchan, Sibambe (where connections may be made for another train to Cuenca), and on to the popular mountain resort village of Alausi, where bus connections to Quito are possible.

At the 103-mile mark the train stops in Palmira, and here on the crest of the Andes, in the clear stimulating air, many of the towering peaks of the Ecuadorian highlands appear.

The rarified atmosphere seems to put Chimborazo, Tungurahua, Sangay, Altar, and Carihuairazo almost within reach. The train soon leaves for Guamote and continues past the shores of Lake Colta and into the agricultural oasis of the Cajabamba Valley.

After Cajabamba dusk usually begins to conceal the dramatic scenery and the train pulls into Riobamba. Many travelers choose to stay here the two nights before continuing on to Quito. Riobamba is the capital of Chimborazo Province and a striking city of graceful stone colonial-style buildings. At night the sky glows with the reflection from Sangay volcano and its ashes often cover Riobamba's cobbled streets. Saturday is market day, and leather goods, baskets, sandals, and Indian wares are very reasonable. The tiny, intricate Tagua carvings are a favorite buy. Try the Andean specialty, baked guinea pig, at the large open-air restaurants.

From Riobamba the line climbs to its highest point, Urbina Pass, and for 26 miles crosses a succession of towering ridges to Ambato, an important town of 45,000 inhabitants, impressively situated at the base of towering Chimborazo. Ambato is an important road junction and home of one of Ecuador's best-known Indian markets.

From Ambato the line skirts the mighty volcano Cotopaxi to Latacunga, another important city of 25,000 inhabitants. Latacunga is dominated by the perfect-coned Cotopaxi, which is 18 miles from the city but still manages to dwarf everything in sight. On a clear day the sharp-eyed can see nine volcano cones from the town. Several tours are operated from Quito to Latacunga for the Saturday Indian market.

The only stop of interest after leaving Latacunga is Machachi, where one of Ecuador's top brands of mineral water is bottled. From the Machachi springs the train descends into the basin where Quito lies, and the final 25-mile run to the capital is rapid.

Bus connections for Quito can be made at either Riobamba (4 hours) or Ambato (2½ hours).

THE GUYANAS

Guyana

Formerly British Guiana, the only British colony in South America, Guyana has two small railways, each of a different gauge and not in the best of repair, although they both now belong to the Government.

One line runs from Georgetown, the capital, for 60½ miles to Rosignol, along the east coast of Demerara and directly across the Berbice River from New Amsterdam.

The other is more interesting, for a large number of middle-aged British and Americans will remember having traveled on it extensively and thoroughly enjoying the ride—but not in its present setting. It was none other than the old Bermuda Railway, which ran in that island-colony from 1931 to 1947 from Somerset to St. George's through Hamilton. This petrol-electric "fun" line was sold, lock, stock, and barrel, to B.G. (as it was known then) and now spreads its aging 18½ miles of track from Vreed-en-Hoop on the left bank of the Demarara River to Parika, in the estuary of the Essequibo River.

There are some freight-only short lines conveying manganese ore in the northwest part of Guyana.

Guyane (French Guiana)

Famous for its "Devil's Island," this self-governing French territory on the South American mainland has never had any railways.

PARAGUAY

River traffic has been the essence of travel and freighting to Paraguay's capital, Asuncion, since the founding of the country by Juan de Salazar de Espinosa in 1537. But the Alto Parna and Paraguay rivers are extremely difficult to navigate due to bends and shallows, and urgent demands for a railway led to the *Paraguay Central's* being opened—but not until 1913 (construction was begun in 1854!).

The line runs now, as it did then, slowly and rather roughly, from Encarnacion on the Alto (upper) Parana for 274 miles to Asuncion. Trains, including the once-weekly through "express" to Buenos Aires, must be ferried across the river from Encarnacion to Posadas in Argentina.

The journey, even by the one good train, is best described as dusty and uninteresting, with speeds averaging less than 20 miles an hour with diesel traction. Some steam remains on freight and mixed services. The line is standard (4 ft. 8½ in.) gauge.

The only other public railway is metre gauge, the *Ferrocarril del Norte,* 35 miles from Concepcion to Morqueta in the northern part of the country. Concepcion is at the extreme limit of navigation by 12-foot-draught passenger vessels on the Paraguay River.

PERU

The highest standard gauge railroad in the world travels between Lima and Oroya with branches to Cerro de Pasco, Huancayo and Huancavelica. The *Southern Railways of Peru* operate between Arequipa-Puno (on Lake Titicaca) with one weekly connection (Wednesdays) by steamer across the lake to Bolivia (returning Fri.), as well as three weekly connections to Cuzco. Check schedules, the boats are often docked for repairs and railway has *summer* and *winter* schedules.

Besides the highest standard gauge railway in the world, Peru can also boast a railway which all travelers, business or pleasure bound, must use, for there is no other possible means of transport.

The *Central Railway* is regarded as one of the wonders of the Americas. A masterpiece by the great American railroad engineer Henry Meiggs, it was built between 1870 and 1893, from the coast to Oroya and Huancayo. This tremendous railway, climbing from Callao (port for Lima), enters a tunnel between Ticlio and Galera, only 107½ miles from the start of the journey, when it is no less than 15,688 feet above sea level. Galera, only 98 miles from Lima, is the highest station in the world, at 15,681 feet!

Everyone traveling from Cuzco, 2¼ miles high, to the Inca ruins of Machu Picchu 110 miles away, must use the railway even if riding in an "autowagon" (which runs on rails). In this high, remote country, there are no roads, although there is an airport at Cuzco.

Peru has 2,214 miles of incredible railway, much of it operating at altitudes so high that oxygen has to be supplied to passengers. The third largest country in South America, Peru has a low density population and some massive Andean peaks. That railways were built at all is something of a miracle—that they still succeed and hold their own against road and air transport despite steep climbs with engines dragging heavy trains three miles up into the clouds, is even more miraculous.

The international train-ship service over the old Peruvian Corporation's *Southern Railway of Peru* from Mollendo on the Pacific to La Paz, Bolivia's capital, actually involves using a ship sailing so high that oxygen is called for!

This is one of the world's great train journeys, leaving Mollendo at sea level in the morning, stopping at Arequipa, third city of Peru situated 7,500 feet up (at the foot of El Misti, the perfect volcanic cone rearing to over 19,000 feet), then climbing to Juliaca, 189 miles and 12,500 feet. Crucero Alto (14,688 feet) is the high point on the line. Puno is on Lake Titicaca, 12,648 feet, and here you take ship for the 12-hour overnight voyage to Guaqui in Bolivia, where another train waits to make the connecting trip to La Paz, the world's highest capital.

In addition to the international train, equipped with restaurant car and saloons and nurses administering portable oxygen (many travelers suffer from "siroche," or altitude sickness), there are other trains to Puno and Huancane and points on the western shore of Titicaca, where hydrofoils operate in daylight across to Bolivia.

The Southern Railway links Arequipa with Cuzco, running along the high spine of the Andes. For those able to stand the heights, it is a marvelously scenic ride, dropping down slightly to the 11,440 foot altitude of Cuzco (former Inca capital) by nightfall. The passenger trains, three times weekly, are well appointed and the track excellently maintained. The restaurant or buffet car requires a ticket, but you can sit there all day if you wish. Experienced travelers recommend eating at the lower altitudes early in the journey.

Lima and Arequipa are not connected by rail; there is a fast motor road over the 640 miles and "collectivos" do the journey in about 15 hours, sometimes only 12.

The *Central Peruvian Railway* makes the most spectacular climbs on its journey from Lima to Oroya, with many zig-zags, no less than 66 tunnels, 59 bridges, and a ruling grade of 4.5%. By contrast, the Southern Railway makes an easy climb, although it reaches an altitude of more than 14,000 feet.

Peruvian trains carry first and second class and on long distance runs offer a sound degree of comfort in both (unusual for South America). Restaurant or buffet cars are provided for runs in excess of five hours. Small diesel units may be quicker on certain stretches, but are noisy, less comfortable, and without meal or medical facilities. We do stress the problem of *siroche;* if insufficient oxygen is taken while on the train, hospital treatment will be called for, and we have a colleague who spent five days in a hospital because he refused whiffs of oxygen in time.

Henry Meiggs built another fine railway in Peru, the *Santa Corporation,* running from Chimbote in north Peru to Huallanca, 88 miles up the Santa Valley to the Canyon del Pato. It climbs to about 2,600 feet, low for Peru, and trains (no meal facilities) take five hours.

One other railway runs inland from Lima to Ancon (the *Northwestern),* and there are short stretches of State Railway from Trujillo and Pascamayo in north Peru, the latter line running inland to Chilete.

SURINAM

An abundance of waterways enabled the Dutch to avoid building their beloved canals, and later they opted mainly for roads instead of railways. There is, however, extremely limited rail service on the only rail line, which runs between Onverwacht and Brownsweg. To take this, you'll have to go by bus from Paramaribo. Since the service is not on an organized basis, and not even daily, you can only make plans after you have arrived in Surinam—and then only if you have plenty of time to wait for arrangements to be made.

(A new railway line, for industrial use, is being constructed in western Surinam, where important new deposits of bauxite have been discovered.)

URUGUAY

The smallest of the South American republics, Uruguay has 1,874 miles of railway. The lines were mainly British-built, like those of neighboring Argentina, from 1868 onwards, and were operated as private companies. In 1948, however, they were sold to the government of Uruguay.

Regrettably, there has been deterioration in recent years, with little money spent on maintenance and renewals. However, restaurant cars and sleeping cars are still found on the longer runs and there are through services to Brazil. The tracks are standard gauge (4 ft. 8½ in.), but average speeds are only moderate even though no major gradients are encountered.

Rail routes radiate from the capital, Montevideo, the one most used by visitors going east along the "Uruguayan Riveria" to Maldonado and La Paloma. The quickest link to Brazil strikes northeastwards to cross the frontier at Rio Branco on the Yaguaron River by a mile-long bridge (the Maua). This is 302 miles from Montevideo, a journey of mainly pastoral character, with plenty of cattle to see and a modest climb through the hills called Cuchilla Grande.

Another line runs almost due north from Montevideo for 316 miles to Rivera on the Brazil border. It passes through the towns of Florida, Durayno, and Santa Isobel, where a branch goes off westwards to Paysandu on the River Uruguay, second city of the country (although this means little, since half the population lives in Montevideo and no other town has more than a twentieth of its inhabitants).

A line runs upriver from Paysandu to split at Baltasar, reaching Brazil's border at two places (Bella Union and Artigas). Argentina is most usually reached on the surface by train or bus from Montevedeo to Colonia, then a hydrofoil directly across the Plate.

VENEZUELA

A large, mineral- and oil-rich nation with a population of nearly nine millions (with over one and a half millions living in the metropolitan area of Caracas, the capital), Venezuela has managed without any significant railway system. There used to be a narrow-gauge British-built rack and pinion line climbing up from the port of La Guiara over the pass to Caracas (3,300 feet) and going on to Maracay. However, this went out of use with the coming of super highways.

Venezuela is now implementing in depth studies on building a modern railway system with commuter lines in and around the capital.

LATE INFORMATION

NORTH AMERICA

U.S.A.

Amtrak's *The Shenandoah* links Washington, D.C. and Cincinnati via Parkersburg, W. Va. Stops include Harpers Ferry, W. Va., and Athens and Chillicothe, Ohio.

Amtrak has designated an experimental route between *Seattle* and *Salt Lake City* via Boise, Idaho, and Ogden, Utah. The train was expected to begin operating in late spring of 1977.

The U.S. Army Transportation Museum at Fort Eustis in Newport News, Va., exhibits historical memorabilia of the Transportation Corps—aircraft, helicopters, trucks, steam locomotives, amphibious vehicles and hovercraft. Also exhibited is an experimental rocket belt and flying saucer. Free. Open to the public daily.

ASIA

Nepal

There is one scheduled passenger service, connecting the Indian Rail railhead at Jayanager (Madhubani) with Janakpur and Bizalpura in Nepal, southeast of Kathmandu. The train runs twice daily from Jayanager to Janakpur and once daily from Janakpur to Bizalpura.

Philippines

A loan of over US$24 million has been made by the Asian Development Bank to rehabilitate the 474 kilometers of line from Manila to Legaspi. Track improvements will enable the journey time of passenger trains late in 1977 to be reduced from 14 to 10 hours. Electrification is in progress to further speed up the route, which carries 85 percent of the total Philippine passenger traffic.

AFRICA

Benin

Passenger service as follows:
1. Cotonou-Parakou: 2 trains daily each way, 3 more trains from Cotonou to Bohicon or Dassa-Zoume.
2. Pobé-Cotonou: 1 train daily each way.
3. Cotonou-Segboroue: 1 train daily each way.

Cameroon

Passenger service operates twice daily (A.M. and P.M.) between Yaounde, the national capital, and Douala, the economic capital and major air and seaport. The Yaounde-Ngaoundere line, completed in 1974, is modern. The Yaounde-Douala line is an improvement on the old German/French construction. Work has been started on major improvements and reconstruction to this line.

South Africa

The *Blue Train* operates once a week all year. In addition, between the end of November and the middle of April it runs one other day a week, and from December to mid-January a third day each week.

SOUTH AMERICA

Panama

The Chiriqui Railroad has passenger service between Colon and Panama City. There are 7 trains on weekdays, 6 on Sundays.

INDEX